WHAT
THE
BIBLE
TEACHES

Contributors

J.M. FLANIGAN

Born into a christian family in Northern Ireland Jim Flanigan was received into the Parkgate Assembly, East Belfast in 1946. In 1972 he felt called of God to give all his time to the work of the Lord. Most of his service has been in ministry of the Word, travelling widely in the British Isles, U.S.A., Canada, Australia and Israel, in which he has a special interest. Jim Flanigan has written *Notes on Revelation* and has contributed various articles to magazines.

WHAT THE BIBLE TEACHES

with
Authorised Version
of
The Bible

IN ELEVEN VOLUMES
COVERING THE NEW TESTAMENT

VOLUME 8

JOHN RITCHIE LTD
KILMARNOCK, SCOTLAND

ISBN 0 946351 06 6

WHAT THE BIBLE TEACHES
Copyright © 1986 by John Ritchie Ltd.
40 Beansburn, Kilmarnock, Scotland

Typeset at Newtext Composition, 465 Paisley Road, Glasgow.
Printed at The Bath Press, Avon.

CONTENTS

PREFACE

Page

HEBREWS

CHAPTER

1	17
2	40
3	62
4	74
5	81
6	100
7	122
8	144
9	163
10	194
11	226
12	252
13	277

APPENDIX

A	295
B	311

ABBREVIATIONS

AV	Authorised Version of King James Version 1611
JND	New Translation by J.N. Darby 1939
LXX	Septuagint Version of Old Testament
Mft	New Translation by James Moffatt 1922
NASB	New American Standard Bible 1960
NEB	New English Bible 1961
Nestle	Nestle (ed.) Novum Testamentum Graece
NIV	New International Version 1973
NT	New Testament
OT	Old Testament
Phps	New Testament in Modern English by J.B. Philips 1962
RSV	Revised Standard Version 1952
RV	Revised Version 1881
TR	Textus Receptus or Received Text
Wey	New Testament in Modern Speech by R.F. Weymouth 1929

PREFACE

They follow the noblest example who seek to open the Scriptures to others, for our Lord Himself did so for those two dejected disciples of Emmaus (Luke 24:32). Whether it is the evangelist "opening and alleging that Christ must needs have suffered and risen from the dead" (Acts 17:3) or the pastor-teacher "expounding ... in all the scriptures the things concerning himself" (Luke 24:27) or stimulating our hope "through the patience and comfort of the scriptures" (Rom 15:4), he serves well in thus giving attendance to the reading of the Scriptures (1 Tim 4:13).

It is of course of equal moment to recognise in the exercise of able men, the continued faithfulness of the risen Head in giving gifts to the Church, in spite of her unfaithfulness. How good to recognise that "the perfecting of the saints ... the work of the ministry ... the edifying of the body of Christ" need not be neglected. Every provision has been made to ensure the well-being of the people of God. And every opportunity should be taken by the minister of Christ and those to whom he ministers to ensure that the saints "grow up into him in all things which is the head, even Christ" (Eph 4:15).

At various times in the post-apostolic period, certain teachers have come to prominence, sometimes because they succumbed to error, sometimes because in faithfulness they paid the ultimate price for the truth they had bought and would not sell. Some generations had Calvin and Luther, others Darby and Kelly, but in every generation God's voice is heard. It is important that we hear His voice today and recognise that He does speak through His servants. The contributors to this series of commentaries are all highly-respected expositors among the churches of God. They labour in the Word in the English-speaking world and have been of blessing to many throughout their years of service.

The doctrinal standpoint of the commentaries is based upon the acceptance of the verbal and plenary inspiration of the Scriptures so that their inerrant and infallible teachings are the only rule of conscience. The impeccability of Christ, His virgin birth, vicarious death and bodily resurrection are indeed precious truths worthy of the christian's defence, and throughout the volumes of this series will be defended. Equally the Rapture will be presented as the Hope of the Church. Before the great Tribulation she will be raptured and God's prophetic programme will continue with Jacob's trouble, the public manifestation of Christ and the Millennium of blessing to a restored Israel and the innumerable Gentile multitude in a creation released from the bondage of corruption.

May the sound teaching of these commentaries be used by our God to the blessing of His people. May the searching of the Scriptures characterise all who read them.

The diligence of Mr. J.W. Ferguson and the late Professor J. Heading in proof-reading is gratefully acknowledged. Without such co-operation, the production of this commentary would not have been expedited so readily.

T. WILSON
K. STAPLEY

HEBREWS
Introduction

1. Introductory Remarks
2. Survey and Theme
3. Authorship
4. Recipients and Destination
5. "Hebrews"
6. Date
7. Key Words
8. Bibliography
9. Outline

1. Introductory Remarks

It was the apostle to the Gentiles who once observed that true ministry was for edification, and exhortation, and comfort (1 Cor 14:3), and the writer to the Hebrews has adhered closely to that pattern. This epistle, which begins rather like a treatise but ends as a letter, is a rich, rare treasury of edification for the genuine believer, of exhortation for the uncertain waverer, and of comfort for the weary sufferer in the path of testimony. But whether edification, exhortation, or comfort, in a sense the substance of the ministry is always the same. It is Christ! In a terse but beautiful title to his exposition of the epistle to the Hebrews, the late J. Charleton Steen of London has admirably summed it all up in two words, *Christ Supreme*. This supremacy of the Lord Jesus will be presented in the epistle as the answer to every difficulty, the solution to every problem, the needed consolation in every perplexing circumstance of life, and the great antidote to backsliding and failure.

The Epistle to the Hebrews is a grand counterpart of, and complement to, the Epistle to the Romans. Both are expositions of fundamental gospel truth. Each of them is a foundational epistle to the eight epistles which follow on consecutively. Perhaps they may have particular appeal, respectively, to Jewish and Gentile readers, but believers everywhere, of whatever religious or cultural background, will revel in, and profit by, both of these letters. Romans will argue, convincingly and conclusively, that grace and law, like faith and works, are incompatible. Hebrews will argue, with equal conviction, that the NT revelation is, in fact, the culmination of the Old. The

3

revelation is progressive. The priests and priesthood of the old order have prepared
the way for a superior Priest and priestly house. The tabernacle itself, in its early
pristine glory, was a foregleam of a greater and more perfect tabernacle. The sacrifices
and offerings of old were foreshadowings of Golgotha. The revelation which began
with the prophets and patriarchs has reached its ordered peak in the coming of the
Christ. The shadows have been – and gone! The substance has come.

Now this NT revelation is not at all at variance with the old Mosaic and Levitical
order of things, but it has superseded that old order. Judaism was introductory and
temporary; it was imperfect and incomplete. But the acknowledgement of this
transient nature of Judaism was a problem for every thoughtful Jew. It was, after all,
a divine institution. It had come to them by the disposition of angels. It had been
delivered to them in glory, and it was theirs, as Hebrews, exclusively. And it was a
beautiful system; aesthetically beautiful. Its ceremonies and its rituals, its architecture
and its furniture, its music and vestments, its priests and prophets, its parchments and
scrolls, its feasts and its holy days, all would have a firm hold upon every proud Jewish
heart. As another has so aptly expressed it, "Israel's magnificent history of more than
twelve centuries, starting with Abraham the father and founder of the race, 'the
friend of God'; Israel's radiant galaxy of the very greatest men, lawgiver, conqueror
of Canaan, priests, judges, kings, prophets, poets, warriors, patriots, statesmen;
Israel's covenant relation with Jehovah, and the mighty future promised the chosen
race; Israel's exalted morality, her unsurpassed system of laws, religious, civil, criminal,
and even sanitary and dietetic – is it any wonder that the heart of a Hebrew
throbbed with exultation and hope when he thought of it all. Is it surprising that such
a people and such a history had for him a strange fascination, a supreme attraction?"
(W. Graham Scroggie).

It is the burden of the writer to the Hebrews to show that all of this was but
emblematical and shadowy; it had served its purpose and was obsolete. Judaism must
now be abandoned. This was a most serious demand to make of any Jew, but the awful
alternative, about which the epistle will constantly warn, was the abandonment of
God's final revelation in Jesus. This human name "Jesus" will be repeated, in singular,
solitary beauty, some eight times in the epistle. A new order of things has come
through "Jesus". If it is to be enjoyed then the old order must be given up. To cling
to the old order is a failure to appropriate the fulness and completeness of the new.
They could not have both. The two orders are not at variance but they are not
compatible. The old was for its day and that day was ended. The choice must be
made, clearly and decisively: it was Judaism or Jesus.

2. Survey and Theme

Two texts from ch. 5 will summarise the writer's exposition of the NT revelation
– "Thou art my Son"; "Thou art a priest". In these two divine pronouncements we
have presented to us both the Person and the work of Christ, and these combined

are the theme of the whole Hebrews Epistle. There is a Person greater than all the great ones of the past, whether human or angelic. There is a work which, in its perfection, has eclipsed and made obsolete all the sacrifices and offerings of the earlier centuries, and which, in another aspect, continues in a present priestly ministry for the saints of this present age. There is indeed, a Son and a Priest unique and supreme, meeting every desire and every demand of God's heart, God's throne, and God's people.

It is perhaps well known that some eleven times in the epistle the writer will say, "Let us ...", "Let us ...", "Let us ...". Two of these would well express the broad message of the letter; "Let us come" (4:16); "Let us go" (13:13). We are urged "inside the veil", and "outside the camp". The first ten chapters will instruct us as to the going in. The remaining three chapters will encourage us as to the going out. As in many epistles of the NT, duty follows doctrine; responsibility follows privilege; practice follows preaching. Indeed it has been well said that the only truth we really know is what we practise.

Chs. 1-2 of Hebrews present Christ in His personal and official glories, These two opening chapters are like strong towering twin pillars of essential truth between which we enter into the magnificence of the epistle. They are like the gold and the wood of the tabernacle furniture. The gold was pure gold; the wood was incorruptible wood. So the great truths of these two chapters are the abiding, essential, fundamental, foundation truths of Christ's deity and humanity. He is the Son of God, numbered with divine Persons, greater than the prophets and superior to angels too, but He has, in grace, taken His place among men. He has voluntarily taken part of flesh and blood, which was the common lot of the children of Abraham. He sanctifies those who believe and stands among them saying, "Behold I and the children which God hath given me". He is not ashamed to call them brethren.

Chs. 3-4 teach us that God will rest in Christ and that He would have us share in that rest. Christ is here greater than Moses in relation to God's house, and greater than Joshua in relation to God's rest. Moses was a servant in God's house; Christ is a Son over that house. Joshua led the people into the land, but not into rest. There is another rest, a future rest, and only those who believe will enter into that rest. The readers are exhorted to be diligent with that rest in view, and for their encouragement and assurance there is a great high priest who has passed through the heavens. There are indeed, three sources of help and succour. There is a priestly ministry; there is an unerring, infallible Word; and there is a throne of grace where to find mercy and grace in times of temptation and trial.

Ch.5 commences a more full and detailed exposition of that priestly ministry which has been but briefly introduced. Our Lord is greater than either Aaron or Melchisedec. He alone among high priests is called a "great" high priest. There follows a treatise on His humanity, His dignity, His authority, His sympathy, His piety, and His unfailing tender ministry for His people.

Ch.6 is parenthetical; it is a warning. There had been a warning about immaturity in ch.5, but this is more serious than immaturity. It is the possibility of apostasy.

Some were in danger of falling away. These would be professors who had arrived where they were in an intellectual sense only. Their profession of Jesus as Messiah was academic. It was not a heart experience of a Saviour but just a mental assent to doctrine. From such a vulnerable position they could easily be lured back to the attractions of Judaism. So the warning.

Ch.7 deals in more detail with Melchisedec. His name and His titles are full of meaning. How great was this man, made like to the Son of God, with no genealogical record of father or mother, beginning of days, or end of life. Christ's priesthood is after this order of Melchisedec. It is superior to the Levitical. Levi, yet in the loins of Abraham, paid tithes to Melchisedec, and in so doing recognised the superiority of the Melchisedec priesthood. It is a greater priesthood too, in that there is no successor. Our high priest lives in the power of an endless life. He is able therefore, to save completely, always, and for ever, those who come unto God by Him.

In ch.8 the treatise on the priesthood continues. Everything is superior. The covenant is new, and better; the ministry is more excellent. It is abiding too, when the very outward semblances of the previous covenant were waxing old and ready to vanish away.

Chs. 9-10 develop further the contrast between the two covenants. A most interesting section recalls some of the arrangement of the furniture and vessels of the old tabernacle system. The way into the holiest was then barred. The sacrifices were not sufficient and had to be repeated, and the consciences of the offerers were never perfect. The new order in Christ has opened the way to a heavenly sanctuary. The blood that made this possible was not the blood of bulls and goats but the blood of Christ, His own precious blood. The work was perfect too; it was once for all, never to be repeated, and He had now sat down in perpetuity. In contrast to the Aaronic priests who ever stood, always ministering, always offering, He had offered once and was now seated forever as far as sacrifice was concerned. But He had not only completed His sacrificial ministry, He had been rejected on earth too, and so the writer appropriately cites Ps 110. The seated Christ would so sit until His enemies would be made His footstool. There is now included another warning. For some of them, apostasy was an ever-present possibility; it was a constant danger. But there was great recompense of reward for those who would hold fast the confession of the hope.

Ch. 11 has often been likened to a roll of honour. It is indeed an illustrious listing of the names of the great, from Abel to Rahab. There are fleeting references after that to six more worthies of faith. Altogether, sixteen persons are mentioned, fourteen men and two women, and there follows also, a stirring account of what others, anonymous, had suffered in the cause of faith.

Ch. 12 begins with the reminder that this great company of testimony bearers is for our encouragement, and, greater than all these, Jesus Himself was the Pioneer and Perfecter of faith, and for the joy that was set before Him He patiently endured and suffered, and was now seated in glory. Considering Him is our safeguard against weariness and fainting. The Lord may chastise us along this pathway of faith. We ought to respond suitably to such chastisement, helping and exhorting each other, and ever remembering that we are associated with a kingdom that cannot be moved. All else may be, and will be, shaken. With becoming grace and reverence and godly fear we serve the God of that immovable kingdom.

Ch. 13 is wholly practical. There are directions and guidance as to our behaviour in the home, in the world, in the assembly, and in the sanctuary. We are exhorted outside the camp of religion which has rejected Jesus. There is much to be done. We must serve and praise; we must do good and be mindful of others. The God of peace, and the Lord Jesus, the great shepherd of the sheep, will perfect us in the doing of His good will.

3. Authorship

It is well known, among all serious students of Holy Scripture, that for many centuries the certain identity of the author of this epistle has been in controversy. For this reason he is constantly referred to just as, "The writer to the Hebrews". The ancient, though uninspired, inscription simply reads, "To Hebrews", giving no hint as to authorship. It seems almost futile and unnecessary, and perhaps indeed unprofitable, to give much time or space to the many and varied claims and avowals that have been made by so many since the 2nd century. Apart from Paul, the names of Barnabas, Apollos, Luke, Silas, Titus, Mark, Aquilla, Priscilla, Clement, have all been advanced. There are many of course who will not doubt the long accepted tradition that it was indeed Paul who wrote it. Among these are such saintly and scholarly writers as J.N.Darby, W.Kelly, F.W.Grant, Sir Robert Anderson, Franz Delitzsch, Adolph Saphir, C.E.Stuart, Samuel Ridout, and a host of others.

It must be stated however, in all fairness, that there are many equally great expositors who will not accept the Pauline authorship at all. Among such are Calvin, Luther, Alford, Bleek, Tholuck, Plumtre, Robertson, Bruce, and, with these, some of the more ancient of the ancients, as Tertullian, Origen, and Clement of Alexandria. Augustine and Jerome, though favouring Paul, dwell in dubiety.

The appealing and interesting suggestion has been made by some expositors that we have, in the epistle, Paul's thought in Luke's language. The polished character of the Greek in which it was written, seems to belong to such an one as Luke rather than to Paul, but the theology and argument and general thought are all very Pauline. J.N.Darby observes that "the apostolic under-current is apparent to a spiritual mind", but this is hardly convincing argument for a Pauline authorship.

Again, the writer's reference to Timothy (13:23), and Peter's reference in his epistle (2 Pet 3:15) to a letter written to Hebrews by Paul, while suggestive, are not conclusive.

Those who wish to pursue the authorship question further will find interesting reading and a detailed treatment of the matter in the expositions of the epistle by Marcus Dods in the *Expositor's Greek Testament*, and F.F.Bruce in the *New International*

Commentary on the New Testament.

Now perhaps the more pressing question for us is, whether we should say, resignedly, as many do, It is not important if we know, or do not know, the identity of the author, or whether we should rather say, It is important that we do not know. May it not be by divine design that the certain identity of the writer of this epistle has been shrouded by antiquity? It has been called by another, "The eclipse of the seer". The human author, be he apostle or not, has indeed been overshadowed by a greater. There is another Apostle in this letter. He is supreme. Let the occupation of the earliest readers, and of those of us who follow, be with the Apostle and High Priest of our confession. Let us consider Him. Like certain Greeks let us say, "We would see Jesus" (John 12: 21). Let not thoughts and disputes and prejudices and arguments concerning the penman, distract or detract from the plain glorious purpose of the epistle, that we should see Him who has become to us the revelation of the heart of God and the fulfilment of every Messianic prediction.

F.W.Boreham says, "I do not know who wrote the Epistle to the Hebrews. Nobody knows. But I like him, whoever he was. I like a man who, sitting down to write a letter, begins with God".

4. Recipients and Destination

If there is doubt as to the authorship of Hebrews, so also is there uncertainty as to the identity and the location of the first recipients of the letter. This much, however, we do know about them.

1. The ancient inscription, as we have seen, reads simply, "To Hebrews". This is not part of the inspired text, but right from the beginning it is the obvious conclusion, even for a casual reader, that the earliest readers were indeed Hebrews, well acquainted with the history, the ceremonials, the vocabulary, and the personalities of Judaism. The epistle being written in Greek, and the quotations of OT scriptures being from the Septuagint Version (LXX), may perhaps indicate that they were Hellenists, i.e. Jews who had settled in Greek-speaking countries, and who spoke the common Greek dialect of those lands rather than the Aramaic of Palestine. They are called "Grecians" in the AV text of Acts 6:1.

2. That they were a local company seems beyond dispute. Much of the epistle may indeed read more like a treatise than a letter, as we have noticed, but the personal references in the closing chapter, and the expressed hope of the writer that he may soon come with Timothy to see them, indicate that this treatise is, nevertheless, a letter to a local assembly, but written in "treatise" style so as to be divinely-preserved for Hebrews and believers everywhere, in every age. Other references too, as 5:12; 10:32-34; 12:4, require there to have been a specific local company of believers in view.

3. They had some Italian connection; "They of Italy salute you" (13:24). This
    admits of two opposite possibilities. For the earliest readers there was no such
    problem with this expression as we now have. It may well indeed simply mean
    that the writer was corresponding from Italy, but if that were the case would it
    not be more likely that he would have conveyed the greetings of the saints from
    whose particular town or city or locality he was writing? This would have been
    more natural than the wide, general, "They of Italy ...". The more satisfactory
    interpretation, for some, is that there were Hebrew believers with the writer,
    wherever he was, whose homeland was Italy. If the epistle was destined, for
    instance, to one of the several assemblies in Rome, (where there was a large
    Jewish element) then it was most understandable that these saints who were now
    with the writer, but who had an Italian background, would want to send greetings
    to their fellow-believers in Rome "They of Italy" would in this case be a natural
    and suitable description.

4. They were a second generation of believers (2:3). Some of their earlier leaders
    had now passed on (13:7 RV). They had indeed been professing Christianity for
    quite some time (5:12), and had suffered for it (10:33-34). They had been
    witnesses of the signs and miracles bestowed by the Spirit in those early days
    (2:4). But some of them were not making progress, and although they were now
    old enough, in their profession, to be teachers (5:12) the writer envisages a sad
    possibility: some of them may not be true believers at all. There may have been
    but mental, intellectual assent to the Messiahship of Jesus and to the truth of the
    gospel. There could be a falling away from such a state (6:4-6). An evil heart of
    unbelief could take them back to the relative ease and respectability of Judaism.
    Some would draw back unto perdition(10:38-39). It was necessary to warn them.

5. The sincere and genuine among them needed great encouragement: "Hold fast"
    (4:14; 10:23); "Let us go on"(6:1); "Cast not away your confidence" (10:35);
    "Run with patience" (12:1); "Consider him ... lest ye be wearied" (12:3).

6. There can be no doubt that whether at Jerusalem, Alexandria, Corinth, Ephesus,
    Rome, or wherever, the earliest readers of this letter were a local company of
    Hebrew believers, in whose midst there were those who, though acknowledging
    the truths of Christianity may have had no personal heart-knowledge of Christ.
    For such there was the ever-present danger of returning to Judaism.

Any uncertainty as to the identity of the first destination of this epistle does not
in any way affect subsequent interpretation. It is now firmly enshrined in the inspired
canon for our edification. Perhaps it is for this reason that the epistle, though indeed
sent as a letter to a local company, is, as we have seen, in the form and nature of a
treatise with wider circulation in view.

Many of us will not be troubled by, or attracted to, Judaism, but there is with us

today a large Judaised Christendom. This, for us, is the camp from which we are
called out, to be a testimony for Him whom religion has rejected. The epistle will
encourage us accordingly.

5. "Hebrews"

The designations "Hebrews", "Jews", and "Israel", have come to be regarded almost
as synonymous terms. They may indeed, sometimes, be used interchangeably, but
they are not, properly speaking, synonymous.

A Jew is, literally, a man of Judah. The term is not found in Biblical usage until
after the division of the kingdom. On the separation of the ten tribes Judah and
Benjamin together formed a kingdom known as Judah, and the men of Judah were
"Jews" (2 Kings 16:6; 25:25). The feminine "Jewess" occurs only in Acts 16:1; 24:24,
and in 1 Chron 4:18 (JND).

The name "Israel" was first given to Jacob at Peniel in Gen 32:28. From the twelve
sons of Jacob there sprang the twelve families and tribes who became known as "the
children of Israel", or simply as "Israel". At the division of the kingdom, referred to
above, the ten tribes were known as "Israel", while the two tribes were "Judah".

The first occurrence in Scripture of the term "Hebrew" is found in Gen 14:13,
where we read of "Abram the Hebrew". It is sometimes supposed that there is a link
with Abram's ancestor Eber, or "Heber" (Gen 11:17-26). The root of the word
"Hebrew", however, is, "to cross over", and it is perhaps more likely that "Abram the
Hebrew" was so called simply because he was a sojourner in Canaan, having crossed
over from his own land. His descendants therefore became known as Hebrews also.
Paul referred to himself as a "Hebrew of Hebrews", meaning that he was a pure
Hebrew, born of Hebrew parentage, with no Gentile or proselyte blood in his lineage.
The designation "Hebrews" is found in the NT only in Acts 6:1; 2 Cor 11:22; Phil 3:5.

So it will be seen that, while strictly speaking there is a narrowing circle from
"Hebrew", to "Israel", to "Jew", it is nevertheless understandable that in many
instances we may correctly use the three terms interchangeably.

6. Date

There is a fairly general, though not complete, agreement, that the epistle was
written between AD 63-68. Perhaps there are two internal indications of this.

1. The verbs of 10:11 are in the present tense. The priests, at the time of writing,
    were still ministering daily. The temple therefore was still standing, so the date
    is earlier than AD 70.

2. The material, visible, tangible things of Judaism, were however, waxing old, and soon to disappear; they were about to vanish away (8:13). This is a clear reference to the pending destruction of the temple in AD 70. After that the sacrifices and ceremonials ceased.

7. Key Words

There are a number of interesting key words in this epistle, which, when studied together, present an excellent indication of the writer's aim and purpose.

1. The word "perfect" is found, in its various forms, some twelve times in the text of the AV (2:10; 5:9; 6:1; 7:11; 7:19; 9:9; 9:11; 10:1; 10:14; 11:40; 12:23; 13:21). In the original text there are further occurrences. These have been obscured in the translation, as e.g., the "full age" of 5:14, the "consecrated" of 7:28, and the "finisher" of 12:2. There was no perfection under the old system. Spiritual maturity, complete assurance, and perfect rest of conscience came only with Christ.

2. The word "eternal", again in a variety of forms, is found many times. There is:
    a. An eternal salvation   5:9
    b. An eternal judgment   6:2
    c. An eternal redemption   9:12
    d. An eternal Spirit   9:14
    e. An eternal inheritance   9:15
    The cognate words "everlasting", "evermore", and "forever", also occur many many times. In this way is emphasised the abiding nature of the new order of things in Christ, in contrast to the transience of old Judaism.

3. Probably the best known key word, the word usually associated with Hebrews, is the word "better", appearing some thirteen times. There is:
    a. A better hope   7:19
    b. A better covenant   8:6
    c. Better promises   8:6
    d. Better sacrifices   9:23
    e. A better country   11:16
    f. A better resurrection   11:35
    And so much more! All this to show that in Christ, who is Himself "better" than the angels (1:4), everything is superior. Better things (11:40) have come to us in Him.

8. Bibliography

Anderson, Robert, Sir. *Types in Hebrews* . Grand Rapids. Kregel Publications, 1978
Bellet, J.G. *The Opened Heavens* . Addison U.S.A. Bible Truth Publishers, 1983.
Boreham, F.W. *The Eclipse of the Seer*. From "Arrows of Desire" (Ch 4). London. Epworth Press. 1951.
Brenton, Sir Lancelot C.L. *The Septuagint with Apocrypha: Greek and English*. (Reprint of Bagster's 1851 Edition). Peabody, U.S.A. Hendrickson Publishers. 1986.
Brown, John. *Hebrews* . The Geneva Series of Commentaries. Banner of Truth Trust, 1961.
Bruce, A.B. *The Epistle to the Hebrews*. Edinburgh. T&T Clark. 1899. Reprint by Klock & Klock, Minneapolis, U.S.A.1980.
Bruce, F.F. *The Epistle to the Hebrews* . The New International Commentary on the New Testament. Grand Rapids. Eerdmans. 1964.
Darby, J.N. *Hebrews*. Synopsis of the Books of the Bible Vol.5, London. Stow Hill. 1965.
Darby, J.N. *Brief Analysis of the Epistle to the Hebrews*. Collected Writings Vol.15, pp.200-237. London. Stow Hill. 1964.
Darby, J.N. *Notes from Lectures on the Epistle to the Hebrews*. Collected Writings Vol. 27, pp.335-414. London. Stow Hill. 1965.
Darby, J.N. *Notes on the Epistle to the Hebrews*. Collected Writings Vol.28, pp.1-34. London. Stow Hill.
Davies, J.M. *Let us go on to Perfection*. Bombay. Gospel Literature Service. 1978
Dods, Marcus. *The Epistle to the Hebrews*. The Expositor's Greek Testament. Grand Rapids. Eerdmans. 1976.
English. E. Schuyler. *Studies in the Epistle to the Hebrews* New Jersey. Loizeaux Brothers. 1955
Gaebelein, Arno C. *The Angels of God*. New York. Our Hope Publications Office. 1924.
Gooding, D.W. *An Unshakeable Kingdom*. Toronto. Everyday Publications Inc. 1976.
Grant, F.W. *The Epistle to the Hebrews*. The Numerical Bible. New Jersey. Loizeaux. 1902.
Kelly, William. *An Exposition of the Epistle to the Hebrews*. (Reprint) Pennsylvania. Believers Bookshelf.
Lenski, R.C.H. *The Interpretation of the Epistle to the Hebrews*. Minneapolis. Augsburg Publishing House. 1966.
Lincoln, William. *Lectures on the Epistle to the Hebrews*. (Reprint) Assembly Writers Library Vol.2. Glasgow. Gospel Tract Publications. 1980.
Maclaren, Alexander. *Expositions of Holy Scripture*. Vol.15. (Reprint) Grand Rapids. Baker Book House. 1974.
Morrish. *Hebrews, Epistle to the*. New and Concise Bible Dictionary, pp 350-354. London. Hammond Trust.
Murray, Andrew. *The Holiest of All*. London. Nisbet & Co.

Newell, William R. *Hebrews Verse by Verse*. (Reprint) Grand Rapids. Baker Book House. 1987.

Ridout, Samuel. *Lectures on the Epistle to the Hebrews*. Kilmarnock. John Ritchie.

Robertson, A.T. *Word Pictures in the New Testament*, Vol 5 (Reprint) Grand Rapids. Baker Book House.

Saphir, Adolph. *The Epistle to the Hebrews, an Exposition*. 2 Vols. Fifth American Edition. New York. Christian Alliance Publishing Co.

Steen, J.Charleton. *Christ Supreme*. Kilmarnock. John Ritchie.

Stuart, C.E. *The Old Faith or the New – Which?* (Reprint) Assembly Writers Library Vol. 5 Glasgow. Gospel Tract Publications. 1981.

Thomas, W.H.Griffith. *Hebrews, A Devotional Commentary*. Grand Rapids. U.S.A. Eerdmans. 1961.

Vincent, M.R. *Word Studies in the New Testament* . (Reprint) Virginia. MacDonald Publishing Company.

Vine, W.E. *Hebrews*. The Collected Writings of W.E.Vine, Vol.3. Glasgow. Gospel Tract Publications. 1985.

Vine, W.E. *Expository Dictionary*. London. Oliphants. 1940.

Westcott, B.F. *The Epistle to the Hebrews* Reprint. Grand Rapids. U.S.A. Eerdmans. 1984

9. Outline

I.   *The Supremacy of the Son of God* (Chapter 1)
     1. Christ Greater than the Prophets   1: 1-4
     2. Christ Greater than the Angels   1: 5-14

II. *The Glory of the Son of Man* (Chapter 2)
     1. The First Warning   2: 1-4
     2. Christ Greater than Adam   2: 5-9
     3. Perfect through Suffering   2: 10-18

III. *God's House and God's Rest* (Chapter 3)
     1. Christ Greater than Moses   3: 1-6
     2. The Second Warning   3: 7-19

IV. *God's Rest and God's People* (Chapter 4)
     1. Christ Greater than Joshua   4: 1-10
     2. The Knife; the Priest; the Throne   4: 11-16

V.   *The Great High Priest* (Chapter 5)
     1. After the Pattern of Aaron   5: 1-5
     2. After the Order of Melchisedec   5: 6-10
     3. Spiritual Immaturity   5: 11-14

VI.   *The Third Warning* (Chapter 6)
      1. Go On – Or Go Back   6: 1-8
      2. Perseverance and Patience   6: 9-12
      3. The Promise and the Hope   6: 13-20

VII. *Melchisedec* (Chapter 7)
      1. King and Priest   7: 1-3
      2. Greater than Levi   7: 4-10
      3. A Superior Priesthood   7: 11-22
      4. An Untransferable Priesthood   7: 23-28

VIII. *A More Excellent Ministry* (Chapter 8)
      1. A Greater Priest   8: 1-6
      2. A Better Covenant   8: 7-13

IX.   *A Greater Tabernacle* (Chapter 9)
      1. The Old Sanctuary   9: 1-5
      2. The Old Ritual   9: 6-10
      3. The Blood of Christ   9: 11-14
      4. The Perfect Mediator   9: 15-22
      5. The Three Appearings   9: 23-28

X.   *The Law is Superseded* (Chapter 10)
      1. The Will of God   10: 1-10
      2. The Work of Christ   10: 11-14
      3. The Witness of the Spirit   10: 15-18
      4. The Way to the Holiest   10: 19-22
      5. The Walk of the Saints   10: 23-25
      6. The Word of Warning (The Fourth)   10: 26-31
      7. The Watchfulness of the Faithful   10: 32-39

XI.   *The Triumphs of Faith* (Chapter 11)
      1. The Character of Faith   11: 1-3
      2. The Antedeluvians   11: 4-7
         a. Abel   v.4
         b. Enoch   vv.5-6
         c. Noah   v.7
      3. The Patriarchs   11: 8-22
         a. Abraham (and Sara)   vv.8-12
         b. Strangers and Pilgrims   vv.13-16
         c. Abraham Again   vv.17-19
         d. Isaac   v.20

        e. Jacob   v.21
        f. Joseph   v.22
     4. Moses, the Passover, and the Exodus   11: 23-29
     5. Rahab and Jericho   11: 30-31
     6. More Victories and Victors   11: 32-40

XII. *Encouragements to Faith* (Chapter 12)
     1. The Supreme Example   12: 1-3
     2. The Chastisement of Sons   12: 4-11
     3. Working, Walking, and Watching   12: 12-17
     4. The Two Mountains   12: 18-24
        a. Sinai   vv.18-21
        b. Zion   vv.22-24
     5. A Closing Appeal   12: 25-29

XIII. *Concluding Exhortations* (Chapter 13)
     1. Concerning Hospitality and Holiness   13: 1-4
     2. Concerning Covetousness and Contentment   13: 5-6
     3. Concerning Grace and Truth   13: 7-9
     4. Concerning Separation to Christ   13: 10-14
     5. Concerning Sacrifice and Submission   13: 15-17
     6. Concerning Intercession   13: 18-19
     7. The Doxology   13: 20-21
     8. A Personal Word   13: 22-23
     9. Salutation and Benediction   13: 24-25

Text and Exposition

I. The Supremacy of the Son of God (1: 1-14)

1. *Christ Greater than the Prophets*
1:1-4

v.1   "God, who at sundry times and in divers manners spake in time past unto the fathers by the prophets,

v.2   Hath in these last days spoken unto us by *his* Son, whom he hath appointed heir of all things, by whom also he made the worlds;

v.3   Who being the brightness of *his* glory, and the express image of his person, and upholding all things by the word of his power, when he had by himself purged our sins, sat down on the right hand of the Majesty on high;

v.4   Being made so much better than the angels, as he hath by inheritance obtained a more excellent name than they."

1   The epistle begins with an alliteration in Greek. The first words are, *polumerōs kai polutropōs*, and this is the only occurrence of these words in our New Testament. In many parts and in many ways, God had spoken. That God had indeed spoken every Hebrew knew well. The gods of the nations were dead, and in their lifelessness they were silent. Gods of wood and stone, or even gods of gold or silver, did not, could not, speak. But the God of the Hebrews was a living God. He could speak; and He did speak. Indeed a living and loving God must speak, for how else should we know His thoughts about us, or towards us? Or how should we come to know Him if there is not a voice, a word, a revelation to us?

For twelve centuries, since the days when Abraham their father had become the friend of God, God had been speaking to the chosen race. That God should speak to men at all was great grace. That He should choose to speak to the Hebrews in particular was sovereign grace. He had indeed chosen to speak to them, and to reveal Himself, but the revelation had been multifarious and fragmentary. Sometimes, whether to the nation, or to favoured individuals, He had spoken in an audible voice. Sometimes He spoke in the sacred writings using inspired prophets into whose minds He had breathed His thoughts.

In dreams and in visions, in similes and in allegories, in types and in shadows, in

17

prophecy and in poetry, at varying times and in this variety of manners, God had formerly made Himself known in a prophetic ministry. The prophets were His instruments. To them, and in them, and by them, He had conveyed His mind to their ancestors, the fathers. To each of the prophets there was a particular, but partial, revelation. To Moses there was one; to Elijah there was another. To Isaiah or to Jeremiah there was something more; to Ezekiel, Daniel, Joel or Amos there was yet more; but all was fragmentary and incomplete.

The designation "prophet" is often used to describe one who foretells the future. This is often correct, but it is not always so. The comment of W.E.Vine is most helpful, "Prophecy (*prophēteia*) signifies the speaking forth of the mind and counsel of God (*pro*, forth, *phēmi*, to speak). Though much of OT prophecy was predictive, ... prophecy is not necessarily, nor even primarily, fore-telling. It is the declaration of that which cannot be known by natural means, Matt 26:68; it is the forth-telling of the will of God, whether with reference to the past, the present, or the future" (*Expository Dictionary*, p.221).

2 But at the end of this period of prophetic ministry, in the last of these days of partial revelation, God had spoken in a unique and supreme fashion, in the Son.

Now we must not here equate the Son with the prophets as being an instrument in God's hand for the making known of His mind. That is not the thought here. The writer is not just saying that God had communicated by prophets and was now communicating by His Son. It is not as simple as that. There is no definite article before "Son", as in the AV. The thought, though difficult to express in English, is that this is God Himself, as Son, who is speaking. The speaker, the Son, is God. Having for so long used the prophets as His instruments, He now, Himself, as God the Son, speaks to men. Here, when once it is understood, is one of the greatest proofs of the deity of Christ. The Godhead is a holy Tri-unity, Father, Son, and Spirit. This God, not as Father, and not in Spirit, but in Son, has been amongst us, and has spoken. God "son-wise", God in sonship, has spoken, in a grand finality of revelation to men. If the manner and method of revelation in old time was incomplete and varied and partial, now there is a revelation which is complete and perfect. There is introduced then, almost immediately, the theme of superiority which will be so prominent in the epistle. The revelation in the Son is superior to the fragmentary revelation given over the centuries through His servants the prophets. It is complete. There is nothing to follow.

This is the first of eleven references to Christ's sonship in the epistle (1:2; 1:5 twice; 1:8; 4:14; 5:5; 5:8; 6:6; 7:3; 7:28; 10:29). In the opening sentence the Son is introduced. In v.5 the sonship is both affirmed and confirmed. After this there may be observed, in the subsequent references, the relation of the Son to the anointed offices of Prophet, Priest, and King. It is important to notice that the relationship is within the circle of divine Persons; it is in the deity; it is eternal. Sonship never implies inferiority, but rather equality, as every Jew knew. To deny the eternality of the relationship on the premise that that would require eternal inferiority, is to betray a gross ignorance, or negligence, of Hebrew thought and culture, and an ignorance too, of the general presentation of sonship in the other NT epistles. (See John 5:18, 23; 19:7.)

Throughout the NT the sonship of Christ is a recurring theme. It is a central truth in the Gospels, in the Acts of the Apostles, in the Epistles, and in the Revelation. He is Son in a beautiful variety of relationships, each revealing some particular glory. There are, indeed, at least ten different ways in which He is viewed as Son.

He is called, Son of God   Luke 1:35
            Son of the Father   2 John 3
            Son of the Highest   Luke 1:32
            Son of the Blessed   Mark 14:61
These titles relate Him to His Father, to God, and to the heavens.

He is called, Son of Mary   Mark 6:3
            Son of Joseph   John 1:45
            Son of the Carpenter   Matt 13:55
These titles relate Him to Nazareth and to the earthly family.

He is called, Son of David   Matt 1:1
            Son of Abraham   Matt 1:1
            Son of man   Matt 8:20
These titles relate Him to Israel, to the kingdom, and to the world.

As the Son in the bosom of the Father, dwelling ever in the affections of the Father, and declaring that divine heart to us, He is also, "The Son of His love" (Col 1:13 JND).

There now follows at once a seven-fold presentation of the Son in His greatness and glory. The writer will portray Him as:

> The established heir
> The creator of the universe
> The effulgence of glory
> The image of God
> The upholder of all things
> The sin-purger
> The seated one

The Son is the appointed heir. The word "heir" (*klēronomos*) is a form, or derivation, of the word "lot". When a father died and property had to be divided, lots were drawn. The property was apportioned accordingly. If there was but one son, then there was one heir; he inherited all. The uniqueness of the only-begotten Son of God requires that He is heir of all things. Nor does He wait for the death of a father, as

other heirs do. He is the established inheritor now; the proprietor of all things. The
Father cannot die, but He has already given all things into the hands of the Son
(John 13:3).

> As Son of Abraham He is heir to the land
> As Son of David He is heir to the throne
> As Son of man He is heir to the world
> As Son of God He is heir of all things

Was not all this beautifully foreshadowed in the beloved Isaac? "And Abraham
gave all that he had unto Isaac" (Gen 24:36; 25:5). There was only one Isaac. He
inherited all. The precious things displayed by the nameless servant (Gen 24:53)
were evidences of the greatness of the father and the son.

There is but one "Only-begotten". There is but one Son like Him. If we have been
brought, by grace, to be heirs with Him (Rom 8:17), it is indeed of grace; He alone
has personal rights because He is not only Son, but the very creator of all that which
He inherits.

The word "worlds" here is, literally, "ages" (*aiōnes*). So often, when reading the
AV, we rightly change the word to "ages". Do we not read, "Lo, I am with you alway,
even unto the end of the age" (Matt 28:20)? Do we not prefer, "Once in the end of
the age hath he appeared" (Heb 9:26)? And do we not read "age" instead of "world"
in Matt 13:39; Rom 12:2; 1 Cor 10:11; 2 Cor 4:4; Eph 1:7, and in other texts also
where the word is the same as here in Heb 1:2?

In the Son, and by Him, and for Him, all the ages have been planned and prepared.
Around Him all the cycles of time revolve. For Him they run their courses for His
glory. He is the Father of Eternity (Isa 9:6 JND) from whom the ages emanate.

But while the primary meaning of *aiōnes* is "ages", and not material worlds, there
is evidence that the word was sometimes used to include the contents of the age in
question, so that it may well mean, not only the cycles of time, but all that they
brought forth as they unfolded. It is the whole universe of time and space. The rabbis
spake of several "worlds" – the world of angels and spirits; the world of sun, moon,
and stars; the world of earth and sea and men. It is irrelevant to contest about the
precise meaning of the word as here in the context. Without Him, the Son, was not
anything made that was made (John 1:3). He is therefore the rightful and appointed
heir of all things. He is the proprietor of everything created. Thrones and dominions,
principalities and powers, things visible and invisible, are all His by inalienable right.
He is the established heir.

3   The Son is the brightness of glory. Note the word "being", early in this verse. It
is but a tiny Greek word, the participle *ōn*, but its importance is far reaching. It
implies absolute and timeless existence. Is it not reminiscent of the "I AM" of other
Scriptures? Eternally the Son is the glorious effulgence; never beginning to be so;
never ceasing to be so. No doubt this glory is divine glory; it is God's glory though

there is no pronoun "his" as in our AV. The word "brightness" is found only here in the NT. It is the word *apaugasma*, an interesting word which is comprised of two words. The first, *apo*, is a preposition meaning "from". The second, *augē*, means "brightness". *Apaugasma* is therefore "a brightness from"; "a shining forth"; "an effulgence"; "a radiance".

"Glory" (*doxa*), is an equally interesting word, but almost indefinable. The Oxford Dictionary has a most lengthy attempt at definition and scans the whole vocabulary for suitable explanatory words and phrases to give the meaning of glory. Greek lexicons too, find the same difficulty in defining *doxa*. It is exalted renown; honourable fame; resplendence; radiance; majesty; beauty; bliss; magnificence; light; splendour; aureole; exaltation. All these, and more, are necessary, to convey to us some little idea of that which is inscrutable. Glory is the out-shining of an intrinsic excellence. Christ is the effulgence of God's glory. This is not a passive reflection but an active out-raying. Moses may reflect the glory and veil his shining face. But the unveiled face of the Son radiates for us the glory of the God who dwells in light unapproachable (2 Cor 3:18; 1 Tim 6:16 RV). The Jew was familiar with glory. To Israel belonged the glory (Rom 9:4). The Shechinah, the visible glory, had dwelt in their ancient tabernacle and in their first temple. But the incarnate Son is the true Shechinah. In Him dwells all the fulness of the Godhead bodily. The message of the gospel is the radiancy of the glad tidings of the glory (2 Cor 4:4 JND). In his Gospel John uses the word "glory" forty times! The glory of God streams forth in the Son. As the solar light brings the very essence of the sun to us, so has Christ brought to us the holiness, the wisdom, the beauty, the perfections, of God.

Such is the completeness, in Christ, of this revelation of the character of God, that this very word, character, is now used. The Son is the express image, the exact expression, the *charaktēr* of God's substance. "Express image" is the one word *charaktēr*, and this is its only occurrence in the NT. It must be distinguished from "image" in 2 Cor 4:4 and Col 1:15. The word there is *eikōn*, which conveys the double thought of representation and manifestation. "Christ is the visible representation and manifestation of God to created beings; the likeness expressed in this manifestation is unique and perfect" (W.E.Vine). So our Lord may say, "He that hath seen me hath seen the Father" (John 14:9).

The word *charaktēr* (cp. our English words "character, characteristic") denotes an impress or stamp as on a coin or seal. An image on a printer's die impresses on the paper its own features exactly. Originally, *charaktēr* came from a word which meant "to engrave; to cut; to scratch; to mark". It was, in fact, at first descriptive of the tool that did the engraving, then of the engraving, and then of the impress made by the engraving. It denotes the reproduction upon the metal coin, or upon the waxen seal, of the exact image of the features which are engraved on the die or on the signet ring. So is the Son the exact expression of all that God is. The substance, the essence, of God, is seen perfectly in the Son. This substance (*hupostasis*) is the reality, the essential being, of God. What God is essentially, is manifested in Christ. There is nothing in the Father which is not in the Son. When "the life" was manifested (1

John 1:2), God was manifested in flesh. Those who saw, and properly appreciated, the Carpenter from Nazareth, could say so beautifully, "We beheld his glory, the glory as of the only begotten of the Father" (John 1:14). The only begotten Son has become to us the exegesis of the God whom men have never seen (John 1:18). Where we cannot understand we may only bow in wonder and worship, and sing with another,

> All the Father's counsels claiming
> Equal honours to the Son;
> All the Son's effulgence beaming
> Makes the Father's glory known.   (J.N. Darby)

The writer now continues to extol the greatness of the Son. He is not only the established heir of all things, and the creator of all things, but He upholds all things by the word of His power. We are often rightly reminded that this "upholding" (*pherōn*) is not, as the mythical Atlas, supporting as a dead weight the pillars of the universe, bowed beneath the burden of it all. The word implies both preservation and government. He is the helmsman and pilot of all things. He marshals them and He orders them, bearing them along, guiding and controlling, sustaining and directing, commanding and carrying. All this He does by the word of His power, or, as it might be rendered, by His powerful word (Pss 33:6-7; 147:15-18; 148:6). He orders, not only the physical universe, but those essential laws which hold it together in arrangement. He can, and He will, if necessary, interfere with these laws (Josh 10:12-13) and with such a thought in mind we remember the noon-day darkness of Mark 15:33.

It was such an One as this who, by Himself, made purification of sins. What a word is this for sinful men! With what confidence and glad assurance we rest in such a work, accomplished by such a person. God's Son, God's appointed heir, creator of all created things, the effulgence of God's glory, God manifested in flesh, the upholder of the universe, Himself, has attended to the question of my sins and has made purgation. This is greater than atonement. He has not covered sins; He has made purification. But there is something more here than my relief from my sins. Note the beauty of the Greek middle voice. There is a reflex action in the verb. As J.N. Darby observes, "The Greek verb has here a peculiar form, which gives it a reflective sense, causing the thing done to return into the doer, throwing back the glory of the thing done upon the one who did it" (*Synopsis* Vol 5, p.182, foot-note). What He has done has come back to Him in glory. There is blessing for others but the glory is His. Even if we omit the words "by himself", as do many of the ancient manuscripts, the remaining grammar requires that we understand the work to be His own work, by Himself and for Himself.

Observe too, that it is not just "our" sins, (see JND and RV), but sins in a more general sense. One day, because of Calvary, there will be a universe purged of sins and the blight they have brought. Then, the message of John Baptist will have been realised fully. The Lamb of God bears away the sin of the world (John 1:29). That will be for His glory.

In the accomplishment of His perfect work of expiation the Man of Calvary is now the Man in the glory. He is seated at the right hand of the majesty on high. "Majesty" (*megalosunē*) denotes greatness (from *mega*, great). It is only here and in 8:1 and Jude 25 in the NT. He sits at the right hand of the greatness in the heights. He sits by invitation (Ps 110:1) but the beauty of the Greek middle voice is here again; He has seated Himself; He set Himself down. Now those who attended to sins and sacrifice in the old dispensation never sat. Perhaps only one OT priest is seen seated, and that with disastrous consequences (1 Sam 4:13-18). Jewish priests stood as they ministered (10:11). Even their high priest, with all the privileges of his holy office, when he had performed his most sacred duties in the sanctuary on the great day of atonement, retired from the presence of the divine glory. There was no seat for those priests of old. Their sacrificial work was never done. But with Christ it is different. He is seated; He is enthroned; He is exalted far above all (Eph 1:21; 4:10; Phil 2:9). Three times more in this epistle we shall see Him seated (8:1; 10:12; 12:2). His work relative to sin is finished.

4   Now this exaltation of the Son to the right hand of God demonstrates Him to be superior to the angels. He is greater than the prophets; He has brought to us a more complete revelation. He is greater than the priests; He has accomplished a perfect work of expiation, and has sat down. But He is, thus, better than the angels. He has a place, and a name, and a relationship with the Father, which angels do not have. In sitting down as He is, raised to these high honours, higher than any angel ever knew, He is "more excellent" than they. The Son has taken a place better than the angels.

That these are angelic beings as we usually understand them, seems beyond question. Yet some have laboured the essential basic meaning of the word angel (*angelos*, messenger) to argue that these angels are none other than the messengers, the prophets, of the first verse. That the word is sometimes used in this way, of men, cannot be denied (see Matt 11:10; Luke 9:52; James 2:5), but in those instances it is obvious that the *angelos* are men. There are thirteen references to angels in this epistle and it is clear in the context that in every occurrence of the word it is heavenly, unembodied, ministering spirits, with which we are concerned (1:14). It is, by the way, somewhat thrilling to notice that if there are thirteen references to angels in the epistle, there are also thirteen occurrences of the word "better" (*kreissōn*), which is here in this verse noticed for the first time. (See also 6:9; 7:7; 7:19; 7:22; 8:6 twice: 9:23; 10:34; 11:16; 11:35; 11:40; 12:24.)

The Son has inherited a more excellent name than the angels. "Inherited" (the verb form of "heir" of v.2) does not imply that this excellent name became His only on His ascension and exaltation. He has, eternally, by personal, inherent right, a more excellent name. The reference is not to any particular name or title. Of these He has a myriad. It is that in His unique exalted sonship, in His person, He is, because of what He is, and because of who He is, and because of where He is, superior to the angels. He has taken a place on high which proves that. But He was already "more excellent" before His enthronement, and before His incarnation. At His incarnation He but inherits in manhood that which was ever His in Godhood. He "shall be called the Son of God" (Luke 1:35), born of Mary but only-begotten Son of God. This then, is the name of v.4. It is the character, the rank, the dignity, of the Son who is now the Redeemer seated at the right hand of the Majesty on high. In His person and in His position He is superior.

Now what tremendous effect should all this have had on believing Hebrews. How familiar they were with the ministry of angels, as were their fathers. Abraham in Mamre (Gen 18:1), Isaac in Moriah (Gen 22:11), Jacob at Mahanaim (Gen 32:1), Moses at Sinai (Acts 7:53), Gideon, Manoah, Elijah, David, Daniel: all could bear testimony to the ministry of the heavenly ones. We have no account of the creation of angels. Neither do we know how many there are. An innumerable company (Heb 12:22); ten thousand times ten thousand, and thousands of thousands (Rev 5:11); a multitude of the heavenly host at Bethlehem (Luke 2:13); more than twelve legions awaiting His command at Gethsemane (Matt 26:53); these give us but a faint idea of the vastness of the angel hosts. But Christ is greater than all. How such superiority to angels should have encouraged and strengthened these Jewish saints. The Christ of the new order of things was more excellent than angels and was therefore more excellent than a Judaism whose glory was angelic in character.

"More excellent" occurs again in 8:6, where Christ has a more excellent ministry. There is also a more excellent sacrifice in 11:4 (AV), but there the word so translated is different from that in 1:4 and 8:6.

2. Christ Greater than the Angels
1:5-14

v.5 "For unto which of the angels said he at any time, Thou art my Son, this day have I begotten thee? And again, I will be to him a Father, and he shall be to me a Son?

v.6 And again, when he bringeth in the firstbegotten into the world, he saith, And let all the angels of God worship him.

v.7 And of the angels he saith, Who maketh his angels spirits, and his ministers a flame of fire.

v.8 But unto the Son he saith, Thy throne, O God, is for ever and ever: a sceptre of righteousness is the sceptre of thy kingdom.

v.9 Thou hast loved righteousness, and hated iniquity; therefore God, even thy God, hath anointed thee with the oil of gladness above thy fellows.

v.10 And, Thou, Lord, in the beginning hast laid the foundation of the earth; and the heavens are the works of thine hands:

v.11 They shall perish; but thou remainest; and they all shall wax old as doth a garment;

v.12 And as a vesture shalt thou fold them up, and they shall be changed: but thou art the same, and thy years shall not fail.

> v.13   But to which of the angels said he at any time, Sit on my right hand, until
>   I make thine enemies thy footstool?
> v.14   Are they not all ministering spirits, sent forth to minister for them who
>   shall be heirs of salvation?"

The seven-fold greatness of the Son having been established, there now follows a seven-fold testimony of OT Scriptures to the Son's superiority over the angels. This superiority has already been intimated in v.4. Christ is "better than the angels". But, quoting now from the ancient writings and particularly from their beloved Psalms (here is something to sing about!), the writer will show that belief in the excelling greatness of the Messiah is founded and grounded upon the authority of the inspired Word. Seven quotations follow. Those who are interested in the accuracy and beauty of Bible numerals will want to emphasise the number "seven": not six quotations, nor eight, but seven. There is a certain completeness and perfection associated with this number. Seven OT Scriptures will speak in a united testimony to the excellence of the Son over the angels. The passages quoted will extol Christ from His incarnation to His millennial reign and indeed into the Day of God.

5   This "for" at the beginning of the verse connects and continues the treatise on the supremacy of the Son. This supremacy having been stated the argument will now be advanced that the prophets and psalmists of the past all concur. The first quotation is from the second Psalm. "Unto which of the angels said he at any time, Thou art my Son, this day have I begotten thee?" Paul's usage of this quotation in Acts 13 will show that it speaks of our Lord's incarnation, of His coming into humanity. God had made promise of a Saviour (Acts 13:23). He had raised up David among them for a king, and of David's seed He had raised up Jesus as a Saviour. This is not a raising up from the dead. It is not resurrection. It is a raising up in manhood, in the nation, of a Saviour. God had raised up David in the nation, and God had raised up Jesus. And this was in fulfilment of Ps 2:7. This, argues Paul, is the glad tidings of the fulfilment of the promise made to the fathers. God had raised up in the midst of them a Saviour (Acts 13:33). Note that the word "again" in the AV rendering of this verse is best omitted. This is not a raising again from the dead, it is a raising up of Jesus in manhood among them. (See JND and RV.) Now it is after this that Paul will proceed to speak of the death and consequent corruption of David, but of the raising up from the dead of Jesus, but it important to see that there two raisings of Jesus in Acts 13. Firstly in manhood, in the midst of the nation (vv. 23, 33) and secondly in resurrection (vv. 30, 34, 37). It is this first that is said to be in fulfilment of the second Psalm.

Now the force of the argument is this, such words were never, and could never be, spoken to any angel. "Thou art my Son" belongs to Christ alone. Angels collectively may be called, "the sons of God" (Job 1:6; 2:1; 38:7), but no single angel is ever called God's Son like Messiah. God has addressed Messiah as "my Son".

But what does this mean, "this day have I begotten thee"? Including the quotation here in Heb 1, the expression is quoted three times in the NT (Heb 1:5; 5:5; Acts 13:32). Some, correctly anxious to guard the truth of Christ's eternal sonship, speak of "eternal generation", and regard the term "this day" as being synonymous with eternity. There is a certain unsatisfactory vagueness about this interpretation which does not seem to be in keeping with the apparent definiteness of "this day".

Others will not see the distinctions we have tried to point out between the raisings in Acts 13, and will interpret "this day" as the day of Christ's resurrection. There is no doubt of course, that our Lord's claim to sonship was vindicated by His resurrection. The empty tomb reverses the verdict of the nation (John 19:7), and powerfully declares Him to be the Son (Rom 1:4).

Still others, who see Christ's priesthood commencing with His ascension, will look to that day of His going up into the heavens as "this day" of these passages.

Now of this there can be no question, that there is no beginning to this unique sonship. "Thou art my Son" is a firm, positive, affirmation of a glorious relationship that already was. Whatever else is here in the word from the second Psalm, it must agree with this, that He ever, always, eternally, was the Son. Have we not seen this proven in the opening verses of this chapter?

There is a golden thread running through the four occurrences of these lovely words, "Today have I begotten thee" (Ps 2; Acts 13; Heb 1; Heb 5). That golden thread is the humanity of Christ. The King of Ps 2 must be a man. The Saviour of Acts 13 is a real man too. The Messiah of Heb 1 is also man. And so is the Priest of Heb 5. He who is the Son, uniquely and eternally, has been begotten into that necessary humanity, and as He makes His advent into real manhood we hear the Father say, "Today have I begotten thee". Is it not all reminiscent of the word of Gabriel to Mary in Luke 1:35?

This then, is the writer's inspired argument, that Messiah is the Son of God, "Thou art my Son"; and that this sonship is publicly saluted as the Son enters manhood, "This day have I begotten thee"; such words never have been, nor could be, spoken to an angel. Christ is unique. He is superior and supreme. His sonship makes Him so.

The second quotation is from 2 Sam 7:14 or from 1 Chron 17:13, but the truth of it is contained also in Ps 89 (see esp. v.26). David had desired to build a house for the ark. He was concerned that he himself should be dwelling in a house of cedars while the ark of God dwelt under curtains. It is Nathan who brings the divine response to David's exercise. It was not in the purpose of God that David should build such a house. But David's son would, and David's house and David's throne and kingdom would be established and preserved for ever in his seed. And in the midst of Nathan's prophecy concerning David's son is this lovely promise, "I will be to him a Father, and he shall be to me a Son". Now the promise is, primarily, to Solomon, and there are indeed parts of Nathan's prophecy which must apply to Solomon only and not to Messiah (see e.g. the warning word which immediately follows the promise in 2 Sam 7:14). Nevertheless, the vision of Nathan looks beyond Solomon to a greater Son of David. Gabriel's word to Mary (Luke 1:32) and the inspired song of Zacharias (Luke 1:68-69) prove this. The Son of Mary is the Son of David, and

He inherits the promises made to David. To Him, to the Messiah, to Jesus, is the promise of Fatherhood made good.

Now to which of the angels could such a thing ever be said? This confirms that the earlier, first quotation, from the second Psalm, relates to the humanity of Christ, and in that real manhood, as the Son of David after the flesh, He lives in the enjoyment of the divine Father-Son relationship. He could say, so beautifully and so tenderly, "The Father loveth the Son" (John 3:35; 5:20). And He could say also, "I love the Father" (John 14:31). In the holy dependence of a perfect manhood He lived in the conscious enjoyment of His Father's love and care, and in the true devotion of a perfect sonship he reciprocated that Father's affection. Truly He alone of the seed of David could experience fully all that was intended in the divine promise, "I will be to him a Father, and he shall be to me a Son". All that the Father desired in a Son He has found in Christ. All that the Son required in incarnation He has found in the Father. Such a Son is greater than angels indeed.

6   The next, the third, quotation, "And let all the angels of God worship him", is preceded by a few simple words which, despite their apparent simplicity, have been a matter of great controversy and disagreement among the most learned of competent commentators. As William Kelly says, "Ancients, mediaevils, and moderns ... differ widely". The quotation is from Deut 32:43 (LXX), and in substance from Ps 97:7, but what does the writer mean when he says, "And again"? Is he but introducing another quotation, and simply saying, "Furthermore", or "Moreover"? Or should the word rather be associated with the bringing in of the Firstbegotten into the world, so as to read, "And when he again (i.e. a second time) bringeth the firstbegotten into the world ..."? Greek grammarians cannot agree and perhaps the controversy has obscured the chief object of the writer, a point which both J.N. Darby and W. Kelly are anxious to emphasise, that the point in time of the bringing in of the Firstbegotten is not in question; it is not a matter of defining a time at all; it is the glory of the Person that is before the writer and not the time of introducing. So that, whether we say, "And again, when he bringeth in the firstbegotten into the world ..."; or, "And when he again bringeth the firstbegotten into the world ...", this great fact must not be missed, that He whom God is bringing in is greater than angels, and greater than all, and the angels are commanded to worship Him.

There can be no doubt that the Scripture being cited relates to a future day. It predicts a day of judgment upon the enemies of God and of Israel prior to the setting up of Messiah's millennial throne. The words are the concluding words of the Song of Moses and they read thus, "Rejoice, ye heavens, with Him, and let all the angels of God worship Him; rejoice ye Gentiles, with His people ...". It will be a day of vindication for the rejected Son, and not only Israel, but angels and Gentiles, will join in the triumph. At His first advent, "a multitude of the heavenly host" praised God (Luke 2:13). At His second advent, "all the angels" are summoned to worship Him.

Now the Son is the "firstborn" (*prōtotokos*). This does not necessarily mean "born first", though it may have that connotation at times, as in Luke 2:7. It is a title of priority, of position, of rank, of dignity, and of honour. It is used five times of our Lord in a four-fold connection. He is:

Firstborn of all creation	Col 1:15
Firstborn from among the dead	Col 1:18; Rev 1:5
Firstborn among many brethren	Rom 8:29
Firstborn in kingdom glory	Heb 1:6

In the midst of His creation He is preeminent. Amongst those risen out from the dead He is supreme. In the midst of His many brethren He is unique. In the day of manifestation God will usher Him into the world as higher than the kings of the earth (Ps 89:27). Then will it be true:

> Throughout the universe of bliss
>   The centre Thou, and Sun,
> The eternal theme of praise is this,
>   To heaven's beloved One.

The word "world" here is not that of v.2. There it is *aiōnes*, but here it is *oikoumenē*. It is the inhabited, or habitable, world. Into this world God will bring His Son in glory. Every knee will bow in acknowledgement of His supreme lordship. Every knee, that is, in heaven as well as on earth, and the angels of God will worship. And they will do this by divine decree. "He saith"! It is a heavenly mandate that they render homage to the Firstborn.

Worship! It is perhaps a surprising discovery that, in such an epistle as this to the Hebrews, this word is found only twice. In the only other reference (11:21) we look back to the man who, first among men, bore the name of Israel. Jacob worshipped, on his staff. In Heb 1:6 we anticipate that day for which Israel has ever since waited, and in that day the angels (who well knew the worshipping Jacob, Gen 32:1) will worship Israel's Messiah and King.

"Worship" is an interestingly beautiful word *proskuneō*. It is comprised of two words, *pros* and *kuneō*. The first is a preposition, meaning "towards". The second means "to kiss". Together they have this lovely idea of moving towards in reverent affection and obeisance. If the actions and movements of Judas in the Garden had been sincere and true they would have furnished for us a most accurate physical illustration of the meaning of *proskuneō*. Alas, it was not there genuine, as we know (see Luke 22:47). "Worship", says J.N. Darby, "is the honour and adoration rendered to God for what He is in Himself, and for what He means to those who render it". The first reference to worship in our AV is in Gen 22:5, but there is an earlier reference in Gen 18:2 where the translation is that Abraham "bowed himself toward the ground". In the NT the first worshippers are the magi from the east. They declared plainly their intention, that they were "come to worship him" (Matt 2:2).

Having found the infant Messiah they fulfilled their declared intention and "worshipped him" (Matt 2:11). When Messiah returns, at His second advent, all the angels will join in the homage. The preciousness and fragrance of true worship, foreshadowed in the gold, frankincense and myrrh which the magi brought, will then be His in a fuller greater way. Perhaps the greatest treatise on worship in the NT is contained within our Lord's conversation with the woman of Sychar in John 4. There are ten references to worship and worshippers in five verses (John 4:20-24).

7   The fourth quotation is again from the Psalms, and again from the Septuagint. This latter point is important since the Hebrew of Ps 104:4 is capable of a slightly different rendering according to whether we make the words "angels" and "messengers" the subjects or the predicate of the sentence concerned. So some will translate, "who maketh the winds his angels (i.e his messengers), and the lightning his servants". If this rendering be used then the argument is that the angels, with all their glory, are not really so great as may be supposed. After all, Jehovah, when He pleases, can make the winds and the lightning His angels. The Son is unique and solitary in His dignity and glory. The angels share their honour with the very elements, with winds and lightning, hence they are greatly inferior to the Son.

Now however true this may all be (and it is true), it is not the argument here used by the writer to the Hebrews. He quotes not from the disputed Hebrew text but from the Septuagint, which admits of no rendering but the one given here in v.7. The correct interpretation of the Hebrew text is here by inspiration settled for us. He "maketh his angels spirits, and his ministers a flame of fire". How gloriously privileged are these angelic servants. They are invisibly swift and powerful as the wind. At His bidding they may effect as the wind irresistible judgments. But not only unseen as the wind do they minister, they may move as the lightning, fearful, frightening, consuming, devouring. Gabriel-like they may run swift as the wind on errands of mercy and goodwill (Dan 8:16-18; Luke 1:19, 26-28). Like Michael they may minister as flames of fire in matters militant (Dan 10:13; Jude 9; Rev 12:7). In either ministries they are His servants, and for Him they serve men, as is perhaps implied in the word here translated "ministers" (leitourgos; a public servant).

What then, and where, and how, is the contrast here advanced between Christ and the angels? It is in the word "maketh". The Son is not "made" anything. The angels are made, created, constituted, spirits and flames of fire. They are so made at His behest and by His will. The Son, it will now be shown in the following verse, is acknowledged for what He is in Himself, intrinsically and eternally.

8   The next quotation is from Ps 45:6-7. The psalm is a marriage hymn for a royal wedding. The psalmist, in a brief opening stanza, introduces himself, speaks of his exercise and of his intention. His heart is welling up, bubbling over, with thoughts of the King, and he would speak of these subjects of his meditation. Soon, however, he will speak no more about himself. He will address the bridegroom, first of all, and then the bride, and perhaps too, the gathered company. In his opening remarks the

psalmist will speak of the King's moral beauty. He will then proceed to the might and majesty and power of official glory. Then we have the ascriptions of dominion and perpetuity which are here quoted, "Thy throne, O God, is for ever and ever". The Psalm is Messianic. It must be, and Heb 1 confirms this. As another has remarked, "A greater than Solomon is here"!

This is one of the most outstanding, irrefutable, unanswerable, proclamations of the deity of Christ. God acknowledges the Messiah as God, and so addresses Him. This is the purpose of the citation, to show that God recognises Messiah as God. It is a fitting tribute to the invaluable nature of this Scripture relative to the deity of Christ, that in the cults that deny the deity of Christ the rank and file of the members are not told of it! The strategy of the cultist teachers of error seems to be that their followers do not need to know of this passage; that it is better if they do not know of it. The hope is that they might never hear it nor see it; but when they do they are confronted with a most powerful avowal of the deity which they have been taught to deny. The King, the Messiah, the Christ, the Son, is God, and is owned as such and addressed as such – by God! And this is not the only place where the Son is directly spoken of as God. See:

Isaiah 9:6	"his name shall be called ... The mighty God"
Matt 1:23	"his name Emmanuel ... God with us"
John 1:1	"The Word was God"
John 20:28	"My Lord and my God"
Rom 9:5	"who is over all, God blessed for ever"
Titus 2:13	"our great God and Saviour Jesus Christ" (JND)
1 John 5:20	"This is the true God"

His throne is established in perpetuity. The throne is the symbol of authority, of sovereignty and of dominion. And this is no tottering unstable throne of unsure duration; it is "for ever and ever", to the age of the age, abiding, eternal. Ps 45 doubtless looks forward to millennial glory, but if there is an appointed end to the millennium, that is only but the end of an earthly phase of rule. There is no end to the kingdom. It is the everlasting kingdom of our Lord and Saviour Jesus Christ (2 Peter 1:11). Of His kingdom there shall be no end (Luke 1:33). He shall reign for ever and ever (Rev 11:15).

The sceptre is wedded to the throne. It is a companion symbol of authority and rule. The earliest sceptres were straight slender rods, often studded ornamentally with jewels or with nails of gold and silver. A straight sceptre was a symbol of impartial rule and righteous administration. The sceptre of Messiah's kingdom is a straight sceptre, a sceptre of righteousness. It is the character of God. Messiah's kingdom is founded on righteousness. The Sun of righteousness ushers in the millennial day (Mal 4:2). The King is "Jehovah Tsidkenu", the Lord our righteousness (Jer 23:6). He is the King of righteousness (Heb 7:2). Righteousness is the girdle of His loins (Isa 11:5). The capital city of His kingdom is Zion, the city of righteousness (Isa 1:26).

Only the righteous enter in (Matt 25:46). In His days shall the righteous flourish (Ps 72:7). He shall judge the people with righteousness (Ps 72:2). It is the character of the King reflected in the kingdom. Righteousness will reign in that day, and in the eternal state will dwell (2 Peter 3:13).

All this sets the Son far above angels, in majesty, in dignity, in royalty, in deity, in glory. But still the contrast is continued in quotations from the same Ps 45.

9   The Messiah's anointing is seen to be consequential upon His moral glory. Our Lord Jesus has not only loved righteousness but has also hated iniquity. There is a dual aspect of His sinless excellence here and it is because of this that God has been pleased to anoint Him. It is the divine recognition in Him of those qualities which are necessary to impartial rule, as that rule must necessarily be, in God's kingdom. As in an earlier tribute in the Ps 45, He is fairer than the children of men. Some men have professed a love for that which is right but in practice have not hated that which is wrong. Others have loudly protested a hatred of that which is wrong but in practice have not always displayed a love for that which is right. But the One whom God anoints has a character perfectly balanced. Every pleasing feature is seen in Him in beauteous blending. He alone among men could say that He did always those things that pleased the Father. He alone could issue the challenge, "Which of you convinceth me of sin?" (John 8:46). His was a unique manhood of perfect sinlessness and unspotted holiness. In Him there was no depraved nature inherited from fallen Adam. But in Him, in glorious union, past comprehension and beyond exposition, there was Godhood and Manhood. He was, in one indivisible personality, God and Man. He therefore did not sin because He would not sin because He could not sin. He loved righteousness; that was His nature. He hated iniquity; it was foreign and loathsome to Him. God has owned with delight these qualities in His Son and accordingly is pleased to anoint Him. "Therefore", i.e. because of this moral excellence, He is anointed to kingship and is given the throne, the crown, and the sceptre. Jehovah has owned both the personal and moral glories of the Son.

The word "iniquity" is "lawlessness" (anomia) as in 2 Thess 2:7-8. One day, for a little while, there will be a usurper upon the throne, whose character will be unrighteous and lawless. His will be a reign of deceit and violence, prior to the manifestation of the the rightful King. The reign of the lawless one will be short-lived however. The throne and the sceptre belong to Him of whom it was written that, "He had done no violence, neither was any deceit found in his mouth" (Isa 53).

The King therefore is anointed, as all kings were. David was anointed three times; once in the house of his father Jesse; again, after the death of Saul, over Judah; and again, at Hebron, over the twelve tribes of Israel. Indeed the "anointed" is Messiah's title (Ps 2:2). Those kings of Israel and Judah were anointed with oil (1 Sam 10:1), as were the priests (Ps 133:2; Exod 28:41), and the prophets (1 Kings 19:16). In this three-fold way our Lord is also anointed. See Isa 61: 1 and Luke 4:18, and compare also Acts 4:27; 10:38. But His anointing is, figuratively, with the oil of gladness. It is the mutual joy of God and Christ in the anointing of the Son for the grace and glory of a unique ministry.

How precious is this word "gladness"! It is not often that we read of the joy of the Man of sorrows, but there are a few references. He speaks of "my joy" in the course of His last evening with His disciples (John 15:11). He rejoiced in spirit at a crisis hour in His ministry (Luke 10:21). He endured the cross for the joy that was set before Him (Heb 12:2). And, when poor lost sheep are recovered, we hear Him say, as the good Shepherd, "Rejoice with me"(Luke 15:6). That day of His manifestation with His bride will be the day of the gladness of His heart (Song of Songs 3:11), and, anointed with the oil of gladness, He will take the throne and the kingdom.

How beautiful and how tender it is that the God who anoints Him is His God. "God, thy God, hath anointed thee". There is an undoubted reference to the dependent Man here. As such He was tested in the wilderness at the beginning of His ministry, but in holy obedience He rejected independence. He refused to be diverted or distracted from a path of implicit trust in God. God was His God and now the God upon whom He leaned in the days of His flesh will vindicate that trust. As W. Kelly says, "The past ... is not forgotten, nor ever can be by God".

But who are His fellows? He is superior to them, whoever they are. This may be descriptive of all those who ever were anointed into any office in the former dispensation, whether prophets, priests, or princes. He is greater than all such. Some expositors will narrow the scope a little and understand these "fellows" as being the earlier kings who have occupied the throne of David. He is superior to these too. Yet others will interpret the fellows as angels. This hardly seems to suit a context in which the Son is being contrasted with the angels, though the argument is true that He is "above" these also. In the original circumstances of Ps 45 the "fellows" of the royal bridegroom could hardly have been other kings of Israel or Judah.

W.E.Vine points out that the word "fellow" (*metochos*) is strictly an adjective describing the persons concerned as "sharing in" or "partaking of". J.N. Darby will translate the word as "companions" and it is to be noted that the word is used twice more in this epistle to describe those who are companions in the heavenly calling (3:1) and who have thus become companions of the Christ (3:14). In the context of Hebrews these companions of the Messiah would have been a Jewish remnant acknowledging Jesus as Lord when the nation had rejected Him. If we, who have been saved out of Gentiledom, are likewise His companions, it is all of grace, and together we delight to see Him exalted above His companions. He is bringing many sons to glory (2:10). In the midst of them He is supreme, but He delights to call them His companions. It is all reminiscent of the golden lampstand of the old tabernacle; a lampstand with six branches, all of the same pure gold. But the central stem has a certain supremacy. The branches with their golden lamps are happy to cast their light upon Him who is greater. What wondrous, matchless grace too, that He whom Jehovah calls, "my fellow" (Zech 13:7), should call us "his fellows", in the day of His rejection.

10   The grand argument continues. The Son is undoubtedly and indisputably and immeasurably greater than the angels. He is the Creator. The sixth quotation is from Ps 102:25-27, and occupies vv.10-12. It is again, as the other quotations, from the Septuagint. The conjunction "and" is to be noticed. It is not part of this quotation but is simply the link with the former quotation. We have read, "unto the Son he saith … ", and there followed the address to the Son in vv.8-9. Now, again, there is a further address to the Son, Jehovah has more to say to Him, so v.10 commences with "and", introducing words also spoken to Christ, in Ps 102:25-27. It is of the utmost importance to keep this in mind, that the address of v.10 is to the Son. This is the force of the argument; "unto the Son he saith … Thou, Lord, in the beginning, hast laid the foundation of the earth". And of equal importance is it to see that He who has been addressed as "the Son", and as "God", is now addressed as "Lord". If it be argued by infidel minds that "God" (the *Elohim* of Ps 45:6) may sometimes be used, in a subordinate way, to describe rulers or magistrates, kings or judges, and therefore does not conclusively prove deity, then no such objection can be sustained with regard to this title "Lord". It is the Septuagint expression of the "Jehovah" of Ps 102, and that belongs to Divine Persons alone. It is a title of deity. "If it be argued", to quote W. Kelly, "that the word 'Lord' *(kurie)* in the LXX, has no counterpart in the Hebrew, the answer is that the truth meant in no way depends on the insertion of that word, but on the attributes of creative and judicial glory … ascribed to the Messiah by Jehovah". The ascription is by Jehovah to Jehovah.

"Thou in the beginning, Lord …". The pronoun "Thou" is emphatic (see JND), and "in the beginning" takes us back at once to Gen 1:1. It is difficult for some of us to comprehend how any honest, open mind could come to this chapter, and to these verses, and read and understand, and still deny the deity of Christ. To the adoring heart, Gen 1:1, John 1:1, and 1 John 1:1, unite with Heb 1:10 to declare this deity in glorious harmony.

"In the beginning" in John 1 takes us back to a "beginningless beginning" in the remoteness of eternity. The human mind staggers in an effort to appreciate this timelessness of the Son. His goings forth have been from of old, from everlasting, from the days of eternity (Micah 5:2 JND). Wherever we begin, in our meditations or contemplations, He is already there. He is before all things in the eternity of His being. He is God.

"In the beginning" in Gen 1 brings us to the morn of creation and He was there. All things were created by Him, and for Him (Col 1:16). This is "the beginning" of Heb 1:10. His superiority to the angels is further established. In the timelessness of eternity He was, when angels were not. In that creatorial beginning of Gen 1 the sons of God shouted for joy as He laid the foundation of the earth and manifested His power and glory. He created the angels who shouted for joy as He created the world!

"From the beginning", as in 1 John 1:1, He has moved towards us, in grace revealing Himself to men. The heavens may declare His glory, and the expanse of the firmament may display His handywork (Ps 19:1), but it is Himself that we would see,

and, in the wonder of incarnation He has granted to us that desire. From the distance
He has come to us. Our ears have heard; our eyes have seen; our hearts have contem-
plated; our hands have handled. He has come to us, who once dwelt in light
unapproachable.

Laying the foundation of the earth is a symbolic, figurative way of describing
creation. It occurs again and again in Scripture. See Pss 24:2, 89:11; 104:5; Job 38:4;
Isa 48:13; Zech 12:1, as well as this quotation from Ps 102:25. The heavens too, are
part of His creation. Some rabbis spoke of seven heavens. Most speak of three. Paul
wrote of paradise as the third heaven (2 Cor 12:2). There is the aerial heaven; the
stellar heaven; and "heaven itself" (Heb 9:24). The aerial heaven is the heaven of
the birds, and of lightning and rain. The stellar heaven is the heaven of sun, moon,
and stars. "Heaven itself" is the dwelling place of God and the angels. Jesus, in
ascension, passed through the heavens. They are the work of His hands. "The work
of thy fingers" says Ps 8:3, as if He had embroidered the firmament with shining
galaxies and created a glorious tapestry with stars and planets.

So, in v.10, the glory of creation is attributed to the Son. All things were made by
Him; and without Him was not anything made that was made (John 1:3). He is the
Creator and therefore He is God. He is consequently greater than the angels. But the
citation from Ps 102 continues.

11   The material creation is neither self-sufficient nor eternal as is its Creator. It
is subordinate and subservient to His will, and one day, at His bidding, it will perish.
"They", i.e. the heavens and the earth, shall perish. "Perish", is the word often
translated "destroy". It is *apollumi*, from which comes that proper name "Apollyon"
given to Satan in Rev 9:11. It signifies destruction or ruin. In one sentence we leap
from the creation to the destruction; from Gen 1:1 to Rev 21:1. But we are not here
occupied with eschatology. We are concerned with the facts, not with the times and
seasons, else we should miss the trend and tenor of the argument. "They" is emphatic;
and so is "Thou". There is a sharp contrast between the creation and the Creator.
"They", the earth and heavens, shall perish. "Thou", the Creator Son, continuest. He
who was before the creation will abide when the creation has gone.

Three times in the three verses of this sixth quotation there is an emphatic
"Thou". The emphasis is important. It is a three-fold declaration of the supremacy
of the Creator over His creation, and therefore over angels.

"*Thou* ... hast laid the foundation of the earth"
"*Thou* remainest"
"*Thou* art the same"
When creation began, He was there. When creation has perished, He will remain.
Angels are a part of that created universe, and if He is greater than it then He is
greater than they.

Such is the insignificance of the earth and the heavens, when compared to the
Son, that they are likened to a garment or a covering. Eventually a garment grows
old. The human wearer outlives his garment. So with the creation; it will wax old.

The Creator will continue on, eternally, abidingly, immutably, unchangeably.

12   As an old garment is discarded, folded up, and changed for another, so shall it be with the creation. Heaven and earth shall pass away. The heavens and the earth, which are now, are reserved unto fire. The heavens shall pass away with a great noise. I saw a new heaven and a new earth: for the first heaven and the first earth were passed away. Such is the united testimony of Peter and John, and of our Lord Himself (Matt 24:35; 2 Peter 3:7, 10; Rev 21:1), and of Isaiah too (Isa 34:4). The old robe will be exchanged for a new. As to the prophetic details, there is much that we do not know, and perhaps, as we have noticed before, this is not the place to enquire; it is not the intent or purpose of the passage to give us an outline of future events, but to show us again and again, the superiority of the Christ, the Son.

When the creation perishes, He remains. When the creation, like a faded garment, is changed, He is the same. He is "the self-existent One who does not change" (JND). Every creature is changeable, but He is always the same. So much is this unchangeableness His character that the Same becomes a divine title. "I, I am HE", is, literally, "the Same" (Deut 32:39). For a further interesting comment on this, and for a long list of OT references, see JND's footnote at Deut 32:39.

The years of the changeless One shall not fail. It is beyond the human mind to conceive eternity. We are creatures of time. Eternity is too much for our limited intellect. The Creator is eternal, the Ancient of Days whose existence cannot be measured in years. But of Him it is said, so that our tiny minds may have some little concept of His eternality, "Thy years shall not fail". He abides for ever and ever; unchanged and unchangeable; eternally independent; independently eternal. He is, beyond any question, greater than His creatures and therefore greater than the angels.

13   The seventh quotation is from Ps 110:1. It will be noticed that this, the final quotation of the seven, agrees exactly with the final part of the seven-fold description of the Son as in vv.1-3. Jehovah's word to His Son is, "Sit thou at my right hand", and we have seen in v.3 that, having made purification of sins, the Son has seated Himself at the right hand of the majesty in the heavens. This parallel between the final quotation and the concluding statement of the earlier description will perhaps stimulate us to observe that there are other parallels also.

Notice that to Him who has been introduced as the Son and the heir it is said, "Thou art my Son", and "I will be to him a Father". To Him who is the outshining of God's character and glory it is said, "Thou hast loved righteousness and hated iniquity". To Him by whom the worlds were made, and who one day will be ushered back into the habitable world to reign, it is said, "Thou Lord, in the beginning hast laid the foundation of the earth". Now, in the final parts of both description and quotation, there is a sealing of the argument. The Son by the oracle of Jehovah will sit at God's right hand.

Ps 110 is unique among the Psalms for at least two reasons. Firstly, it is quoted more often in the NT than is any other Psalm, and indeed, perhaps more often than any other OT passage. It is quoted in the Gospels, in the Acts of the Apostles, and in the Epistles, and the spirit of it is in the Book of the Revelation. It is, as we shall consider later, quoted several times in this epistle to the Hebrews. Secondly, this psalm is wholly and entirely Messianic, with no primary reason for its being written other than this. It is pure poetic prediction of Messiah. It is altogether and completely Messianic. Other Messianic psalms may have initial application to David or to Solomon, and to events and circumstances of those days of the monarchy, but it is not so with Ps 110. This psalm sings of Messiah only. There is no other reason for its existence.

In Matt 22:44 it is quoted by our Lord Himself in a most interesting confrontation with the leaders of the nation. Matt 22 is a chapter of questions. A strange alliance of Pharisees and Herodians brings the first question (v.16). Jesus rebukes them and answers them. These are followed by the Sadducees (v.23) who pose another question based on a most grotesque and unlikely hypothesis. The Lord rebukes these too, for their double ignorance of God and His Word, and then answers their question also. Yet another question is brought by one of the lawyers (v.35). This too, our Lord answers. Now, having heard and answered this series of questions, Jesus will ask a question of them. It is as if He would say, "I have heard your questions, and I have answered. Now I would ask a question of you". And so He asks, "What think ye of Christ? whose son is he?" (v.42). Now He is not asking, (as is sometimes suggested), "What do you think of Me?". His question is about the Messiah. "What do you think of Messiah? When He comes, whose son will he be?". They answer quickly and correctly, "The Son of David". "Now", says the Lord, "I have another question for you; how then doth David in spirit call him Lord, saying, The Lord said unto my Lord, Sit thou on my right hand, till I make thine enemies thy footstool? If David then call him Lord, how is he his son?" For this they had no answer. This was, in fact, the end of both their questions and their answers! (v.46). Our Lord has, confirmed for us, incidentally, both the authorship and the inspiration of Ps 110. "David" wrote this psalm, "in spirit" (v.43). Nor has the true believer any difficulty in answering the question which silenced the Pharisees. Messiah is the Root and the Offspring of David. He is before David and He is after David. David sprang from Him and He sprang from David. He who acknowledges the deity of Christ has no problem here (Rom 1:3-4; Rev 22:16).

The first line of the Ps 110 is not quoted here in Heb 1, but would not the very reference to the psalm send the thoughtful believer back to that opening word, "The Lord said unto my Lord"? The first "Lord" is *Jehovah*. The second "Lord" is *Adonai*. To which of the angels has Jehovah ever spoken as He has spoken to Messiah, saying, "Sit thou"? It is a rhetorical question. This divine oracle is addressed to the Son only, and to Him whom David calls, "My Lord". How privileged are they who similarly call Him, "My Lord", like Elizabeth (Luke 1:43); like Mary (John 20:13); like Thomas (John 20:28). The argument is, however, that angels do not sit. It is their privilege to "stand in the presence of God" as Gabriel (Luke 1:19). Once they were allowed to sit in His empty tomb! (John 20:12), though even then, as they sat, they served: they sat in angelic testimony that He was now risen, in virtue of His perfect and accepted sacrifice. Now the risen, ascended One takes His seat, by divine decree, at God's right hand.

It is, however, the day of His rejection. He has enemies on earth. Nor is He yet seated on His own throne. Rejected by Israel and by the nations He is now, in glory, sharing His Father's throne (Rev 3:21). The true Son of David He awaits the day when the throne of His father David will be His (Luke 1:32). In the meantime He sits at the right hand of the majesty on high, the place of honour. In sovereignty, Jehovah will prepare the nations for His revelation in glory. In the days of vengeance prior to the manifestation of the King, Jehovah will pour out His wrath and prepare the nations like a footstool for the feet of the Messiah. That day of manifestation will be a day of vindication and triumph, and His enemies will be beneath His feet. All this, though glorious and true, is not the specific purpose for this citation from Ps 110. It is to show once again the superiority of Christ over angels. Never, at any time, has a single angel, no matter how glorious, ever been invited to sit at God's right hand, but there He sits. who is greater than the angels.

14   The chapter closes with yet another question touching the angels. The answer is implicit in the question. Angels do not sit; they are ministering spirits, too busy to sit! The word for "ministering" is most interesting. It is a form of the word *leitourgos*, a word used by the Greeks to denote one who discharged a public office; a public servant. The word is used of our Lord (Heb 8:2). He is a Minister of the sanctuary. It is used of His apostles (Rom 15:16), as Paul ministering the gospel to the Gentiles. It is also used of magistrates or rulers in Rom 13:6.

Angels then, are ministering spirits, serving others at the divine command. But now another word for "minister" is used. They are "ministering spirits", sent forth to "minister", but the two words are different. The second word is *diakonos*. It may be easily recognised as the word from which we get our word "deacon", meaning a servant or attendant. Angels are not new to deacon work. They were His deacons in the wilderness! (Mark 1:13). Now they are sent forth in such service for others. This "sent forth" is from *apostellō*, akin to our word "apostle" as will be clearly seen. But who are these "heirs of salvation" to whom, and for whom, the angels minister? And what is the nature and the form of their ministry?

It is interesting to note that in this chapter both Christ and Christians are viewed as heirs. It is the same word in v.2 as in v.14. Christ is the appointed heir of all things. Christians inherit salvation. Now this may mean that, prior to conversion, we have in some way been the objects of angelic ministry with a view to our preservation for eventual salvation. Do we not sing –

> Preserved by Jesus when
>   My feet made haste to hell ...

and is it not conceivable that those heavenly deacons ministered to us and for us at His bidding when we knew it not, protecting us along our unregenerate way?

There is, however, an aspect of salvation which is yet future. It will be our salvation from the very presence and plague of sin altogether. It will be a deliverance from an old world that has opposed us; from an old body that has hindered us; and from an old nature that has troubled us all along the way. So we say with Paul, "Now is our salvation nearer than when we believed" (Rom 13:11), and later, in this very epistle we read of Christ that He will appear a second time, apart from sin, "unto salvation" (9:28). It will be an eventual deliverance, both for believers of this present age at the rapture of the Church, and for a believing remnant after the rapture who will look and wait expectantly for the Redeemer. But this has well been called an "eschatological" salvation. It belongs to the future and there may be, for many of the saints, a difficult pathway before the ultimate enjoyment of that salvation. Without doubt, they shall all inherit salvation. Of that they are truly heirs. It is their final destiny. But until then, how much shall they be in recurring need of a sustaining and comforting and protecting ministry, and may not the Lord of the angels send forth His angels in ministry to these heirs?

It is the privilege of angels to serve the Lord by serving His people. At His behest they have ever so ministered. Were they not interested in Cornelius and his salvation (Acts 10:3)? Were they not concerned with Philip and his service (Acts 8:26)? Did they not assist Daniel in his study (Dan 9:21-22)? Have they not ministered for the believers' safety (Dan 6:22; Acts 12:7-10)? And did they not arrange the safe arrival of Lazarus in paradise (Luke 16:22)? Throughout successive generations, patriarchs and prophets, priests and princes, and pilgrims all, will testify to the ministry of angels, and in how many instances they ministered of which the saints were not even aware, we know not.

But again we remember that it is not the point or purpose of the passage to explain or expound angelic ministry but to emphasise that the angels are indeed ministers; they are but servants. Messiah is greater; He is Son, and He is Lord. He sits while they serve. They are sent; it is He who sends.

Notes

The Septuagint (LXX)

It may here be in order to give a brief account and explanation of this version of the OT, from which perhaps every OT quotation in Hebrews is drawn.

The Septuagint is an ancient translation of the text of the OT from its original Hebrew into Greek. It is perhaps the earliest version of the OT Scriptures now extant, and appears to belong to the third century BC, probably to the period 285-247 BC.

The name Septuagint comes from the Latin "septuaginta", which means "seventy". It is usually referred to by the Roman numerals LXX.

This name has arisen from a tradition that the translation was made by seventy (or perhaps seventy-two) Jewish scholars. It is believed to have been made at Alexandria and it early became the Bible of Greek-speaking Jews.

Although it is admitted that very little is known with certainty as to the origins of, and the reasons for, the Septuagint, it is well-known that our Lord Himself, and His apostles, and most of the NT writers, quoted from it extensively.

For us it has been translated into English by Sir Charles Brenton. This English translation, with the accompanying Greek text of the Septuagint, referred to in the Bibliography, was first published in 1851 by Samuel Bagster & Sons, London, and more recently by the Hendrickson Publishers of U.S.A.

Messianic Psalms

The word "Messianic" is obviously an adjective derived from the proper noun "Messiah". There are some sixteen psalms which are referred to as "Messianic Psalms". See Pss 2, 8, 16, 22, 24, 40, 41, 45, 68, 69, 72, 89, 91, 102, 110, and 118. Your counting of the Messianic Psalms will be influenced however, by your definition of what exactly is meant by "Messianic".

When we say that a psalm is "Messianic", in general we mean that, whatever the original reasons for writing, or whatever the primary associations of the psalm, if the psalm awaits the coming of the Messiah, the Christ, for its ultimate fulfilment, then it is Messianic. There are psalms which have an obvious immediate application to David, or to Solomon, but in some cases, even where this primary association cannot be denied or doubted, it is similarly obvious that the complete fulfilment of the psalm did not come with David or with Solomon. In these psalms referred to there is a waiting for Messiah. The ultimate reference is to Him. They are Messianic.

Some, in defining what is Messianic, will insist that the psalm is Messianic only when it is quoted with reference to Christ in the NT. This mode of definition is deficient, as will be proven by noting that the Pss 24, 72, 89, are obviously Messianic but are never quoted in the NT at all.

The sixteen Messianic Psalms mentioned trace the Messiah from glory to glory; from eternity to eternity. They follow Him through incarnation and crucifixion to resurrection and ascension and exaltation, and on to millennial glory. His glories, personal, creatorial, moral, ministerial, mediatorial, and official, are all to be found somewhere in these beautiful portions of Holy Scripture.

Those interested in pursuing further study of the Messianic Psalms will probably find nothing better than that delightful meditation entitled simply, *The Messianic Psalms* by T. Ernest Wilson, as referred to in the Bibliography.

II. The Glory of the Son of Man (2:1-18)

1. *The First Warning*
2:1-4

v.1   "Therefore we ought to give the more earnest heed to the things which
      we have heard, lest at any time we should let *them* slip.
v.2   For if the word spoken by angels was stedfast, and every transgression
      and disobedience received a just recompence of reward;
v.3   How shall we escape, if we neglect so great salvation; which at the first
      began to be spoken by the Lord, and was confirmed unto us by them that
      heard *him;*
v.4   God also bearing *them* witness, both with signs and wonders, and with
      divers miracles, and gifts of the Holy Ghost, according to his own will?"

1   The warning of these early verses of ch.2 is a parenthesis. The theme of Christ's
superiority over the angels will be resumed in v.5, but there is now a serious and
solemn interlude in which the writer will warn regarding any neglect of the great
salvation. It is as if he would pause in his meditations in personal enjoyment of the
greatness of Christ, but in the consciousness of this, that the carelessness of some
might result in their eternal loss. Such warnings will be repeated again and again
throughout the epistle (see 3:7-19; 6:1-8; 10:26-31).

The warning begins in the AV, with "therefore". It is a simple and safe principle
in reading the Holy Scriptures, that every time we read "therefore", we should ask,
"wherefore?". It always precedes some powerful conclusion, or some strong practical
application of what has just been written. It is a well-known pattern in Paul's epistles
that he will expound great doctrines, then say, "therefore", and forthwith demand
practical godliness on the basis of what truth he has just expounded. In Romans, the
word "therefore" may be counted almost fifty times, in keeping with the inspired
argument which runs right through that epistle.

Now this word, here translated "therefore" is not quite the same as that so often
found in the Romans, but the intent and purpose is just the same. J.N.Darby will
translate, "For this reason ..." In view of the greatness of Christ, so well established
in the earlier chapter, the message of salvation is correspondingly great, as is the
responsibility of those who hear. We have seen the greatness of His Person; we have
seen the grace of His coming to Golgotha; we have considered the glory of His
exalted position, and the grandeur of His supremacy over the angels, and in light of
this surpassing excellence it is incumbent upon those who hear the message that they
receive it. The message is grand and glorious; it is unparalleled and unequalled;
therefore, for this reason, we must give heed.

Much discussion and disagreement have prevailed concerning the pronoun "we".
Who are these? The simple answer appears to be that it is we who have heard, we
who hear, the glad tidings of a great salvation in Christ. All who hear bear heavy
responsibility to respond, no matter who they are. But in the immediate context the

writer is speaking as a Jew. To Israel first the gospel came. The principle will apply, of course, to all, but the initial warning here is for those of that nation to whom the Messiah came. Note that the writer says "we", and not "ye". He includes himself, imposing upon himself what he will urge upon others. As J.M.Davies so interestingly remarks, "Five times the pronoun 'we' occurs in these verses, and 'us' once. It is to be understood in the same way as Peter used it when he and John were before the Sanhedrin .... He charged them with having been the builders who had rejected the stone which is become the head of the corner. Neither is there salvation in any other, for there is none other name under heaven given among men whereby *we* must be saved. (Acts 4:5-12)".

What things, in grace, have we heard about the Son. What an exalted glorious gospel has come to our ears. It is imperative that we give heed; nay, earnest heed; yea, more earnest heed; that we should give heed more abundantly. The message demands it. It is only but right and proper and reasonable that we give earnest attention to the revelation of One so great as the Saviour is. But sadly it is envisaged that some will let slip, or slip away from, the things that they have heard.

The picture may be of a leaking vessel. Water has been poured in but is being lost; it is slipping away. How many there are into whose minds the truth of the gospel has been poured by earnest friends and preachers, but they will not take heed. The call of the world is strong; its sights and sounds are too appealing; its cares and customs are too demanding; and the precious words of gospel truth are neglected and lost. But some will see another picture, and the text will allow it. The hearers are slipping away from the message. They drift like a ship without pilot or anchor. They slip out of, or past, the safety of the harbour, with no mooring. The end for such is shipwreck and tragedy. For some it will be the indescribable, unthinkable tragedy of apostasy, a falling away from the privileged position to which grace has brought them.

Of course the genuine believer can not apostatise. The true child of God can never be lost. But the warning is necessary because now, as then, there are those who have given but mental assent to the truth of the gospel; who have appeared to believe it and receive it; who company with Christians and even look like Christians and talk like Christians and yet have never had any heart experience of true repentance and a knowledge of Christ as Saviour and Lord. It is important to remember that these Hebrews may have been second generation Christians, who had been brought up in Jewish-Christian homes, where the parents were undoubted believers. Intellectually they consented to the gospel in which they had been instructed, but they were Jews at heart and in constant danger of yielding to the call of Judaism and letting slip the things that they had heard. Hence the repeated warnings of this epistle that we should search our hearts and make our calling and election sure.

2 The warning is now continued and fortified with a renewed reference to the angels, who had been so much in evidence in ch.1. "For", says the writer, "... the word spoken by angels". This is an obvious reference to the presence of angels at the giving of the law. Did not every Jew know that their law had been ordained by angels

(Gal 3:19), and received by the disposition of angels (Acts 7:53)? The Jew had a certain glory in the fact that the nation had ever been the object and subject of angelic interest and ministry. Had not even Michael and Gabriel in a special way been dedicated to the cause of Israel (Dan 9:21; 10:13)? Had not thousands and tens of thousands of these holy ones attended at Sinai (Deut 33:2; Ps 68:17)? This was all true, and this ministration of angels had indeed imparted a certain dignity and glory to the word then spoken at Sinai.

Some have supposed a difficulty here in that the words of the law were actually spoken by Jehovah, and not by the angels (Exod 20:1; Deut 5:22). But the difficulty is not insurmountable. Whether the audible voice is that of angels or prophets or apostles or evangelists, or that of the Son Himself, it is God who is speaking. In what particular manner the angels mediated at the giving of the law we know not, but in some way there was an angelic agency at Sinai; thus the law becomes "the word spoken by angels". The argument is going to be that if that which was spoken by angels demanded obedience, how much more is it necessary that we give heed to that which was spoken by the Lord Himself.

That law was an inflexible, unbending, unyielding, law. It was written on stone! It was steadfast and firm; it was sure and certain; it was strong and unwavering; and it took notice of every deviation from what was right and proper. It condemned sins of every kind and character. There is a play upon words here, an alliteration in Greek. "Transgression and disobedience" are *parabasis* and *parakoē*. The first describes deliberate violation of known law; transgressing beyond a forbidden line, wilful sins of commission. The second implies sins of omission, a failure to do what ought to be done, a refusal to hear and obey. But whether transgression or disobedience, every Jew knew that the law of Sinai condemned every sin and demanded proportionate punishment. Moreover, it was "every" transgression and disobedience. There was nothing too trivial to be overlooked. Nothing was excused. There was, however, a discriminatory judgment. Some sins were punishable by death. Those that did not call for the capital punishment of the offender were nevertheless dealt with in the death of a substitute, an offering, an animal sacrifice. "The soul that sinneth, it shall die" was the consistent demand of their law. There was, in every case, a just recompense. The prescribed penalty was commensurate with the seriousness of the violation. But no sin was excusable. Under the law handed over by the angels every transgression and disobedience must be dealt with. There would be a just and righteous and proportionate but inescapable recompense. There would be payment in full.

3   Now the logic and argument continues, that if all this was so with the word brought to us by angels, how much more so with that word of the new dispensation which at the first began to be spoken by the Lord Himself? How shall we escape if we neglect such a word as this. Here again, as in v.1, is the pronoun "we". It is, as we have seen, the general "we", embracing all those who hear the message of grace. How shall we escape, if we neglect, if we treat carelessly, if we disregard, such a

message as this that we have heard? The word "neglect" (*ameleō*) is the word of Matt 22:5, "they made light of it". The question is rhetorical, for there is no escape. There is nowhere to flee for those who are careless of the great salvation. The important contrast in these verses must be noted. There is "the word spoken by angels", and that "spoken by the Lord". If that spoken by the angels required response and obedience, how much more that which was spoken by the Lord. Notice too, that it is not here said to have been spoken by Jesus, nor by Christ, though either of these would be true. It is "the Lord" – not angels now, but the Lord of the angels; not servants or delegates now, but, as we have seen in ch.1, the Son Himself   It is a great salvation. It is more, it is "so" great. It is as if the greatness is immeasurable, like the love of Him who provided it, who "so" loved the world (John 3:16). How earnest evangelists have revelled in this greatness and have sought to expound it to us! For so many reasons is this salvation great.

1.   It is great in its scope. It reaches out not only to Israel but to the nations, not only to Jew but to Gentile. This wide scope was intimated in the Lord's commission to those earliest preachers of the message (Mark 16:15; Acts 1:8). "All the world"! "Every creature"! "The uttermost part of the earth"! It is a great salvation indeed that, in its greatness, reaches far beyond the bounds of Judaism to the strangers and aliens of Gentiledom. Peter had difficulty in grasping and accepting this great scope of the message, until a special vision helped him to Caesarea and to Cornelius with the saving words (Acts 10:1-23).

2.   It is great too in its power. It brings justification and reconciliation. It removes sins; it does not just cover them. It is the message of a perfect sacrifice, a propitiation accomplished, and a Saviour risen from the dead and exalted. It preaches a finished work and a complete forgiveness.

3.   Then it is great in its effect upon those who receive it. The conscience can now be set at rest. There can be perfect peace in the soul, and an assurance of acceptance. It is an eternal salvation too, which can never be lost, so the mind is always at rest. Such peace of conscience was never possible in the old dispensation. This is a great salvation.

4.   But it must follow, that if this salvation is so great in these several respects, it must of necessity be great in its cost. That which is now offered so freely, so gratuitously, cost more than the blood of bulls and goats and lambs and doves. It cost the death of Christ. God gave His Son. The Son gave Himself. The cost is infinite, incalculable, the precious blood of Christ. How solemn, how serious, how tragic, to neglect so great salvation. How shall they escape who so neglect?

Whether this is neglect by unbelievers, to whom the message is being offered, or whether it is an abandoning in apostasy by those who, like certain of these Hebrew readers, had made a profession of belief, it does not materially matter. In the context it can hardly be doubted that it is the latter, but the principle is always true and applicable that for those who hear and neglect and refuse there can be no escape from the appropriate judgment.

Further, that which at the first began to be spoken by the Lord, was confirmed to another generation by those who heard Him. The word "confirmed" is similar to the "stedfast" of v.2. Our Lord's spoken ministry has been attested by witnesses who actually heard His gracious words. They were "ear-witnesses"! They have made firm to us the glad tidings which they heard from Him.

4   Now if the Saviour Himself had introduced this great salvation, and if others who heard Him confirmed the message to these Hebrews, and so to us of a later day, God too had borne witness with them. There had been a miraculous visitation in a ministry of the Holy Spirit that had produced signs and wonders and a variety of miracles. This had been predicted by the Lord (Mark 16:17-18). It had come to pass. These three words, "signs, wonders, miracles" are grouped together on several occasions in the NT. W.E.Vine, in his *Expository Dictionary*, defines them as follows.

1.   Signs (*sēmeion*): A sign or mark or token attesting authenticity or authority.

2.   Wonders (*teras*): Something strange, causing the beholder to marvel. It is always used in the plural.

3.   Miracles (*dunamis*): Power, inherent ability, works of supernatural origin and character, such as could not be produced by natural agents and means.

Vine continues, "A sign is intended to appeal to the understanding, a wonder appeals to the imagination, a power indicates the source as supernatural" This combination of these three words is used again, though in a different order, of God's approval of the ministry of Jesus, "A man approved of God among you by miracles and wonders and signs, which God did by him in the midst of you" (Acts 2:22). They are found again, but once more in a different order, in connection with the man of sin, "whose coming is after the working of Satan with all power and signs and lying wonders" (2 Thess 2:9). Satan will counterfeit the heavenly means of approving the ministry and the men, but in this case the wonders are "lying wonders" or "wonders of falsehood".

Apart from the intrinsic value and inherent greatness of the message itself, there are now three reasons adduced as to why it ought not to be neglected. Firstly, that it was initially introduced by the Lord Himself. Secondly, that it has been reliably and firmly brought to us by those who actually heard Him. Thirdly, that there has been the added witness of heaven in the miraculous events of those early days. As Marcus Dods so beautifully remarks, "The salvation was at first proclaimed not by angels sent out to minister, not by servants or delegates ... but by the Lord Himself, the Supreme. The source then is unquestionably pure ... God testifies to its purity.

There is only one link between the Lord and you, they that heard Him delivered the message to you, and God by witnessing with them certifies its truth". What a message is this that has come to us by the witness of men, by the witness of God, and by the witness of a Man who was God. We must not neglect such a gospel.

Many of the "divers miracles", the "various acts of power" (JND), here referred to are specifically recorded for us in the Acts of the Apostles. See, for instance:

> The healing of the lame man at the gate Beautiful (Acts 3:1-11).
> The deaths of Ananias and Sapphira (Acts 5:1-12).
>   (This narrative actually ends with the observation that "many signs
>   and wonders" were wrought among the people).
> The healing of the sick in Jerusalem (Acts 5:16).
> The opening of prison doors (Acts 5:19).
> The cure of the palsied man (Acts 9:32-34).
> The raising of Dorcas (Acts 9:36-41).
> The opening of prison gates (a second time) (Acts 12:5-10).
> The fearful death of Herod (Acts 12:21-23).
> The blindness of Elymas the sorcerer (Acts 13:8-12).

All these, and many other signs and wonders and acts of power, some recorded in detailed account, others recorded in general terms, were God's approval of the early preachers, as earlier He had approved His Son (Acts 2:22).

These supernatural works which accompanied the early preaching are now referred to as "gifts of the Holy Ghost". The word here translated "gifts" is not the much used *charismata*, but *merismos*, meaning a dividing or distribution, and is found only once more in the NT, in Heb 4:12. There is much argument and disagreement among scholars as to the expression "of the Holy Spirit". Is this objective, or subjective? Are we to understand this as God distributing the Holy Spirit, in which case it is an objective genitive? Or should we understand it as a subjective genitive, in which case it is the Spirit Himself who apportions or distributes. Commentators do not agree in interpreting the grammatical construction, but perhaps the controversy is not of great importance since both things are true. Does not the Spirit divide to every man severally as He will in 1 Cor 12:11? And does not God, in another place, supply the Spirit and work miracles (Gal 3:5)? The end result is the same. It is the united testimony of divine Persons in miraculous manifestations of the Spirit.

All is according to the will of God. The word "will" (*thelēsis*), in this exact form, is found only here in the NT. It is God's sovereign pleasure. According to the will of God there had been a sovereign distribution of spiritual manifestations among those early saints. The apostles confirmed to others the word spoken by the Lord and God has likewise confirmed the word spoken by the apostles.

So concludes this first parenthetical portion of the epistle and with it the first of several warnings; if such warnings were necessary to these first readers it is good to remember that they are equally relevant to us who live in this later day.

2. *Christ Greater than Adam*
2:5-9

> v.5 "For unto the angels hath he not put in subjection the world to come, whereof we speak.
>
> v.6 But one in a certain place testified, saying, What is man, that thou art mindful of him? or the son of man, that thou visitest him?
>
> v.7 Thou madest him a little lower than the angels; thou crownedst him with glory and honour, and didst set him over the works of thy hands:
>
> v.8 Thou hast put all things in subjection under his feet. For in that he put all in subjection under him, he left nothing *that is* not put under him. But now we see not yet all things put under him.
>
> v.9 But we see Jesus, who was made a little lower than the angels for the suffering of death, crowned with glory and honour; that he by the grace of God should taste death for every man."

5   The warning digression being ended, the writer will now return to the subject of Christ and the angels. Not that he has ever completely left that subject for even in the digression we have had a reference to the angels in v.2. But now, in a fuller way, there is both a resumption and an expansion of the theme and a continuing contrasting such as we had in ch.1. The writer will continue to prove the supremacy of Messiah over the angels, but he will also proceed to show that Christ, as the second Man, has precedence over the first man. In ch.1 the Lord was consistently portrayed as the Son of God whereas now He will be presented as the Son of man, in relation to the rule of man over the habitable world to come. In this connection there is now advanced this further instance of the superiority of Christ. If the administration of this present world has been committed, in some respects, to the care of angels, it is not so with respect to the world to come.

The connecting particle "For", with which v.5 commences, has presented to some a difficulty. Perhaps the most satisfactory explanation for it is to emphasise the parenthetical nature of vv.1-4, in which case there a natural and easy transition from 1:14 to 2:5. Put brackets around the first four verses of ch.2 and notice the ready connection between the closing verse of ch.1 and 2:5. Angels serve. They do not reign, though they do have certain responsibilities of administration in relation to this present world. The earliest reference to this is in the Song of Moses as we have it in the LXX version of Deut 32:8, which reads, "When the Most High divided the nations, when He separated the sons of Adam, He set the bounds of the nations according to the number of the angels of God". This concurs with what we have later, in the book of Daniel, where we read of "the prince of Persia" and "the prince of Greece" (Dan 10:13, 20). These are most obviously angelic rulers or governors of the nations, divinely appointed, though some are now in rebellion with Lucifer.

But in the world to come it will not be so. It has ever been the purpose of God that the administration should be in the hands of man. It was so at the beginning, in Eden, as the chapter will proceed to show, but there has been a hiatus, an interruption. The dominion was threefold. Beasts of the field, birds of the air, and fish of the sea (Gen 1:26; Ps 8:7-8), were but expressive of the vast kingdom originally given to man. The earth, the heavens, and the sea were, to use the word of this verse, in subjection. Then came temptation, seduction, and rebellion in Eden, and man forfeited the dominion. The world, in disorder now, in the interim period has been entrusted in great measure to the angels for administration. They are not kings; they are administrators. But God does not abandon His original purpose and this will be realised in the world to come. This is undoubtedly the same "habitable world" (*oikoumenē*) of which the writer has spoken in 1:6. It is the millennial world or earth into which God will usher His Son in glory and majesty at the appointed time. In that day the Son will inherit His rights and the purpose of God will be fulfilled in that the creation will be in subjection to a Man. In His purpose He has not put that world in subjection to angels.

6   The writer now quotes extensively from Ps 8 (LXX) in support of what he has just stated, but in a strangely interesting way he does not identify the source of his quotation. He says, "One in a certain place testified". Quite literally what he says is, "Someone, somewhere, has testified". It is not, of course, that he did not know, or that he had momentarily forgotten, that the words were from Ps 8. Nor is it that he has any doubt as to the authorship of the Psalm. It is by divine design that he omits the explicit information. To him all the OT writings are equally inspired of God. The human author is not very relevant. What he is quoting is God's Word, no matter who he may have been who was privileged to write it at the time. We know however, and his readers knew, that it is to the eighth Psalm that he wishes to draw our attention. The indefinite manner in which he introduces the quotation is also an oblique way of acknowledging that they knew very well from where he was quoting.

This Psalm is quoted four times in the NT and being a Messianic Psalm, is always quoted in reference to the Lord Jesus (Matt 21:16; 1 Cor 15:27; Eph 1:20-22; Heb 2:6-8). The writer to the Hebrews is particularly interested in vv. 4-6 but the Psalm ranges, in its wide vision, from heaven to earth; from the majesty of God to the simplicity of babes; and from Eden to the millennium. The Psalm begins as it ends, with ascriptions of praise to Jehovah. The first and last words are exactly the same. They are like golden clasps which hold this jewel of a psalm firmly in place while it radiates the glory of the Lord. But in the early part of it, and in the background, there is a reference to the enemy. This is undoubtedly Satan, who intruded into that early scene of glory in Eden and invaded a sphere of worship and communion between God and the man.

The Psalmist looks up into the night time skies. In the Ps 19 he admires the daytime sky and describes the journeys of the sun. Here it is the moon and the stars. Our tiny minds cannot understand it. Stars as the sand of the sea are innumerable. Vast, immense stretches of universe are immeasurable. Planets and galaxies are incomprehensible. The beauty of it all is indescribable. T.E.Wilson, in his book *The Messianic Psalms* speaks of "the fathomless immensity of the universe", and quotes

Carlyle as saying that it is "the silent palace of the Eternal, of which our sun is like the porch lamp!" He goes on to say, "And our earth is like a grain of sand on a mighty seashore". With such glory and majesty in his vision the Psalmist bows in wonder and exclaims, "What is man, that thou art mindful of him?" How gloriously inexplicable that the God and Maker of this universe should take notice of puny man and say, "Let them have dominion" (Gen 1:26). Someone has spoken of "The greatness and the littleness of man!" How true this is in this passage. The repetition of the word "man" in v.6 is not an exact repetition in the Hebrew of Ps 8. There the first word "man" (*enosh*) is man in his feeble frailty; man in his mortality and insignificance. The second, the son of "man" (*adam*), though still man of the dust, man of the clay, is, nevertheless, man in his conferred dignity, head of the creation. God, in all His greatness, has been pleased to visit man, in a gracious providential visitation of care and of kindness, and, may we say it, with affection.

There is now introduced the designation "son of man". This is the expression with which the Psalm moves from Adam to Christ; from the first Adam to the last Adam; from the first man to the second Man. The primary reference is to Adam in his innocence but there must be a prophetic view which looks on to the second Man in whom the purpose of God will eventually be realised. The title Son of man occurs some eighty times in the Gospels. It is almost always used by the Lord Jesus, and of Himself. The only exceptions are in John 12:34, and even these are not true exceptions. Our Lord had predicted His death by speaking of being "lifted up". The multitude replied that they had always been taught that Christ would live forever. "How sayest thou", they asked, "The son of man must be lifted up? who is this Son of man?" They were but quoting His own words and asking, "What kind of Son of man is this, who is to die?". All the other occurrences of the title in the Gospels are in the ministry of the Lord Himself. Outside of the Gospels and the passage here under consideration, we have it only three times more in the NT, in Acts 7:56, Rev 1:13; 14:14. In the latter two instances "the absence of the article in the original serves to stress what morally characterises Him as such" (W.E.Vine).

The title is a Messianic title and for us it has a triple purpose. It will point us back to the days of His flesh, to His ministry, His sufferings, and His death. It will also point us upward to the risen exalted Man, and then point us forward to His return in power and glory. All the references combined bring us the story of the dignity of the past, the glory of the present, and the authority of the future, all invested in the Son of man. But we anticipate! The first application of the title in Heb 2:6 is to the first man, Adam, and to God's ways with him in Eden.

7   There are now advanced three particulars which demonstrate the fact just stated, that God has been mindful of man and has indeed visited him. These were all true of Adam in Eden.

1.   He was made a little lower than the angels.
2.   He was crowned with glory and honour.

3.   He was set over the works of God's hands.

Now it is important to see, and to emphasise, for a subsequent right interpretation of this passage, that all of these things were true of the first man in Eden. It is to him, to the first man, that Ps 8 immediately refers. That Christ is in view is beyond dispute but the psalm has a first application to Adam. It is of the first man Adam that we are presently speaking.

He was made a little lower than the angels in that he was a material being, and consequently finite and mortal. If, in the Hebrew of Ps 8, the word for angels is *elohim*, Hebrews 2 settles for us the correct interpretation that it is angels who are in mind. Man is not a spirit being. He is therefore, in his corporeal restrictedness, inferior to the angels.

He was crowned with glory and honour. Man was a king. He had a crown and a throne. He ruled with a certain glory. He reigned with that honour divinely bestowed upon him. He had a conferred sovereignty. He was God's vicegerent, exercising delegated power and authority.

He was set over the works of God's hands in that the whole creation was under his feet. His kingdom was vast. His territory was wide. His dominion was over land, sea, and air, as we have earlier noticed in v.5. He gave names to the cattle, and to the fowl of the heavens, and to every beast of the field. Jehovah brought the creatures to the man, and the man named them, with the apparent acquiescence of his God. This was an early demonstration of his divinely-given authority and of his superiority to the brute creation.

8   The continuing quotation from Ps 8 maintains and reinforces the argument for man's greatness in the creation. Jehovah has put all things under his feet. In v.7 we see man set over the creation. In v.8, we see the creation put under man. It is a dual way of stating the same truth. Man, in God's purpose, is superior. The creation, in that same purpose, is subject. This was the divine intention, and this is how it was in Eden. It was "all things" too. There was nothing excepted. Now in 1 Cor 15:27, Paul quoting this same Scripture, will add, "it is manifest that he is excepted who did put all things under him". Paul is emphasising the fact that the sovereignty committed to man was a delegated sovereignty. It was over created things, and of necessity did not include the God by whom the sovereignty had been given. For a helpful comment on this, and for a clear elucidation of the many difficult pronouns in that Corinthian passage, see the exposition of 1 Cor 15:27-28 by J. Hunter in *What the Bible Teaches*, vol.4. Eden was a fair scene. The man was sovereign and the creation was subject. The man was supreme and the creation was subordinate. The man was responsible and the creation was responsive. There was superiority and submissiveness, and all in perfect harmony. It was indeed a garden of delights, for such is the meaning of the name. It was innocence. It was pleasantness. It was paradise. But it was not to last.

This was altogether too fair a scene for Satan to contemplate. Of all the sad words in our Bible, these must be among the earliest, "So he drove out the man" (Gen 3:24). The man in whom the authority had been vested had sinned. The man in whom the divine purpose was to have been realised had failed. Man, like the tempter himself, had succumbed to pride and its desires. He had rebelled against the sovereignty which had given sovereignty to him. It was the end of a blissful era. And now, "we see not yet all things put under him".

Now notice carefully these words, "not yet". Jehovah does not depart from an original purpose. That purpose may be interrupted by sin and Satan. It may look as though it has been thwarted, but it has not been given up. "Not yet" may be a sad word, but there is a measure of triumph in it. If it is Jehovah's intent that man will rule in the creation, then man will rule. The divine intent will yet be realised and creation accordingly will be subdued. But now, in this present, we do not see it. Creation rebels against the rebel man. The man is humiliated in the very sphere over which he was to govern. A mouse will frighten him! A mosquito may kill him! His own dog will bark at him! He has lost his crown and his throne and his authority. But God has another Man. A second Man will replace the first fallen man, and the purpose of God will be realised in Him who is uniquely, "The Son of man". This second Man now becomes the focus of our attention and the Messianic fulfilment of Ps 8.

9   We see Jesus! How blessedly refreshing to turn aside from occupation with the failure and humiliation of the first man to behold the glory of the second Man, the last Adam. We are not now looking at man in general, but at Jesus in particular, and we see Him crowned with glory and honour. There is a well-known difficulty in the interpreting of this "glory and honour" in connection with the Lord Jesus. Are we to see this as a present glory and honour of the risen Man? Is it a glory in the heavens, subsequent to, and consequent upon, His tasting of death? Are we to understand this as that glory of which Peter speaks when he says, "God, that raised him up from the dead, and gave him glory" (1 Pet 1:21)? Or that of which Paul speaks when he writes, "Wherefore God also hath highly exalted him, and given him a name which is above every name" (Phil 2:9)? That this is the most usual and the more popular view of this glory and honour of cannot be disputed, but, as A.B.Bruce remarks, "The traditional view is beset with insuperable difficulties, especially this difficulty, that it is not easy to assign a natural sense to the words in the last clause of v.9. What clear satisfactory sense can one attach to the statement that Jesus was exalted to heaven in order that He might taste death for everyone?" He goes on to say, "It is pathetic to observe the expedients to which interpreters have recourse to get over the difficulty". He charges such interpreters with subjecting the sentence to violent dislocation so as to bring out their sense. There is another view therefore, which demands consideration and which is not without its strong advocates.

Do the verses not read the more easily if we understand this as a glory and honour which was our Lord's prior to Calvary? Is it not on earth, during His lifetime, that we see Him, as a Man, wearing again the crown which the first man lost? And is it not this that qualifies Him, alone among all men, to go into death on the behalf of others? To many it seems as if the context requires that we should see Jesus, right here in the midst of the dominion that Adam lost, regaining and wearing the insignia of man's authority, crowned with the glory and honour of a unique manhood. This makes for easy reading of this whole passage, which, in an expanded paraphrase with this understanding of it in mind, would now read like this, "As yet, we do not see the realisation of God's purpose, that is, that all things should be put under man. But we do see Jesus, who also has been made a little lower than the angels in order that He might suffer and die; we see Him crowned with glory and honour, that glory and honour of anointed manhood which the first man lost. So fitted and qualified, He is able, by the grace of God, to taste death for every man". "The construction of the sentence", says Marcus Dods, "is much debated. But it must be admitted that any construction which makes the coronation subsequent to the tasting death ... is unnatural". Two things are said of our Lord here, and they are followed by two reasons.

1. He was made a little lower than the angels.
2. He was crowned with glory and honour.

Why was He made lower than the angels? So that it would be possible for Him to suffer and to die.

Why was He crowned with glory and honour? So that by His death the whole fallen creation might be reached. He tasted death for every "thing". Only by the death of One so crowned with the glory and honour of such a manhood could the dominion be recovered to man.

But, it will be asked, how are we to see Jesus crowned with glory and honour during His lifetime? Were those days of His flesh not rather days of humility and of humiliation? Was He not a Man of sorrows? Have we not read that He made Himself of no reputation, that He humbled Himself? Let us contemplate that, and view Him as wearing the crown of glory and honour even during such days.

> He was with the wild beasts in the wilderness (Mark 1:13)
> He made water wine, and manifested forth His glory (John 2).
> He calmed the elements (Luke 8:24).
> He walked on the sea, putting it beneath His feet (John 6:19).
> He bade a fish bring a coin for Him (Matt 17:23).
> He multiplied fish and bread to feed a multitude (John 6).
> He withered a barren fig tree with a word (Mark 11:13-20).
> He healed leprosy, paralysis, blindness, and deafness.
> He commanded demons and they obeyed Him.
> He raised from the dead, a man, a youth, and a girl.

Is it not abundantly evident that He who was with the wild beasts at the beginning of His ministry, and who rode upon an unbroken colt at the close of His ministry, was in control even during those days of His flesh on earth? When He was born, a star appeared. When He died, the sun disappeared. At His death the earth shuddered and the skies went into mourning. We may well write across the whole story, "We see Jesus, crowned with glory and honour". It is the recognition of His Messiahship, and of His authority, by His Father, by the creation, and by a remnant of the nation. Of course it is true that the world knew Him not (John 1:10), and that His own received Him not (John 1:11), but this in no way detracts from that glory and honour which was His. He wore the crown then; He will yet wear it with universal recognition in that world to come. Meantime He sits in glory, sharing His Father's throne (Rev 3:21). He must reign, and He will, but that is not the immediate point of the passage we are reading just now. It is His glory down here in the days of His flesh.

3. *Perfect through Suffering*
   2:10-18

v.10 "For it became him, for whom *are* all things, and by whom *are* all things, in bringing many sons unto glory, to make the captain of their salvation perfect through sufferings.

v.11 For both he that sanctifieth and they who are sanctified *are* all of one: for which cause he is not ashamed to call them brethren,

v.12 Saying, I will declare thy name unto my brethren, in the midst of the church will I sing praise unto thee.

v.13 And again, I will put my trust in him. And again, Behold I and the children which God hath given me.

v.14 Forasmuch then as the children are partakers of flesh and blood, he also himself likewise took part of the same; that through death he might destroy him that had the power of death, that is, the devil;

v.15 And deliver them who through fear of death were all their lifetime subject to bondage.

v.16 For verily he took not on *him the nature of* angels; but he took on *him* the seed of Abraham.

v.17 Wherefore in all things it behoved him to be made like unto *his* brethren, that he might be a merciful and faithful high priest in things *pertaining* to God, to make reconciliation for the sins of the people.

v.18 For in that he himself hath suffered being tempted, he is able to succour them that are tempted."

10   The writer continues in contemplation of the glory of Messiah but will show us that the ultimate perfection and glory is arrived at by an avenue of suffering, even in the case of Messiah. The particle "For", which is repeated so many many times throughout the argument of this epistle is now used again. It here precedes the justification of the concept of a suffering Messiah. Such a concept required to be justified to the Jewish mind. The very thought of Messiah suffering was foreign to the thinking of the Jew. This is seen so clearly in the reaction of Peter when our Lord

announced His impending suffering and death. Peter took Him, and began to rebuke
Him, saying, "Be it far from thee, Lord; this shall not be unto thee" (Matt 16:22).
And did not our Lord gently rebuke the couple of the Emmaus road when He charged
them with being "slow of heart to believe all that the prophets have spoken" (Luke
24:25)? They were happy to believe the glory side of it: that He should have
redeemed Israel. But they were reluctant to believe all. Had not the prophets also
predicted that Christ should suffer, and then, after that, enter into His glory? To
Hebrews in general Christ's sufferings were a stumbling block. So, now, to these
Hebrew readers in particular, the writer will explain that the sufferings of Christ were
in perfect keeping with the character and the nature of God. "The intention is to
ascribe to God, in connection with the sufferings of Christ, an end indisputably
worthy of Him who is the final end of all things" (A.B.Bruce).

"It became him ..."; it befitted Him; it was worthy of Him; it was fit and seemly
and comely, and in accord with all that He was, that Christ should suffer. The One
"for whom are all things, and by whom are all things" is not here the Son, but the
Father. It is the Father who is bringing many sons to glory and who will make the
Captain of our salvation perfect through sufferings. Notice the holy interchange of
glories between divine Persons. What is here attributed to the Father is attributed in
Col 1:16 to the Son. In Heb 1:10 the glory of creation is ascribed to the Son, but here
the same glory is ascribed to God the Father. All things are for Him. He is the sole
reason for the existence of the universe. He is the cause. It is for His glory. And all
things are "through" Him ("by" Him, AV). He is the divine agent through whom this
same universe came into being. Compare the majestic parallel passage in Rom 11:36,
ex autou kai di' autou kai eis auton. The universe comes "out of God, by means of God,
for God" (see A.T. Robertson). By "all things" we are to understand just that – "all
things"! It is the universe of created things. Observe the repetition of the expression
in 1:2; 2:8 (twice); 2:10.

Now this same God, the Supreme, Possessor of heaven and earth (Gen 14:19) is
bringing many sons to glory. We have seen that there is a unique Son, an only-
begotten; and we have read that, being the Son, He is the appointed heir. Sonship
and heirship are inseparably linked together. "If sons, then heirs" says Paul (Rom
8:17). Here the writer to the Hebrews reasons inversely; we are heirs (1:14), therefore
sons (2:10). And God is surely bringing these many sons to their divinely-appointed
glory. What high dignity and destiny is this, that we should be brought to share with
Christ, sonship and heirship, and all the attendant glory. To be His servants would
be a privilege. To be His saints is precious too. To be His children is an inestimable
favour. But to be His sons is supremely blessed. Sons of God! It is the word *huios*,
"sons", not "children". The word is characteristically Pauline and this fact has
sometimes been used in argument for a Pauline authorship of this epistle. Probably
Paul alone, among all the other NT writers, calls Christians sons of God, until Rev
21:7. We shall find the word again in ch.12.

The Lord Jesus is now called "the captain of their salvation". This word "captain"
(*archēgos*) is found only four times in the NT: in Acts 3:15; 5:31; Heb 2:10; 12:2. In

the AV it is variously translated "captain", "prince", and "author". Both Thomas Newberry and J.N.Darby prefer "leader", and J.N.Darby's note on the word at Acts 3:15 is worth quoting. He says, "The word is difficult to render in English. It is a 'leader', but it is more … it means, 'he began and finished the whole course'; 'the origin' or 'originator', though the word is harsh in connexion with life. The word is only used of our Lord". He takes the lead. He takes the precedence. As the Captain of our salvation He goes before. He leads the way and will conduct us to our inheritance in glory, the ultimate in our salvation.

Now the chief point of the argument is this, that the Captain of our salvation has been made perfect through sufferings. But in what sense can we understand our Lord to have been "made perfect"? Every believer knows that there was no moral imperfection in Jesus. There was no deficiency in His character. In Him was neither fault nor flaw, nor blemish nor stain. How then could He be "made perfect"? Of the word *teleioō*, W.E.Vine's *Expository Dictionary* says, "*Teleioō*, to bring to an end by completing or perfecting, is used (I) of accomplishing; (II) of bringing to completeness; … of Christ's assured completion of His earthly course, in the accomplishment of the Father's will, the successive stages culminating in His death (Luke 13:32; Heb 2:10), to make Him perfect, legally and officially, for all that He would be to His people on the ground of His sacrifice". If we, the sons being brought to glory, are to travel there by a pathway of suffering, then is it necessary that He who is our Leader to that glory should also arrive there through sufferings. This He has done, and having trodden the path of sufferings before us He is now perfected as the Captain of our salvation. In the priestly ministry which will later be expounded He is able to sympathise perfectly with us. Through incarnation, poverty, obedience, rejection, sufferings, and death, He has learned experimentally what sorrow is, and can succour accordingly. He is a perfect Leader. He is a complete Saviour.

11 Another "for" now continues and advances the explanation and the argument, and we are introduced to the Sanctifier and the sanctified. Christ is the Sanctifier, setting His people apart by His sufferings and death. The subject of sanctification is not here dealt with in detail but it is developed throughout the epistle. It is the setting apart of God's people for Himself. It is a call to holiness and to separation from the evil around (10:10; 12:14; 13:12). He that sanctifieth and they who are sanctified are all of one. What does this mean? It is not said that they "are one" as if it were the truth of the oneness of the Body as in the epistle to the Ephesians. It is "of one", and this has presented a difficulty. Of one what? Since the Sanctifier and the sanctified are all sons it may be natural to say, "of one Father". This is undoubtedly true but if this were the whole sense of the expression then what would be the point of saying, "He is not ashamed to call them brethren"? This would seem to be superfluous since they would indeed be His brethren. Many, taking into account the verses gone before and the OT Scriptures about to be cited, will understand the expression to mean "of one humanity". But this brings problems too since then there would be the implication (taught in much of Christendom) that all men are His brethren. It is difficult to improve upon the words of J.N.Darby, which we quote at length.

"This shews us Christ standing in the midst of those who are saved, whom God brings to glory ... Observe that it is only of sanctified persons that this is said. Christ and the sanctified ones are all one company, men together in the same position before God. But the idea goes a little farther. It is not of one and the same Father; had it been so, it could not have been said, 'He is not ashamed to call them brethren'. He could not then do otherwise than call them brethren.

"If we say, 'of the same mass' the expression may be pushed too far, as though He and the others were of the same nature as children of Adam, sinners together. In this case He would have to call every man His brother; whereas it is only the children whom God has given Him, 'sanctified' ones, that He so calls. But He and the sanctified ones are all as men in the same nature and position together before God. When I say 'the same', it is not in the same state of sin, but the contrary, for they are the Sanctifier and the sanctified, but in the same truth of human position as it is before God, as sanctified to Him; the same as far forth as man when He, as the sanctified One, is before God".

This position is, of course, fully arrived at by His resurrection. It is the risen Man who says, "My Father, and your Father ... my God, and your God" (John 20:17). And two other important considerations must be emphasised. Firstly, that although through grace the Saviour deigns to call us brethren, we must on no account dare to call Him brother. We have no scriptural example or mandate for this. If He so calls us, then we are humbly grateful, but it would be outside the bounds of scripture language for us to so address Him. Secondly, that while He did instruct His disciples to pray saying, "Our Father" (Matt 6:9), yet He Himself never used the pronoun "our" when speaking to the Father in prayer. He spake of "my Father" and of "the Father". He addressed God as "Father" and "holy Father" and "righteous Father" (John 17), but He never said "Our Father" as including Himself with the disciples.

12   Once more, as is his wont, the writer turns to the OT Scriptures to support and sanction what he is saying. Three OT quotations follow to show Messiah's real humanity and His consequent close relationship with His people. The first of these is, again, a quotation from the Psalms. Ps 22, so much associated with Messiah, from which he now quotes, is naturally divided into two parts. It has been said that the whole psalm is "A Sob" and "A Song" . It is a psalm of the sufferings of Christ and of the glory that should follow. The verse now cited (v.22) is the opening verse of that "Song" section of the psalm. The Holy Sufferer is now singing. He speaks of declaring God's name to those whom He calls "my brethren". This is the spirit, and indeed the very language, of John 17:26, but it is particularly for the word "brethren" that the writer refers to the psalm. This is in proof of what he has just said at the end of v.11. But he gives the full quotation and continues, "In the midst of the church will I sing praise unto thee". Note the word "church" or "assembly". It is a principle that there are no direct references to the NT assembly in the OT Scriptures. It was a mystery hid in God (Eph 3:9) and unknown to the OT writers (Eph 3:5). In vain do we look there for direct predictions or prophecies about the assembly, yet here, in the Psalms, the writer to the Hebrews finds that word "church" (AV). The Hebrew word of Ps 22:22 is, properly, "congregation", but the Holy Spirit, with the rights of divine authorship, transports the word into the NT writings from the Septuagint, and there it is the word *ekklēsia*. Correctly now we translate it "church". Better still, we say, "assembly". In the midst of His assembly the Lord now sings. He is the great Precentor. He is the leader of the praise. Once, in the relative sadness of the Upper Room, He sang in the midst of a little remnant company (Mark 14:26). Here it is better. His sufferings are past and He sings with gladness and joy in the midst of those whom He calls His brethren, His assembly.

13   In the two OT quotations that now follow the writer turns from the Psalms to the prophets and he quotes from Isaiah. Although the two citations are continuous in Isa 8:17-18, the writer here introduces them separately so as to bring out two different aspects of Messiah's life and service. They are introduced individually with the words "And again", "And again".

The first quotation directs us to One who was truly a dependent Man, saying of His God, "I will put my trust in him". In the Ps 22, just quoted, this holy dependence is cast at the Sufferer in mockery. But like so much of what men said in mockery, how true it was, "He trusted on the Lord" (Ps 22:8). In the same Psalm He insists on His dependence, and says, "I was cast upon thee from the womb" (v.10). From His birth to His burial; from the manger to the cross; from Bethlehem to Golgotha He lived in simple dignified trust and dependence upon His God. It was so in Nazareth (Luke 2:49). We see it also in the wilderness (Mark 1:12). And it was so until His latest breath, "Father, into thy hands I commend my spirit" (Luke 23:46). Notice how closely the Messiah is associated with the godly remnant of Israel. He may use the language of the remnant at any time. So does the writer to the Hebrews freely attribute remnant language to Christ.

The quotation which now follows is continuous, as we have seen, in Isa 8:18. Isaiah personally refers to his own family, his own children, whose persons and whose names were of prophetic significance. Had the quotation been extended it would have read, "Behold, I and the children whom the Lord hath given me are for signs and wonders in Israel". Isaiah's children were a testimony to his obedience and his trust in God. They were a vindication of the prophet's confidence in Jehovah. This is expressed in the very meanings of their names (Isa 7:3; 8:3). The prophet and his children were a witness to the nation of the faithfulness of the God in whom they had trusted. So it is with the Messiah. His people are the witness to the truth of His Person and His work. They are His vindication. He Himself is no longer in the world, but He has left "children" in the world who testify to Him and for Him, and who rejoice in their association with Him, even in His rejection.

Observe that they are not now, "my brethren", as in the previous quotation, but "the children". It is the word *paidia*, a diminutive, a term of affection, of endearment, like "dear children". And how reminiscent is it of Isa 53:10, "he shall see his seed". Nor can we read "the children which God hath given me" without thinking of John 17, where several times the Lord will speak of His disciples as the Father's gift to Him (see vv. 2, 6, 9, 11, 12, 24).

14 The words "Forasmuch then" continue the theme. Perhaps "Since then" (RV) or "Since therefore" (JND) might be better, but in any case it is obvious that the subject still is to be that of Christ and the children. He will be associated intimately with these, and because they are blood and flesh, so He will be too. It should be remarked that "blood and flesh" is the order preferred by many manuscripts rather than the "flesh and blood" of our AV. The reason is not clear but it may simply be that since the shedding of blood is to be a prominent theme in the epistle, accordingly the blood is given precedence in the term. Christ will be a sharer in this humanity, but with a most important reservation. The children are "partakers" (*koinōneō*), He "took part" (*metechō*). The words are different, and are intended to be. The children are partakers by common lot, without choice; He will take part voluntarily, in something outside of Himself. He will become their Kinsman. He will enter into humanity in like manner as they. Some will see, in the word "likewise" (AV), simply a reference to His holy birth. He who was conceived miraculously nevertheless entered the world by the gateway of birth as did the children. This is true, but see here also a safeguarding of the uniqueness of our Lord's humanity. It is real; it is true; He is Man as truly and as certainly as others. But there is an essential difference. The children partake, in a common, equal sharing, of a humanity with a fallen nature. It is their common lot to inherit at birth the nature of their fallen progenitor. Jesus is different. He takes part in their manhood as similarly as is possible without inheriting anything of fallen Adam. He came near to them; He came close to them. Such is the force of the "likewise" of the AV. For the clear meaning of the word see Phil 2:27 where Epaphroditus was sick, "nigh unto" death. How near he was to dying, without dying! How close has our Kinsman come; how near to us He has come in a real humanity, so similar to ours, but neither innocent nor fallen. His is a unique holy humanity, divinely-prepared and voluntarily-chosen (Heb 10:5).

Now the point and purpose of Christ's taking of humanity was that He might die. The Son of God became the Son of Mary and the Son of man so as to be able to enter into death, the fear of which held men in bondage; and so that by death, through death, He might render powerless him that had the power of death.

15 The devil (*diabolos*) is a murderer from the beginning (John 8:44). It was he, in serpent form, who beguiled Eve and brought about the downfall of Adam. With that downfall came death and ever since that entrance of sin and death men have lived their lives in fear of dying. The devil, who introduced sin, introduced with it a bondage (John 8:34). Sin when it is finished bringeth forth death (James 1:15). In every human breast there is a dread of death. Some there are, who with a glib nonchalance profess an indifference to it, but such an attitude usually is revealed eventually to be but a veneer and a facade. There is, in the natural heart, a lurking fear of death and of dying and of the afterward. But the Saviour has annulled him that had the power of death. "Destroyed" as in the AV is inexact. The devil is obviously not destroyed yet. But his doom is certain and already he has been robbed of his power as far as the believer is concerned. The Saviour has abolished death and has brought life and incorruptibility to light through the gospel (2 Tim 1:10). The children are set free. One day, in the full enjoyment of it all, they will sing

> O death, where is thy sting?
> O grave, where is thy victory?
> (1 Cor 15:55).

The deliverance has been accomplished through death. He who, alone among men, was entitled not to die; upon whom death had no claim because He had no sin; He it was who went into death, and by means of death brought to nought him that had the power of death. Goliath has been slain with his own sword! (1 Sam 17:51).

> "He hell in hell laid low,
> Made sin, He sin o'erthrew,
> Bowed to the grave, destroyed it so,
> And death, by dying, slew."

16   "Verily" in this verse is not the familiar "verily" of the Gospels, the double form of which, "Verily verily", is found twenty-five times in the Gospel according to John. The word, *dēpou,* is found only here in the NT. It means "indeed", "doubtless", "so", and the writer uses it here as a prelude to remarking upon something which they all knew very well. He is about to state a truism. We would say, "As you know", or, "It goes without saying", or, "It need hardly be said". The familiar truth now stated is that when the Son came down to be Saviour and Helper, it was not of fallen angels that He took hold with a view to helping. Why the AV translators rendered this verse as they did is somewhat of a mystery. There is nothing in the text about "the nature" of angels. That is misleading. It is "For verily not of angels doth He take hold" (RV), or, "For He does not indeed take hold of angels" (JND). If the italicised words of the AV are omitted the sense is clearer; "For verily he took not on angels; but he took on the seed of Abraham". The word signifies here (though not always) "to take hold of to help". See the meaning brought out so clearly in 8:9 of this epistle, where, "I took them by the hand to lead them out of the land of Egypt". Now these Hebrew believers knew this well, but for what reason does the writer now draw their attention to the well-known truth? Is it not in preparation for the introduction of the high priestly ministry of Christ? He who would stoop to save must also be able to keep. To be their Helper in any or either of these matters the Son must become, as far as may be possible, as the children. He who would so help men must become a Man, and so He did. He passed angels by and came into manhood to lay hold of men. What stirrings of gratitude ought this to stir in our breasts. We know relatively little about the angels and their sin, but we do know that some have fallen. And we know their awful present condition and their terrible future. God has not spared them. They are reserved for judgment. They are kept in eternal chains in gloomy darkness (2 Pet 2:4; Jude 6). They have not been offered salvation. There is no provision for them. For men it is different. Christ indeed has not taken hold of angels to help them, but has taken hold of the seed of Abraham. He who is better than angels in ch.1 becomes lower than angels in ch.2 that He might bring salvation to sinful men.

But why "the seed of Abraham"? It is evident that coming into humanity our Lord must of necessity attach Himself to some particular family. In the sovereign purpose of God He came of the seed of David (Rom 1:3) and as the son of Abraham (Matt 1:1). So does this confine His saving ministry to that people? Is it to the seed of Abraham only that He brings help? The answer is, Yes, and No! The glad tidings and the offer of salvation in Christ is not for Jews only, in the natural and national usage of that word. He is "the Saviour of the world" (John 4:42). In this sense the promise is wider than that nation. However, those who believe are "blessed with faithful Abraham" (Gal 3:9). They are reckoned as his sons and his seed (Gal 3:7, 29). Many of us are not the natural descendants of Abraham, but he is the father of the faithful (Rom 4:11) and we who believe have thus come into blessing through faith. We are, by grace, the true "seed of Abraham". It is open to every man to become, by grace, a son of Abraham.

17   The word "wherefore" leads us on. The writer takes the opportunity now to introduce that theme which is to become predominant and peculiar to the Hebrews, the high priestly ministry of Christ. This is another compelling reason for the humanity of the Lord Jesus. It was necessary, it behoved Him, to be made like unto His brethren. To be the merciful and faithful high priest that we needed He must know, experimentally, the sorrows of the way. Priests were taken from among men (5:1). They must be such as know the difficulties and problems of manhood. So in all things He would be made like His brethren of v.12. But this "all things" requires to be qualified. There will be a full qualification later, in 4:15, where the impeccability of that holy manhood of our Lord will be expounded emphatically. It is a unique humanity, as we have seen, ever apart from, separate from, sin and sinning. There is not even the possibility of sinning with Him. He is untouchable, unreachable, by even the suggestion of sin. He is not vulnerable as we are.

> Without a trace of Adam's sin,
> As Man unique in origin,
> All fair without, all pure within,
> Our Blessed Lord !

What then does "all things" mean? He suffered all things apart from sin. Our Lord was a Man of sorrows. He was acquainted with grief. He knew poverty and pain, weariness and loneliness, hunger and thirst, but not sin. He was misrepresented and misunderstood, He was mocked, and maligned. He was hated without a cause, and His own friends failed Him and forsook Him. But He did not sin. We may not, we cannot, and we would not, attribute sin or the possibility of it to our Lord. So is He able to sympathise with His suffering brethren. He knows the path they tread, for He trod it too. He is therefore merciful, pitiful and compassionate towards us. He is faithful too to us and to God, as He was in the treading of that pathway of suffering when He was here. He trod it faithfully to the end.

As a high priest Christ ministers for us in things relating to God. "High priest" implies and assumes a priesthood, and so it is. There is a royal and holy priesthood of men who have responsibilities toward God. He is our high priest. He ministers for us in matters for which we are responsible to God. He has therefore, first of all, attended to the question of our sins. He has made propitiation (not reconciliation as in the AV). God has been propitiated in that His holy and righteous character has been vindicated by the expiatory sacrifice of Christ. Thus propitiated, God can move toward men in mercy and with forgiveness. For the believing sinner the sin-question has been settled and he may now move toward God in priestly exercises. In such priestly ministry we have a high priest. He brings us to God. He brings God to us. He is merciful and faithful.

18   Our Lord's trials were real. He suffered being tempted. It must be repeated, and emphasised, and understood, that this was not, for Him, temptation to sin. There may indeed have been propositions from Satan and from men which we call temptation but they never reached His heart (see Matt 4:1; 16:1; 19:3; 22:18, and parallel passages). There was nothing in Him to respond to sinful temptings. He might be tried and tested and proved, but He cannot sin. Now in all of these trials He suffered. He can therefore succour those that are similarly suffering. He does not sympathise with our sinning, but He does with our suffering. Indeed He hastens to our aid, for such is the meaning of this word "succour". The verb *boētheō* is a compounding of two simple words: *boē*, "a shout", and *theō* "to run". Our faithful high priest runs to help those who call. We shall find the word again in the well-known 4:16. where there is grace to "help" in time of need.

So He who has been portrayed in all His personal greatness as the Son in ch.1 is indeed a Man in ch.2. The eternal One has come into time. The Ancient of Days has come to Bethlehem and to Nazareth, and to Golgotha. He has become truly human that He might be capable of sufferings and death. And having trodden the path of righteousness and testimony before us He is now perfectly qualified to represent us. The upholder of all things is now a Man in the glory. His personal sufferings are past but He is the high priest of a suffering people and He cannot, and will not, forget them. He who is our Saviour, is our Sympathiser, and our Succourer.

Thus has the great subject of His high priestly ministry been introduced. It will now be developed in a most orderly way through the very heart of the epistle.

Notes

"A little lower than the angels"

It is conceded by all commentators that the words translated "a little" in vv.7, 9 (*brachu ti*), may relate either to degree or to time. If the relation to time was agreed then a fair translation would be, "made for a little while lower than the angels". Some would interpret v.7 in the former way, "a little (in degree or rank) lower than the angels", and v.9 in the latter way, "for a little while lower than the angels". This appears to be rather inconsistent. The context of Ps 8, which is being quoted, would seem to require the first sense, i.e. "a little (in degree) lower than the angels". So we have understood it in our exposition.

Propitiation

It is important to note, as pointed out in the exposition of the text, that the word "reconciliation" in 2:17 AV, ought to be "propitiation". It is equally important to understand the difference between propitiation and atonement. Atonement is, strictly, an OT word and an OT truth. The word is never found in our NT except in Rom 5:11 AV, and there the Greek word is not atonement but reconciliation. Propitiation, however, is not an OT word, nor is it, in its fulness, an OT truth, although the mercy seat was, indeed, the "propitiatory". Atonement covered sins. Propitiation does more; it implies complete expiation of sins by an acceptable and accepted sacrifice, and the consequent vindication and satisfaction of God so that His holy wrath and righteous anger against sins may be stayed. (See Rom 3:25; 1 John 2:2 and 4:10.) Atonement needed to be repeated again and again. It was never complete. Indeed even the Day of Atonement was, literally, the Day of Atonements, in the plural. But propitiation was made once for all by the expiatory sacrifice of the Lord Jesus and took into account those sins of the past which had been but covered in view of His death (Rom 3:25). There had been, from Eden to Calvary, a suspension of God's retribution through a system of sacrifices and offerings which allowed God to go along with the people in prospect of Golgotha. Now, at this present time, the righteousness of God is declared in that He can justify the believing sinner, and yet remain just, because propitiation has been made.

It is also important to see that propitiation was made at the Cross and not in heaven. The view, that propitiation was made in heaven, is prevalent in some parts, perhaps made popular by such writers as Sir Robert Anderson and Sir Walter Scott, of an earlier generation. It was a necessary doctrine for them because they taught that our Lord's priesthood began in heaven. They could see, however, that propitiation was necessarily a priestly work, and so, to reconcile the two ideas they taught that propitiation was made, not by blood shed, but by blood sprinkled. This is based upon a sad misunderstanding, even by such men, of the typical teaching of Leviticus and other related Scriptures. For a full and detailed treatment of this important and interesting question, see a booklet by the late Thomas H. Lyttle of Belfast, entitled *Was Propitiation made at the Cross or in Heaven?*

III God's House and God's Rest   (3:1-19)

1. *Christ Greater than Moses*
3:1-6

v.1 "Wherefore, holy brethren, partakers of the heavenly calling, consider the Apostle and High Priest of our profession, Christ Jesus;

v.2 Who was faithful to him that appointed him, as also Moses *was faithful* in all his house.

v.3 For this *man* was counted worthy of more glory than Moses, inasmuch as he who hath builded the house hath more honour than the house.

v.4 For every house is builded by some *man;* but he that built all things *is* God.

v.5 And Moses verily *was* faithful in all his house, as a servant, for a testimony of those things which were to be spoken after;

v.6 But Christ as a son over his own house; whose house are we, if we hold fast the confidence and the rejoicing of the hope firm unto the end."

1 With a repeated "wherefore" (2:17), the writer continues his argument which is now to take the form of an appeal. Having introduced the subject of a priestly ministry which for Hebrews really began with Aaron, he will now go on to compare and contrast Christ, not only with Aaron but first of all with Moses of those early days. In a tender but powerful manner the writer will appeal to them to consider the superiority of Jesus. There is indeed an inherent appeal even in the form of address which he now uses. There is a fourfold recognition and reminder of their status and their dignity. They are brethren; and they are holy; they have a calling; and it is heavenly. In this very mode of address there are strong incentives to an occupation with Him who has made it all possible.

In the one small phrase "holy brethren" is a combination of privilege and dignity. That they are Christ's brethren has already been shown in 2:11, 12, 17. And if they stand, each of them, in that relationship to Christ, then they are also in that relationship with one another. In the difficulties of the way and in face of persecutions and oppositions and reproach for Christ, what can be more immediately helpful and encouraging than this, to know that they are brethren together, united with family ties greater than ever they had known in Judaism.

But these brethren are holy. "Holy" is a cognate word with the sanctified and the Sanctifier of 2:11. In the purpose of God, they had been set apart. They were different, not only from the nations, as God ever desired Israel to be, but also now from unbelieving Israel, and as they were in God's mind and purpose, so should they be in daily practical living. Holiness, which characterised Christ, ought now to characterise the brethren. They are holy brethren. This is perhaps a unique expression. We read of holy apostles, of holy prophets, of holy men and holy women, of a holy nation and a holy priesthood, but with the doubtful exception of 1 Thess 5:27 this is the only time we read of holy brethren.

In a heavenly calling they were "partakers". This is the word of 1:9, "fellows". They were companions (*metochos*). Note the important difference between this word and the word partakers of 2:14. There they were partakers (*koinōneō*) of flesh and blood, sharing by common lot in the human condition of all Israel and of all men. Here they are companions in a heavenly thing which is exclusive to those who are Christ's. It is a "heavenly" calling. Israel's calling nationally was an earthly one. As Israelites the earlier ambitions of these Hebrews would have been related to earthly advantages. They had a land and a country, a kingdom and a throne, a temple and a priesthood. But they were sharers now in a heavenly calling. There is no definite article here, as in the AV. It is the nature and character of the calling which is being stressed. Heaven now, and not earth, was the source and the object of their affections and their hopes. It is a holy calling in 2 Tim 1:9; a high calling in Phil 3:14. Here it is a heavenly calling.

To such people, endowed with such dignity, the writer now appeals for a contemplation of Jesus. The dignity conferred on them demanded a response to his call. "Consider" (*katanoeō*) means to consider closely, to perceive clearly, and to understand fully. He will not have them in the slightest doubt as to the greatness of Christ. He is the Apostle and high priest. Is this dual title of our Lord not reminiscent of Moses and Aaron? Is not the writer really saying, "Consider the Moses and Aaron of our confession"? The Apostle is the sent One (*apostolos*). As such He was sent forth to us. As high priest He has now gone back. The Apostle comes out. The high priest goes in. He has represented God to us and now He represents us to God. The ministries of Moses and Aaron are now invested in one Person. It is imperative that we should diligently and earnestly contemplate such an One. Note that "confession" (RV; JND) is better than "profession" as in the AV. He is the One whom we confess (Rom 10:9). The word *homologia* will appear twice more in the epistle (4:14; 10:23).

This confession is of "Jesus", which is in perfect accord with Rom 10:9 just mentioned. Many MSS, with those considered to be the best, omit "Christ" here, retaining only the single name "Jesus". The usage of the single name of Jesus is a characteristic of this epistle. It is the human name of Him who was Jehovah. It is the name of Him whom the nation rejected. It is not always reverent or spiritually intelligent to use the single name "Jesus", without "Christ" or "Lord" attached. But sometimes it is so used and where it does appear like this there is some reason for it which we do well to observe. This is the second such occurrence (see 1:9). The writer is obviously intent on showing that in the despised and rejected "Jesus" God has invested a ministry and an authority such as had not been seen before, neither in Adam, nor in Moses, nor in Aaron. Jesus is the second Man, the Apostle, and the high priest in the new order of things associated with the heavenly calling.

2   Further mention is now made of the faithfulness of Christ. This had already been remarked upon in 2:17. Now it is of course true and very beautiful that Jesus was ever faithful during His life and ministry on earth, but here we need to change the past tense of the AV. It is not that He *was* faithful, but that He *is* faithful. Perhaps indeed it is in this present faithfulness that we are now urged to view Him. If we read the exhortation as, "Consider Him being faithful", we shall get the real point of it. This is a present faithfulness of our Lord in His ministry relative to the house of God and there is a comparison now with the faithful ministry of Moses. There is an obvious reference to Num 12:7, and an obvious parallel too, between the murmurings of the people against Moses and complaints and murmurings in our day. Moses was their appointed leader. God had made him so. He was, in language used of Christ, the captain of their salvation, but as he led them through the wilderness on the way to Canaan they grumbled constantly. In the midst of all this discontent Moses remained faithful to God and to the people. And so it is with us. In spite of all our failings and grumblings on the way to glory, there is One who ever remains faithful. This fidelity of Moses was a faithfulness both to God and to God's people. It was in God's house. "His" house in vv.2, 5, 6, is always God's house.

This mention of God's house now raises a difficulty of definition and a difference of interpretation among commentators. What was the "house of God" in which Moses was found faithful? What is the "house of God" now? Many will interpret the house in which Moses served as the "household", meaning the people, the nation. They will argue that *oikos* ("house") may denote either the house or the household, the dwelling or the family. Others understand the house to be the tabernacle, and this may be the preferable view. The difference, however, is not so large as may at first appear. Moses served the people as he served the tabernacle. His divinely-appointed ministry in connection with the tabernacle was likewise a ministry to and for the people. It is his faithfulness in the ministry which is here emphasised, and as Moses was faithful to the divine appointment, so is Christ, whose house are we. This is developed more in a later verse.

3   But if Moses has been introduced here, it is not that we should be found contemplating him. We are to consider Christ, for He has been counted worthy of greater glory than Moses. Moses has been introduced to compare the faithfulness of Christ and Moses in relation to God's house, but now comparisons are over; there must be contrasts. Perhaps in the hearts of some of these Hebrew readers there was yet a yearning after Moses. Earlier Jews had boasted, "We are Moses' disciples" (John 9:28). In the heart of every Jew there was an inherent natural veneration of the lawgiver. This was understandable but it could prove to be a danger and a snare to the believing Jew. They must see the superiority of Christ even over their great prophet. The writer will proceed to demonstrate this superiority. A grasp of it would keep them firm in their christian confession and would lessen the attraction of Judaism. Christ is worthy of greater glory than Moses. He is not just worthy of *more* glory, as in the AV rendering, as if to say that there was glory for Moses and a little more glory for Christ. Christ is worthy of greater glory. It is not merely an advance; it is a contrasting glory; it is a greater glory. The measure of the superior glory of Christ is the measure of the honour which is afforded to the builder rather than to the house. The magnificence of a building brings honour to the architect and builder.

The builder is to be praised, not the building. Proportionately so is Christ greater than Moses. Moses was himself but a divinely-ordained part of the old order of things. Christ was the builder of it.

4 Every house must have a builder. The word translated "builded" and "built" in vv. 3, 4 is not the common word for building. It is *kataskeuazō* and implies more than constructing. The word appears three times more in the epistle and each time is translated differently. Perhaps a combining of the various renderings in the AV will bring out the full meaning. Here it is translated "builded"; 9:2 "made"; 9:6 "ordained"; 11:7 "prepared". Now while it is true that every house must have such a builder, a designer, an architect, He that so prepared all things is God. And since the creation of all things has been attributed to Christ already in the epistle (1:2, 10), it follows that here in these verses, in an almost incidental manner, we have been given a further attestation to the deity of Christ. He is the designer, the planner, the maker, who has ordained and established all things. He is therefore God.

5 The contrast between Moses and Christ is now resumed in v.5 and and pursued in v.6. It may be summed up like this.

Moses	a servant	in	God's house;
Christ	a Son	over	God's house.

Moses was a servant. He was a good servant; indeed he was a faithful servant. But he was a servant neverthless. The word *therapōn* rendered "servant" is found only here in the NT. It is an old word akin to the verb *therapeuō* which appears many times in the NT and is almost consistently translated "to heal". Thus Moses is not here viewed as a deacon (*diakonos*), nor as a bondservant (*doulos*), but as an attendant of high rank with responsibility for the healthy ordering of things relative to the house. W.E.Vine regards the term as denoting dignity and freedom in the house management. But yet withal he was a servant! Christ is a Son! Every Jew knew that a son was superior to a servant. Even the prodigal knew that. He returned in repentance to the father with intentions of saying, "I am no more worthy to be called thy son: make me as one of thy hired servants" (Luke 15:19).

Moreover, this faithful service of the man Moses was actually but anticipatory and preliminary. It was prophetic of the greater ministry that was to come with Christ. In faithfulness Moses served, labouring with all diligence in that tabernacle system of things so that it might all be a true foreshadowing of that which was to come after. The house in which he served was typical of things then future. It was a shadow of good things to come (10:1) and its testimony to better things was true, as this epistle will later endeavour to show.

6 Now observe the contrasting prepositions. Moses was "in" the house. Christ is "over" the house. Moses the servant may be in the house, attending and ordering, but

Christ is over the house as the author and originator of all. And we who have
confessed His name are that house, taking for granted that we are truly His and that
this is being proven by our holding fast of the hope which we have professed.
Provided that we do hold fast the boldness and the boast which belong to true
believing, then we may profess to be that house. It is not presumptuous to be bold
in this hope. It is not pride to boast in Christ. This is not vainglory. It is the simple
glad assurance and willing testimony of every true confessor of Christ. The warning
which is inherent in the "if" of this verse, "if we hold fast ...", is for those who may
be but professors, in constant danger of yielding to the call of Judaism and abandoning
their earlier profession of Jesus as Messiah. The genuine believer would have a settled
confidence. He would have an assured hope of glory in Christ. But there were many
distractions and dangers even for those who were sincere and genuine among these
Hebrews. If persecutions and difficulties and the attractions of old Judaism proved
too much for the false professors and exposed their unreality, it was sadly possible that
true saints also might be side-tracked and stumbled. So the "if" is a sad necessity for
all. The underlying exhortation, mingled with the warning, is that we hold fast.
Perseverance is the proof of reality. There can be no "if" regarding God's faithfulness,
or Christ's greatness. There is no doubting His grace, His power, His love, or His
provision. The hope is secure and firm (6:19). But there cannot be a returning to
Judaism, or to the world, or to the old life and its habits, and at the same time a
confident testimony to that hope. His house are we, assuming that life and lip agree;
taking for granted that what we are agrees with what we say.

It may be profitable, and necessary, at this juncture, to ask, What is the house of
God? In the days of Moses it was, undoubtedly, the tabernacle. But what is the house
of God now, when both tabernacle and temple have served their day and have
gone?

There are three basic reasons why a man builds a house. He desires a place where
he may dwell. He seeks a sphere where he may rule, in exercise of his responsibility
of headship. He wants a home where, when the labour of the day is ended, he may
rest. A man's house is where he resides, where he rules, and where he rests. The house
of God may be viewed similarly. It is the place where God may dwell. It is the place
where His authority and government are recognised and where He rules. It is the
place where, in complacency, He may rest.

It is important to remember, in the study of this epistle, that we do not have in
it the church which is His body, as we have in Ephesians. Indeed the word *ekklēsia*
("assembly") is found only twice in the whole letter (2:12; 12:23) and these but
incidentally and not in the form of exposition. That assembly of Eph 2:22,23; 3:10;
5:32, is viewed there as being already safe at home, seated in the heavenlies, in glory,
with Christ. This is not the background of the Epistle to the Hebrews. Here the saints
are pilgrims, travelling through a wilderness to Canaan. They sing as they journey:

'Tis the treasure I've found in His love
That has made me a pilgrim below;
And 'tis there when I reach Him above,
As I'm known, all His fulness I'll know.

The saints then, in Hebrews, are viewed as being on earth, and accordingly they are seen as God's house. They are in testimony. They are in responsibility. They remember the threefold purpose of the house as above stated, and they seek to order things aright for His pleasure and for His glory. The house, however, with so much attendant profession, unreality, and failure, has become a great house (2 Tim 2:20). It is like the great tree of Luke 13:19. It is therefore our privilege and responsibility to build locally assemblies with "house of God" character. No particular individual local assembly will claim to be either "the" house of God, nor "a" house of God, but each will so arrange its affairs according to the word of God so as to make that assembly a place where He may reside and rule and rest. This is the local view of the house (1 Tim 3:15). The house here in Hebrews is viewed in a wider context. It is all saints on earth at any given time. It is the body as subsisting on earth.

Having compared and contrasted Christ and Moses, and having established the superiority of Christ over Moses, the writer has shown simultaneously that discipleship to Moses was now a thing of the past for these Hebrew believers. Once having known Christ in His greatness, an Apostle greater than Moses, it was unthinkable that anyone should go back. But the warnings and exhortations were necessary and are now continued and intensified.

2. The Second Warning
   ### 3:7-19

v.7 "Wherefore (as the Holy Ghost saith, To day if ye will hear his voice,

v.8 Harden not your hearts, as in the provocation, in the day of temptation in the wilderness:

v.9 When your fathers tempted me, proved me, and saw my works forty years.

v.10 Wherefore I was grieved with that generation, and said, They do alway err in *their* heart; and they have not known my ways.

v.11 So I sware in my wrath, They shall not enter into my rest.)

v.12 Take heed, brethren, lest there be in any of you an evil heart of unbelief, in departing from the living God.

v.13 But exhort one another daily, while it is called To day; lest any of you be hardened through the deceitfulness of sin.

v.14 For we are made partakers of Christ, if we hold the beginning of our confidence stedfast unto the end;

v.15 While it is said, To day if ye will hear his voice, harden not your hearts, as in the provocation.

v.16 For some, when they had heard, did provoke: howbeit not all that came out of Egypt by Moses.

v.17 But with whom was he grieved forty years? *was it* not with them that had sinned, whose carcases fell in the wilderness?

v.18 And to whom sware he that they should not enter into his rest, but to them that believed not?

v.19 So we see that they could not enter in because of unbelief."

7   God has spoken in ch.1. The Son has spoken in ch.2. We are now exhorted to listen to the voice of the Spirit. The writer will quote from Ps 95 but notice that he does not say, "as the Psalmist saith", but "as the Holy Ghost saith". Notice the definite and unequivocal recognition of the inspiration of the Holy Scriptures. They are the voice of the Spirit. Now while the exhortation that follows is applicable to all believers, of whatever age and of whatever background, yet how solemnly would it come home to these Hebrews who were a remnant of the very nation to whom the Ps 95 was first given. And were they not also the descendants of that nation which had so provoked God in the wilderness on the way to Canaan? "Wherefore", says the writer, "take heed ...". The AV will indicate a parenthesis between the "Wherefore" of v.7 and the "take heed" at the beginning of v.12, while Ps 95 is being quoted. The parallel which is being drawn now is unmistakable. There had been a past generation on the way to Canaan. They had been delivered from Egypt. They had been given the promise of a better land. They had a divinely-appointed leader. Jehovah was graciously and miraculously providing for them along the way. But that way to Canaan led through a wilderness and the desert conditions were not always acceptable to the people. They murmured. They rebelled. They complained against Moses and against the Lord. And, in the end, unbelief deprived them of the land to which they were professedly travelling. The appeal of Ps 95 to the nation of the Psalmist's day was to remember the failings of the fathers, and not to be like them, or to do as they did. The exhortation of the Psalm is to rejoice, to sing, to be thankful, and to worship, and to obey.

For the earliest readers of this epistle (and for us) the appeal was exactly the same, "Today ... hear his voice". For them, and for us, there are so many similarities to the experiences of the people who left Egypt in the great exodus. Christ our passover is sacrificed for us (1 Cor 5:7). In baptism we have crossed the Red Sea and left Egypt behind. We are bound for a better country. Christ is our manna and our Rock, our meat and drink in the wilderness through which our path lies to the heavenly rest which has been promised us (1 Cor 10:2-4). Let us, today, in our day, hear His voice, heed the warnings, and in simple trust believe His word whatever the difficulties of the way.

8   The words "provocation" and "temptation" are a sad commentary on Israel's behaviour in the wilderness. The warning now to us who have confessed Christ is that we be not like that "church in the wilderness" (Acts 7:38). Let us take heed to our hearts indeed, lest we repeat the tragic failures of that people. The Hebrew word for "provocation" is *Meribah* (literally, "strife"), and the word for "temptation" *Massah*. J.N.Darby will actually put these names into his translation of the text of Ps 95:8. What painful memories would the mention of these names evoke in the hearts of all thoughtful Hebrews. The story of this provocation was a continuous story. It was not just one isolated sad lapse into bitterness and strife. It was characteristic of them. It began as early as Exod 17. They contended and disputed, and murmured against Moses, and they tempted the Lord. He gave them water from the smitten rock and Moses called the name of the place Massah, and Meribah, memorials of their contentions and provocations. But the spirit and conduct of Massah persisted until

Num 20. The events of Exod 17 are there repeated. The patience of Moses is exhausted. The meek man is angry. In haste he strikes the rock instead of speaking to it. Jehovah still in grace gave water in abundance from that rock, but a beautiful foreshadowing of Christ had been marred. The rock, once smitten, must not be smitten again. It is sufficient now to speak to the rock. The waters that now issue from the rock in Num 20 are again called, "the waters of Meribah", where the children of Israel contended with Jehovah (Num 20:13).

9   That this unbelief, this mistrust of Jehovah, was characteristic of that generation, and not just occasional backsliding, is now confirmed. They constantly "tempted" God, by "proving" Him, and this over a period of forty years. "Tempted" (*peirazō*) infers that they tried God by their unbelief, and by their persistent refusal to trust Him and believe His promises; "proved" (*dokimazō*) that they put Him to thorough trial, even though He had powerfully delivered them, and graciously cared for them. They had tried Him by proving Him, for those forty years. In the Hebrew text of Ps 95, which is being quoted, the "forty years" is linked with the "I was grieved", so as to read, "Forty years was I grieved with that generation". Here in Heb3 the "forty years" is linked with "your fathers saw my works", so as to read "your fathers... saw my works forty years". Perhaps together they tell the whole story. For forty years they saw His works and knew His care, and for those same forty years they continually provoked Him and refused to trust Him.

Forty years! Should there not have been, to these Hebrew readers, something ominously prophetic in these words? Forty years! Would not the thoughtful among them realise that it was now almost forty years since the commencement of the Lord's ministry? The shadows of AD 70 were now looming large. Forty years of unbelief had passed since Jesus had appeared among them with the glad tidings. Were the earlier forty years now being duplicated? The pending judgment of AD 70 would indeed be a righteous judgment on the nation. How solemn if among them there were those whose hearts were not right.

10   Jehovah was grieved. The word *prosochthizō* is more intense than the "grieved" of the AV. To quote W.E.Vine (*Expository Dictionary*), "'Grieved' does not adequately express the righteous anger of God intimated in the passage". "I was wroth with this generation" (JND); "I was displeased with this generation" (RV); "I was indignant" (Newberry), are other translations of that sad phrase. Jehovah's wrath was righteous, for there had been continuous provocation for forty years. It was habitual. Is this not emphasised in the words that follow, "They do alway err in their heart"? Observe the singular "heart", as if to say that the very heart of the nation was wrong. And it was "alway" or "always". Perpetually, incessantly, invariably, repeatedly, continually, they erred in heart. "Err" (*planaomai*) is a wandering from what is right and proper; a going astray. It is the word from which we get our English word "planet". It is the word used by Jude when he describes some as "wandering stars". That generation wandered in heart, and consequently in their ways, from the path that Jehovah had intended for them. He was righteously indignant that they did not recognise His ways but wandered in their own. It was not simply that they did not know His ways. They ignored His ways. They would not know. They refused to know. There is an echo of an earlier indictment of the nation in Isa 55:8, "My thoughts are not your thoughts, neither are your ways my ways, saith the Lord". Jehovah and His people were at variance in thoughts and ways. So the sad history has been repeated. They had ignored His ways for their own.

11 So, righteously so, consequently so, Jehovah turned from those who had turned from Him and swore in His wrath that they would not enter the Canaan He had intended for them. It was a solemn sentence. They could not enter into His rest while in unbelief they persisted in their own ways. There must be an abandoning of self-will and of human effort if there is to be an enjoyment of God's rest. Failing this, the word is unalterably final, "They shall not enter". For the nation that left Egypt, this rest was Canaan. For the Hebrews the rest was a future rest in glory. It was a rest which would be fully realised when God Himself would rest. It was, after all, God's rest. It will be a millennial rest, which will be but the prelude to an eternal rest in an eternal day. There is, of course, for the believer, a rest now. There is a rest of conscience, given when we first come to the Saviour (Matt 11:28), and there is a rest of heart in the daily circumstances of life, to be had when we take His easy yoke (Matt 11:29). "Peace I leave with you," He said, "My peace I give unto you" (John 14:27). We dare not minimise the preciousness of such rest. These are blessed foretastes, but they are not the rest of God. They are not what Jehovah calls "my rest". The context requires that the rest of these two chapters, 3 and 4, be a future rest, when God Himself will cease from work. When sin, with all the blight it has brought, will have been subdued, and when creation will groan no more, and when the Prince of Peace will reign, God will rest. To quote Wm. Kelly, "Heaven and earth shall be united in a chain of descending goodness and universal blessing, when Christ is no longer hid in God, and His sons are revealed for the deliverance which the long enthralled creation awaits. Till that day God works, because there is still unremoved sin and misery; and we work in the communion of His love. When it comes, we shall be in the rest of God".

12 The parenthetical quotation from Ps 95 is now ended and v.12 follows naturally from the "wherefore" of v.7. "Wherefore, take heed, brethren". "See, brethren" (JND) is the intensified exhortatory warning. The writer gets to the solemn root of the matter. What happened to those who came out of Egypt could happen to some of them. Could there be some, outwardly journeying with the people of God, travelling in company with the saints, whose hearts were not right with God? "Take heed, brethren …". "An evil heart of unbelief" was the problem with Israel of old. A wicked heart of unbelief and a falling away; this was the sad story of that earlier generation. And the story was being repeated. It was up to every individual among them to search his heart. "Any one of you" may be in that self-same condition, and though ostensibly journeying with a believing people, there could be within the wickedness of unbelief and a heart unchanged. The end of such a condition is apostasy. "Departing"(AV); "falling away" (RV); "turning away" (JND) is *apostasia* or *aphistēmi*, indicating a deserting, a defection, an apostasy.

Unbelief departs from the "living" God. It prefers the lifeless deities of man's own imaginations. But the God of Israel is *El Chai*, the living God (Ps 84:2). The believing heart cries out for *El Chai*. "The living God" is a title occurring so frequently in the NT that it would scarcely be feasible just now to list every reference. It occurs in the Gospels and in the Acts; is in the epistles to the Romans, to the Corinthians, to the Thessalonians, and to Timothy. It is four times in Hebrews and once in Revelation. Christ is the Son of the living God. The Church is the Church of the living God. We belong to the City of the living God.

This then was the solemn possibility, that as Israel of old had done, so might they, in forsaking the living God. The appeal of Judaism was strong to the heart that had no firm trust in Jesus as Messiah. The ceremonies and rituals of Judaism were somewhat easier than the path of faith. Judaism was visible and tangible and beautiful. It was attractive to a man in the flesh.

13 They were therefore to exhort one another daily. Indeed it is rather "encourage yourselves", which seems to imply not only an encouraging of each other but an encouragement, by each man, of himself, as David had encouraged himself in the Lord (1 Sam 30:6). Day by day such encouragement was a recurring necessity and safeguard, and it is for us too. As long as "today" continues we must exhort and encourage and help each other. Unbelief is wicked and sin is subtle. Unbelief and sin are not compatible with faith and holiness. We cannot live for that which is visible and sensual and temporal and yet be in the enjoyment of things which are unseen and spiritual and eternal. Temptation to an easier path may touch even the true believer, hence we must encourage each other, and God in grace restores and preserves. But where there is a wicked heart, unchanged and unregenerate, then sin with all its deceitfulness will lead that soul astray into an eventual abandonment of the earlier profession. As is often pointed out, the genuine believing soul will cry out, "To whom shall we go?" The trusting heart to Jesus clings. For Israel in the wilderness the way of faith was too difficult. They hardened their heart in unbelief and the price of that unbelief was that they lost Canaan with all its promise.

14 The particle "For", with which v.14 commences, is again an important conjunction. The warning is about to be reiterated, that the proof of reality is perseverance. True companions of the Christ will continue. The assurance and confidence which marked the beginning will be maintained until the end.

> Simply trusting every day;
>   Trusting through a stormy way;
> Even when my faith is small –
>   Trusting Jesus, that is all.

> Trusting Him while life shall last,
>   Trusting Him till earth is past,
> Till within the jasper wall –
>   Trusting Jesus, that is all.

This does not necessarily mean a life of remarkable evidences of faith. It does not mean that we shall all do exploits for God. But it does mean that the genuine companions of Christ will be manifested by a sturdy going on as they began. We are not of them that draw back (10:39). "Partakers" or "companions" (*metochos*), are "fellows", as in 1:9 and 3:1. There is a holy fellowship of those who love the Christ and who pursue the heavenly calling, looking for the promised rest when wilderness days are past. Already we have tasted of the grapes of Eshcol and in the enjoyment of this we will travel together, encouraging each other in the wilderness of the world until we arrive in Canaan.

Now the words "we are made partakers" (AV) may be a little misleading. We should not think that we must persevere, and so, by perseverance, be made partakers. A better rendering would be "we are become companions". By faith, we are already companions of Christ. Our patient continuance does not obtain this privilege for us; it only proves that we have it. Holding fast is not a means of salvation but an evidence of it. The word "confidence" (AV) is "assurance". It is strange to observe that there are those in Christendom who say that we cannot be sure! They say that it is arrogant and presumptuous to imagine that here and now we can have assurance of salvation and of heaven. How do such answer this exhortation, that we must hold firm our assurance, from the beginning to the end?

15 Do this indeed, exhorts the writer. Hold your confidence firm while it is said "Today if ye will hear his voice". But how are we, today, in our day, a day of pilgrimage, to hear His voice? Is it not in the reading of His word and in our attendance to the ministry of it? By such means His people hear His voice today. He calls us to service and to worship, to separation and to fellowship, to communion and to holiness. One day, someday, when "today" is over and gone, He will call us to Himself. While it is "today" let us give heed to His voice, and as we hear, obey. By such constant diligent hearing of His will for us we shall guard our hearts against any hardening of them and so be saved from provoking Him, as others did.

16 This hearing of His voice, however, must of necessity be an obedient hearing, for some of old, when they had heard, did provoke. They heard His voice indeed, and heard His will for them made known to them, but so hearing, they did not respond. It was as if they had not heard at all. They did not hear with the hearing of faith and with a consequent obedience. They heard; but they did not hear; and they provoked.

In the latter part of this v.16 the AV is at variance with the RV and with JND. In the AV rendering it is stated that not all that came out of Egypt provoked the Lord. This is true indeed if we exclude those who had not reached an age of responsibility and accountability (and, of course, Caleb and Joshua). The alternative rendering however, makes the statement an interrogative, "Who on hearing did provoke? Was it not all who came out of Egypt by Moses?" This is very solemn. A whole generation, six hundred thousand men with their families (Num 1:46) came out of Egypt and fell in the wilderness and never entered Canaan. With most of them God was not pleased (1 Cor 10:5 RV). They heard His word. They heard His promise. They saw His mighty works. They ought not to have doubted. But they did. They mistrusted Him and provoked Him and perished.

17   For forty years, it is again emphasised (see v.9), God was grieved with them. Again "grieved" is too weak, as in v.10. He was indignant; He was wroth; He was displeased and He was angry. Their unbelief was sin. Their mistrust was wicked. To disbelieve His word was, in essence, to slander His character. To refuse Him was to slight Him, and this they did. Not once, but many times over did they sin the sin of unbelief. The Lord Jesus predicted that when the Spirit was come He would indict the world. One of the three charges with which the world stands indicted is this, "Of sin, because they believe not on me" (John 16:8-9). Unbelief is sin, and the wickedness of unbelief was a sad but real possibility in the hearts of some of these Hebrews.

Note that with that generation that came out of Egypt "their carcases fell in the wilderness". This is a strange statement, "their carcases fell"! Usually we employ the word to describe that which is dead, "a carcase". Their *carcases* fell! Is this a solemn suggestion that they were dead before they fell? Unbelief had slain them. To God they were already dead, and the carcases fell in the desert, monuments, like that pillar of salt (Gen 19:26; Luke 17:32) to the tragedy of unbelief and disobedience.

18   Another question is now asked concerning them. To whom did God sware that they should not enter His rest? The question is answered with another question. Was it not to them that believed not? The sin and seriousness of unbelief is emphasised once again. It is ironical that the gospel preacher delights to preach the simplicity of the way of salvation as "Only believe"! "Believe on the Lord Jesus Christ and thou shalt be saved" (Acts 16:31); "He that heareth my word and believeth" (John 5:24); "He that believeth on the Son hath everlasting life" (John 3:36); "Whosoever believeth" (John 3:16). Yet this simple exercise becomes such a difficulty to some. A refusal to believe is really a refusal to hear. "They hearkened not to the word" (JND). This is almost certainly a quotation from Num 14:43 (LXX). The story of that chapter is an intensely sad one. That generation had known Jehovah's greatness and His grace. They had experienced His goodness and they had seen His glory. Yet they murmured, they despised, they transgressed, and they refused to hearken. "They shall in no wise see the land", was the divine judgment. "They have not hearkened to my voice" (Num 14:22). "None of them shall see it". "In this wilderness shall your carcases fall". All that were numbered, from twenty years old and upwards, who had responsibly and wilfully refused to hearken, perished in the desert. Caleb and Joshua had obeyed and followed fully.

19   So because of this refusal to hear, this unbelief, this mistrust, they forfeited the land. On account of unbelief they could not enter in. How terrible is unbelief. What an indescribable tragedy it was that a journey of only eleven days would have brought them from Egypt to Canaan (Deut 1:2), but instead of this short pilgrimage and a happy entry into Canaan's fruitfulness, unbelief barred them out. They spent forty years in the wilderness, and died there and never arrived at that which God had intended for them.

IV.   God's Rest and God's People   (4:1-16)

1.   *Christ Greater than Joshua*
   4:1-10

   v.1   "Let us therefore fear, lest, a promise being left *us* of entering into his rest, any of you should seem to come short of it.
   v.2   For unto us was the gospel preached, as well as unto them: but the word preached did not profit them, not being mixed with faith in them that heard *it.*
   v.3   For we which have believed do enter into rest, as he said, As I have sworn in my wrath, if they shall enter into my rest: although the works were finished from the foundation of the world.
   v.4   For he spake in a certain place of the seventh *day* on this wise, And God did rest the seventh day from all his works.
   v.5   And in this *place* again, If they shall enter into my rest.
   v.6   Seeing therefore it remaineth that some must enter therein, and they to whom it was first preached entered not in because of unbelief:
   v.7   Again, he limiteth a certain day, saying in David, To day, after so long a time; as it is said, To day if ye will hear his voice, harden not your hearts.
   v.8   For if Jesus had given them rest, then would he not afterward have spoken of another day.
   v.9   There remaineth therefore a rest to the people of God.
   v.10   For he that is entered into his rest, he also hath ceased from his own works, as God *did* from his."

1   It is important, for a proper appreciation of this section of the epistle, that we understand this rest of God to be a future rest. There are eleven occurrences of the word "rest" in these two chapters and we do well to have a clear understanding of the writer's intent when he uses it; he is indeed speaking of a future rest. Again it must be said that this does not in any way minimise the sweetness of that rest which we now enjoy. "I will give you rest", the Saviour said. "Ye shall find rest", He continued (Matt 11:28-29). There is a blessed rest for the conscience from the burden of sin and guilt. There is also a rest for the heart in a submissive acceptance of God's will along the pathway of faith. Both rest of conscience and rest of heart may be ours to enjoy now, but there is another rest to which we travel – God's rest, and the very word is different from that of Matt 11:28. There the word is *anapausis*, indicating ease and refreshment; here the word is *katapausis*, meaning a settled repose, an undisturbed rest.

"Let us fear" would be a strange exhortation for one who was looking for the rest of Matt 11:28. But the exhortation is most understandable once we see it to be addressed to people professing to be travelling on the difficult road to Canaan, some of whom, alas, may never arrive there. It is the solemn exhortation repeated, that we should remember those who left Egypt. They heard the glad tidings of a good land. They set out, travelling with the redeemed, but they failed to reach the promised land. "Let us therefore fear". Might not the same thing happen to any of you? We too have the promise. The possibility of entering into God's rest has been proffered to us. But some who set out may never arrive. It is sadly possible that some will fail, that they will fall short of it. That is exactly what happened to the fathers of these early Hebrew readers of this epistle. Their problems have been assessed in a threefold way. There was distrust, despair, and desire. There was the continual, habitual, characteristic distrust of Jehovah. With the hardship of the way there came a despair of ever reaching Canaan. Out of this despair there was born a desire for a return to Egypt. They failed. They came short. And they perished in the desert.

2   Now we, as they, have had glad tidings presented to us. Just as that nation of bondmen heard, in Egypt, the glad message of a better land and a Canaan rest, so the gospel has borne to us the promise of a future rest when life down here is over. Through the wilderness of this world we travel. There is nothing for us here. We have abandoned Egypt and we look for the land of promise where we shall enjoy God's rest in Christ. The true believer sings,

> This world is a wilderness wide,
>   I have nothing to seek or to choose;
> I've no thought in the waste to abide;
>   I have nought to regret nor to lose.
>
> With Him shall my rest be on high,
>   When in holiness bright I sit down,
> In the joy of His love ever nigh,
>   In the peace that His presence shall crown.

For those who come short the consequences are tragic. "Let us therefore fear". If, as they, we have heard glad tidings and a good word, then it behoves us to enquire why they fell short of the promised rest in Canaan. The answer is simple. The word of the report which they heard was not mixed with faith in those who heard it. A revised rendering of v.2 will say, "because they were not united by faith with them that heard". This would indicate that they did not join in faith with Caleb and Joshua who believed. Whichever rendering is preferred, the point being pressed is quite the same. They heard, but they did not believe. The glad tidings of the better land were borne to them, but they would not receive the message in simple trust, so the word did not profit them. As in the parable of the sower (Matt 13; Mark 4) the seed is always good, but however good the seed may be, if there is not the proper ground to receive it there is no fruit. Hearts there may be like the hard trodden wayside. Stones and thorns there may be to prevent the good result. Only when the good seed is received into good ground in simple faith will there be the desired growth. This was not so with the generation that left Egypt. This is an ever present danger in our day, just as in the days when this epistle was written. For though these earliest readers were undoubtedly Hebrews, yet are these principles equally applicable to Gentile believers also. If the word is not mixed with faith there can be no profit, neither then nor now, neither for Jew nor Gentile.

3 The translation "We which have believed do enter into rest" tends to misunderstanding, seeming to imply that we who have believed have already entered into the rest. J.N. Darby's rendering is preferable, "We enter into the rest who have believed", or Wm Kelly's reads, "We that believe enter that rest". The verse is not saying that we do, here and now, enter the rest, nor that we have already entered into it. It is the statement of the absolute principle that those who enter are believers, or, conversely, that only believers enter. The rest is for believers only. It is God's rest, and His purpose is to share it with those who will trust Him. There is nothing in the verse of a present rest. Whatever other aspect of rest we may enjoy (and do enjoy), this is a future rest with God, reserved exclusively for those who believe. It is not yet entered. It "remains", as we shall see later in v.9.

With this principle the early history is in complete agreement. "They shall not enter into my rest" (RV). "See if they shall enter into my rest". Such is the meaning of the strange and difficult AV rendering of v.3. The doubt, and the negative "if" is a way of saying positively, "They shall not enter", and this although there was, indeed, a rest available. There was a creation rest. God had rested in a finished work. It was all very good. It was completed. And the Creator rested.

4 "He spake in a certain place". We know, and the writer knew, that this certain place was Gen 2:2. We have remarked before on the reason for this indefiniteness in quoting OT Scriptures. It is neither doubt nor ignorance nor uncertainty, but a simple acknowledgement of the inspiration of every part of Holy Scripture. What matters if it is David, or Moses, Pentateuch or Prophets or Psalms. It is all God's good word and God's mind. God rested on that seventh day. The earliest Scriptures thus show that God desired rest.

5 God delights to call it "my rest", but this verse indicates also that He would have men share that rest with Him. Man did not, however, and could not, enjoy that early Eden rest. It was marred by sin. God cannot rest in sin, and sinners cannot rest with God. The message of this verse is that God would enjoy rest and would rejoice to share that rest with men, but the principle is abiding and unchanging that unbelief cannot enter God's rest. The phrase, already quoted, "They shall not enter into my rest", is quoted in this instance to emphasise the pronoun "my". It is God's rest.

6-8 The proposition therefore remains that God has a rest in view in which He would have men to share. That promise of this rest has already been offered to men who refused it. They were disobedient and failed to enter. This is a renewed reference to Num 14, and to the generation that came out of Egypt. They first heard the gospel, the glad tidings of God's rest. But they would not hearken, and they did not enter in. Some must enter; this is God's purpose; but these did not.

So, after so long a time, Jehovah fixes another day, and calls again. If those whom He first called refused, He will call others. In the Ps 95 of a much later day, He appeals again, as He had appealed before, "Today if ye will hear his voice harden not your hearts".

Now this only proves that if David, long after Joshua, speaks about another day, then Joshua did not really lead them into God's rest. (For "Jesus" of the AV here, read "Joshua", as in the RV and others. "Jesus" (*Iēsous*) is a Greek transliteration of the Hebrew "Joshua".)

Whatever Israel enjoyed under Joshua, it was not the realisation of the rest as God had intended it, else David would not have been offering it again in his day. As it had been in Eden, so it was in Canaan, God would rest, and would have men enjoy that rest with Him, but sin and unbelief and the wicked character of the human heart have delayed the fulfilment of the divine purpose.

9 There remaineth therefore, a rest for the people of God. A different word is now introduced for "rest". It is an unusual word. Indeed it is unique. F.F.Bruce says that "this is the earliest attested occurrence of the word in extant Greek literature". It is a Greek suffix added to a Hebrew word to make *sabbatismos*, literally "a sabbath-keeping". It is so very reminiscent of the lovely Hebrew seventh-day greeting, *Shabbat Shalom*! It is peace and rest, tranquility and repose. Such was God's intention and purpose from the beginning. A finished work! God at rest! and man sharing. But it had not been so. Neither in Eden nor in Canaan was it realised. Nor indeed in David's day, after so long a time. And still is the word being borne to men in the gospel, that one day God will rest, and those who believe shall rest with Him. Then shall we have truly entered our *sabbatismos*. We shall hear Him say to us, *Shabbat Shalom*! Such remains for the people of God. For this we hope, and for this, in patience, we wait. Creation groans for it, as we do (Rom 8:22-24), and in a glorious future day it will be fully known, for His pleasure and for His glory.

10 The writer now states a principle which is well and often stated in the NT epistles. A man who enters into rest is a man who has ceased from his labours. Now this is the principle that we emphasise in gospel preaching. "Not of works" (Eph 2:8). "To him that worketh not, but believeth" (Rom 4:5). This, however true, is not quite the emphasis of this verse. It is a simple assertion that rest will be enjoyed when work is done, as in Gen 2:2. But as sin has marred that rest so now God works (John 5:17), and will work, until that coming day when He will rest to enjoy the fruits of all His labours and His love. Then will He rest in His love (Zeph 3:17). Until that day the work of Father and Son continues, and in this we are privileged to share. As another has said, "When they rest, so shall we". We shall rest in perfect holiness and happiness. All the toils and trials of the path of faith will be ended. The wilderness and the warfare, the waiting and the watching, will be past forever. It will be a blessed rest.

2. The Knife; the Priest; the Throne
   4:11-16

v.11 "Let us labour therefore to enter into that rest, lest any man fall after the same example of unbelief.

v.12 For the word of God *is* quick, and powerful, and sharper than any twoedged sword, piercing even to the dividing asunder of soul and spirit, and of the joints and marrow, and *is* a discerner of the thoughts and intents of the heart.

v.13 Neither is there any creature that is not manifest in his sight: but all things *are* naked and opened unto the eyes of him with whom we have to do.

v.14 Seeing then that we have a great high priest, that is passed into the heavens, Jesus the Son of God, let us hold fast *our* profession.

v.15 For we have not an high priest which cannot be touched with the feeling of our infirmities; but was in all points tempted like as *we are, yet* without sin.

v.16 Let us therefore come boldly unto the throne of grace, that we may obtain mercy, and find grace to help in time of need."

11   Let us therefore be diligent, with that rest in view. We must not look for too much ease down here, nor contemplate a settling down. We do not rest yet. The "let us labour" of the AV is inappropriate. This is rather a call to diligence. Nevertheless we are conscious that in such diligence we must earnestly serve Him until we enter into rest with Him. And in all earnestness too, we keep remembering the sad example of that unbelieving generation that fell in the wilderness so long ago. Christendom, as we call it, all that which takes upon itself the name of christian, must have many in its ranks whose profession is profession only. The call to diligence is so very relevant to all who profess His Name. For a final time in this chapter we are reminded of that large company that left Egypt. (And how large is Christendom!) What disobedience and unbelief was harboured in that company, and it remains as a solemn warning to all who profess to be travelling to the better land.

   The burden of these first eleven verses of Heb 4 is well summarised by J.N.Darby. It is, he says, "... 1st, That Israel had failed of entering into rest through unbelief; 2nd, That the rest was yet to come, and that believers (those who were not seeking rest here, but who accepted the wilderness for the time being) should enter into it".

12   The writer having spoken much of obedience and disobedience, and of hearkening and refusing to hearken, there is now an easy transition to some particulars regarding the word of God. It is this Word that will enable us to judge our hearts and properly assess our state before God. The true believer will welcome it. The false professor will fear it. Being God's word, it is of necessity like God, and it judges all that is not according to God. Five things are said about this Word. It is living; it is powerful; it is sharp; it is penetrating; it is discerning.

1.   *It is living.* It is essentially, intrinsically, possessed of life, even as He is, whose Word it is. "The words that I speak unto you, they are spirit, and they are life" (John 6:63). It is alive and will ruthlessly judge that which is dead.

2.   *It is powerful (energēs).* It is energetic, active, efficient, effectual. There is nothing and no one beyond the reach of its energy. It will expose the weakness of the unbelieving heart as it is applied in power.

3.   *It is sharp.* It is sharper than any two-edged sword. Its double-edged ministry both commends and condemns, rebukes and restores, approves and disapproves. Our Lord uses it in His approach to the assembly at Pergamos (Rev 2:12), that assembly being much mixed up with things which He hated, and from which they needed to be severed.

4.   *It is piercing.* It penetrates where we can not. It searches into the deepest recesses of a man's being, distinguishing in matters which, with us, are intimately linked together. The Word will separate for us that which is "soulish" from that which is "spiritual". It will divide for us the external "joints" from the internal "marrow". It will assist us in determining what is emotional and what is truly spiritual. It will judge that which is but formal.

5.   *It is discerning.* With infallible accuracy, it can make a difference between thoughts and intents. It has an ability to judge every movement and feeling of the heart. It can judge our thoughts before they become words, and our intentions before they become actions.

It may be painful and humbling to submit ourselves to this sacrificial knife, but it is the way to blessing, and as another has said, "Such is the true help, the mighty instrument of God to judge everything in us that would hinder us from pursuing our course through the wilderness with joy, and with a buoyant heart strengthened by faith and confidence in Him. Precious instrument of a faithful God, solemn and serious in its operation, but of priceless and infinite blessing in its effects".

13   And from this living word of the living God there is nothing and no one hidden. There is not a created thing that is not apparent to the God of that word. Everything appears as it is. All is manifested. All things are naked and opened, laid bare to His gaze, exposed before Him. To Him with whom our account is, everything is known. Hypocrisy is foolish. Veneer is to no avail. This is the *bēma*, the Judgment Seat, before the time.

14   Being so laid bare in all our weakness, and so being made conscious of our potential for unbelief and disobedience, we do need help. "Having then a great high priest ... let us hold fast". Jesus, the Son of God, the captain of our salvation, has gone on before and has passed through the heavens for us. He alone, of all the high priests that Hebrews ever knew, is called a "great" high priest. The theme was but briefly intimated in 2:17. From this point it will be developed through several chapters as a main theme of the epistle. We are in the wilderness, with all its trials. So were they to whom Aaron as high priest was first given. Just as Aaron passed through the outer court of the tabernacle, and through the holy place and into the holiest, for them, so has Jesus passed through the heavens for us. He has gone from this world, through the aerial heavens and through the starry heavens, and into heaven itself (9:24).

15   Now "we have not an high priest which cannot be touched with the feeling of our infirmities". The double negative is an interesting, emphatic way of stating the positive. The truth is that we do have a high priest who can, and does, sympathise with us in our infirmities. He can sympathise, for He too once lived down here and was tested and tried as we are. It is important to note, however, that He who was tempted as we are was never tempted to sin. "Yet without sin", as in the AV, is most misleading, and has been responsible for deeply derogatory thoughts and statements touching the person of Christ. So many have read the AV rendering only, and have interpreted it as meaning that our Lord was tempted but did not sin. This is not only far from the meaning, but it is essentially and fundamentally erroneous. He was in all points tempted like as we are, apart from sin. Or, He was in all points, apart from sin, tempted like as we are. There was nothing in Him to respond to sin or to be enticed by it. Sinful temptings could not reach Him. He was not vulnerable. He was impeccable. It was impossible that He could sin. How then, and in what way, has He been tried as we are? In all points apart from sin. He knew pain and poverty; He suffered weariness and loneliness, and hunger and thirst. He was misunderstood and misrepresented. He was mocked and molested. He was a Man of sorrows. He shed tears and He shed blood. But He could not sin, nor could He so be tempted. In all the trials and troubles of the path of faith He has been before us.

> In every pang that rends the heart
>   The Man of sorrows bears a part.

He is therefore well able to sympathise with us in our trials. That this has nothing to do with sin may be clearly seen in the word "sympathise" (*sumpatheō*). This is the word which the AV translators have rendered "to be touched with". It means, "to suffer with" or "to be affected similarly" or "to have compassion upon". Now I do not need such sympathy or compassion when I sin. I need the Word which will judge both it and me, ruthlessly and unsparingly. This is not sympathy in my sin, it is sympathy in my infirmities. And so I have the Word to judge me and a great high priest to sustain and succour me. And I have more!

16 There is a throne of grace. To this we are invited to come with boldness. There is a throne of glory. There will be, one day, a throne of government and a throne of judgment. But for us now there is a throne of grace. We may approach with boldness. We do not come cringeing, or in fear and dread. There is mercy and grace. There is timely, seasonable help for us, and we come by divine invitation.

V. The Great High Priest (5:1-14)

1. After the Pattern of Aaron
5:1-5

v.1 "For every high priest taken from among men is ordained for men in things *pertaining* to God, that he may offer both gifts and sacrifices for sins:

v.2 Who can have compassion on the ignorant, and on them that are out of the way; for that he himself also is compassed with infirmity.

v.3 And by reason hereof he ought, as for the people, so also for himself, to offer for sins.

v.4 And no man taketh this honour unto himself, but he that is called of God, as *was* Aaron.

v.5 So also Christ glorified not himself to be made an high priest; but he that said unto him, Thou art my Son, to day have I begotten thee."

Having returned, in ch.4, to the subject of Christ's priesthood, from the earlier fleeting reference to it in 1:17, the writer now enters upon the grand theme in some detail. Here begins the great doctrinal development of that priesthood, and this, with kindred truths, will be pursued until the middle of chapter 10. So much of this priestly ministry of Christ was foreshadowed in Aaron that, looking back to Aaron, we can find great principles there, albeit we must find much contrast as well as comparison. Christ is greater than Aaron, just as He is greater than Moses and greater than Joshua. Jehovah gave these three men to the nation for a threefold purpose, each man with his distinctive and particular ministry. Moses led them out. Aaron led them on. Joshua led them in. We have seen the superiority of Christ over Moses and over Joshua. We must now see that He fulfils a priestly ministry which, for Israel, began with Aaron. Christ's ministry is after that Aaronic pattern, but, as we shall later find, it is not after that order.

1   The first great principle is that every high priest was taken from among the ranks of men. He must, of necessity, be able to understand men, and at times sympathise with them in their weaknesses. This necessitates that he himself must be a man. We have earlier seen that neither Michael nor Gabriel, with all their angelic greatness, could so enter into the feelings and frailties of mortal men. It has often been remarked upon also, that not Moses, but Aaron, was the man chosen for the priestly office. Perhaps Aaron was the one who, the more definitely, was taken from among their very ranks. While they made bricks in Egypt, and languished under the lash of their taskmasters, Moses had enjoyed much of the luxury and comfort of the palace and the court. But Aaron had been with his fellow Israelites. Would there not have been, with Aaron, an experimental knowledge of the sufferings they had endured? Was he not the more conversant with the conditions under which they had lived and suffered for all those years? Moses, of course, later chose to suffer with them, but Aaron had always been with them, and out from among these fellow-men he was raised up to be their priest and high priest. So has our Lord become our true kinsman: "The Word was made flesh and dwelt among us" (John 1:14). "He also himself likewise took part" in our blood and flesh (2:14). Our great high priest is truly man. By the assumed weakness of babyhood and boyhood He came into our society and grew into manhood. He knows, by experience, what difficulties there are down here. If He has now gone up, a Man in the glory, He was once down here, a Man of sorrows. He has indeed been "taken from among men".

It must be remarked here, that some excellent commentators (e.g. W. Kelly; F.W. Grant) will object to any relating of this expression "taken from among men" to Christ. They argue that it has reference only to the high priests of the Aaronic order and that the reason for the expression is to emphasise the human weakness and limitations of those priests. They see it only as a means of contrasting those priests who were but men and only men, taken from among men, with our great high priest who is the Son of God. Most others, however, will agree that while the phrase primarily looks to the Aaronic priests it also indicates a basic principle in priesthood, that, to suitably represent men, the priest must himself be a man. While most strenuously contending for the deity and personal glory of the Lord Jesus, and while jealously guarding the uniqueness of His manhood, nevertheless it seems an unavoidable implication here that there must be manhood if there is to be priesthood.

Being taken from among men the high priest was ordained, or appointed, for men. This appointment is in things pertaining to God. It is in relation to matters for which men are responsible to God. It is the same expression as commented upon in 2:17. For these men whom he represented, the high priest was able to offer both gifts and sacrifices for sins. "Gifts" and "sacrifices for sins" are not just two ways of expressing the same thing, as some will argue. It may be helpful to see that those who bring "gifts" are in truth giving. On the other hand, those who bring "sacrifices for sins" are really receiving, in the sense that what they bring is with a view to their forgiveness and an atonement, and their own blessing. "Gifts" (dōron) means "gifts presented as an expression of honour". The principle of first mention takes us to Matt

2:11. This is very beautiful. The first mention of the word is associated, in the same verse, with one of the earliest references to worship. "They opened their treasures"! The adoring heart will ever want to give to God. This is our privilege. The gifts mentioned here, in our chapter, were undoubtedly those oblations which are sometimes called the eucharistic or thanksgiving offerings. "Sacrifices for sins" needs little comment, except to remark that, since it is high priestly ministry that is in view, perhaps the day of atonement is particularly in mind. This will be developed later in the epistle.

Briefly then, is the chief design and purpose of high priestly ministry summed up in this verse. There were other ministries too, however, for which, ideally, certain qualities and characteristics were necessary in the priest.

2   A priest dealing with failing men was required to be a man of some compassion. But with his compassion he must be discerning and discriminating. He needed firmness with tenderness. He must have wisdom and knowledge and understanding in equal measure. Men were, and are, weak and frail, and often like sheep they get out of the way. Every high priest must have compassion. The word here rendered "compassion" has been variously rendered by others. It is not the usual word for compassion, but is a rather beautiful word, *metriopatheō*, which has been created by compounding two words: *metrios* meaning "moderation", and *paschō* meaning "to suffer". *Metriopatheō* means "to treat with mildness or moderation". The various translations taken together are helpful in bringing out the full import of the word: "who can bear gently with" (RV); "able to exercise forbearance towards" (JND); "reasonably bear with" (AV margin). Now men were ever ignorant and erring and in every high priest there had to be that ability to deal firmly with the sin and yet tenderly with the sinner. Such a balance was necessary, but difficult. There must be no compromising with sin. There must be no lessening of judgment of what was wrong. But there must be also a gentle remembrance of the frailty of those who were erring, and a pity for their persons, if not for their sins. Sins committed in ignorance (*agnoēma*) were sins nonetheless; (see the same word in 9:7, translated "errors"). The man who is, in this verse, "out of the way", is a wanderer (*planōmenos*). With such unwitting sinners, so wandering into errors, there must be a certain priestly gentleness which did in no way disregard the sin but yet dealt moderately with the offender. The Pharisees of later years than Aaron were renowned for their hardness, and for their often uncaring and unpitying attitude to others. We recall the attitude of the Pharisees towards the publican of Luke 18 and the women of Luke 7 and of John 8. The true priest must not be such a callous onlooker at the sins of others.

Indeed, the writer now observes, those earlier high priests, being themselves but men, should "naturally" have shown forbearance to the ignorant and erring, since the same tendencies to sin were in them too. How freely Aaron himself ought to have admitted a proneness to err and a potential for sin. Even the high priest was compassed with infirmity. "Compassed" is *perikeimai*, "bound, tied, fettered", and this with infirmity (*astheneia*, "weakness"). Remembering his own weaknesses every high priest of Aaron's order should have been gentle with others.

How delightfully are the comparisons and contrasts fulfilled in the Lord Jesus. He who was God's Son lived as a Man among men. He knows what men are. But He was not possessed of our old nature, nor was He bound with our moral weakness. Yet He sympathises and is gentle as none other. He will expose to us our sinning, and He will require confession of it, but in great tenderness He will assist us back towards the Father and into restored communion. Such is the true meaning of 1 John 2:1 and such is the ministry of Christ the Comforter, the *Paraklētos*, our helper and succourer, our great high priest, sinless but sympathising.

> O hope of every contrite heart,
>   O joy of all the meek,
> To those who fall how kind Thou art;
>   How good to those who seek.

3   High priestly ministry involved also offering for sins. This undoubtedly has specific reference to the Day of Atonement (Lev 16) when the high priest was so personally and particularly and prominently active in all the detailed ceremony of that great annual event. The exercises of that Day of Atonement began with the killing of a bullock, the offering of a sin offering in atonement for Aaron himself. Even the Jewish high priest was a sinner. He was personally compassed with moral infirmity, as was his house. He was bound with sinful weakness, and for this reason it was necessary, even though he was the high priest, that he offer first for himself. A high priest who was about to function for others must himself have acceptance before God, and by reason of his sinful nature Aaron, as also his sons and successors, had to atone for their own sins before offering for the people. One who will function in a representative high priestly capacity, himself must stand in purity before God. This was always applicable to Aaron and to the priests of his order. Not only on the great Day of Atonement, but at all other times and on all other occasions they must stand purified if they will suitably represent the people. So had Jehovah ordained a particular sin offering for the sinning priest (Lev 4:3-12). It was incumbent upon the priest that he stand in purity in his holy ministry.

Now Jesus in His spotlessness stands in contrast to all this. He who, at Golgotha, was to offer Himself for sins once for all (7:27; 9:25-28; 10:11-12), required no sin offering for Himself. He was holy, guileless, and undefiled (7:26). His was an impeccable, incomparable, and incorruptible humanity which needed no offering and no atonement. It is important to state again and again that some of the typical foreshadowings of Christ are interpreted by comparison, but, of necessity, some must be interpreted by contrast. Such is the case with Aaron. There are many beautiful ways in which he is a picture of Him who was to come, but in respect of his personal human failings and need for atonement, we must mark most definitely the contrast with Him whom the demons called "the Holy One of God" (Mark 1:24).

Now Jesus did, for the people, if not for Himself, offer for sins. The magnitude and the value of this offering of Himself will be the subject of later passages. The preciousness of the blood that He shed and the eternal efficacy of His death on the cross will be the theme of the very heart of this epistle. The point being made just now is, that Christ must be excluded, in His holiness, from that observation, that the high priest who offered for the sins of the people, must also offer for himself. This applied to Aaron, and to Eleazar, and to some fourscore high priests who followed over the centuries, but not to Christ.

4   A further qualification for this high priestly position is now advanced. We have already seen that the high priest must be capable of sympathy for weak and failing men. To be so capable it was necessary that he should be a man himself. But not any man could properly fill this high office. To such a ministry a man must be called of God. It was a divinely-given privilege, that a man should occupy this holy place in the ordering of God's house and God's people.

The writer here is speaking, of course, of the ideal and of the divine purpose, for it was on clear record that not all those who had functioned as Israel's high priests had been called of God. Some of them had taken this honour to themselves, and some had received it by the arrogant decree of heathen despots and governors. To quote, partially, the interesting comments of F.F.Bruce on this, "In 174 B.C., Jason and later Menelaus were appointed to the high priesthood by Antiochos IV; Alcimus was appointed by Demetrius I in 162 B.C.; the Hasmonaean Jonathan was appointed by Alexander Balas, putative son of Antiochos IV, in 152 B.C.; his brother Simon and his successors were appointed by decree of the Jewish people in 140 B.C. With the fall of the Hasmonaean house the high priests were appointed successively by Herod the Great (37-4 B.C.), Archelaus (4 B.C.-A.D.6), Roman Governors (A.D.6-41), and members of the Herod family (A.D.41-66). The last high priest, Phanni, son of Samuel, was appointed by popular ballot during the war against Rome (c.A.D.67)".

This is all a sad reflection on the barren state of the nation at these times, that to such a high and holy office in Israel priests should be appointed at the whim of pagan rulers. It was into this "dry ground" (Isa 53:2) that He was to come who would be the great high priest, of whom the others were but faint shadows.

But Israel's first high priest was truly called of God. Aaron was the divine choice, and for Aaron this was honour indeed. Called of God to represent a redeemed people, he wore the garments which had been prepared for glory and for beauty. With blue and purple and scarlet on fine linen, and with a golden thread inter-twining, and a golden crown upon his mitre, he was invested with a dignity as he went in on behalf of the people, interceding, sacrificing, bearing on his shoulders and his heart the names of all of them, responsible for their guidance and spiritual well-being along the wilderness way. It was a high honour but a heavy responsibility, and in all of this he was a foregleam of a greater to come.

In a solemn but glorious ceremony of consecration Aaron and his sons were dedicated to the priesthood in Lev 8. With the fragrance of the holy anointing oil and with the blood of the peculiar offering of that day of consecrations, they were anointed. Having earlier been washed, now robed and anointed, the holy priesthood then set themselves apart for God and the ministry, on holy ground feasting upon the ram of consecration and unleavened bread from the basket of consecrations, while God's portion was being consumed upon the great altar.

A sanctified priesthood then had been inaugurated, "called of God", with Aaron in the most elevated position in the nation. His gorgeous priestly apparel, unknown to him, held prophecies of the glories of the Christ who would come centuries later, and who would fulfil perfectly all that was being foreshadowed in this early imperfect Levitical order.

Aaron's call therefore, was a divine call. His appointment was by the will of God. Some of the very people whom Aaron represented were later to criticise and challenge his appointment (Num 16). The consequences were disastrous. Two hundred and fifty men who sought to intrude into the holy ministry without a call were destroyed in a fearful divine intervention, and fourteen thousand of Israel who sympathised were likewise cut off in a solemn judgment at that same time. Jehovah then confirmed Aaron's divine appointment in a miraculous budding and blossoming and fruit-bearing of Aaron's staff, of which mention is made in this epistle (9:4). Still later in the nation's history, king Uzziah also intruded into the priestly domain without authority. He attempted to burn incense, which was the peculiar ministry of the priesthood. There was again an immediate divine judgment. Uzziah was smitten with a leprosy which plagued him until the day of his death (2 Chron 26:16-21). In all of this it would seem that Jehovah would emphasise this which has just been stated by our writer, "No man taketh this honour unto himself, but he that is called of God". Some indeed have tried, but no man can function legitimately in this holy sphere with divine approval, but he who has the divine call, as had Aaron.

5   Now all this is but leading us to consider the divine approval of the Christ in His high priestly ministry. "So", or "Thus", has it been with Him who has been introduced as our great high priest. He is not without heavenly authority in His ministry. In entering such ministry, he has not sought glory for Himself. There is no presumption with Him. There is no intrusion into a forbidden sphere or into functions which belong to another. But if He has not glorified Himself, there is glory nevertheless. He has been glorified in it. He wears the glory of a high priesthood, in the functioning of which there will be displayed something of His own personal glory. God has invested Him with this priestly honour. He has the acknowledgement and approval of heaven, as Aaron had, and as we contemplate the perfection and grace of a priesthood which is after the pattern of Aaron, we are soon to learn that this is a priesthood superior to Aaron's order, and a priest greater than Aaron.

Who then, has glorified the Christ in His appointment to this honour? None other than He who said, "Thou art my Son, today have I begotten thee". What then has this reference to sonship to do with priesthood? Just this, that our Lord's priesthood is as surely and as certainly acknowledged by Jehovah as is His sonship. He who said "Thou art my Son", is the same who says "Thou art a priest". The divine recognition of our Lord's priesthood is as definite and as authoritative as the divine recognition of His sonship. The one is as great as the other. The God who acknowledges Messiah as His Son in Ps 2, and proclaims Him so, is the same God who acknowledges Him as high priest in Ps 110, and likewise proclaims Him so.

Our Lord's rights then, to such priesthood, are undisputed and undoubted. They are unchallengeable, except it be on this ground, that He was not of the tribe of Levi, but of the tribe of Judah. This objection the writer will deal with briefly and incidentally in the next verse, and will expound in more detail in ch.7.

There is however, a tender and interesting connection between "Thou art my Son", and "Thou art a priest". We have seen, in 1:5, in consideration of the quotation from Ps 2:7, that this declaration of our Lord's sonship is always linked with His incarnation. He who is the Son from eternity has come into humanity, into manhood, and as He makes His advent into that humanity Jehovah says, "Thou art my Son". He is not being made Son. He is not becoming Son. He is not being constituted Son by coming into flesh and blood. This is not the beginning of His sonship. He has ever, eternally, been the Son. But He had now been begotten, uniquely and miraculously, into a holy manhood which is so essentially linked with His gracious ability to be our great high priest. And in that manhood He is acknowledged as the Son. Son of Mary He might indeed be, and He is, but He is saluted as Son of God in that day of incarnation. The Son of God has become Man and that blessed Man is suited completely to be a high priest for us. This is very precious, that He who said, "Thou art my Son", is the same who says, "Thou art a priest".

2. *After the Order of Melchisedec*
   ## 5:6-10

v.6   "As he saith also in another *place,* Thou *art* a priest for ever after the order of Melchisedec.

v.7   Who in the days of his flesh, when he had offered up prayers and supplications with strong crying and tears unto him that was able to save him from death, and was heard in that he feared;

v.8   Though he were a Son, yet learned he obedience by the things which he suffered;

v.9   And being made perfect, he became the author of eternal salvation unto all them that obey him;

v.10   Called of God an high priest after the order of Melchisedec."

6   The characteristic vagueness with which the writer has made reference to OT Scriptures is now repeated (see particularly 2:6; 3:7; 4:4). Now he writes, "also in another place". It is not that he does not know from where these quotations are culled. It is neither from ignorance nor from carelessness that he has not yet identified any of the sources of his many quotations. There is a two-fold reason. Firstly, he graciously assumes that his Hebrew readers will know. He gives them credit, as Hebrews, and now as believers in the Lord Jesus as Messiah, for a certain knowledge of God's word. He presumes a certain knowledge of that Word on their part. Secondly, he is acknowledging the divine inspiration of all of Holy Scripture. Neither the specific place nor the particular writer is of great importance. They are incidental. All the Word is God's word, therefore it is sufficient to quote any portion of it from anywhere in its pages. This he does again and again with scant regard for the human penman of any portion that he cites. There is of course no disrespect intended for the inspired writers, but simply a holy recognition of the one mind of deity behind all the sacred writings. Anything from anywhere, in the Holy Scriptures, may be cited confidently to extol Christ, and this the writer freely and frequently does throughout his epistle.

Now this "other place" of which he speaks, is in the Ps 110. It is here, for just the second time in the OT, that we read of Melchisedec. This man was a priest before Aaron was. He was also a king. He wears both the mitre and the crown. He is a foreshadowing of the Christ of whom Zechariah wrote "He shall be a priest upon his throne" (Zech 6:13). Ps 110 is quoted in the NT more often than any other Psalm, and indeed more often than any other OT passage. It is appealed to some fourteen times in the NT, both by our Lord and by the apostolic writers. We have remarked before that it is quoted in the Gospels, in the Acts, and in the Epistles, and the spirit of it is in the Book of the Revelation. The Psalm is wholly and purely and exclusively Messianic. There is no other primary association or reason for its being written. It is all prophetic of Christ. The writer to the Hebrews has already quoted from it in 1:13, and will do so again. We are first introduced to Melchisidec in Gen 14. He does not appear again in the OT until Ps 110. These are the only references to him in the OT, and in the NT he is mentioned only in this epistle. Now this is all very beautiful. Genesis is the first and greatest book of history in our Bible. The Psalms constitute the greatest book of poetry. Hebrews is one of the greatest books of pure doctrine. It seems as though neither history, nor poetry, nor doctrine, is complete without Melchisedec. Christ, of whom he speaks, is the centre of all history. He is the sweetness of all true poetry. He is the subject and substance of all true doctrine. Such is the greatness of the One who represents us in the heavens.

It is, however, the order of Melchisedec's priesthood which is here of present interest to us. This order of priesthood is antecedent, and superior, to the Levitical order. It both precedes and succeeds it. It comes before and it remains after. Aaron has provided us with a pattern, and all that Aaron ever was or ever did has been perfectly fulfilled in Jesus. But the Aaronic order was flawed by the weakness and mortality of men. Those priests of Aaron's order were not able to continue endlessly. They had to die. Of Melchisedec we never read that he died. In the records there is no account of his decease or burial. He is therefore a suitable picture of Christ in a ministry which will never be interrupted or terminated by death. Christ lives in the power of an endless life. He is a priest for ever after the order of Melchisedec. This will all be developed in more detail later in the epistle. It is now introduced because a dual type of Christ is necessary to picture properly His priestly ministry and person.

Both Aaron and Melchisedec are needed to bring to us the fulness of the teaching on priesthood which has begun in this chapter.

7 There now follows an interesting blending of the pattern of Aaron with the "order of Melchisedec". Having been assured of the glory and majesty of One who is both Son and priest, and, by implication, king also, we are now taken back in memory to "the days of his flesh". If the Man who represents us is now in the heavens, it was not always so. If we now delight to call Him "the Man in the glory", again, it was not always so. He was once a Man of sorrows. How tender are the memories of "the days of his flesh", between the manger and the cross. The Word became flesh and tabernacled among us. Luke uses several words to describe the holy development of that lovely life which began at Bethlehem and was offered up at Golgotha.

1. The "babe" wrapped in swaddling clothes (Luke 2:12, 16) is *brephos*, a word so tender as to be used of an unborn foetus.

2. The "child" of Luke 2:21 is *paidion*, a little child, recently born, and in this case but eight days old. This is the word used also some weeks later (Luke 2:27). The *paidion* in Simeon's arms is forty days old (see Lev 12:1-4).

3. The "child" of Luke 2:43, however, is a different word. He is a boy (*pais*) now, of twelve years.

4. But He is Mary's *teknon* in Luke 2:48, the One whom she has borne, her "bairn".

Twenty-one years later Pilate calls *Ecce Homo!* Behold the Man! "The days of his flesh" were unique and wondrous; impeccably holy; thirty-three years of fragrant spotless perfection mingled with the myrrh of suffering.

It was in those days of His flesh that He offered up prayers and supplications (*deēsis*, supplications; *hiketēria*, "entreaties"). These are the holy exercises of a dependent man and our Lord was ever this during those days of His flesh: "I was cast upon thee from the womb" was prophetically true of Him (Ps 22:10). "Thou didst make me trust upon my mother's breasts" (Ps 22:9 JND). There can be no doubt that this dependence characterised Him always. It would be wrong to limit these "prayers and supplications" to any confined period within "the days of his flesh". How often did our Lord withdraw Himself to the solitary place to be engaged in holy converse with His Father. It was His wont, His custom, to retire often to the Mount of Olives to pray (Luke 22:39). However, the words which follow here probably indicate that it is to Gethsemane in particular that we are now being drawn. Dependence means submission. Submission may mean suffering. It was so for Him, and we are brought to the "strong crying and tears" of the garden to witness the anguish of One who has come so very near to us in our sorrows and can therefore suitably exercise a high priestly ministry for us. He who had dried the tears of so many, Himself wept. He who had raised others from the dead would Himself go into death, voluntarily and obediently.

The adjective "strong" is a powerful one, *ischuros*, strong; powerful; mighty; boiterous: describing the might of angels (Rev 5:2), the power of the wind in a storm (Matt 14:30), and even the strength of the Lord (Rev 18:8). Such was the character of His crying and tears in Gethsemane.

"Crying" and "tears" are different words. "Crying" (*kraugē*) implies sound or noise. It is a crying aloud. It is a wailing which may be heard. "Tears" (*dakruon*) is a silent weeping. It is the quiet trickling of tears down the cheek. Tears were shed, flowing silently; sorrow was seen but not heard. So did the Saviour weep in the garden. Oh the mystery of Gethsemane!

> Garden of tears that never
> > Mortal could ever weep!
> Not of the common river:
> > Drawn from a deeper deep!
> Drawn from a depth unsounded,
> > Coursing toward the sod,
> Telling of love unbounded,
> > Sourced in the heart of God!

In such anguish of soul, exceeding sorrowful, our blessed Lord anticipated death and cried to Him who was able to save Him out of it. Death was foreign to His deathless nature. Death was essentially associated with sin, and with sin He had had nothing to do. In His piety there was an understandable shrinking from it all.

Now it is most important to see that our Lord does not pray to be saved from dying. He cries in holy dependence to Him who was able to save Him "out of" death. It is "out of", not "from". The preposition is undoubtedly *ek*. Yet there is a strange and sad interpretation sometimes advanced that the Gethsemane prayers were a plea of our Lord to be saved from premature death in the garden, where Satan was about to make an attempt upon His life. We must reject such a suggestion. We ought to resist any idea of His dying before the appointed hour at Golgotha. We ought to reject the possibility of His premature death as firmly as we reject the possibility of His sinning. One is as unthinkable as the other. In the context, the preposition *ek* ought to settle the matter for us. He was delivered out of death. God raised Him. Resurrection was the answer to His strong crying and tears and the divine recognition of His piety.

"He was heard". How like Ps 22 is all this. That Psalm, we are often reminded, is in two parts. There is a sob and a song. The sob of the holy Sufferer is described in the first twenty one verses. But in the heart of that v.21 the song begins with these words "Thou hast heard me"! His God "who was able", was the God of Shadrach, Meshach, and Abed-nego (Dan 3:17). He may choose, in His sovereign ways, not to deliver them from going into the furnace, but He saved them out of it nevertheless. He was the God of whom Paul would write, "He is able" (2 Tim 1:12). He may not deliver Paul from the anguish of suffering and eventual martyrdom, but He would deliver Him out of it, keeping safe all that ministry which Paul had committed to Him.

He was heard "in that he feared". The word here translated "feared" is found, in this exact form, only twice in the NT. Both of these are in this epistle (see 12:28). The word *eulabeia* signifies reverence, godly fear, holy fear, piety. It is so fittingly commented upon by Trench, in his *Synonyms of the New Testament*. He says, "That mingled fear and love which, combined, constitute the piety of the man of God; the OT places its emphasis on the fear, the NT on the love, though there was love in the fear of God's saints then, as there must be fear in their love now". In this Heb 5:7 that piety is seen in Christ. In ch.12:28 it is to be seen in the saints. The prayers of such as are characterised by this sincerity and reverence are surely heard of God (James 5:16). And such indeed characterised Him who was the perfect Man, walking ever and always in the dignity and holiness and reverential love and piety which should be the mark of all those who profess to be dependent upon God as He was in the days of His flesh.

8   "Though he were a Son" is a reference to that which has just been stated in v.5, a citation from Ps 2. We are reminded that all that He suffered, He suffered even though the glory of a unique sonship was His. Our Lord has added a new dimension both to service and to sonship. It is not without significance that in that Gospel of the perfect Servant (Mark's Gospel), the first title given to the Lord Jesus is " Son of God" (Mark 1:1). Now in the Jewish household sons were not servants and servants were not sons. As has before been remarked, even the prodigal knew this (Luke 15:19). But He who served as no other servant ever served was God's Son. He may be Son over the house of God (3:5), but He serves that house as none other. Notice the absence of the article here in the Greek text. It is not "a Son", nor "the Son", but simply "though he were Son". The emphasis is on the sonship. It has sometimes been translated, "Son though He was", and this is perhaps the proper emphasis: "Son though He was, yet learned He obedience".

In suffering the things which He did suffer, He learned obedience. Obedience was new to Him. Before His incarnation, in glory, He directed, He decreed, He commanded, and others obeyed. In the days of His flesh it was different. He was a perfect Man and a perfect Servant. Voluntarily He became so, even though He was the Son. Now perfect manhood and perfect service require perfect submissiveness and complete obedience in dependence. This He rendered, and experimentally He learned obedience. He never learned to be obedient. He never learned to obey. We must learn to obey as sons of God, because we were once sons of disobedience (Eph 2:2). The unique, sinless Son humbled Himself and "became obedient" (Phil 2:8). How rightly do we often say that He became what He had not been before but did not cease to be what He had always been. The Son has become Servant and Sufferer, not ceasing to be the Son.

"The things which he suffered" are a tender meditation. In the suffering of these things He experienced the cost of the implicit and full obedience which He rendered.

William Kelly has expressed it so beautifully, "If ever prayers and supplications, if ever strong crying and tears, were realities for the heart of God, His were. For His divine nature screened Him from no pain, grief, or humiliation, or suffering, but rather gave competency of person to endure perfectly, while all was accepted in absolute dependence on, and subjection to, His Father.... It was no small thing for His love to have hatred and contempt, to be despised and rejected of men; not only not to be honoured by the people of God, and His people, but to be esteemed stricken, smitten of God, and afflicted; to be deserted by all His disciples, denied by one, betrayed by another; and, far the most terrible of all and wholly different from all, to be forsaken of God just when He most needed His consolation and support". Such were the sufferings He endured, and more. He was a Man of sorrows indeed. He gave complete and absolute obedience because He was completely and absolutely dependent and devoted, and in sufferings of spirit, soul, and body, He learned the cost of such obedience. But it was early related of Him, "He shall not fail" (Isa 42:4), and He did not. He was obedient unto death. Such utter submissiveness involved death, in the plan of God, and to this He was willing to go. He did not obey death. That is not the meaning of "He became obedient unto death" (Phil 2:8). His obedience was rendered to His God, to His Father, and it extended as far as to death itself, and even to the shameful and cruel death of the cross. So did He who was Son learn the cost of obedience by suffering. Angels saw Him in the wilderness and in the garden. What a sight was this for holy angels. In the wilderness they became His deacons and ministered to Him (Mark 1:13). In the garden they strengthened Him (Luke 22:43). What encouragement was this for suffering Hebrew believers, whose obedience to the faith had been the cause of their sufferings. What comfort indeed to know that He, their Lord, had suffered for obedience too. And what consolation to know that heaven is witness to the sorrows of those who suffer for righteousness sake, and, at the appropriate moment, will minister the necessary help and strength.

9   In the path of suffering our Lord was perfected. This word "perfect" appears several times in Hebrews. We have already noted it in 2:10, and we shall find it several times more. In fact, we shall find a different form of it, an adjectival form, in the last verse (14) of this very chapter, though the AV rendering there conceals the fact that it is the same word essentially. The Greek word *teleioō* signifies a bringing to a desired end. It is accomplishment, completeness, perfection, fulfilment. It does not suggest any prior moral or personal imperfection in the Lord Jesus. It has to do with His being suitably and practically and perfectly qualified to be to His people what they need Him to be. Through sufferings our Lord has been perfected as a Saviour and Succourer of His people.

He has become, to all that obey Him, the Author of eternal salvation. This word "author" (*aitios*), is not the same as that which is translated "author" in 12:2. This, in 5:9, is the only occurrence of *atios* in the NT. There is, however, another form of the word in Luke 23:22, which perhaps throws light upon its true meaning. Pilate says, "I have found no *cause* of death in Him". This is *aitia*, the noun form of *aitios*.

Christ is the cause, literally the causer, of our salvation, the One who caused it to be. W.E.Vine says, "It is difficult to find an adequate English equivalent to express the meaning. Christ is not merely the formal cause of our salvation. He is the concrete and active cause of it. He has not merely caused or effected it, He is, as His name "Jesus" implies, our salvation itself". Did not Simeon, looking at the Child, say, "Mine eyes have seen thy salvation"?

Our salvation is eternal. There are so many eternal things mentioned in Hebrews. Was it intended as an encouragement to those who had abandoned the transient things of old Judaism? Did they look as though, having given up Judaism, they had nothing? Judaism would pass; it was temporal; it had already been superseded; it had been displaced and replaced. The outward semblances of it may have been at that time still in evidence but even the temple with all its glory was about to vanish. Their salvation was eternal. It would abide. It was like the eternal redemption (9:12), and the eternal inheritance (9:15), and the eternal covenant (13:20), and with the very character of the eternal Spirit Himself (9:14). They would still be in the enjoyment of all these things when the disobedient would be enduring eternal judgment (6:2). Eternal salvation cannot ever be lost. That pathetic doctrine that we may be "saved today and lost tomorrow" is incompatible with the truth of eternal salvation. Eternal salvation is eternal security. If we have become true possessors of a salvation which is eternal we cannot lose it. Otherwise it is not eternal!

This salvation is for them that obey Him. Here is an aspect of the gospel which we do well to keep in mind. The gospel is not all invitation and appeal and promise. It is that, but it is more. It is a command (Acts 17:30), and a demand (Acts 3:19). It demands obedience, and obedience is the evidence of true faith. Obedience is faith in action. Obedience presumes that there is a knowledge of God's word which faith believes. As another has said, "He obeys Christ, then, who, crediting God's testimony concerning His Son, submits to be saved by Him in the way of His appointing; and, trusting to Him as the only Author of eternal salvation, acknowledges Him as his Lord and Master, and pays a conscientious regard to all things whatsoever He has commanded him" (John Brown). And to quote another, "There is something appropriate in the fact that the salvation which was procured by the obedience of the Redeemer should be made available to the obedience of the redeemed" (F.F.Bruce). Note that there is salvation for "all" who thus obey. This little word "all" measures the wide scope of the glad tidings. There are no religious, racial, social, moral, cultural, political, intellectual or ethnological, or any other form of boundaries to the scope of the message. The only requirement is this, that we obey the gospel. The terrible alternative is envisaged by Peter in the form of a question, "What shall the end be of them that obey not?" (1 Pet 4:17).

10   Our present section concludes as it commenced, with another reference to "the order of Melchisedec". The One who is to be obeyed in the gospel has been viewed in these three verses as a suppliant, a Son, a sufferer, and a Saviour. He was a weeping intercessor; He was an obedient incarnate Son; He was a silent uncomplaining

sufferer; and through all this He is a merciful and faithful high priest. God salutes Him as such. "Called" is misleading. The word "called" here in v.10 is not the same as the word "called" in v.4. The word of v.4 is from the verb *kaleō* and signifies an appointment. The word of v.10 is completely different; *prosagoreuō* means "addressed by God", or "saluted of God". Christ is being saluted or named or acknowledged by God for what He already is, a high priest according to the order of Melchisedec. He is not here being called to office as those Aaronic priests were. Christ is not here being appointed to a priestly office. As we have observed, and as we shall have reason to observe again, He must be a priest at Calvary. In the historical records, of course, Melchisedec offers no sacrifice, but ministers bread and wine to the warrior pilgrim. It will be conceded that it is in resurrection that our Lord's priesthood assumes the character in which Melchisedec represents Him, but that in no way invalidates the truth that Golgotha was a priestly work. This, however, belongs to a later chapter.

Saluted He is then, a high priest after the order of Melchisedec. How touchingly appropriate is this, that between the two references to Melchisedec in vv.6, 10, we should have memories of the Lord relating to the days of His flesh. There are recollections of His prayers and His tears, His obedience and His suffering, His piety and His death. How did these Hebrew believers, as we, need such an high priest, who knew by experience all that was involved in being holy in this sinful environment. This was their encouragement and their comfort, that the One who now represented them in an abiding priestly ministry, was Himself experimentally conversant with conditions down here. He had lived here. If He was now in scenes of glory, in a royal priesthood, He had once lived in scenes of poverty and sorrow and tears. He was perfectly suited to be their great high priest. He knew exactly what they were suffering in the world that had cast Him out, and what rejection they were enduring from their own nation, the very nation that had rejected Him.

The priesthood of Christ then has brought to us all that substance of which Aaron's priesthood was but the shadow, and the priesthood of Christ is after a different order. It is after the order of Melchisedec. This will be developed later in the epistle, after another parenthesis.

3. *Spiritual Immaturity*
5:11-14

v.11 "Of whom we have many things to say, and hard to be uttered, seeing ye are dull of hearing.

v.12 For when for the time ye ought to be teachers, ye have need that one teach you again which *be* the first principles of the oracles of God; and are become such as have need of milk, and not of strong meat.

v.13 For every one that useth milk *is* unskilful in the word of righteousness: for he is a babe.

v.14 But strong meat belongeth to them that are of full age, *even* those who by reason of use have their senses exercised to discern both good and evil."

11 It would have seemed a natural progression, from this point, for the writer to have now expounded in more detail the interesting subject of Melchisedec. Having mentioned the Melchisedec priesthood twice in the few verses preceding, it would not have been surprising if we should now have had a more thorough treatment of it in the verses to follow. But instead of a progression there is to be a digression. There will be indeed a development later, in ch.7, but the writer chooses now to defer that exposition of the subject until he has raised again the warning note. There was no hesitation or doubt or difficulty about the grand theme, but it was again necessary to sound a warning about the spiritual condition of his readers. Their condition was the deterrent to advanced thoughts about Melchisedec and Christ at this particular moment.

Much as the writer desired to console and comfort and encourage these Hebrews, there was an ever-present danger. Some of them, perhaps many of them, were not making progress as they should have. Spiritual immaturity was a sad condition. The more grave possibility was that some of them were not making progress because they had not really made a start. It was solemnly possible that some of them had had no real heart experience of Christ as Saviour. The writer therefore will keep this always in mind, and while encouraging some he will warn others. All, in fact, should search their hearts and be aware of their condition and state.

The "of whom" of this v.11 apparently may be rendered "of which". The writer may be referring to Melchisedec's person, "of whom" he had many things to say. Or he may have been referring to Melchisedec's priesthood, "of which" he had much to say. The difference of course is negligible for the person and the priesthood are intimately related. Concerning Melchisedec there was indeed much to say. After all, he was, in their Scriptures, an historic figure of some magnitude. He was both a king and a priest. He had early associations with ancient Jerusalem, and also with their father Abraham. The grandeur of a priesthood that pre-dated the Aaronic priesthood was not to be overlooked. There was perhaps a certain mystique about the man, but even this evoked desires for a closer study of him. Yes, there were many things to say, and the writer knew that the things that could be said would be for the exaltation and glory of Christ, of whom Melchisedec was a foreshadowing. But the things that could be said, could not be said just now.

The things he had in mind were difficult of interpretation. They were hard to be uttered. But the difficulty was with the readers and not with the writer. Had there been an assurance with him of a more mature spiritual condition on their part it would have been easier to have continued. The rich things he had to impart were perhaps too rich for spiritual immaturity. His mind and heart were full, and he longed to give to others what he himself had received, but they were not in the right spiritual condition to apprehend and appreciate. The subject was glorious, and it would be helpful to many, but first he must rebuke and reprove the sad state of some of them.

They were "dull of hearing". Note that they had "become" so. It is not simply "ye are", as in the AV. It is, more accurately, "ye are become" (RV, JND). There is a sadness about this. Does it not imply that there was at one time a more ready ear for divine things? Is the implication not this, that they were slipping? Is there not, implicit in the expression, a warning to them that they were being overtaken by an increasing deafness to the very voice of God? "Today, if ye will hear his voice"! It is all reminiscent of the condition of the assembly at Ephesus in Rev 2. They had known better days and a better love. There is not so much a stern rebuke nor a severe reprimand. It is rather a touching appeal, "Remember! Repent! Return!" They had become, then, "dull of hearing".

"Dull" (*nōthros*) means slow, sluggish, and indolent. They were lazy hearers. *Nōthros* is only here and in 6:12 in the NT. W.E.Vine, quoting Trench's *Synonyms*, compares it with "slow of heart" in Luke 24:25. The word there is not quite the same, but perhaps the thought is. "Hearing" is a plural word. In "hearings" they had become listless and slow. To such a condition of mind and heart it was difficult to explain anything. "Dull of hearing and slow of heart" was not a condition conducive to the unfolding of the rich and good things which the writer wanted to bring to them concerning Melchisedec. And, again we say, what made it the more sad, was that they had not always been like this. They had become so.

12 "For", he says, to demonstrate and prove his point. He will show them, to their shame if possible, what they could have been, and what they should have been, had they not grown sluggish. It is a well-known principle that there is no standing still in the spiritual life. If there is no progression, then there is retrogression. If there is no growth, then there is positive dwarfing of the person concerned. If we are not going forward, then, in real terms, we are going backward, for the time that we have lost in our indolence requires that we should have been that much further forward. This is what had happened to them. For the time they had been professing Christ they ought to have been teachers. Instead, they were still babies.

Now the writer does not necessarily mean "teachers" in the technical sense of Eph 4:11 or Rom 12:7. It is not expected that every Christian will be a teacher in such a sense. But, for the time that had elapsed since their first confession of Christ, they ought to have made sufficient progress in divine things to be able to impart to others the knowledge of what they had received in Christ. This was not so. They had not grown. They had not developed proportionately with the time that they had professed Christianity. They were yet like infants. They stood in need of being taught. The writer does not offer any explanation here for their lack of spiritual growth. C.E.Stuart makes the following interesting observation. He quotes the words of James to Paul in Acts 21:20, "Thou seest, brother, how many myriads of Jews there are which believe; and they are all zealous of the law". Then he remarks, "Abiding in Jerusalem, the cradle of Christianity, had tended to keep believers in a state of spiritual infancy, instead of leading them on to become mature Christians. And if we may draw the natural conclusion from James' words above quoted, and from his manifested desire to conciliate Jewish prejudices, he and the elders with him were not in a condition to minister truth that would foster true spiritual growth and a full apprehension of divine things. So the Hebrews were like babes, desiring milk, not solid food". It would appear to be another principle, so evidently seen in Christendom, that religion as a system always hinders healthy growth towards spiritual maturity. To quote J.N.Darby, "We may observe that there is no greater hindrance to progress in spiritual life and intelligence than attachment to an ancient form of religion, which, being traditional and not simply personal faith in the truth, consists always in ordinances, and is consequently carnal and earthly … under the influence of such a system piety itself – expended in forms – makes a barrier between the soul and the light of God; and these forms which surround, preoccupy, and hold the affections captive, prevent them from enlarging and becoming enlightened by means of divine revelation".

Notice the word "again"! It was not just that they needed to be taught. They needed to be taught again! They needed, as it were, to be sent back to the infant classes. They had not only failed to make progress, but the implication is that, through neglect, they had forgotten what they had learned in those earlier days. Like one who may learn a foreign language, and, through disuse, forget all that he has learned, and when again interest is revived in that language, he needs to begin at the beginning and learn again. They had need that one teach them again. They needed to be taught again what were "the elements of the beginning of the oracles of God" (JND). Or, as the RV has it, "the rudiments of the first principles of the oracles of God". Three words require comment: "the elements"; the beginning"; "the oracles".

1.   "Elements" (*stoicheia*) comes from a word which means a straight rod, a straight line, or rule, or element, or rudiment.

2.   "Beginning" is from *archē*, and means the first, the original, the commencement.

3.   "Oracles" (*logion*) is a diminutive of *logos*. It is a word, an utterance, a doctrine

This then, was what they needed to be taught again, "The elements, the rudiments, the basics, of the first, the early, original, doctrines of God's word and God's gospel". They had failed to make progress. They had not grown in a knowledge based on these very first principles of the gospel, and they needed to be re-established in those things which had become clouded in their minds and hearts. How sad, that instead of strong meat and solid food they were lingering in an infant state and were able only for infant's food. It was a serious condition indeed, where a failure to develop rendered them incapable of receiving anything but milk. What they needed was solid food, but the solid food which they needed was not suited to their immature condition. Occupation with the types and shadows and ceremonies of Judaism had stunted their growth. It had dwarfed them, and robbed them of strength and maturity. It is a severe rebuke which continues into the next verses.

13   Milk is infants' food, and for infants it is good. When Peter makes reference to it, it is in a different context, and for a different reason from the reference here. He has in mind the instinctive hungering of a newborn infant after milk. So it should be with us. There should ever be an instinctive intense desire after the word of God. This is the believer's food. We should hunger after it like a child after milk. But Paul's mention of milk-food in 1 Cor 3:1-2 is quite different. There he is administering rebuke to the Corinthians as the writer does here to the Hebrews. The carnality of the Corinthians had stunted their growth and hindered their progress to maturity. Paul's lament is so akin to the lament of this writer to the Hebrews. "I have not been able to speak to you as to spiritual ... but ... as to babes ... I have given you milk to drink, not meat, for ye have not yet been able, nor are ye yet able; for ye are yet carnal". It is not good that those who should be full-grown men should still be incapable of digesting anything but milk. We must repeat that milk is good, but there ought to be such development of physique and strength and growth, that, physically, the body desires something more substantial than the food of babes. Milk is for infants and invalids, and for them it is nourishing and good. The believer who has not so developed spiritually as to enjoy the richer strong meat of the deeper things of God is still in the infant state. Notice again, that these Hebrews had "become" such as had need of milk (v.12). By neglect of proper nourishment suited to progress and growth, they had lost appetite and the ability to assimilate the deeper things.

Now the believer who was still using milk was displaying his unskilfulness in the word. "Unskilled" (apeiros) is found only here in the NT. The word peira means "a trial" or " experience". The prefix a negatives this, so that apeiros literally means "no experience". Exactly thus does the RV translate, and reads, "is without experience". Such then was the sad condition of these Hebrews. They were without experience, unskilled, in the greater and deeper truths of the gospel.

What exactly are we to understand by "the word of righteousness"? It is like a phrase lifted out of the Epistle to the Romans or the Epistle to the Galatians, and had we found it there we would have associated it, without hesitation, with the great doctrine of justification and with the righteousness of God as we have it in those two letters. Justification, however, is not a theme of this Epistle to the Hebrews, but nevertheless, the gospel which had brought them salvation was that same "word of truth" (2 Cor 6:7). Had they gone on with this, doctrinally and experimentally, they would have reached by now an adult state in christian experience. Instead, they apparently had lingered with the childish, infantile, noisy things of Judaism and the law, and consequently were without experience in the more advanced principles of righteousness and the gospel. Again the writer says it: they were babes.

Some expositors will not relate this "word of righteousness" directly to the gospel. They will interpret the expression as "a principle of righteousness", meaning that these Hebrews, in their immaturity, had not built up in the course of experience a principle or standard of righteousness by which they could pass discriminating judgment on moral situations as they arose (see F.F.Bruce). This lack was, in any case, a failure to come to maturity in a knowledge of the gospel. Such knowledge would have brought with it a right perception of righteous conduct which would be compatible with that gospel. They could have been living out the very requirements of the law, occupation with which appeared to be hindering them. The demands of the law are instinctively met in the lives of those who have nothing to do with the law, but who, because of increasing occupation with Christ, bear His likeness and so live as to please Him and bring Him glory. They had not entered fully into the enjoyment of this. They should have been teachers, but infants can neither understand nor teach the things of that life of which they have had no experience.

14 How the writer was longing to give them "strong meat". He had introduced the grand subjects of Melchisidec and priesthood. There was a priesthood greater than that of their Aaron, and the writer yearned to expound it. And he will, of course, for the spiritual immaturity which he is lamenting would not apply to every single one of them. He necessarily will rebuke the lack of progress of some of them, and also will show the greater danger which might befall others of them, but he will return, in a little while, to extol the glories of that priest who was after the order of Melchisedec. This will be solid food.

The strong meat which he had for them was for full-grown men. It was solid food indeed, and herein lies a challenge and a warning for every believer. Can we receive this strong meat? Do we enjoy it? What exactly is this "strong meat"? Oh, by how many grand names is it all described for us in the Word: justification! propitiation! reconciliation! atonement! predestination! election! sanctification! grace! righteousness! holiness! worship! And all this is but the beginning. There are the glories of our Lord to be enjoyed: His personal glory! His creatorial glory! His virgin birth! His moral glory! His crucifixion! His resurrection! His ascension! His exaltation! His kingdom glory! There is so much. There is too much. And there is little time down here during our pilgrimage. How it behoves us to redeem the time, and to make what progress we can while we are able. These Hebrews had not done so; and were not doing so. They had not developed the habit of occupation with Christ in glory, and with the great doctrines related to Him and to the gospel. So, because of a failure to use their spiritual faculties, they were not yet full-grown. They ought to have been. But they were not.

There is a physical principle, that as we exercise our senses, they become more acute; they develop with use. The same principle obtains in the spiritual realm also. A man, by reason of use, so learns to employ his senses as to be able to discern between what is good and nourishing and what is to be refused. It is the same with regard to things spiritual. The believer who is engaged habitually with the great things, develops the ability and appetite for more great things. And with this constant occupation with Christ and the gospel there comes an ability to rightly discern between the good and the evil. Whether this be the morally good and evil, or the doctrinally good and evil, is a question of little importance. The God-given ability to discern and discriminate applies in all spheres. The sincere and serious Christian, who, on account of habit, has his sensitivities exercised, will be able to distinguish between right and wrong in every department of life, in the world, in the home, and in the assembly.

The parenthesis, begun at v.11, now continues to the end of ch.6. After that the

writer will resume the meditation upon Melchisedec and upon that priesthood which
is greater than the Levitical, great as that may have been in the thinking of every
Hebrew.

VI.   The Third Warning (6:1-20)

1.   *Go On – Or Go Back*
   6:1-8

> v.1   "Therefore leaving the principles of the doctrine of Christ, let us go on
> unto perfection; not laying again the foundation of repentance from
> dead works, and of faith toward God,
> v.2   Of the doctrine of baptisms, and of laying on of hands, and of resurrection
> of the dead, and of eternal judgement.
> v.3   And this will we do, if God permit.
> v.4   For *it is* impossible for those who were once enlightened, and have
> tasted of the heavenly gift, and were made partakers of the Holy Ghost,
> v.5   And have tasted the good word of God, and the powers of the world to
> come,
> v.6   If they shall fall away, to renew them again unto repentance; seeing they
> crucify to themselves the Son of God afresh, and put *him* to an open
> shame.
> v.7   For the earth which drinketh in the rain that cometh oft upon it, and
> bringeth forth herbs meet for them by whom it is dressed, receiveth
> blessing from God:
> v.8   But that which beareth thorns and briers *is* rejected, and *is* nigh unto
> cursing; whose end *is* to be burned."

1-2   The "therefore" with which this chapter begins, continues, in a lovely blending
of argument and appeal, the warnings on the perils of immaturity and sloth, and offers
encouragement to the readers to press on to full growth. Since immaturity, inexperience
and lack of growth are so undesirable in the true believer, "therefore", the writer says,
"let us go on". We must leave the "word of the beginning", the elementary doctrines,
the rudiments, and from them move on to maturity.

   Now we do not leave these first principles in the sense of giving them up or
abandoning them as unwanted. We leave them as a plant leaves the root or the bulb,
still depending upon it for its nourishment and growth, but growing up from it into
foliage, flower, and fruit. We leave these rudiments as a child leaves the alphabet,
leaving the letters and the simple "ABC" beginnings, yet ever depending upon these
same letters for acquiring or imparting future learning, and for intelligent development.
We leave these early principles as a building, in course of erection, will leave the
foundation. The builder will not stay forever labouring at the foundation, but having
laid it will move onward and upward from it, yet ever resting dependently upon it.
So are these first principles, the word of the beginning of the Christ; they are
foundational. We leave them, yet ever rest upon them. They are a beginning, but

they are only a beginning, and as another has said, "Beginnings belong to a stage which ought long since to have been left behind". We must press on. We must advance. We must make progress. The "perfection" to which we must move is the "full age" of 5:14. It is the same word. It is full growth or maturity.

But what is this "word of the beginning of the Christ" (JND)? What are these "principles of the doctrines of Christ"? It is important to see that all of these principles were enshrined in Judaism. The writer will enumerate six doctrines or particulars, which, although they are the very beginnings of the christian faith, are not exclusively or distinctively christian. They were all to be found in the OT writings and were well known to every thinking Jew, apart from Christianity at all. To the believing Jew they now took on a new dimension and importance, but the snare for the believing Jew was to remain occupied with these rudiments and not to make progress to things associated with the Man who was now in the glory. Though important, these were all but preparatory and foundational. It was now up to every soul desiring full growth and maturity to move on from these things and to enjoy the rich inheritance of association with the heavenly Man. There were increasing blessings to be had in a deepening knowledge and appreciation of Him, who, having been foreshadowed in the OT writings, in virtue of His finished work was now enthroned in the heavens. This was true progress, to get to know Him better. These first principles were the foundation of greater things. The six principles are listed in three pairs, moving from what was fundamental to what was experiential, and on to what was final and eternal. Some think that the writer may well have been referring to, or quoting from, an early Hebrew catechism. They are:

1. Repentance and Faith.
2. Baptisms and Laying on of Hands.
3. Resurrection and Judgment.

The principles need to be considered individually and also in the couplet form in which they are presented.

Repentance from Dead Works. These are not, as is sometimes suggested, the works associated with law and law-keeping and the old ceremonials and rituals. That such could, and did, become "dead works" is not denied or disputed, and it must be conceded that many expositors will equate these dead works with the ritualistic observances of the ceremonies of old Judaism, thus seeing a contrast between them and faith. But that is not what we have here. These are works which issue in death. They are evil works. They are sins. They are the works of the flesh, such as might be listed by Paul in Gal 5:19-21. The end of such is death (Rom 6:21). Repentance from these is neither exclusively nor peculiarly nor originally christian. The OT prophets all demanded such repentance, until he came who was the last of the prophets, and this was the very basis of John Baptist's wilderness preaching, "Repent ye ..." (Matt 3:1-2).

Repentance alone, however, is, in a sense, a negative exercise. It is "from" dead works. So there must be a necessary link with the positive, which is "faith toward God". Notice that in the preaching of Jesus, as in the preaching of the apostles, repentance and faith are linked together. "Repent ... and believe", our Lord preached in Mark 1:15. "Repentance ... and faith", Paul testified in Acts 20:21. Repentance (*metanoia*) is a change of mode of thought and feeling, bringing remorse and contrition for one's past actions. It has been described as "taking sides with God against myself", and the prodigal of the parable of Luke 15 has often been cited as a perfect picture of true repentance. Repentance, in itself, is of no saving value, but it is a necessary preliminary to that faith in God which brings salvation to the penitent.

Faith toward God. This is, perhaps more accurately, "faith in God". It is again a well-known OT principle. The great example is Abraham, of whom it is said so simply and so beautifully that "he believed God" (Gen 15:6). He so became the father of the faithful, and as such he is held up to the Romans in Paul's great exposition of the righteousness which is of faith (Rom 4:16-23). Among the OT prophets Habakkuk is the preacher of faith. "The just shall live by faith", he wrote (2:4), and this word is quoted by Paul in Rom 1:17 and in Gal 3:11, as also by the writer to the Hebrews in 10:38. Faith then, was not something new. It had not been introduced with Christianity. These Hebrew believers had the advantage of knowing that the rudiments of the gospel which they had believed were embodied and enshrined in the pages of their OT. These principles were good, but they were just a foundation. Believers would not make progress while they were occupied only with rudimentary things which were the common lot or heritage of all Jews, whether believers in Christ or not.

The Doctrine of Baptisms. This has been regarded by many of the older expositors as a reference to christian baptism. There are two objections to that interpretation. Firstly, the word "baptism" is in the plural. Secondly, it is not the word which is usually employed when NT baptism is in view. The word here is *baptismos*, which is "washings". Indeed the AV translators have so rendered the same word in 9:10 of this epistle. Why they did not so translate it here is difficult to understand. It may have prevented difficulties and errors of interpretation had they rendered "washings" instead of "baptisms". The plurality of the word militates against it being a reference to christian baptism unless we see a plurality by counting John's baptism and the baptism of believers as practised later in the Acts of the Apostles as two baptisms. Some get over the difficulty of the plurality by saying that it is a reference to the dual baptism of water and of the Spirit. But this would warrant an unusual and unfair elasticity of thought and expression. "Divers washings" as mentioned in 9:10 were well-known to every Jew. Apart from the washing of persons, cups, pots, pans, tables and such things also had to be washed repeatedly (Mark 7:2-4). There were many and varied rules and regulations regarding ablutions and rites of cleansing. Ceremonial purity was an essential element in the national and religious life, and ceremonial washings were necessary to provide and maintain such purity. This had been taught them as early as Num 19, where we have described the ceremony associated with the red heifer, and indeed even earlier than that, the very priesthood itself had been inaugurated with washings, as in Lev 8:6. These "washings" then, were an integral part of Jewish ceremonialism from the very beginning, and were but teaching, in a preparatory, shadowy, temporal way, the need for cleansing and purity for those who in any way were concerned with testimony and with holy things.

Laying on of Hands. This is rendered by J.N. Darby, "imposition of hands". That this was a practice among early believers, cannot be denied. In Acts 6, having chosen out seven good men to oversee the daily administration, the apostles laid their hands on them, thus giving them apostolic fellowship and approval in the ministry for which they had been chosen. In Acts 8 the apostles likewise laid hands on the believing Samaritans. It was an apostolic welcome into the bosom of Christianity for these of Samaria. There are further references to the laying on of hands in Acts 9:12, 17; 19:6, and also in 2 Tim 1:6. But this, like the "washings", predates the apostles. In Num 27:23 Moses laid his hands on Joshua, and this is recalled in Deut 34:9. It was too an essential part of the sacrificial ritual. In the early chapters of Leviticus it is instructed again and again that the offerer should "lay his hand" on the head of his offering, and in Lev 16, on the Day of Atonement, Aaron did the same. The thought is always that of identification with the person or with the offering upon whom the hands are being laid. It was a preparatory ceremonial; it was in that foundation from which we must move on in spiritual progress.

Resurrecton of the Dead. This too, was a doctrine of the OT, well-known by Jews of that earlier dispensation. Martha speaks for such when she says of her deceased brother, "I know that he shall rise again". The resurrection of the dead was clearly taught and believed. But observe, however, that it was resurrection "*of* the dead" that the OT taught. With the resurrection of Christ and the further revelation given to and through the apostles, there came an even greater hope of resurrection *out from among* the dead. This was an advance on the OT doctrine of a resurrection of the dead but it does not invalidate what is here being said, that resurrection of the dead was something known and believed by every intelligent Jew before Pentecost and the apostolic era. The Pharisees were in perpetual contention with the Sadducees about the resurrection of the dead. Paul skilfully used this contention to his advantage in Acts 23:6-9.

Eternal Judgment. With the doctrine of resurrection there was associated the doctrine of judgment. There may well be further light and greater knowledge of detail in the NT with regard to this judgment, but, nevertheless, eternal judgment was clearly taught also in the OT. Jehovah is described as the "Judge of all the earth" as early as Gen 18:25, and there it is asserted that His judgment is righteous judgment. The great scene of judgment is described so vividly by Daniel in 7:9-10. The fearful description in Rev 20:11-15 is but a NT confirmation of an OT doctrine. Eternal judgment was indeed an OT truth. The judgment is eternal. It is timeless in its results. Its issues stretch out into the endlessness of the ages to come. There is no end.

So we see that these six particulars were together a foundation which had been laid in OT times, and in OT writings. It was no evidence of great progress to believe these. Every thoughtful and serious Jew believed them. They were fundamental. They were a beginning. The true believer took their message to heart, and, building upon them, sought to advance in the knowledge of things now associated with that Man who had come, and had been rejected by Judaism, and had now gone up on high. Full growth was attained in knowing Him. True spiritual manhood, full age, maturity, were found in a corresponding increase of appreciation of the glorified Man. Let us leave the word of the beginning and press on to this full growth.

3 The apparently simple statement, "And this will we do, if God permit", has occasioned much difficulty of understanding. Would God indeed do anything other than permit advancement in a knowledge of Christ? Is it not unthinkable that God would not assist and encourage every movement on our part towards spiritual maturity? Would He not indeed delight to see the endeavours of His children towards deeper and greater appreciation of His Son? What then does the writer mean when he says "if God permit"?

Some think that the writer is simply referring to his intentions with regard to this epistle, as if he were saying that he had in mind to press on to these weightier things, and, God willing, this is what he will now do in the letter. This may be indeed an intimation of his present determination to continue with an exposition of advanced things. He has no desire to enter into any further statement of the foundational matters just listed but will now proceed, God willing, to other things. But the unavoidable connection rather seems to be with the exhortation of v.1. "Let us go on", he had written. His exhortation had the spiritual growth of his readers in view. He desired their advancement, their progress in divine things, their going on to christian maturity. "This we will do", he now avows. We will go on. This is not just a proceeding with the epistle. It is a pressing on towards the desired full-growth. And when he says, "if God permit", is this not just a reminder that everything that we do, or intend to do, must be subject to the sovereign will of God, so that even our highest ambitions and our noblest intentions are dependent upon God's gracious help? There is no doubting here of God's willingness. It is a conscious acknowledgement of human inadequacy and of dependence upon God in every detail of our lives. The writer is in full agreement with James who says, "ye ought to say, If the Lord will, we shall live, and do this, or that" (James 4:15). See also 1 Cor 16:7.

Some then will enquire as to the plural pronoun "we". This will "we" do, if God permit. Is the writer not including himself with those whose maturity he desires, by using the plural pronoun? We have already seen, as early as 2:1, that there is a writer's way of identifying himself with his readers. It is a humble, unassuming way of appealing to others, to include oneself in the exhortation. Some expositors will regard the pronoun as proof that the writer is simply speaking of his intention with regards to the epistle. They argue that such a man as the writer to the Hebrews was already matured, that he is not speaking at all of going on to full growth, but simply stating his intention with respect to his writing. He will go on with a fuller exposition of deeper things. To them the "we" is a courteous way of saying "I".

Whichever thought was in the mind of the writer (and the Hebrews probably knew exactly what he meant), either intention is good. Let us go on indeed, whether it be in our reading of the epistle, or in our progress towards personal progress and maturity. "Let us go on", is the appeal. "This we will do" is our response. And all is governed by His gracious will.

4–8   With this verse we now enter upon a passage of Scripture which has occasioned much dificulty, if not distress, for many believers. It has become a stronghold of those who deny the eternal security of the believer, or, as it is sometimes called, the perseverance of the saints. A misapprehension of the passage implies that the people here described are true saints, genuine believers, who fall away and are irretrievably lost. Now it is an essential principle in the interpretation of Holy Scripture that we cannot ever interpret a passage in a way which brings it into variance with any other part of Scripture. The doctrine of the believer's eternal security is well-proven. It is indisputable, irrefutable, unquestionable. However therefore we are to interpret these verses, our interpretation must not conflict with the truth of the perseverance of the saints, so clearly taught in other parts of the Word. Whatever understanding we finally arrive at must concur with this established truth, that the believer in Christ is saved and safe, eternally and forever. We must not be afraid of the passage, nor dare we avoid it because of difficulties. When once it is rightly understood and its meaning properly grasped we shall find it in complete agreement with all other parts of Holy Scripture and we shall be well rewarded for a careful enquiry into it.

There are four considerations in the vv. 4-8. There is:

1. A Description
2. A Possibility
3. An Impossibility
4. An Illustration

We shall consider them in this order, looking firstly at the description of the people concerned, and enquiring as to who and what they are. But notice first the connecting particle "for" which is recurring so often in the argument of the epistle. Whatever the writer has in view to say, it is essentially connected with what has gone before. What has gone before is an appeal for us to "go on". The connecting "for" will now introduce the perils of going back. If we do not "go on", we really must consider the terrible implications for those who "go back".

1. A description
The description that now follows is fivefold. It is a description of a highly-privileged people who had been brought under the power and influence of the gospel and of the presence of the Holy Spirit. Possession of spiritual life is not supposed at all. It is a state of privilege and of advantage. There is revelation and corresponding responsibility, but there is no life. A careful and particular study of each facet of the description will confirm this. A correct understanding of the description is necessary to a correct understanding of the writer's argument.

The phrase "once enlightened" need not cause difficulty in any mind. It was apparently common with those who are called "the Fathers" to refer to baptism as illumination, and those who were baptised were called the illuminated. There is no reason, however, to introduce baptism here. The word "enlightened" (*phōtizō*) needs little comment. It is found again in 10:32. It means "to give light"; "to bring light"; "to shine"; "to illumine"; "to enlighten". It will be observed that this does not necessarily mean salvation. Many dwell in darkness. Others have been enlightened. Many live in ignorance of the glad tidings while others are privileged to hear. But the enlightenment which comes with the hearing of the gospel is not always accompanied by the response to the light that brings salvation. To be enlightened is a great blessing indeed, but it is not to be equated with salvation.

"The heavenly gift" is the gospel. Well might it be described as "heavenly". It is "the gift of God" of John 4:10 and Rom 5:15. The word is *dōrea*, meaning a free gift. "The stress", says W.E.Vine, "is on its gratuitous character". Now these people had "tasted" of the heavenly gift. Does this not imply that they were true believers? Not so. The comment of Dr Owen is hard to improve upon in this connection. He says, "Tasting does not include eating, much less digesting and turning into nourishment what is so tasted; for its nature being only thereby discerned, it may be refused, yea, though we like its relish and savour, on some other consideration. The persons here described, then, are persons who have to a certain degree understood and relished the revelation of mercy: like the stony-ground hearers, they have received the word with a transient joy". These people have observed the blessing that comes with conversion. They have so companied with the saints and are so conversant with the joys of salvation as evidenced all around them, that they have virtually tasted of this heavenly gift but have not received it for themselves. Tasting of the heavenly gift does in no way mean that they are saved.

The word "partakers" (*metochos*) is interestingly translated "partners" in Luke 5:7. This rendering may give the sense here. Here are persons who have been brought under the power and influence of the Holy Spirit. In a solemn "partnership" they have gone along with that divine Person in His gracious dealings with them. Is it not He who has enlightened them? Have they not been brought by His ministry under some personal conviction of sin and need? And in His ministrations to them, has He not brought them to a certain knowledge of the truth (10:26)? Do they not know, because of His divine enlightenment granted to them, that Jesus is indeed Lord and Christ and Saviour? Have not the pages of their OT now become illuminated as He has convinced them that all these Messianic predictions have been fulfilled in Jesus? All this, indeed, they have learned as they have moved along experimentally in a path of "partnership" with the Spirit of God striving with them. But this is not salvation. How is this all repeated so often in our own day, causing us to sing solemnly,

> Oh sinner the Spirit is striving with thee;
>   What if He should strive never more,
> But leave thee alone in thy darkness to dwell,
>   In sight of the heavenly shore?

The next part of the description, "tasted the good word of God", is also possible apart from salvation. The "good word of God" is perhaps a more embracive term than "the gospel". If it were only the gospel, the glad tidings, then perhaps that would make "the heavenly gift" and "the good word of God" almost synonymous terms, which is hardly likely in the one short section. "The good word of God" then, would be a wider expression, including all the promises and predictions of Holy Scripture from the beginning. How many Messianic promises there were with which these Jews were familiar. How many predictions and prophecies and warnings and entreaties they had in the writings of those inspired prophets of theirs of earlier generations. These Hebrews had been privileged to "taste" of all this. It was the good word of God and they had not only been taught it as Hebrews, in a Hebrew environment, but they had heard from christian teachers the correct and proper exposition of it in relation to Jesus the Messiah. That Jewish couple with whom Jesus had walked to Emmaus were a perfect illustration of all that had happened to them. They had been shown that Christ was in all the Scriptures. They had learned that both Moses and the Psalms and all the Prophets spake of Messiah, and they now knew that that Messiah was Jesus. There could be no doubting of whom the prophets spoke. Whether in His suffering and rejection or in His glory and vindication, He was the grand theme of their OT writings. This was "the good word of God". They had tasted of it. They had seen that God had been faithful to all His promises and had fulfilled them in the coming of the Saviour. This they knew, but such knowledge is not salvation. Such knowledge is good, but in itself it falls short of true conversion.

Moreover they had tasted "the powers of the world to care". They had experienced works of power (*dunamis*) that belonged to an age (*aiōn*, AV "world") to come when Messiah would return and reign. After all, the King had visited Israel. He had been, in person, with the nation. And while He was here he had told them that the kingdom of God was among them (Luke 17:20-21; Matt 12:28). Where the word of a king is, there is power, and that power had been demonstrated to the nation both by the King in person and by His apostles in those early Pentecostal days. How

vividly had Isaiah described that age to come. "Behold, your God will come ... He
will come and save you. Then the eyes of the blind shall be opened, and the ears of
the deaf shall be unstopped. Then shall the lame man leap as an hart, and the tongue
of the dumb sing" (Isa 35:4-6). And how exactly had all this been fulfilled when the
King was here. The King's message to His imprisoned ambassador was this, "Tell John
what things ye have seen and heard; how that the blind see, the lame walk, the lepers
are cleansed, the deaf hear, the dead are raised, to the poor the gospel is preached"
(Luke 7:22). The works of power which would be characteristic of a future age when
the King would come to reign had been seen when the King was here in the days of
His flesh. They had been graciously continued to the nation in the ministry of the
apostles. These miracles were a partial anticipation of the complete and glorious
deliverance which would be accomplished when the King would come in power and
subdue every enemy. The Hebrews had tasted of the powers of the age to come. But
all this was possible without life or salvation. Indeed some had so shared in this
mighty privilege that they would one day say to Him, "Lord, Lord, have we not
prophesied in thy name? and in thy name have cast out demons? and in thy name
done many wonderful works?" (This word "works" is the same *dunamis* as here in Heb
6:5, "works of power".) But these who so cry were never saved. The Lord will say to
them, "I never knew you; depart from me" (Matt 7:22-23).

And so we see that this description does not imply or indicate a saved people.
These are privileged people. Beyond measure they have been privileged above many.
But they have no life. They had had proofs and evidences; incontrovertible proofs,
that the Messiah had come, and that Jesus was that Messiah. They had been
enlightened, and by the gracious ministry and power of the Spirit they had tasted of
the gospel, and of the good word of God, and of the powers of a coming age. But they
were not possessors of the life everlasting.

It is a principle that privilege brings responsibility and that advantage is accompanied
by greater accountability. It is likewise a principle that to be "very near" may yet
result in being "far away". Do we not solemnly sing to the privileged sinner,

> Yes, "not very far" from salvation by grace,
>   But beware, Oh sinner, beware!
> For "not very far" is a perilous place,
>   Thou art lost if thou linger there.

2.   A possibility

A possibility is now introduced. It is a sad and serious possibility that persons who
have been so described in the foregoing verses may fall away from the heights of
privilege to which they have been brought. How near to Canaan were the children
of Israel when they arrived at Kadesh Barnea, but "so near" was to be "so far". They
never entered. They saw the evidences of a good land. They had the sure word of God
that the land was for them. They had His promises. They had divine assurances. But

they perished in the wilderness. Is it not so with the people described in these verses. They are spiritually at Kadesh Barnea. They are on the very borders of a blessed experience of salvation. But the awful possibility is that they will never enter the good land. It is possible to fall away from such a position of privilege and advantage, never to be saved. How solemnly does John Bunyan put it when he writes, "Then I saw that there was a way to hell, even from the gates of heaven". How many have been brought to these privileged border-lands of enlightenment and knowledge, only to deliberately reject all that in grace has been offered to them. How many, like Esau, have lost all for a morsel of meat (12:16). How many like Judas have sold all for a few paltry pieces of silver.

3.   An impossibility

An impossibility is now associated with this possibility of falling away. It is the impossibility of renewing that person again to repentance. Now we must not be tempted to minimise this word "impossible". It is not just "difficult", or "very difficult", or "improbable". It is "impossible". It is the word found again in this chapter in v.18 where it is stated that it is "impossible" for God to lie. Just as certain as is the impossibility of God lying, so certain is the impossibility of renewing these to repentance who have fallen away. Here is seen the inconsistency of interpretation and practice on the part of those who teach from these verses that a true believer may fall away. Such persons tell constantly of those who were "saved", and fell away, and were "saved" again. And sometimes again, and again! None of this is the teaching of Heb 6:4-6. These are people brought to the verge of salvation, mingling with the saved in a sphere of illumination and blessing and power. As J.N.Darby puts it, "The light of God was shining, the good word of grace was being preached, the heavenly gift was being tasted; and the sensible power of the Holy Ghost made itself known". Such were the heights of privilege to which these persons had been brought, until many of them indeed would have professed to believe all that they had heard, acknowledging the truth as truth.

But who are these who "fall away", and for whom repentance is impossible? These are undoubtedly those who, for one reason or another, reject the revelation which has been given them. They have been convinced intellectually and academically of the truth of what they have heard. Mentally they have given assent to it, and may even have been reckoned among the Christians, because moving in that sphere. But they have deliberately, wilfully, intelligently refused and rejected, and they will return to Judaism. They are verily guilty of the sin of their fathers. They crucify the Son of God. Only they do it in the full and conscious knowledge of what they are doing. With open eyes and hardened heart they repeat for themselves the sin of Golgotha. They acquiesce in an intelligent and awful acquiescence with the rejection and crucifixion of Jesus. They side with Judaism and they share in the guilt of those who put our Lord to shame. They are repeating for themselves the sin of the nation. It is, in the words of W.E.Vine, "a damning sin".

What can be done for such people? Nothing! It is impossible to bring them to repentance. The terrible fact is that they have rejected every means of salvation. They have rejected all the proofs that have been shown them. They have rejected the word of God, the people of God, the Spirit of God, and Christ Himself. They have refused everything in an apostate return to Judaism. By what means therefore can we now renew them to repentance? There are no such means now. There is nothing left. They have refused all. It is impossible to renew them again to repentance. It is like attempting to lay another foundation.

Many therefore will be brought, by the power and grace of God, to this sphere of privilege. Many of these will respond to God's gracious dealings with them and will go on to bring Him pleasure and glory in an acknowledgement of Christ's Messiahship and Lordship. Some, however, will fall away from this high ground of enlightenment, never to be restored to it again.

4.   An illustration

An illustration from nature now describes the blessing of the saved and the doom of the apostate. Two plots of land are envisaged. Alike these two pieces of ground share the sun and the rain. It is the same sun that shines on both. It is the same rain that waters both. The first piece of ground responds suitably to the refreshing rain and to the attention bestowed upon it by those who till and tend it. It brings forth fruit. It yields useful herbs for the dressers. It partakes of blessing from God in the sense that it is producing that for which it was intended and God blesses it with prosperity accordingly. To the Jew, rain was ever an emblem of divine blessing, of heavenly influence in the life of the nation (see Isa 44:3; 55:10). This ground of the parable had drunk of the rain which came oft upon it. The blessings and privileges and teachings which have been enumerated in vv.4-5 had been bestowed upon them like refreshing showers. God had been good to them. He had rained much blessing and had lavished much care upon them. Many from the nation had responded. There had been fruit for God with heaven's pleasure and approval.

But not all had responded. Some there were like the other plot of ground. In spite of all the care and attention, and the sun and the rain, the only sad result was the bringing forth of thorns and briars. Now the persons so envisaged here are not living in ignorance, as we have seen. They have been "drinking in" the message of the new dispensation. They have been the recipients of glad tidings which offered to them the possibility of spiritual fruitfulness. They have a great measure of understanding. But though so much care has been lavished upon them they will produce nothing for God. How sadly reminiscent is all this of Isaiah's "Song of the Vineyard" (Isa 5:1-7). Having done so much for His vineyard, Jehovah asks, "What more could have been done to my vineyard, that I have not done in it?" But the pleasant fruits for which He looked were not forthcoming from His vineyard. So it was with these who had rejected Messiah. Jehovah would reject them. They were apostate. They were reprobate. Instead of spiritual fruitfulness they had produced only thorns and thistles.

How near to the curse they are may be seen in the first reference to thorns and thistles in Gen 3:17-18, to which there must be an intended allusion here. The end was to be burned. It is so eloquently descriptive of the utter worthlessness of a life in which there is nothing for God. Whether the burning here is of the thorns and thistles, or, as some will have it, of the land itself, to keep down its worthless produce, is immaterial. The lesson is that if there is no response to divine dealings, if there is nothing for God in the life, then the end is fearful. Our God is a consuming fire (12:29). The burning up of useless ground is, however, a scriptural symbol of divine judgment as in Nahum 1:10 and Mal 4:1.

How aptly is all of this illustrated for us in the tender story of those two girls from Moab, Ruth and Orpah. Were they not, alike, brought under the influence of the life of Naomi? Did they not, together, listen to her tales about Israel, both of the land and the nation? Did not Naomi instruct each of them and both of them concerning Jehovah? Had they not, both of them, seen and heard how El Shaddai dealt with His people? And did they not together hear the glad tidings that God had visited His people and was giving them bread? So, together, with Naomi, they set out along the path and travelled the Bethlehem road in company. Then came the moment of decision. They arrived together at the place of choice. They both wept. They both kissed Naomi. They both wept again. Oh how much they seemed to have in common, until through their tears they made conflicting decisions. How touching are those sad sad words of Naomi to Ruth, "Behold, thy sister-in-law is gone back". "Gone back"! From that place of opportunity and privilege and potential blessing Orpah went back into oblivion. Her name is never mentioned again. "Gone back"! To what? To where? To the darkness of Moab. To its idols and its idolaters. Poor poor Orpah. So near, yet so far. Lost! while Ruth goes on to a glorious association with the Messiah.

It cannot be disputed that these solemn verses have a direct and immediate bearing on the Jews of that generation. Neverthleless there must be, in the great mass of profession in Christendom today, so many in exactly the same position as these Hebrews. They are enlightened, instructed, blessed, and privileged beyond measure, but, in the appropriate circumstances it might well be proven that there is really no possession of life, and for many there would be a giving up of all that they have learned and a returning in apostasy to the bosom of that infidel world which has rejected Christ. How it behoves those who are truly the Lord's to ask, "What fruit am I producing for Him?" As Jesus said, "Herein is my Father glorified, that ye bear much fruit". That this is both God's desire and the desire of the writer concerning his Hebrew friends, he now proceeds to develop.

2. *Perseverance and Patience*
6:9-12

v.9   "But, beloved, we are persuaded better things of you, and things that accompany salvation, though we thus speak.

v.10 For God *is* not unrighteous to forget your work and labour of love, which
      ye have shewed toward his name, in that ye have ministered to the
      saints, and do minister.
v.11 And we desire that every one of you do shew the same diligence to the
      full assurance of hope unto the end:
v.12 That ye be not slothful, but followers of them who through faith and
      patience inherit the promises."

9 Such a weighty and solemn warning as the writer had been giving carried with
it the danger of possible discouragement to those who were genuine but perhaps weak
in faith and feeble of spirit. This he will now counteract in a word of comfort and
reassurance. "Beloved", he calls them. It is a tender affectionate form of address used
only here in the epistle. Lest they should be tempted to think that he stood in doubt
of them, he will make haste to reassure them. In faithfulness he was showing the
danger inherent in not going on. The lack of progress to maturity, may, in some cases,
be a sign that there is no possession of life. He must warn them of this, and that he
has done in the strongest of language. They must all, as individuals, search their
hearts. But he will think the best of them nevertheless. In spite of their failure to
grow as they should have grown, there had been other evidences in their lives that
they were truly the Lord's, and he will reassure them.

The writer was "persuaded" better things of them than the things he had just been
enumerating in vv.4-5. Those things fell short of actual salvation. He had observed
in them the better things that accompany salvation. Of "persuaded" (*peithō*), W.E.Vine
says that it signifies a prevailing upon, "a winning over", "an influencing of the
reasoning or consideration" of the person so persuaded. The writer had been so
influenced by their behaviour and manner of life and by their works, as to be
convinced of the reality of their profession. There were things about them connected
with salvation. There was behaviour which was the corollary of salvation, and which
witnessed to the genuineness of their confession of Christ. He had been prevailed
upon by what he knew of their life and love and labour. He was assured, and now he
would reassure them. If he had been moved to speak so strongly about apostasy it was
not that he regarded all them as such, but it was a necessary warning in that some
who were not going on, inevitably would go back.

10 There has come then into his heart what someone has called "a rush of
affection". Anxious as he has been to warn, he is equally anxious to encourage and
comfort. What beautiful balance he will maintain in his address to them, faithful in
his warnings to some, but careful, at the same time, not to discourage others.

"God is not unrighteous to forget" is a negative way of saying things; we have met
it before in the epistle (see 4:15). It is the writer's way of saying that God *is* righteous
and *will* remember. The God who will not remember our sins will not forget our
service (8:12). It is the same righteousness that obtains in both matters. We may rely
confidently upon God in His righteousness to put from the divine mind every
thought of sins that have been forgiven, and to retain forever in that mind a remem-

brance of every little thing that has been done for His glory. God will remember those things now, and they will not be forgotten at the Judgment Seat of Christ where in His grace suitable recompense will be made for all that has been done for Him and for His people. How rightly do we sing:

> Deeds of merit, as we thought them
>   He will show us were but sin:
> Little acts we had forgotten
>   He will tell us were for Him.

Now God would not forget their work nor their love. Many manuscripts omit the word "labour" here, and it is omitted by the RV and JND. But there was work nevertheless, and there was love, and there is a principle here which had been earlier stated by the Lord Jesus Himself. "Inasmuch as ye have done it unto one of the least of these my brethren, ye have done it unto me" (Matt 25:40). That which is done in sincerity for His people is done for Him. The kindred principle is that love for Him is truly manifested in ministry to His people. Their love then, was towards Him, and that love expressed itself in ministry to the saints. The work was prompted by the love and the love was manifested by the work. How very similar it seems to Paul's commendation of the Thessalonians for their "work of faith and labour of love" (1 Thess 1:3). Work and love are forever conjoined.

These Hebrew believers had "ministered" to the saints. The word rendered "ministered" is the verb *diakoneō*, from which we get our word "deacon". It signifies a waiting upon others, attending to them in their needs, rendering assistance, helping in any way to serve another's interests, supplying their needs, relieving their distresses. What privileged people are we who are so served by other saints, and by the angels too, for the same word is applied to them as they minister to those who are heirs of salvation in 1:14.

This ministry which the writer is commending was not a thing of the past. He is careful to say "Ye have ministered ... and do minister". Literally he says, "Ye have served the saints and are still serving". Whatever was the exact form of this ministry to the saints is not here enlarged upon, but the writer himself had personal experience of their love and care, and he will recall this later, in 10:34. They had had compassion of him in his bonds and he remembers their attention to him in his suffering even though they were then suffering themselves. He is grateful for a service which they had rendered in the past, and which, he knew, was yet continuing. God would not forget. Because of all this he was persuaded concerning them that they had indeed evidenced the features of those who were truly saved.

11 Having remembered their service of the past, and having assured them that he knew that that good work was continuing in the present, the writer will now look to the future. His expressed desire for them is not just a general thing, viewing them abstractedly as a company. His concern is for "each one" of them. His ambition for them is a noble one and he uses a very strong word for "desire", *epithumeō*, that same word used by the Saviour on the night of His betrayal, "With *desire* I have desired to eat this passover with you before I suffer" (Luke 22:15). When used in an evil sense the word would be translated by the word "lust" (Matt 5:28; 1 Cor 10:6; James 4:2). This but brings out the strength of the word and of the inner feeling which is implied. It is an intense earnest desire. With such feelings the writer anticipates the future for these saints whom he loves.

Like as there has been a continuance in work and love he desires for them a similar perseverance in diligence. "Diligence" (*spoudē*) signifies zeal and earnestness and carries also the thought of the careful haste which is appropriate when there are things requiring to be done. How beautifully is this meaning expressed in the case of Mary, who, having heard of the joyful happenings to her cousin Elizabeth, arose at once and went into the hill country "with haste" (*spoudē*). It is the same word. The word is also translated "forwardness" in 2 Cor 8:8. Forwardness in other circumstances may not be an attractive or desirable feature, but when there is business requiring to be done with diligence then Paul will commend such forwardness to the Corinthians. The writer here earnestly longs that such zeal and forwardness in spiritual things would characterise these Hebrews in the days that lay ahead.

In such diligent continuance in well-doing they could enjoy the fulness of the hope that was theirs. A patient diligent pursuit of deeds of kindness and labours of love is the way to the real enjoyment of that full asurance of hope. This joy is not to be had in idleness or sloth, but in busy ministering to others. In such loving ministries the writer desires that they should continue, until, eventually, their hope is realised. He will speak of this hope again, further down this same chapter (v.18), but his immediate desire for them is that they should be in the fulness of the joy of it, and the sure way to this enjoyment is to be engaged busily in the work of the Lord. The hope is certain. It will be realised one day. For the present, while we await the fulfilment of it, we are to be in the fulness of the joy of it. And this exhortation is but a repetition of that similar exhortation of 3:6. "Hold fast", he had there exhorted, "the confidence and rejoicing of the hope firm unto the end". We must persevere. We must continue. "The end" is undoubtedly the end of our pilgrimage. The realisation of our hope will come when we shall see Him, whom we have loved without seeing. In the certain hope of His coming and in the equally certain hope of a resurrection out from among the dead for those who have died in Christ, we live and labour and wait and watch, and thus engaged we arrive even now at the full enjoyment of all that for which we hope.

12   "Be not slothful" is better, "Do not become slothful". In desiring their positive perseverance in diligence and in loving ministry, the writer now speaks rather negatively. He would not have them become slothful. Such sloth would be the very opposite to the diligence he had been exhorting. Perhaps "sluggish", as in the RV and JND, is a better rendering. It is the same word *nōthros* as is translated "dull" in 5:11. He had already charged them with being dull in "hearing". He would not have them become dull in "doing". The great preventative would be a constancy in the ministry for which he had commended them. We have noticed earlier in ch.5 that they had "become" dull of hearing because they had not been exercising their spiritual faculties. It is a principle that if one does not use a faculty, then that faculty may become atrophied. The principle seems to obtain in the spiritual realm also. These Hebrews, by reason of disuse, had become dull of hearing. At least it was to their credit, and the writer accordingly has praised them, that they had continued busily in ministry to their fellow-saints. In such labour he would encourage them still to continue so that there would be no sluggishness in this respect. Their intellectual sluggishness was to be regretted. To add practical sluggishness to this was to be prevented by maintaining their diligence in ministry.

"Faith and patience" would be their great safeguard too, against the dreaded sluggishness. And it would be for their encouragement to remember those who, through such faith and patience, had become the inheritors of God's promises. This in no way conflicts with 11:13, nor with 11:39, where we shall read that those men of faith died, "not having received the promises". This present v.12 of our chapter is describing the character of those who inherit. They are men of faith and patience. It is characteristic. That in their lifetime they did not receive the promises, we know. But they have entered long since into the bliss and joy for which they had hoped, and while they lived and waited and hoped they were marked by faith and patience. They believed, and they patiently waited for that which they believed. This has all been rewarded in glory.

Now we are to be imitators (mimētēs) of these who have gone before in the path of faith. W.E.Vine's comment is interesting. "In 1 Cor 4:16; 11:1; Eph 5:1; Heb 6:12, it is used in exhortations, accompanied by the verb ginomai, to be, become, and in the continuous tense, except in Heb 6:12, where the aorist or momentary tense indicates a decisive act with permanent results". We must follow these who have gone before. They are our examples. This the writer will develop later in the epistle.

What encouragement this should have brought to these Hebrew readers. There was much to discourage. There were many trials and troubles. But the patriarchs had trials too and they came through them in faith and patience. So should these readers. So should we. To us, many of the promises have been made good, but there are promises yet to be fulfilled. Faith should lay hold on these. Patience should wait for them. And eventually every promise ever made will be redeemed and we shall be glad that we persevered in faith and patience like the patriarchs.

3.   *The Promise and The Hope*
6:13-20

v.13   "For when God made promise to Abraham, because he could swear by no greater, he sware by himself,

v.14   Saying, Surely blessing I will bless thee, and multiplying I will multiply thee.

v.15   And so, after he had patiently endured, he obtained the promise.
v.16   For men verily swear by the greater: and an oath for confirmation *is* to
       them an end of all strife.
v.17   Wherein God, willing more abundantly to shew unto the heirs of promise
       the immutability of his counsel, confirmed *it* by an oath:
v.18   That by two immutable things, in which *it was* impossible for God to lie,
       we might have a strong consolation, who have fled for refuge to lay hold
       upon the hope set before us:
v.19   Which *hope* we have as an anchor of the soul, both sure and stedfast,
       and which entereth into that within the veil;
v.20   Whither the forerunner is for us entered, *even* Jesus, made an high
       priest for ever after the order of Melchisedec."

13   It is well known that each man of God has an outstanding characteristic or feature. We remember Moses for his meekness; Job for his patience; Solomon for his wisdom; Paul for his knowledge; Peter for his zeal; John for his love. When faith is the subject in hand we are inevitably reminded of Abraham. He is the father of the faithful. Over and over again, in the Epistle to the Romans, in the Epistle to the Galatians, in the Epistle of James, and in this Epistle to the Hebrews, this good man is presented to us as the great example of simple unwavering faith in God's word and God's promises. So Abraham is introduced here for the encouragement of the Hebrews. Was not Abraham the first Hebrew? He becomes the grand example for all who will follow. The father of the faithful walked by the very same principles which the writer is now urging upon these Hebrews. He believed God and rested upon promises and waited patiently and confidently for their fulfilment.

"God made promise to Abraham". Indeed God made many promises to Abraham. Some of these were of things temporal; some were of things spiritual; some were personal; some were familial and national. But there is a specific promise here, a particular promise, made with reference to Isaac. In Gen 12:2 the initial promise was, "I will make of thee a great nation ... and make thy name great". This was a stupendous promise to a man who had no heir and whose wife was barren (Gen 11:30). But Abraham believed God and in due course, in fulfilment of the promise, an heir was born. In the ecstasy of holy joy Abraham called his son Isaac ("laughter"). Faith, however, is always tried and tested. The trial of Abraham's faith comes in Gen 22, "Take now thy son, thine only Isaac whom thou lovest, and get thee into the land of Moriah, and offer him there for a burnt offering". Abraham was being asked to give up the heir upon whom hung all the promises of a future name and nation. But God had promised and Abraham obeyed. Obedience is the evidence of faith. Even as Isaac still lay upon the altar Jehovah said, "Now I know that thou fearest God". At the same time God made Himself known as "Jehovah Jireh". He who had promised would provide. His word was faithful. He would acknowledge faith and obedience and would make provision accordingly. Abraham's precious heir was received back as "from the dead" (11:19).

The promise of a great nation was therefore now still intact and Jehovah now repeats and restates it. The affirmation of the promise is accompanied by the divine oath. God "sware by himself". He could swear by no greater, therefore He says, "By myself have I sworn" (Gen 22:16). This is reward indeed for Abraham's faith, that God should not only reaffirm the promise made in Gen 12:2, but should reinforce it with an oath. Men are inherently weak and potentially failing. Even the father of the faithful will appreciate this confirmation. It is for Abraham's assurance and for the renewal of his faith (and ours) that we now have both the promise and the oath. It is for the encouragement of these Hebrew believers, and for all who will believe God, to see that the divine promises are always fulfilled.

> The Lord hath declared, and the Lord will perform;
>   "Behold ! I am near to deliver,
>   A refuge and fortress, a covert in storm";
> He keepeth His promise for ever.
>   For ever ! for ever ! O not for a day !
> He keepeth His promise for ever !
>   To all who believe, to all who obey,
> He keepeth His promise for ever !

This is the first time in Scripture that God's word is accompanied by His oath. It has been described as "a gracious condescension" that God should add His oath to His word. Man ought not to need more than God's word. If God promises, it is enough. Such is His righteous character that whatever He promises He will perform. What He says He will do. His word is sufficient and does not require an oath. But in this divine condescension to assure the faith of Abraham, and of us, He gives His word and His oath. It is a double assurance to the human heart so prone to unbelief and to doubt.

14   The word "surely", translating a variety of words, is an oft-recurring word in God's promises to His people: "Surely he hath borne our griefs and carried our sorrows" (Isa 53:5). "Surely goodness and mercy shall follow me all the days of my life" (Ps 23:6); "Surely I come quickly" (Rev 22:20). Here is divine assurance relative to our past, our present, and our future. The word is akin to the "verily" of the Gospels, and to the "amen" of other Scriptures. God who promises is the God of the Amen (Isa 65:16). He is the God of truth, whose name is a synonym for truth. Christ Himself is the Amen (Rev 3:14). To quote another on 2 Cor 1:20, "Christ ... the Amen to God's promises, the verity and realisation of them. Whatever promises there had been on God's part, the Yea was in Him, and the Amen in Him. God has established – deposited, so to speak – the fulfilment of all His promises in the Person of Christ. ... it is in Him that all is true – Yea and Amen". He is faithful and true, the character of God. This is the God who declares to Abraham, "Surely blessing I will bless thee". It is the word of the God who cannot lie because He is the God of truth, and when the word of such a God is accompanied by His oath then any doubting or disbelief on man's part is a serious slander of the very character of God.

"Blessing"(*eulogōn*), from which is derived our English word "eulogise", means, "to speak well of; to confer a favour upon". "Blessing I will bless thee" was a most gracious promise to the patriarch. It was a promise full to capacity of God's avowed intention to make Abraham an object of divine favour because he believed God. In what large measure has such blessing come to us also, so that we in turn speak well of God and say, "Blessed (*eulogētos*) be the God and Father of our Lord Jesus Christ, who hath blessed (*eulogēsas*) us with all spiritual blessings (*eulogia*) in heavenly places in Christ" (Eph 1:3). We bless the God who has blessed us and we enjoy the promise given to the father of the faithful.

The promise given to Abraham in Gen 12:2-3 was confirmed to him in Gen 22:16-18, and it is this word that is now being quoted by the writer to the Hebrews. God had promised a posterity to Abraham when there was no heir apparent. When the heir did come then God asked that he should be offered in sacrifice upon an altar. To the patriarch who gave all to God, the promise was reaffirmed and accompanied by God's oath. Note the repeated "I will". In this we too can rest, with believing Abraham. When Jehovah says "I will", then doubt not that He will. "I will bless", He promises, and, "I will multiply". The multiplication promise was of a dual nature. Abraham's seed was to be like the stars of the heavens and like the sand of the seashore. So has the promise been made good. The posterity of faithful Abraham cannot be counted. Heavenly saints and earthly; stars and sand; they are innumerable; they are the fulfilment, in a dual manner, of that early promise, "I will multiply thee".

15   Abraham not only believed but he "patiently endured". This "patiently endured" is but one word in Greek. He had "long patience" (*makrothumeō*). It is fortitude in suffering. It is a patient continuance. It is prolonged endurance linked with expectation. All this was true of Abraham, and, after he had so endured in patience, he obtained the promise.

But in what sense are we to understand the statement, "he obtained the promise"? Interpreters are not agreed. Some understand it to mean just the verbal promise itself, and not the fulfilment of it. They refer us to Heb 11:13. They point out that Abraham received the verbal spoken promise of Gen 22 after his patient endurance in the sore trial of offering up Isaac. They say that he never received the fulfilment of the thing promised and that this is in keeping with Heb 11:13 just mentioned. Others think that in fact he did, in a measure, see the fulfilment, in that he lived to see the marriage of Isaac to Rebecca, and the birth of his grand-children through that marriage.

Perhaps there is a measure of truth in both interpretations. Abraham did receive the spoken promise of Gen 22 because of his faith in the trial. And he did live to see a partial fulfilment of that promise, and yet, there is no disagreement with 11:13. Abraham is counted among those who died in faith, not having received the ultimate fulfilment of the promise of a coming Messiah, but having seen that fulfilment afar off. So, he obtained the promise; he saw the beginnings of the fulfilment of it; now, with those other men of faith, he has inherited the promise in a fuller sense in association with Christ in glory.

16   However interesting it may be though, the writer does not here engage us with the details or with the terms of the promise to Abraham. He would fix our attention on the fact that God had promised, and that He had confirmed His word with His oath. It is a principle with men that they swear by a greater and that their oath is a confirmation of their word. This principle, however, obtains among natural, unregenerate men of the world and not among believers. Believers are exhorted by the Lord Jesus to "swear not at all" (Matt 5:34-37). In the world, and among the men of the world, the believer's word should be his bond. Such should be his known character among his neighbours that a Christian's word should be enough. We should be known as those who mean what they say and who say what they mean, and whose word does not need the assuring oath which may be required of others whose word is not always reliable or trustworthy. But the oath, for confirmation, is, among men, an end of the matter. A man makes a statement, or gives a promise. He gives it with his oath. He is not now to be doubted. He must be believed, for he has given his oath. There is no argument now. There is no gainsaying. There is no doubting and no disputing. The writer is showing the importance to men of the oath. It is confirmatory. There is something final with it. And men swear by the greater. They involve the honour of one greater than themselves to give due value and validity to the oath. God, in gracious, wondrous condescension, comes to the ground with which men are familiar and He gives His oath with His word.

17   Now this is condescension indeed. God's word is not to be doubted at any time. Such is His character that we ought to believe unhesitatingly whatever He may say. But in grace He will come down to the level with which men are accustomed, and confirm His promise with His oath. This, says the writer, but demonstrates the abundance of the divine willingness and desire that men should believe Him. It delights God that men should trust Him. He will do everything on the Godward side of the promise to make it easy for man to believe. To the heirs of promise God will show that they have a right to believe. His word alone would guarantee their faith. Now they have His oath as well.

Who are these "heirs of promise"? Abraham, Isaac, and Jacob, were of course, heirs together of the same promise (11:9). But these Hebrew readers of the epistle, and all those, including us, who have followed, are the heirs intended here. We have inherited the fulfilment of the promises given to them. They died in faith. We, by faith, have experienced in the gospel, the fulfilment of that which was promised to the patriarchs, though we have not yet entered into glory.

Notice in v.17 the beautiful and interesting play upon the word *boulē* and its derivatives, (*boulē,* "counsel; will; purpose; design; decree"). Now God is "willing" more abundantly, to show unto the heirs of promise the immutability of His "counsel". God is "willing" (*boulomenos*) to show us His "counsel" (*boulē*). It is His purpose to show us His purpose! It is His will to reveal to us His will! He decrees to make known to us His decree! Wondrous, sovereign grace.

But He not only shows to us His purpose, His will, His decree. He wants us to see the immutability of His designs and plans for us. "Immutable" is an interesting word, and an assuring one. The Greek word *metatithēmi* means "to change". When *a* is prefixed to it, this negatives it. So then *ametatheton* signifies "unchangeable". W.E.Vine says that examples from the papyri, the ancient manuscripts, show that the word was used as a technical term in connection with wills. God's designs are unalterable. They are unchangeable. They are immutable.

Now God, willing more abundantly to let us see this immutable, unchangeable nature of His purpose, confirmed it with an oath. This word "confirm" here, is not the same as that in the previous verse. There the word is *bebaiōsis*, the noun form of the verb meaning "to make firm; to establish; to make secure". Our AV translation "confirmation" adequately gives the sense, in that the oath is confirmation of the promise, making it firm. But "confirmed" in this v.17 is different. This word is from the verb *mesiteuō* , meaning "to act as a mediator; to interpose oneself". What wondrous, marvellous, almost inexplicable grace is this: literally, God interposes Himself as a mediator by an oath. The comment of A.B.Bruce is very beautiful. "The idea is very bold but also a very grand one: that God, in taking an oath, made Himself a third party intermediate between God and Abraham. Men, as is remarked in v.16, swear by the greater, and so in a sense did God. God swearing became inferior in His condescension to God sworn by, 'descended as it were' (to quote Delitzsch) 'from His own absolute exaltation, in order, so to speak, to look up to Himself after the manner of men, and take Himself to witness; and so by a gracious condescension confirm the promise for the sake of its inheritors. Thus God, in taking an oath, does a thing analogous to God becoming man ... God stoops down from His majesty to the weakness and want and low estate of man. In taking an oath, He submits to indignity, imposed by man's distrust, and, instead of standing on His character for truthfulness, puts Himself under oath, that there may be an end of gainsaying'".

18   Now we have two immutable things. We have God's word, and His oath. It is impossible for God to perjure Himself. He cannot lie (Titus 1:2). His word is as unchangeable as His oath. His oath is as immutable as His word. The promise is thus made doubly sure to us. And as it is impossible for God to lie, so accordingly it ought to be impossible for us to doubt. To faith, God's bare word is enough. For the encouragement of the weakest faith He has given His oath. There are two immutabilities, His promise and His oath. It must surely be a dishonouring thing to doubt.

These two unchangeable things give us a strong consolation. *Paraklēsis* is variously translated "comfort; exhortation; encouragement". It is akin to "Paraclete", that great title of "Comforter", given four times to the Holy Spirit in John 14:16; 14:26; 15:26; 16:7, and to our Lord Himself in 1 John 2:1. The consolation is "strong" (*ischuros*) or mighty. It is as strong as our Lord's crying and tears in 5:7; or as the valour of the valiant of 11:34. The word is used for the strength of the Lord God in Rev 18:8; for the strength of strong angels in Rev 5:2; 10:1; 18:21; for the power of a boisterous wind in Matt 14:30; and for the might of a great famine in Luke 15:4. We who trust in the immutability of God's promise and God's oath have in this a powerful encouragement. We have fled for refuge. Like one fleeing to the sanctuary to lay hold upon the horns of the altar, or as one fleeing to the city of refuge, we lay hold upon the hope which has been set before us in Christ. It is a hope of glory. It is more than safety, though it is that. It is the assurance of all the promised glory associated with Christ in the heavens. We lay hold on that hope. We grasp it firmly. And the sure word of God encourages us so to do.

19 This hope is our anchor, and it is fixed immoveably within the veil. There are two metaphors in this verse. Life is like a troubled sea and the soul is like some frail barque, tossed and drifting in the turbulent world system. But our hope, our anchor, is fixed upon the promises of a God who cannot lie, and we are safe. The two metaphors are now tenderly mixed. This mooring place is within the veil. Life is like the outer court of the old tabernacle structure. Our hope is behind the veil, in the holiest, where Jesus is. It is sometimes argued as to whether "sure and stedfast" describes the anchor or the hope. The argument is unnecessary and irrelevant because the hope is the anchor; the anchor is the hope. "Which hope we have as an anchor"! Our anchor-hope is "sure and stedfast". It is *asphalēs* and *bebaios*; safe and secure; fixed and firm; certain and settled. It is as stedfast as the law given at Sinai (2:2). It is as sure and as certain as God's word and God's oath can make it.

> We have an anchor that keeps the soul
>   Steadfast and sure while the billows roll,
> Fastened to the Rock that cannot move,
>   Grounded firm and deep in the Saviour's love.

20 Our hope is therefore anchored where Jesus is, in the sanctuary itself. This gives character to our hope, making it a heavenly hope. Whereas the nation had cherished ambitions and hopes of an earthly kingdom, and this too will be realised in a millennial reign yet future, nevertheless the hope of these Hebrew believers was now heavenly and into the heavens the Forerunner had already entered.

That the high priest should be a forerunner was a completely new concept to the Jewish mind. In the old economy of things the high priest went where none else could follow. He entered alone; he was not a pioneer. He went in, but no other went in, either with him or after him. For us it is different. Our high priest is a forerunner. He has entered for us, meaning that He has prepared the way for us. "I go to prepare a place for you" (John 14:2). "Forerunner" is *prodromos*, a precursor; one who goes in advance; one sent before to prepare the way. This is the only occurrence of the word in the NT, though a similar thought is expressed in Matt 11:10; Luke 9:52. Now the entrance of the forerunner is the pledge that one day we too shall be there with Him. He who said, "That where I am there ye may be also" (John 14:3) has already assured that for us, in that He has gone where we are going. He has entered and we shall follow.

The forerunner is "Jesus". Note the single unadorned, unattached name. It is not always intelligent or reverent to call Him simply "Jesus". Since the triumph of His resurrection and the glory of His ascension those who love Him have delighted to call Him "the Lord Jesus", a title first given to Him at the empty tomb (Luke 24:3). The last title of all given to Him in the NT is "our Lord Jesus Christ" (Rev 22:21). Nevertheless the lovely name "Jesus" by itself may sometimes be used with great intelligence and reverence and beauty. The writer to the Hebrews uses it so again and again. We are reminded by it of the Saviour's lowly pathway, His sojourn down here. It is His human name. But having trodden that earthly path He has now ascended, a real Man, into the heavens. He has entered too, upon a priestly ministry which is now of a heavenly character. This has superseded the old Aaronic order. Our Lord ministers after the pattern of Aaron, but, as we have seen, and as now will be developed further, His priesthood is after the order of Melchisidec. He is a high priest for ever after that order, and this surely was for the abiding comfort of these Hebrew readers.

So ends the chapter which began in sombre tones and with solemn warning. The heavy notes of warning have given way to the glad notes of encouragement and consolation. There is a promise, an oath, a hope, an anchor, and a high priest. With so much in our favour it behoves us indeed to be followers of those who through faith and patience inherit the promises.

> The path where my Saviour is gone
>   Has led up to His Father and God,
> To the place where He's now on the throne;
>   And His strength shall be mine on the road.

The chapter which follows expounds in more detail that heavenly priesthood which has been alluded to again in these closing verses of ch.6.

VII. Melchisedec (7:1-28)

1. *King and Priest*
7:1-3

v.1 "For this Melchisedec, king of Salem, priest of the most high God, who met Abraham returning from the slaughter of the kings, and blessed him;

v.2 To whom also Abraham gave a tenth part of all; first being by interpretation King of righteousness, and after that also King of Salem, which is, King of peace;

v.3 Without father, without mother, without descent, having neither beginning of days, nor end of life; but made like unto the Son of God; abideth a priest continually."

1   The parenthetical section which was commenced at the beginning of ch.6, or indeed, towards the end of ch.5, is now concluded. The writer, having voiced his complaint about their immaturity, and having raised his warning about the danger of their going back, is now free to resume his dissertation on the priesthood. This subject had been introduced at the end of ch.4 and had continued into ch.5, but necessarily had been interrupted for the warnings of ch.6. The mention of Melchisedec again in 6:20 has now prepared the way for the interesting exposition which follows in ch.7. He will speak of Melchisedec relative to his person and his priesthood.

The first three verses of this chapter are one whole compacted sentence. To condense the sentence, omitting the intervening clauses and punctuations, the message is, "This Melchisedec abideth a priest continually". But the subordinate clauses are a necessary exposition both of the dignity of this royal personage and of the uniqueness of his priesthood which was of an order entirely distinct from that of Aaron's. Between the opening words of v.1 and the closing words of v.3, which constitute the sentence, ten interesting observations are made regarding Melchisedec.

1.   He was a king
2.   He was a priest
3.   He met Abraham
4.   He blessed Abraham
5.   He received tithes from Abraham
6.   He is King of righteousness
7.   He is King of peace
8.   He is without father, mother, or genealogy
9.   He is without beginning of days or end of life
10. He is assimilated to the Son of God

Omitting, for the present, all these adjuncts and participial clauses, the main proposition is, as we have seen, "This Melchisedec abideth a priest continually". Notice now the important connection with the close of ch.6. The often repeated particle "for" recurs again and provides a conjunction not to be overlooked. At the close of ch.6 we have read of Jesus, "an high priest for ever after the order of Melchisedec". Hence the "for" with which ch.7 begins, and the argument will now be continued that this is an order of priesthood which abides for ever. It is to this abiding order that Jesus belongs. The long sentence of these first three verses consists of facts, drawn from Gen 14, and of the writer's observations and commentary upon these facts, and also the inspired interpretation of the silences as well as of the utterances of that Genesis story.

Melchisedec, contemporary with Abraham, was King of Salem. There seems to be little reason to doubt that Salem is Jerusalem. "Salem" is but an ancient abbreviation of Jeru-salem, but more about this later. Melchisedec was king there. We therefore, immediately, are introduced to royalty. If priesthood is the main thrust and point of these verses, nevertheless we are so soon reminded that this priest was king also. He is a priest upon a throne. Jerusalem, destined to become the very centre of priestly ministry and the city of the future temple, is to be also the city of the great King (Ps 48:2), as it was the city of Melchisedec's throne. This first mention of Jerusalem in our Bible (Gen 14:18), is therefore appropriately associated with priesthood and with monarchy.

Melchisedec was "priest of the most high God". We do not know what light (or lack of it) Melchisedec possessed in his capacity as priest. We do not know how much he knew or enjoyed of that *El Elyon* whose priest he was. Did he have a sanctuary? a holy house? an altar? So much has been hidden from us, but for the writer's purpose in hand it is sufficient to know that Melchisedec was indeed priest of God Most High. This is one of the many divine names and titles by which God makes Himself known. It is important to note that this *El Elyon* is not limited or confined to God's dealings with Israel. He is "the most high over all the earth" in Ps 83:18, and He is "possessor of heaven and earth" in Gen 14:19.

Melchisedec met Abraham, and that at a most opportune moment. The whole interesting story is rehearsed in Gen 14. Four allied kings had descended on the area around Sodom. They had raided and plundered and had carried off a large number of captives among whom was Abraham's nephew Lot. Abraham was at the time at Mamre, near Hebron, but immediately on hearing what had happened he set off, with more than three hundred trained men, in pursuit of the marauding kings. The patriarch travelled far and fought well. He fought and won and recovered the stolen goods and delivered the prisoners. He had journeyed from Hebron up through Judaea, Samaria, and Galilee, and over the Syrian border to Damascus; it was a fair journey. He was now returning victorious, but he must have been battle-worn and weary. He was a pilgrim-warrior, and in his weariness he must have been vulnerable. It was well indeed that at this moment Melchisedec met him. The king of Sodom was on the way to meet him too, with a tempting proposition, but Melchisedec, priest of the Most High God, met him first.

Melchisedec blessed Abraham. The writer is soon intent on showing, not only the greatness of Melchisedec, but his superiority over Abraham. He will reason on the principle that "the less is blessed of the better". The superior blesses the inferior. It is therefore an important statement, essential to the further discourse, that Melchisedec "blessed Abraham". With the blessing he gave the weary patriarch bread and wine. We sing of "bread to strengthen, wine to cheer", and so it was to Abraham. The proposition of the king of Sodom was to be that Abraham should deliver over the released captives but retain the goods as the spoils of battle. Abraham however, strengthened and blessed by the priestly ministrations of Melchisedec, was enabled to refuse the offer of the ruler of Sodom. Abraham would be enriched only by the Most High God, not by the gifts of the king of Sodom. Abraham's God was the Possessor of heaven and earth. From Him alone would Abraham receive riches. The king of Sodom would never be able to say that he had made the patriarch rich. The timely intervention of the priest of Salem had strengthened him for the meeting with the king of Sodom. There is a spiritual lesson for us.

2 The argument continues as the author notes that Melchisedec received tithes of Abraham. If the greater gives to the lesser in the way of blessing, then the lesser gives to the greater in the way of tithing. The greater has a right to bless, the lesser has a duty to give. Abraham gives, Melchisedec receives; Abraham divided the spoils with him, giving him a tenth of all. The writer will show, in later verses, the typical significance of this, in that it demonstrates Melchisedec to be not only superior to Abraham but superior also to Levi, and therefore to the Levitical order of priesthood.

Melchisedec is King of righteousness. How readily would these Hebrew readers recognise the meaning of Melchisedec's name, as also the lovely meaning of the name of his city. To quote A.B.Bruce, "He did not need to tell his Hebrew readers the literal meaning of the words Melchi; Zedec; Salem. He interprets them because he wishes to suggest ideas entering into the 'order' of which these words are the symbols, the ideas of royalty, righteousness, and a royal priesthood resulting in peace, or exercised in a region of peace remote from the passion, temptation, and strife of this world".

Melchisedec is King of peace, because he is King of Salem. Salem, abbreviation of Jerusalem, is cognate with *Shalom*. Jerusalem, in Israel today, is *Yerushalaim*. Its earliest meaning may have been, "Foundation of Shalem" or "City of Shalem". Its obvious association with *Shalom* makes it the City of Peace. Melchisedec is King in the city of peace. Righteousness and peace are therefore joined together in his personal name and the name of his city. Righteousness and peace have kissed each other in Melchisedec (Ps 85:10). They are descriptive, so suitably, of Him who one day will be a priest upon His throne (Zech 6:13). Righteousness and peace will be the characteristics of the millennial kingdom of the Lord Jesus (Ps 72:3). The kingdom of peace is established upon righteousness. The kingdom of righteousness will be blessed with an abundance of peace (Ps 72:7). The King is *Jehovah Tsidkenu*, the Lord our righteousness (Jer 23:6), but He is also "Prince of *Shalom*" (Isa 9:6), Prince of Peace. The same features characterise the true sons of the kingdom today, righteousness and peace (Rom 14:17). The fruit of righteousness is sown in peace (James 3:18).

3 The writer so far, in recounting the story of Melchisedec, has been rehearsing the facts as recorded in Gen 14. It is now, however, that he begins to call upon the silences of that narrative. In the wisdom and providence of God, and in the plan of inspiration, certain considerations have been purposely omitted in Gen 14. The Epistle to the Hebrews, being similarly and equally inspired, will now appeal to the inspired omissions.

Melchisedec is without father, without mother, and without genealogy. To argue the literalness of the first two expressions is childish. Of course he had a father. Of course he had a mother. But in the accurate records of Judaism he did not. The archives of Israel held no account of Melchisedec's father or mother. Nor was there any genealogy of this priest in the registers of these Hebrews to whom genealogies were of the utmost importance. Every Jew knew that on the return from Babylon certain men were excluded from the priesthood for this very reason, that they could not find their genealogies (Ezra 2:62; Neh 7:64). The writer is thus appealing to the silence of Scripture regarding the human generation of him of whom the Psalm had declared that there was an order of priesthood that bore his name. Messiah of Ps 110 was to be a priest "after the order of Melchisedec". For how long had this isolated reference to Melchisedec remained unnoticed and uninterpreted. But He who inspired this solitary reference in Ps 110 now inspires the appeal to Gen 14, to prove that there is an order of priesthood which precedes the Aaronic order. Melchisedec's sacerdotal dignity and office do not depend upon Jewish genealogies. Melchisedec's priesthood predates all that.

Melchisedec is without beginning of days or end of life. If there is no account of Melchisedec's mother, neither is there any record of his birth. Of the circumstances of his nativity we know nothing. Neither have we any account of his death or of his burial. The facts, dates and circumstances are unrecorded and unknown. This is all by divine and sovereign design.

Melchisedec is made like unto the Son of God. He is assimilated to Him who, likewise, is without beginning of days or end of life, the Son of God. Melchisedec is symbolically and typically what the Son of God is essentially and intrinsically. No beginning! No end! Are there not here sufficient grounds for the belief, denied by some, in the eternal sonship of Christ. Of that sonship there is neither beginning or ending. Sonship does not imply or demand inferiority. Rather was it understood by the Jews to be a claim to equality with the Father (John 5:18; 19:7). To argue that eternal sonship requires eternal subjection and eternal inferiority is a sad misunderstanding of the greatness of sonship. Melchisedec is made like unto that Son who has neither beginning of days nor end of life.

Thus Melchisedec, in the records, abides a priest continually, in perpetuity, and forever.

2. Greater than Levi
7:4-10

v.4 "Now consider how great this man was, unto whom even the patriarch Abraham gave the tenth of the spoils.

v.5 And verily they that are of the sons of Levi, who receive the office of the priesthood, have a commandment to take tithes of the people according to the law, that is, of their brethren, though they come out of the loins of Abraham:

v.6 But he whose descent is not counted from them received tithes of Abraham, and blessed him that had the promises.

v.7 And without all contradiction the less is blessed of the better.

v.8 And here men that die receive tithes; but there he *receiveth them*, of whom it is witnessed that he liveth.

v.9 And as I may so say, Levi also, who receiveth tithes, payed tithes in Abraham.

v.10 For he was yet in the loins of his father, when Melchisedec met him."

4 Melchisedec having been now more fully introduced, the writer invites his readers to a further consideration of the man's greatness. "Consider" (*theōreō*) is a strong word, signifying "to ponder intensely; to behold diligently; to weigh thoroughly". W.E.Vine in his *Expository Dictionary* states that it indicates a careful observation of details; beholding with interest and for a purpose. It is the desire of the writer (and of the Spirit) that due careful consideration should be given to the greatness of this great man. Let us not be misled by the brevity of the Genesis narrative, nor by the fleeting character of that reference in Ps 110, nor by the fact that there is no other account of Melchisedec. He is great nonetheless: there is a symbolic greatness; there is a typical greatness. There are royal, sacerdotal, and moral significances here, which, being foreshadowings of the Messiah, are of special and compelling interest. He who is both King of righteousness and King of peace in the city of peace must not be overlooked or neglected by any serious student of the greatness of the Messiah. But for the present purpose it is the excelling character of Melchisedec's priesthood that is of importance to the writer to the Hebrews.

"The patriarch Abraham"! How would this strike a chord in proud Jewish hearts! All that they were as Hebrews could be traced back to that illustrious forefather of the race. The long, remarkable, and often tortuous history of the nation had begun with him whom God had called out of Ur of the Chaldees. He was the father of Isaac, from whom had come Jacob, from whom had come the twelve sons, from whom had come their twelve tribes. Abraham, whose bones now rested in Hebron in the Machpelah cave – the very mention of his name touched the heart of every Jew. But there was, even in their own sacred Scriptures, a greater than Abraham. To this Melchisedec their august ancestor had paid tithes. Abraham had given the tenth part of the spoils of battle to Melchisedec. Now Melchisedec had no legal entitlement to such tithes from Abraham. This action on the part of the patriarch was a voluntary, spontaneous recognition of the superiority of the King-Priest of Salem. Abraham, their greatest, the progenitor of their race, had acknowledged a greater. He had paid tithes to Melchisedec.

5 The practice of tithing, of dedicating one-tenth, especially of the spoils of war, became an accepted practice among the nations. The tithe was offered to a chosen deity through the medium of a priest of that deity. In Israel, Jehovah required an annual tithe of the produce of the land. One-tenth, year by year, was devoted to the practical support and upkeep of the tribe of Levi (Num 18:2). Jehovah gave to the people the increase of the land, fruit and corn and wine and oil, and by the commandment of Him who gave the increase the sons of Levi took tithes of this produce (Neh 10:34-39). Now not all the sons of Levi were priests, so of that which was tithed for the tribe of Levi there was a tenth part taken for the priesthood. This was known as the "tithe of tithes" (Neh 10:38; Num 18:26). The Levites had no personal inheritance or possession of land and accordingly were supported by the tithes of those who had, so that they, in turn, could devote themselves to the service of the house of God. The priests then, by commandment, were similarly kept by the "tithe of tithes", one-tenth of all that which had been given to the Levites.

The writer is intent upon showing that those Levites in the priestly office did receive tithes from their brethren. It was, however, a legal, ritualistic arrangement; it was by commandment. It did not at all indicate that either the priests, or the Levites in general, were any better than their brethren, for they all alike had come out of the loins of Abraham. In Israel those who paid the tithes and those who received the tithes were descended from the same father Abraham. The receiving of the tithes in their case was not because of any superiority or other greatness. It was a legality; nothing more. It was their right only because of the commandment.

6 But this priest of Salem of the earlier verses had no Hebrew genealogy. He had no natural or tribal or national link with Abraham or with Levi, and yet had received tithes from Abraham. The writer now repeats, perhaps with even more definiteness, what he has already stated, that Melchisedec had both received from Abraham and given to Abraham. He had received tithes and had bestowed blessing, and in these two respects he had demonstrated his greatness. Melchisedec had accepted tithes, not because of any legal rights to them, as the sons of Levi. They had been offered voluntarily by the patriarch in a spontaneous acknowledgement of the king's superiority. Abraham recognises a greater than himself, and accordingly pays tithes. Melchisedec then blessed Abraham. The wording of the blessing was majestic and beautiful and fitting for the occasion, "Blessed be Abram of the most high God, possessor of heaven and earth". The writer to the Hebrews though, does not recount the words of the blessing. It is sufficient for his present argument that Melchisedec did bless Abraham. These two facts then prove the superiority of Melchisedec over Abraham, he received the tithes and he gave the blessing. These were the prerogatives of a superior. He who had no legal entitlement, either conferred or inherited, received Abraham's offered tithes. He who was greater essentially than Abraham, pronounced the blessing upon the patriarch. In a dual way Melchisedec's greatness is established, both in the history of Gen 14 and in the commentary of Heb 7.

And yet there is even more. Melchisedec blessed the man who had the promises! He was not just magnanimously and graciously bestowing his blessing upon some common Bedouin shepherd or tribesman. This Abraham was the depository and custodian of divine promise. He was to become the father of a nation. In him, in God's time, all nations of the earth would be blessed. It was therefore no small matter that Melchisedec should elect to bless such a man. This was greatness indeed. A greater greatness than the greatness of the man who had the promises. It enhances the bestower of the blessing to consider who he was who received the blessing.

7 It is a well-known axiom that "the less is blessed of the better". This is a universally accepted principle. It is not open to question; it cannot be disputed; it is beyond all gainsaying. Such is the meaning of the word "contradiction" (*antilogia*) here. Not a word can be spoken against it, and this principle is observed in the narrative of Gen 14: the less, Abraham, is blessed of the better, Melchisedec; the superior blesses the inferior. It is the prerogative of old age to bless youth; of fathers to bless sons; of dignitaries to bless the poor and humble. Jacob blesses his children (Gen 49) and his grandchildren (Gen 48:9). Simeon blesses Mary and Joseph (Luke 2:34). Jacob will even bless Pharaoh (Gen 47:7-10), but that because of his hoary head and length of days. Melchisedec blesses Abraham, for Melchisedec is superior.

8 The writer now introduces another facet to his argument regarding Melchisedec's superiority. He speaks of a "here" and a "there": "here", in the customs and practices of Judaism; "there", at the meeting of Melchisedec and Abraham, men received tithes – but with an important difference. Here, in Judaism, it is dying men who receive the tithes; there, in Gen 14, the tithes are received by one who, in the records, never dies. There can be no doubt of course, that the actual, historical Melchisedec did die, but we have no account of his death. In the records Melchisedec lives on. While we have the history of successive generations of priests who received tithes and died, we have no history of the death of the priest of Salem. Here, in Judaism, the priests are mortal and they die; there, in the Genesis narrative, we have a priest who never dies, in so far as the records are concerned. As touching life and death, living and dying, of Melchisedec it is asserted only that "he lives". This will be developed further down the chapter when Jesus is contrasted with the high priests of Israel, but meantime the writer's intent is to show that the order of Melchisedec is indeed an abiding, undying order. It bears the name of one, who, in all that we know of him, never dies. It is testified only of him that he lives.

9 But there is yet another facet. Like as every added facet increases the brilliance of the diamond, so does the writer's argument increase in brilliance with every new observation that he makes. If Abraham paid tithes to Melchisedec, and he did, then, so to speak, so also did Levi, his great-grandson. Abraham may often be viewed as a representative man. When God called Abraham out from Ur of the Chaldees, it was, in the divine purpose, a call to Israel. When God blessed him it was a blessing for Israel, and indeed for the nations. Abraham, patriarch and progenitor, is the representative of all his descendants. If he offers tithes to Melchisedec, he may be regarded as offering not only personally but representatively. Levi then, though unborn, has, through Abraham, paid tithes to the priest of Salem! Abraham however, tithed voluntarily. Levi "has been made to pay" (JND). Levi, father of Israel's priestly tribe, involuntarily has paid tithes through Abraham. And it is not just that he has "paid tithes"; he "has been tithed"; he has been "made to pay".

This is the more remarkable when we remember, as in this verse, that Levi himself, i.e. the tribe of Levi, received tithes from his brethren. He who received tithes, paid tithes. The receiver of tithes was tithed. How forcefully and eloquently then, this greatness of Melchisedec over Levi is demonstrated.

10 For Levi, explains the writer, was yet in the loins of his father when Melchisedec met him. Levi, unborn, has been compelled by Abraham's tithing to recognise an order of priesthood superior to his own Levitical order. Aaron's sons, the sons of Levi, the priestly house, had been tithed, representatively, by Melchisedec at that memorable meeting with the patriarch, their father Abraham. Melchisedec had received the tithes. Abraham had received the blessing. The priesthood of the priest of Salem is greater than the Levitical priesthood and Jesus is a priest after that superior order of Melchisedec.

3. A Superior Priesthood
   7:11-22

> v.11 "If therefore perfection were by the Levitical priesthood, (for under it the people received the law,) what further need *was there* that another priest should rise after the order of Melchisedec, and not be called after the order of Aaron?
> v.12 For the priesthood being changed, there is made of necessity a change also of the law.
> v.13 For he of whom these things are spoken pertaineth to another tribe, of which no man gave attendance at the altar.
> v.14 For *it is* evident that our Lord sprang out of Juda; of which tribe Moses spake nothing concerning priesthood.
> v.15 And it is yet far more evident: for that after the similitude of Melchisedec there ariseth another priest,
> v.16 Who is made, not after the law of a carnal commandment, but after the power of an endless life.
> v.17 For he testifieth, Thou *art* a priest for ever after the order of Melchisedec.
> v.18 For there is verily a disannulling of the commandment going before for the weakness and unprofitableness thereof.
> v.19 For the law made nothing perfect, but the bringing in of a better hope *did;* by the which we draw nigh unto God.
> v.20 And inasmuch as not without an oath *he was made priest:*
> v.21 (For those priests were made without an oath; but this with an oath by him that said unto him, The Lord sware and will not repent, Thou *art* a priest for ever after the order of Melchisedec:)
> v.22 By so much was Jesus made a surety of a better testament."

11   How important and powerful must the continuing argument have been to these Hebrew readers. The epistle will now argue compellingly the imperfection and transient nature of the Levitical priesthood, and the necessity for the ideal order bearing Melchisedec's name. Having appealed to, and commented upon, the historical narrative of Gen 14, the writer will now appeal to the Messianic prophecy of Ps 110, the only other reference to Melchisedec in the OT.

The main proposition of this lengthy sentence of v.11 may be expressed thus, "If then perfection were by the Levitical priesthood, what further need was there that a different priest should arise according to the order of Melchisedec?" The additional clauses, which for the moment we have stripped from the main proposition, are a further comment upon the word "perfection", and the phrase, "the order of Melchisedec". The "if then" with which the interrogatory sentence begins is a rhetorical way of arguing that perfection did not come with that Levitical order. It was the purpose of priesthood to perfect, if possible, the conscience of the worshipper, thus enabling him to draw near. This perfection the Levitical priesthood had not been able to produce or provide. Under this priesthood, or in connection with it, and based upon it, the nation had received the law. The demands of that law could be summed up in one word – perfection! There was but one law. The distinctions of "ceremonial law" and "moral law" are the innovations of commentators and preachers. The law is one. Nevertheless, there were ceremonial and moral demands within that law and these necessarily required priestly ministry. Therefore the law was based upon the principle of priesthood. But the perfection which was demanded by the law was never attained or attainable, not even with the priestly ministry which was always available. Not all the ceremonies and rituals and ordinances and offerings associated with that priesthood could bring the people to perfection. Altars and lavers, incense and blood, sacrifices and feasts, sabbaths and holy days, all were necessary adjuncts to priestly service, but all were inadequate. It was a fact to be faced that under the old Levitical system there was no perfection. There was indeed a certain beauty and glory, and a mystic religious attractiveness that captivated the very soul of every proud Hebrew, but there was no perfection. Indeed, far from removing the conscience of sin, the Levitical offerings were but perpetual reminders of sin. Neither nationally or individually was there to be perfection under this system.

Now comes the appeal to Ps 110. That Psalm speaks prophetically of a Messiah who would be "a priest after the order of Melchisedec". Now what need was there for another order of priesthood if the Levitical order could have brought the desired perfection? That the Ps 110 was predictive of the Messiah they would not, could not, doubt. That the coming Messiah would be King they also knew. He would be a King-Priest! A priest upon His throne! There is an almost unavoidable remembrance of that earlier king-priest, Melchisedec. The Messianic priest would be a priest after the order of Melchisedec. This was the inspired reason for the Gen 14 narrative and the inspired meaning of Ps 110:4.

12   But there was another consideration. If the law was based upon the priesthood, and if the priesthood was to be changed, this would require, of necessity, a change in the law. If a new or different order of priesthood was to be introduced then there must be a corresponding legal adjustment. The institution of another priesthood would require a revolutionary change in the law which was so intimately connected with the Aaronic or Levitical order. A change of priesthood meant a change of law also. Now this was no mean consideration. It is not just a matter of superseding one order of priesthood with another. It is not as simple as that. That priesthood had been inaugurated under the Mosaic law, and that law was founded upon the priesthood. The law and the priesthood were together integral parts of the same system. The law had provided the priesthood . The priesthood maintained the law. They would stand or fall together. If the priesthood was temporary and transient, then so was the law. If the priesthood was preparatory and provisional, then so was the law. A similar argument is advanced by Paul in his Epistle to the Galatians where he likens the temporary provision of the law to the service of a tutor, teaching us our sinfulness until He would come who is our Saviour (Gal 3:24). Undoubtedly the proclamation of Christ as a priest after the order of Melchisedec necessitates a change in the law.

13 Again the particle "for" both connects and continues the argument as it does throughout the epistle. It is the thread which draws together the many propositions and considerations which belong essentially to each other and to the whole pattern and design of the letter.

"He of whom these things are said" is obviously our Lord, acclaimed as a priest for ever after the order of Melchisedec (Ps 110:4). He "belongs" to a different tribe (JND); He "pertaineth" to another tribe (AV). The word translated "belongs" or "pertaineth" is an interesting word with a beautiful connection in this epistle. It is the same word *metechō* as in 2:14 where we read of the Saviour that He "took part in" flesh and blood. It was a voluntary, willing assuming of that of which the children were partakers by common lot. He who took part in flesh and blood has chosen also to take His part in a particular tribe of Israel, and that a tribe of which no man gave attendance at the altar. That tribe which did give attendance at the altar, or (as JND) was attached to the service of the altar, was, of course, the tribe of Levi, but He who is a priest after the order of Melchisedec did not belong to that tribe. He has no link either with the house of Aaron or with the tribe of Levi.

14 It is evident, as our author says, that our Lord sprang out of Judah. It was common knowledge even then, that He was of that royal line. To us of a later day it has been well established. The genealogies of Matt 1 and Luke 3 confirm it. The apostles preached Him as the Son of David (Acts 2:29-32; 13:23). They wrote of Him as the Son of David (Rom 1:3; 2 Tim 2:8). It is the earliest title attached to His name in the NT (Matt 1:1). One of the last things said of Him is that He is the "offspring of David" (Rev 22:16). It is clear then that Jesus is of the tribe of Judah.

He "sprang" out of Judah. There is some question about this word "sprang". It is similar to the word "arise" in v.11. It may allude to the rising of the sun, and indeed the dayspring from on high has visited us with the coming of the Saviour (Luke 1:78). It may however suggest the springing up of a plant, in which case we are reminded of Him who grew up as a tender plant and whose name is "the Branch" (Isa 53:2; Jer 23:5; Zech 3:8). But whatever other glory or dignity may have been attached to this princely tribe of Judah, Moses spoke nothing of it regarding priests or priesthood. Judah may have crowns and thrones and sceptres, but the priestly privilege belonged to Levi. To his great cost one of the kings of Judah learnt this. King Uzziah, not content with the crown and the sceptre, coveted the altar and the censer as well and tried to invade the priestly domain. He was smitten with leprosy for his trespass. Standing in the sanctuary beside the golden altar, in his pride and anger, he was smitten by the Lord and remained an isolated leper unto the day of his death (2 Chron 26:16-21).

15 But the inadequacy of the old Levitical order becomes even more abundantly evident as the argument is pursued. It is perhaps unfortunate that the word "evident" is used by the translators both in v.14 and here in v.15. The words are cognate and similar, but they are not the same. That which is now regarded as "far more evident" or "abundantly evident", is not that which was evident in v.14. There, in v.14, the evident thing was that our Lord sprang out of Judah. Here, in v.15, what is becoming yet far more evident is the insufficiency of the Aaronic priesthood. It must be superseded. It has been superseded, and that by a different priest of a different order. The fact that a different priest arises proves the inadequacy and insufficiency that the writer has been arguing. His argument has been strong, but the arising of a different type of priest, a priest after the similitude of Melchisedec, is conclusive evidence of the failure of the Levitical priesthood to bring the desired perfection. From the fact that a new order is deemed necessary we must conclude that the old order was inadequate. The priest who arises in this verse is not just "another" priest, as in our AV, but a "different" priest (*heteros*), i.e. another of a different sort. He is a priest after the order of the priest of Salem whose superiority over Levi has already been established.

16 What will be further established now is the eternal, abiding character of the new order. There is a most sharp contrast made between the two priesthoods. One is associated with the law of a carnal commandment; the other with the power of an endless life. The contrast is actually a dual contrast. One order is associated with legality; the other with power. One is associated with a commandment which is fleshly; the other with a life which is indissoluble and indestructible. One is according to law; the other according to power. Law is an external imposition of binding regulations. It is a directing from without. Power is an inherent energy propelling from within. Law is compulsion. Power is propulsion. The law which governed the Levitical priesthood was a carnal commandment. "Carnal", of course, is not here used in the moral sense in which we so often use the word. It does not mean evil or sinful; it is simply "fleshly". The old priesthood was ever associated with physical, fleshly considerations. The genealogies which were required were physical. The priest himself must be free from physical deformity or blemish (Lev 21). The sanctuary in which they ministered was a "worldly" sanctuary (Heb 9:1). The house was visible. The sacrifices and offerings were animal and material. Almost everything associated with the old system was visible, tangible, audible, edible, and therefore temporal. It was a fleshly commandment indeed. Associated as it was with the weakness of flesh and fleshly things, it must be evident that the Levitical system could neither succeed nor endure. It was only as strong (or as weak!) as the flesh with which it had to work.

The new order is different: not law now, but power; not fleshly commandment but indissoluble life. In Christ there is inherent essential energy and fitness for His priestly work. It is the energy and power of eternal life. Our great high priest is man, but He is not mortal. His sanctuary is not carnal. His priesthood is not temporal. All has changed now, with the arising of this "different" priest of another order. These Hebrews must be assured that if things were not now visible and tangible and audible and sensual, as they had been before, nevertheless they did have a priest, and they did have a sanctuary, and they did have an effective representation before God. It was infinitely superior. It was enduring.

> No temple made with hands
>   His place of service is;
> In heaven itself He stands,
>   A heavenly priesthood His.
> In Him the shadows of the law
>   Are all fulfilled and now withdraw.

17 Once more the writer appeals to Ps 110. He has already quoted it more than once. He will quote it yet again, making a total of six references in the epistle to v.4 of the Psalm (5:6; 5:10; 6:20; 7:11; 7:17; 7:21). This text has been likened to a bell, ringing out the old order and ringing in the new. With the clearest and most majestic of tones it rings out the transient and rings in the permanent. It sounds the death-knell of the Levitical system and announces the birth of an entirely new dispensation. The old priesthood is finished. It is the end of an era, the end of golden altars and brasen lavers, of veils and curtains, of vestments and lamps and incense and offerings. They were all preparatory, provisional, and temporal. They were shadowy and typical. Who needs them now, or wants them? The Psalm testifies to the introduction of something better, "Thou art a priest for ever after the order of Melchisedec".

This pronouncement had been enshrined in their sacred writings for a thousand years. It nestled in the heart of a Psalm that was purely and completely Messianic. They must have known, with all intelligent Hebrews, that the throne of David was awaiting the coming of the Messiah-Prince. Did they not know too, that the Messiah would also be a priest? And did they not wonder how a Messiah of the royal tribe of Judah, a Prince of the house of David, could be a priest? Did the spiritually discerning among them not sometimes conclude that there must, eventually and inevitably, be an end of the priesthood of Levi at some time? For those who wished to know it, the Psalm declared it. There would arise a different priest, after the order of Melchisedec. If the prediction was lacking in details and if the readers were lacking in light, at least this should have been clear, that there was to be a priest after the order of Melchisedec, who would also be a king of Judah's line; there would have to be a setting aside of their Aaronic, Levitical order. These Hebrew readers had lived to see it happen. They now had light which their fathers lacked. Jesus, risen from the dead, ascended and exalted, was that priest which the psalmist had predicted, a priest for ever after the order of Melchisedec.

18   The writer persists in his argument that the law governing the Levitical priesthood has now been disannulled. It has been "set aside" (*athetēsis*), signifying a displacing; an abrogation; an abolition. It is found again in 9:26 where we read that the Saviour has been manifested for the "putting away" of sin. As surely then as the sacrifice of Christ has made an end of our sin, so surely has the inauguration of the new priesthood meant the abrogation of the commandment which had instituted the old order.

Two contrasting things are being treated of in vv.18-19. There is the "putting away" of one thing, and the "bringing in" of another. Stripped of the several parentheses and adjuncts the main proposition of the sentence concerns the putting away of the old commandment and the bringing in of a better hope. The old commandment is the ancient law which had required and instituted and regulated the Levitical priesthood. It has been set aside. It has been annulled. This has been the subject of earlier verses (from v.12), but the writer pursues the matter. It is no light thing that a divinely-given law should be set aside. This is almost like a countermanding of divine orders. The law too was essentially and intrinsically holy and just and good (Rom 7:12). There was however, weakness and unprofitableness. This was not because of any inherent defect in the law itself. It was weak due to the weakness of the flesh of the men to whom it was given. The law could direct and command and condemn. It could demand what was right and proper but it could not impart either the willingness or the power to obey. In that, it was weak. It was by this law, and upon it, and because of it, that the old order of priesthood had been established, but the ceremonials and rituals of that old system only became barriers, hanging a veil between God and men. Rather than fitting men to draw near, they only reminded man of his unfitness, and closed him out. It was not only weak, but unprofitable also. What the law demanded was perfection. But in making such a demand upon men with fallen natures and sinful propensities the law only magnified the sinfulness of sinful men until many a man would cry out, "O wretched man that I am!" (Rom 7:24). The law was powerless to help towards the perfection it was demanding. The priestly system which it had ordained allowed God to go along with the nation, there being a continual covering up of the sins which the law was exposing. This good law, because of what man was, was weak and unprofitable. It was powerless to give the power to rise to its demands. It had to be annulled. It must be set aside.

19   The opening words of v.19 are a parenthesis. The law demanded perfection but could not produce that perfection in a man. The law provided a priesthood but could not provide perfection. The colourful accompaniments and adornments of that priesthood were full of beautiful emblems and symbols of the desired moral perfection. There were precious metals; sweet incenses; fragrant anointing oils; lambs without blemish; cleansing laver waters and holy vestments with their priceless gems. All these lovely things were but typical pictures of a perfection that was so desirable. But the law could only preach it; it could not produce it. One Man alone magnified the law and made it honourable. He was, incarnate, the very God of Sinai who had given the law. His life was the living example and exposition of all that the law was demanding (and more).

> As in holy contemplation
>   We review His ways,
> Full-orbed manhood in perfection
>   Fills our gaze.
>
> Ever "altogether lovely".
>   Ever, all, most sweet,
> Richest fragrance ever rising
>   Round His feet.
>
> Contemplating every aspect,
>   Every feature fair,
> Find we precious, peerless beauty
>   Everywhere.

But for poor fallen man the law made nothing perfect. Neither in behaviour nor in conscience was perfection to be had by it or under it. It must therefore give way to something better. That better thing these Hebrews now enjoyed. It was a better hope. It was too:

1. A heavenly hope   Col 1:5
2. A glad hope   Col 1:23
3. A glorious hope   Col 1:27
4. A saving hope   1 Thess 5:8
5. A good hope   2 Thess 2:16
6. A blessed hope   Titus 2:13
7. A sure hope   Heb 6:19
8. A living hope   1 Pet 1:3
9. A confident hope   2 Peter 3:15
10. A purifying hope   1 John 3:3

The old commandment then is set aside. A better hope is introduced.

With such a hope it was now possible to draw nigh to God. Was not the central glory of the old system the beautiful veil? It was beautiful indeed, but it barred men out. Even the privileged priestly family, who were allowed to come nearer than other men, were prohibited by the veil from proceeding beyond the Holy Place. Behind that veil was the Shechinah, the dwelling glory. But only one man, only once a year, and only in a particularly specified manner, could go beyond that veil. It was not inviting; it was prohibitive; it closed men out. It was the door through to glory, but men were not permitted to enter. The thousands of Israel never even saw that veil. Others saw it but could not pass beyond it. "Drawing near" was hardly one of the privileges of Judaism! The Holiest was inaccessible. A better hope has changed things for us. How blessed a realisation must it have been for these Hebrew readers, that now it was gloriously possible to "draw nigh to God". Who would exchange the privileges of the new order for the prohibitions of the old? The words "draw nigh unto God" have been called "the dogmatic centre of the epistle", and so they are. This is the grand predominant truth of this letter, that we may now draw near: "Let us come boldly" (4:16); "Let us draw near" (10:22).

20   Now there is yet another argument to advance the truth of the superiority of Christ's priesthood, and of the new dispensation. This priesthood is not, as the Levitical, without the swearing of an oath. When they of Aaron's order, and Aaron himself, were constituted priests, their constitution did not require an oath. Aaron was chosen, sanctified, washed, robed, anointed, but there was no oath. Aaron's sons and posterity inherited the privileges of the priestly family just on account of their natural link with Aaron. There was no inaugural oath. Jehovah, who later will "swear and will not repent" did not thus institute the Levitical system. Of course He knew, in His wisdom that it was but a temporal order which He was introducing with Aaron. The priesthood was preparatory and temporary; it was pictorial and provisional; it would not be in keeping with its purpose or character to inaugurate it with an oath. An inaugural oath would have imparted to it an importance which belonged to an abiding, permanent order of things, and such it certainly was not intended to be.

21   If we are to try to measure the extent to which the new is superior to the old we must measure by this rule, that one is established without an oath, but the other with an oath, according to Ps 110. This distance between "without an oath" and "with an oath" is the measure of the supremacy of the priesthood of Christ over the priesthood of Levi and Aaron.

So are we directed back yet once more to Ps 110, "Jehovah hath sworn and will not repent". We have before remarked upon the significance of Jehovah's oath, when commenting on His blessing of Abraham (6:13-17). The word of the God who cannot lie is sufficient. But when that word is accompanied by the swearing of an oath, then, as we have seen, there is a double assurance. By these two immutable things, His word and His oath, we have been assured of our hope in ch.6. By these same two immutable things is Jesus declared to be a priest for ever after the order of Melchisedec. Jehovah has declared it, and has sworn to it, and will not repent of it. There is a new, abiding, permanent order of priesthood in Him who is after the order of the priest of Salem.

22   Observe now, how much is involved in the bringing in of this new order. It is not just a superseding of an old order of priesthood, but the supersession of everything associated with that old order. There is a setting aside of the whole system; of the law

which required it; of the very dispensation to which the law gives its character and of the covenant itself. We have a better order of priesthood. We have a better hope. And Jesus is the surety of a better covenant. This is the first reference to the covenant in the epistle. The excelling character of the better covenant will be developed in ch.9. There are at least seven contrasts to be noted between the old covenant and the new.

1. The old was written on cold unyielding tablets of stone. (Exod 31:18).
    The new is written in hearts (2 Cor 3:3), so the law's demands are now the desires of the new people of God.

2. The old was a literal letter of law and could be observed with a diligence devoid of devotion.
    The new is a spiritual thing. Spiritual aspirations are now wrought into the very being of the believer.

3. The old was a ministry of death; "the letter killeth" (2 Cor 3:6); "the commandment came … and I died" (Rom 7:9)
    The new is associated with life and liberty: "the Spirit gives life" (2 Cor 3:6).

4. The old covenant was doubtless introduced with glory. There were thunderings, lightnings, voices, angels, at Sinai.
    The new covenant is more glorious. It subsists in a glory which is not just inaugural but abiding (2 Cor 3:11).

5. The old was a covenant of condemnation. The law which it brought was merciless and severe in its judgments.
    The new is a covenant of mercy, providing in righteousness both reconciliation and redemption.

6. The old, as we have seen, was transient and temporal; its glory faded; it waxed old, decayed, and passed away.
    The new is eternal, as sure as Jehovah's very throne.

7. The old covenant would ever be associated with the veiled face of Moses, veiled to hide the fading of the glory.
    The new covenant is associated with the unveiled face of Christ. We have the knowledge of the glory of God in the face of the Saviour (2 Cor 4:6).

Of this new and better covenant Jesus is surety (*enguos*). He is the pledge, the assurance, the guarantor, that it will never fail. Some have observed a possible allusion, though an oblique one, to the word earlier translated "draw near". That word is *engizō* akin to *engus*, meaning "near". The two words probably have the same root so that we might understand the surety as "the one who insures permanently near relation to God". Some express doubt as to this suggested connection, but A.B.Bruce, while acknowledging the doubts of others, seems personally happy that there is an intended play upon words.

Whether it is so or not does not in any way affect the beauty of this lovely title now given to the Saviour. He is our "surety". He is the assurance to us of the unalterable new covenant privileges which have come to us, and in particular that privilege of "drawing near" to God in the holy confidence of being accepted in the Beloved. There is then, a better hope and a better covenant.

There seems to be a pattern in Hebrews, as in Romans, that there is often an allusion to something, perhaps a fleeting, almost isolated reference, but a more detailed development later. So it is here with the covenant. There will be more in ch.8.

4   An Untransferable Priesthood
7:23-28

> v.23 "And they truly were many priests, because they were not suffered to continue by reason of death:
> v.24 But this *man,* because he continueth ever, hath an unchangeable priesthood.
> v.25 Wherefore he is able also to save them to the uttermost that come unto God by him, seeing he ever liveth to make intercession for them.
> v.26 For such an high priest became us, *who is* holy, harmless, undefiled, separate from sinners, and made higher than the heavens;
> v.27 Who needeth not daily, as those high priests, to offer up sacrifice, first for his own sins, and then for the people's: for this he did once, when he offered up himself.
> v.28 For the law maketh men high priests which have infirmity; but the word of the oath, which was since the law, *maketh* the Son, who is consecrated for evermore."

23   Yet one more instance of the superiority of Christ's priesthood will now be presented. It is untransferable and intransmissible, which the Levitical priesthood certainly was not. The priests of the Levitical order were multitudinous. They were legion. Thousands of them served successive generations. They were indeed "many priests", as this verse states. Even the high priests were many. It is estimated that between Aaron and AD70 there were some eighty-three high priests of Israel. Between Aaron and Caiaphas, who rent the priestly garments, there may have been eighty-one. The reason for there being so many is simple: they had to die. Death hindered their continuance. Death forbade their remaining in priestly office. Aaron wore the ephod and carried the people in his priestly care during several years of the wilderness journey. But he had to die. His priesthood was transferred. Another became high priest. Another wore the robes. And after Aaron's successor there was

another, and another, and another. They were not allowed to continue because they
had to die. The change must at times have been traumatic. Well might the nation
mourn at the death of Aaron. They knew him, and he knew them. It would have
been happy for the nation if he could have continued, but he died. They had to get
to know another high priest, but they knew, even at the time of his appointment,
that he too would one day have a successor. The Levitical order of priesthood has
been shown already to be defective. This is another aspect of that imperfection: the
best of priests were mortal and had to die.

24 The "But" with which this verse commences continues the contrast. "But this
man" says the AV. "But He" says JND and RV. It is Jesus, the priest in perpetuity after
the order of Melchisedec. He, in contrast to Aaron and all the others, has a
priesthood which is not transferable. He will never have a successor. How sadly
Moses must have ascended Mount Hor on that memorable day in Num 20:25. With
Aaron and Eleazar, Aaron's son, together they went up with Aaron's death in view.
"Moses stripped Aaron of his garments, and put them upon Eleazar his son; and
Aaron died there" (Num 20:28) It was the end of an era. Israel mourned for thirty
days. Aaron was gone! Eleazar now carried the burden of the high priestly ministry.
But this Man, Jesus, has an intransmissible priesthood. It is not that He does not
know what death is. He too ascended a hill one day, and died. But death did not have
power or jurisdiction over Him. The power was His. He said Himself, "I lay down my
life, that I might take it again. No man taketh it from me, but I lay it down of myself.
I have power to lay it down, and I have power to take it again" (John 10:17-18). This
He did, and as another has so beautifully observed, "He rose again, and after forty
days ascended another hill, not to die, but to be translated to the celestial sanctuary,
there to abide a priest for ever". He went up from Olivet to an undying, inviolable
ministry of intercession. So can He say to those who need His priestly care, "I am ...
the living one; and I became dead, and behold, I am alive for evermore" (Rev 1:18
RV). The Man in the glory will not, cannot die. He continues ever, and His
priesthood will never pass to another. Our case and our cause are permanently safe
with Him.

25 "Wherefore", whence, because of this, He is able to save completely. "He is
able"! What glorious truth is this; what grand words. How often do they appear in
Holy Scripture.

He is able to deliver	Dan 3:17
He is able to make grace abound	2 Cor 9:8
He is able to subdue	Phil 3:21
He is able to keep	2 Tim 1:12
He is able to succour	Heb 2:18
He is able to save	Heb 7:25

Now the Saviour's ability here is that He saves completely, perfectly, to the uttermost, to the end. The thought is the same as that in John 13:1, "Having loved his own which were in the world, he loved them unto the end". He loved them completely, perfectly. He loves completely and He has power to save completely. How rightly then do we sing,

> His love is as great as His power
> And knows neither measure nor end.

But this ability to save completely is based upon the fact that He continues for ever. He will not carry us through the wilderness for part of the journey, only to hand us over at some stage to the care of another. He will carry us all the way. He will save completely and to the end.

This salvation is not salvation from the penalty of sin only. It is an on-going, continuing, daily salvation from the power and plague of sin until we reach home. His gracious intercession on our behalf is our shield and protection from temptation and defilement as we make our way heavenward. By how much we have been preserved we may never know until we are safe in glory. Those who approach to God by Him need never doubt His ability to keep. He ever lives to make intercession for them. It is the same truth as in Rom 8:34. He is at the right hand of God and "maketh intercession for us". It is a continuation of that ministry begun on earth. Did He not say to His Father, "I pray for them"; "Holy Father, keep ... those whom thou hast given me"; "Keep them from the evil"; "Sanctify them" (John 17:9, 11, 15, 17)? And did He not say to Peter, "I have prayed for thee" (Luke 22:32)? Neither does He plead these things for us as if begging from a God who is unwilling to hear and who needs to be implored or invoked by an advocate. It is not that kind of intercession or representation. He asks as a Son on equal terms with the Father and what He wills He receives for those for whom He intercedes. Which of us knows from what we have been delivered by the faithful, continual intercessory ministry of Him who is even now at the right hand of God for us?

26   In view of what we are, on account of what God has made us, and because of the near and privileged position into which we have been brought, we do need such a high priest as Jesus is. We are in a nearer relationship than Judaism ever was. We are a heavenly people with heavenly hopes and aspirations, and accordingly we need a high priest greater than Aaron, a high priest in keeping with what we are. Such a high priest we have, who is holy, harmless, undefiled, separate from sinners, exalted above the heavens. No legal priest could ever have been so described. They were mortal men with the same tendencies and propensities and failings as other men. Our high priest is different.

1.   *He is holy.* JND's footnote here is most helpful. He reminds us that there are two Greek words used for "holy" in the NT. The word here (*hosios*) is not the word

most commonly used. Darby says that this word conveys the thought of piety. "It speaks of God in mercy and grace, and of Christ, in whom all gracious qualities are concentrated, as well as perfect piety. When applied to men it is in general the sum of qualities which suit and form the divine character in man, as opposed to the human will".

2. *He is harmless.* This lovely word signifies "guileless; innocent; free from evil thought; blameless; artless; a pure simplicity". Such was He when here – a tender plant in a parched ground indeed. And this pure manhood He has taken up into glory. Such high priest became us, who has lived without guile in our sinful world.

3. *He is undefiled.* He is unstained, unsoiled and unblemished. He is chaste, pure and sincere. He is irreproachable and incomparable. Yea, He is altogether lovely. He lived for thirty years amid the defilement of Nazareth. He walked its streets; attended its synagogue; saw its sin; but was undefiled. Well do his saints sing of Him –

Thy stainless life, Thy lovely walk,
    In every aspect true,
From the defilement all around
    No taint of evil drew.

Morning by morning Thou didst wake
    Amidst this poisoned air;
Yet no contagion touched Thy soul,
    No sin disturbed Thy prayer.

4. *He is separate from sinners.* And yet, as we have seen, He moved daily in the midst of those who were sinners. How different He must have been. It was a moral difference. A real man He was, and truly man, but a lovely Man morally separated from the men among whom He lived. He hungered as they hungered, and thirsted as they thirsted. And He laboured and toiled and slept and woke. But He was separate from them. "My beloved Son", said the Father, at the end of those thirty years, "in whom is all my delight". His life was as a cloud of fragrant human incense ascending constantly to God.

5. *He is exalted above the heavens.* He who brought Godhood to earth has taken manhood into heaven. There is a Man in the glory! "far above all principality, and power, and might, and dominion, and every name that is named" (Eph 1:21). He who came down has now gone up. He humbled Himself and God exalted Him.

WHAT THE BIBLE TEACHES / HEB 7

How rightly do we read, "Such an high priest became us".

27   Being what He is, our Lord has no need of sacrifice for Himself. Aaron, with all the dignity of his office, was not personally sinless. He had to offer for himself before offering for others. It is not so with the One who is both guileless and guiltless. While the word "daily" is used here, there was no explicit command for a daily sin offering for the high priest. For the people, however, the offering for sin was a continual daily ritual. Particularly on the Day of Atonement was the high priest involved (Lev 16). He, personally, would attend to the ritual of the two goats. But first there was a bullock to be offered and slain for himself and his house. Then there were those sad occasions when a priest would sin. A certain offering was prescribed for the sinning priest in Lev 4:3-12. Day by day the priests were engaged in the making of atonement, for themselves and for the people. It is not so with Christ. He who is impeccably pure required no offering for Himself, and, as far as the people are concerned, He offered once for all when He offered up Himself. His work relative to sin is finished. Once again we have the principle which we have already observed in the epistle, that there is an earlier allusion to a truth which will be developed later. This once-for-all character of our Lord's all-sufficient sacrifice will be expounded in more detail in chs.9-10.

28   There are three contrasts in this closing verse of the chapter: the old law stands in contrast to the word of the oath; the legal priests stand in contrast to the Son; the infirmities of those legal priests stand in contrast to the Son's eternal perfections.

We have seen already that the ancient legal system which required and provided the Aaronic priesthood had its limitations. Here is another. The only men who were available for the priesthood were mortal, failing men. They were not only dying men, but they were men prone to sinning while they lived. The law constituted its high priests from the ranks of such men. It had no option. It required priests, but all the available men were encompassed with personal weakness. But the order of priesthood which supersedes the Aaronic order is different. It is inaugurated with an assuring oath, giving it the character of permanence. And it introduces a Son who is for ever associated only with perfection. All that He ever was; all that He has become; all that He has done; all that He has suffered; all that He is now; all has but assured His perfect suitability for the ministry in which He is now engaged.

The chapter concludes on this high note. The chapter which follows will summarise and then go on to deal more fully with the excellencies of the new covenant.

VIII. A More Excellent Ministry   (8:1-13)

1. *A Greater Priest*
8:1-6

v.1   "Now of the things which we have spoken *this is* the sum: We have such
an high priest, who is set on the right hand of the throne of the Majesty
in the heavens;

v.2   A minister of the sanctuary, and of the true tabernacle, which the Lord
pitched, and not man.

v.3   For every high priest is ordained to offer gifts and sacrifices: wherefore
it is of necessity that this man have somewhat also to offer.

v.4   For if he were on earth, he should not be a priest, seeing that there are
priests that offer gifts according to the law:

v.5   Who serve unto the example and shadow of heavenly things, as Moses
was admonished of God when he was about to make the tabernacle: for,
See, saith he, *that* thou make all things according to the pattern shewed
to thee in the mount.

v.6   But now hath he obtained a more excellent ministry, by how much also
he is the mediator of a better convenant, which was estabished upon
better promises."

1   The commencement of a new chapter does not indicate any break or hiatus in
the argument concerning the superiority of Christ's priesthood. The writer will pause
only to emphasise the chief point, a summary of what he has been saying. He will
then continue in a pursuance of the pre-eminence of our great high priest. "The
things which we have spoken", or, better, "the things which we are saying", or, "the
things of which we are speaking", are thought by some to be inclusive of the whole
epistle until this point. Others think that the writer means only those things that
have been written relative to priests and priesthood. The difference is not of great
importance. There has been an early allusion to our Lord's priestly work in 1:3 where
He made purification of sins, and another brief reference in 2:17 where we were
introduced to a merciful and faithful high priest making propitiation for the sins of
the people. In 3:1 we were exhorted to consider Him, the Apostle and high priest of
our confession. The consideration of Christ's superior priesthood does not commence
properly, however, until 4:14. From that point in the epistle practically all that has
been written has had some bearing on His priestly ministry. Even the parenthetical
ch.6 leads up to a due appreciation of that priesthood.

The word translated "the sum" (*kephalaion*) in the AV, has occasioned some
difference of thought among commentators. It is rendered "the chief point" in the
RV, and "summary" in JND. Marcus Dods says of it, "*kephalaion* is used to denote
either the sum, as of numbers added up from below to the head of the column where
the result is set down ... or, the chief point, as of a cope-stone or capital of a pillar.
This latter sense alone satisfies the present passage". There is also a most helpful
comment by F.F.Bruce, who says, "Our author may feel that his argument about the
superiority of the Melchisedec priesthood has been too involved for some of his

readers to follow, so he sums it up by saying: 'What all this amounts to, what it all leads up to, is this'." An explanatory note by J.N. Darby reads, "The difference is small; it expresses what it results in, in the writer's mind, as the substance of the things of which we are speaking ... it heads up in this".

Now the sum, or summary, or chief point, is this, that we have such a high priest. "Such an high priest" became us, in 7:26, who is holy, harmless, undefiled, separate from sinners, and made higher than the heavens. And just "such an high priest" as we need, we have. This indeed is the chief point of all that he is saying. We who are a heavenly people, with privileges of near relationship to God that Israel of old never knew; we who belong to the very place where God is; we who are related to the heavenly sanctuary; we needed such a high priest. And such we have. We have such a one as is suited to us, and He is at the right hand of the throne of the Majesty in the heavens.

The thoughts here expressed are reminiscent of 1:3, and are an obvious allusion to, if not a citation from, Ps 110:1. For the second time in the epistle our Lord is seen seated in the heights. As in 1:3, the force of the expression is that He has "set Himself down". He has set Himself down with rights in the place of honour and authority, at the right hand of God. "Majesty" is, "greatness" or "dignity" as in 1:3. The throne is here introduced to indicate the royal character of His Melchisedec priesthood. He is seated as expressive of the perfection of the sacrifice in virtue of which He has gone in to where He now is (9:12). No high priest of Israel ever sat. A sitting priest was unknown in Judaism, except perhaps once, and then associated with weakness and with disaster (1 Sam 1:9; 4:13-18). There was really no such provision made for Israel's priests. But our high priest, though still engaging in a ministry of intercession for His people, nevertheless is entitled to sit, in that there is no more sacrificing for sins. That aspect of His work is finished. He accordingly may sit. This will be developed in a later chapter.

> Jesus in the heavenly temple
>   Sits with God upon the throne,
> Now no more to be forsaken,
>   His humiliation gone.
>
> Dwelling in eternal sunshine
>   Of the countenance of God,
> Jesus fills all heaven with incense
>   Of His reconciling blood.

The change in the tenor of the writer's argument will now become apparent. He is still arguing the superiority of Christ's priesthood, but whereas he has formerly been expounding the greatness of Christ's person, now he will dwell upon the superiority of His heavenly sphere of ministry. If the Person was superior, so also is the place. Indeed the surpassing majesty and dignity of the heavenly sanctuary required a superior priest. Perhaps the whole message of this section of the epistle is summed up in those words from v.6, "a more excellent ministry".

2   Christ is a minister of the sanctuary. "Minister" (*leitourgos*) we have observed before in 1:7, in relation to angels, who are God's ministers. The word signifies a public functionary, one who serves on behalf of others; Paul uses the word of himself in Rom 15:16. As a preacher of the glad tidings he is a minister of Jesus Christ to the nations. It is also used of earthly rulers who, though often not aware of it, are God's ministers nevertheless (Rom 13:6). Our Lord is here such a one in the sanctuary, serving for, and on behalf of, others. He is graciously engaged in a representative ministry for His people.

His ministry is in the sanctuary. The word "sanctuary" is a neuter plural. The RV renders "sanctuary" in the text, as does the AV, but gives as a marginal reading "holy things"; JND has "the holy places". The word is literally "holies", which perhaps is not acceptable English, hence the translators may supply either "things" or "places". W.E.Vine comments that since there are no compartments in the antitypical and heavenly sanctuary where Christ ministers, the textual rendering of both AV and RV is to be preferred, i.e. "sanctuary". Even though the word is a plural word, with Westcott he would appear to think that the word has been uniquely chosen to fix attention on the most holy character of the sanctuary.

This sanctuary where our Lord ministers for us is "the true tabernacle". "True" is not used here in contrast to something false or untrue, but rather to emphasise that the celestial sanctuary is abiding and real, whereas the old tabernacle of Israel was but a temporary, provisional foreshadowing of the true. There was nothing false about the tabernacle in the wilderness; it was God's provision for the time then present, but it was not the ultimate. It pointed forward to the true, genuine sanctuary where Christ would minister. A consideration of the word "true" used in the same sense in the fourth Gospel is helpful; Christ is there -

1. the true Light   John 1:9
2. the true bread   John 6:32
3. the true vine   John 15:1

He is the true Light in contrast to John Baptist. Now there was nothing false about John, but he was not that Light; he was but a lamp, shining until the true Light came. Our Lord is that true Light when compared or contrasted with John.

He is the true bread in contrast with the manna. There was nothing wrong with the manna, it was God's gracious provision for the time, but it was not the true bread; it was but a foreshadowing of Him who was to come as God's purposed provision for the people's need.

Christ is also the true vine, in contrast to Israel. Israel was a noble vine but because of human, moral weakness could not give to God the joy for which He was looking. He did that who was the true vine.

Our Lord's sphere of ministry then, is the true tabernacle. Again, Israel's tabernacle in the wilderness was suited to the time and to the circumstances, but it was not the true sanctuary. It was but a shadowy copy of the celestial sanctuary where Christ now ministers.

It may be fitting to notice here that the background and basis of the Epistle to the Hebrews is the wilderness and the tabernacle, and not the land and the temple. This is both interesting and important, and, as another has observed, it is full of instruction which Christendom has chosen to overlook and abandon. It is instruction for pilgrimage here, and help for the desert journey. This wilderness background then is more suited to us who travel towards our rest, our Canaan. There is nothing established for us here in the desert of this world. We are but passing on and passing through. Ornate and grand cathedrals are not in keeping with our present circumstances. The rich, adorned edifices and sacred buildings of Christendom are in essence a denial of this pilgrim character of the believer which is so much a part of this epistle.

That old tabernacle was a beautiful structure, but it was just a tent. It was skilfully made by divinely-gifted men; but it was man-made; it was material; it was "pitched" by man. God dwelt there emblematically, in symbol. This is the only occurrence in the NT of the word here translated "pitched" (*pēgnumi*). It signifies to fix, to make fast, as when·pitching a tent. For such the old tabernacle was, a tent, man-made, and but a shadow of that spiritual reality which is called in ch.9 a greater and more perfect tabernacle, and in the same chapter, "heaven itself" (9:24). It is here that Christ now serves for His people, where everything is transcendent and superior.

3   There is now therefore no earthly priest or place of worship. "Places of worship", a common expression among men, do not exist now on earth. Tabernacle and temples have served their day and their purpose and have been displaced and superseded. Other "places of worship" have no divine approval or sanction or mandate. There is, however, a holy place, a sanctuary, and it is there in heaven itself, that our Lord ministers for us. He is the Man in the glory.

Now our Lord being a high priest and a minister of the sanctuary, it follows that, as the high priests who foreshadowed Him, He must have somewhat to offer. Every high priest of Israel was constituted for this purpose, that he might offer both gifts and sacrifices. It is almost impossible not to hear in this verse an echo of 5:1. It will be re-echoed in 9:9. But what is the difference, if any, between "gifts" and "sacrifices". There is an acceptable sense in which any offering may be viewed as a gift or as a sacrifice, but when the two terms are employed together as here, then an intelligent distinction is intended. As Westcott remarks, "The two ideas of eucharistic and expiatory offerings are distinctly marked". The eucharistic offerings were those of a thanksgiving nature, as meal offerings and incense. The expiatory offerings were those associated with sin and with the shedding of blood. Israel's high priests were ordained, appointed, constituted, with such a ministry in view, especially on the annual Day of Atonement.

If Christ then is a high priest after the pattern of the typical priests; if they were honest shadows, then it is needful that He too should have somewhat to offer. The writer simply suggests this thought without any further development of it. Why? Was this to make his Hebrew readers ponder what he had already said? Was it to keep their interest and stir their memories? Indeed an answer to the unspoken query had already been given. What has Christ to offer? The answer is in one word – Himself! Such had been so recently affirmed in 7:27. Our Lord is not only priest, but the sacrifice too. He is both offerer and offering. And He is the glorious antitype of every offering, of every kind, for every purpose. All the sweet savour of burnt offerings with their accompanying meal offerings; all the fellowship and preciousness of peace offerings; all the efficacy of every kind of guilt offering; the drink offerings; the fragrance of the incenses; the loaves of shewbread; bullocks and goats and lambs and turtle-doves; first-fruits and fine flour and cakes and wafers; all were but foreshadowings of Himself, and when He came He was the perfect fulfilment of all that the shadows were proclaiming in their typical language.

This is not to suggest that our Lord is engaged in a continual offering of Himself in the heavens. As F.F.Bruce observes, "The tense and mood of the Greek verb 'to offer' in this clause also exclude the idea of a continual offering". As far as sins are concerned Christ has offered Himself once for all and His presence before the throne as a Lamb freshly slain (Rev 5:6), indicates the eternal abiding value of that one sacrifice, never to be repeated. This will be further developed in a later chapter in the epistle.

There may be, however, a representative ministry also suggested here, in which the high priest offers for others, or assists others with their offerings. The typical priest of Israel was a mediator, to bring to God the gifts offered by the people. Does our high priest then take our offered worship, our praises, our thanksgivings and our prayers, and make them acceptable to God for us? Is not this the picture given to us in Rev 8:3-4? And do we not rightly sing:

> To all our prayers and praises
>   Christ adds His sweet perfume,
> And love the censer raises
>   Their odours to consume.

Yet still everything that we offer may be comprehended in this one word – Himself! We come in priestly exercise to offer, in the smallness of our appreciation, Christ. He is the Leader of the praise. He is the subject of our song. We enter the holiest boldly, yet conscious of our weakness and ever grateful that we have a great high priest who will take our feeble expressions of appreciation and worship and make them acceptable with the fragrance of His own Person. It is a principle then, that high priests are appointed to offer, and Christ, in this respect, is no exception. But His ministry is superlative and superior; superseding and all-sufficient. We have such a high priest.

4   There has ever been controversy among the most scholarly and saintly of expositors as to the commencement of our Lord's priestly ministry. Many there are who would date that ministry only from His resurrection and ascension, and for them this verse has been a basis and stronghold for their argument. Others insist that, since our Lord needs no inaugural or initiation ceremonies or anointings, but ever and always possessed, inherently, priestly qualities, there is no commencement, as such, of His priestly ministry. This implies that we may view Him in a priestly ministry during the days of His flesh, prior to the Cross. For such as see it this way, this verse has sometimes presented problems.

It is well to see what the verse does not say. It is often misquoted by those who use it to deny that our Lord was a priest on earth. It does not say that, "When He was on earth He was not a priest". Rather does it say, "If he were on earth he should not be a priest". This is quite different. To quote W.R.Newell, "The contention of some that v.4 sets forth that Christ's priesthood began only after resurrection and the Lord's ascension, is strange indeed. For in this verse the apostle is speaking of Christ risen from the dead and now in glory, who had sat down on the right hand of the throne of the Majesty in the heavens, a Minister of the sanctuary. It is of this One in that ministry that it is affirmed, 'If He were on earth, He would not be a priest at all' (RV). For there were at that moment those of the Aaronic order, in the temple which was then standing, carrying on the service which the Law, the copy and shadow of heavenly things, prescribed".

The comments of F.W.Grant are also valuable. "It is just here however that a mistake has been made in another direction which needs to be pointed out. It is that which would ascribe to the apostle a doctrine of the Lord not having been a Priest on earth, not even when offering up Himself upon the Cross; in direct contradiction of the whole typical system. His words are very different from this ... he does not say the the Lord was not a Priest on earth; but having set Him before us as Minister of the true (antitypical) Tabernacle, he says, if He were on earth there would be no room for Him in the earthly one: for there the sons of Aaron fill everything according to the law. Surely nothing could be much more simple than such a statement".

This observation of F.W.Grant, that a denial of priestly ministry at the Cross would be in direct contradiction of the whole typical system, is most important. There were no sin offerings before priesthood. All offerings prior to the institution of the Levitical priesthood were burnt offerings or approach offerings, as with Abel, Noah, and Job. Sin offerings are essentially a priestly ministry. Hence we have those well-known Scriptures in this very epistle which tell us of our Lord that He made propitiation (2:8); that He offered up Himself (7:27) to bear the sins of many (9:28); that He made one sacrifice for sins (10:12). All this was done on earth, outside Jerusalem. When He went up and entered into the holy place He had already obtained eternal redemption for us. On His ascension and at His entering in He is "saluted" a high priest. This is not an appointment. It is not an inauguration. It is not the beginning. He is saluted, addressed, acknowledged, for what He already is. But such recognition would not be afforded Him on earth.

Then, of course, there is that other aspect of priestly ministry to be remembered. Christ is not only a sacrificing priest but a comforting, consoling, healing, restoring priest as well. Was He not this on earth? Ask those who felt His gracious touch and heard His tender voice. Ask the family at Bethany. Ask Peter. Ask the widow of Nain, or the house of Jairus, or those many lepers, or the deaf and maimed and halt and blind who, in their multitudes, experienced His kind and powerful ministrations. Was this not priestly ministry? Was He not a priest on earth? This surely is not in question here in Heb 8:4. If He were on earth, says the writer, there would be no place for Him in the earthly sanctuary, which was then still standing, for there were priests there, of the Levitical order, who served there according to the law. Christ's present ministry for us is, as we have seen, the ministry of a risen Man, in glory, in the heavenly sanctuary.

5   At the time of the writing of this epistle the legal priests were still serving. This is one of the internal evidences that the epistle was written prior to AD70 and before the destruction of the second temple. It was still standing. There is a certain sadness in the use of this word "serve". It is not the word *diakoneō*, from which we get our word "deacon". Nor is it *douleuō* from which comes our word "bond-slave". It is the word *latreuō*, which is a priestly word, associated often with worship, and sometimes translated so by the RV (Luke 2:37; Heb 9:9). It is sad that at that time there were still so many thousands of priests engaged fruitlessly in a "service" which was now to no purpose. It was a priestly ministry that was out-dated and superseded, and was producing nothing either for God or for the people. Further usage of the word in the epistle indicates that the true "service" has now been committed to believers in the Lord Jesus. It is they who "serve" the living God (9:14). It is they who "serve" Him acceptably now (12:28). The "service" of the legal priesthood then, as the service of the pseudo-priests of Christendom, is to no avail. It has no divine mandate, nor sanction, nor acceptability, and brings no pleasure to God.

Those legal priests of an obsolete Judaism were engaged with a form of things which, as we have already observed, was but provisional and temporary. Two words are used in this verse to indicate the transient nature of the old system. It was:

1.   an example.
2.   a shadow.

1.   As an example (*hupodeigma*), the old tabernacle was a copy of heavenly things. It was therefore not in any sense permanent, nor intended to be. It was but a copy of what was in the heavens, to serve its purpose for an earthly people until the realisation of the heavenly reality would come with Christ.

2.   As a shadow (*skia*), the old system was an outline of those heavenly things. As by observing the form of a shadow cast we may discern the outline of a man or of a tree or of some other object, so by a proper understanding of the old order of things

we may discern what God had in mind and in purpose for His people. It was though, but a shadow. All its ceremonies and rituals, its altars and offerings, were but an outline of the spiritual substance which was in Christ and in the heavenlies. The word is used again in 10:1.

The writer now refers us to the divine admonition given to Moses when he was about to construct the tabernacle. This admonition was rather more than instruction; it was a warning. It was absolutely necessary that everything be made after the pattern shown to Moses on the mount. This warning was repeated to Moses several times (Exod 25:40; 26:30; 27:8). It was of the utmost importance that the tabernacle should be a true copy of that which Moses saw. Many expositors think that Moses may have seen an actual visible representation of what he was directed to build, and that the verbal instructions are but a commentary on what he saw. Whether this be so or not, there can be no doubt that Moses was given clear instructions and an intelligent insight into the divine requirements regarding the building, and that he was to construct accordingly.

This is an unvarying principle, that we are ever responsible to build according to the divine pattern shown us. Moses was not free to make adjustments or modifications as he may have thought desirable. The admonition was clear, "See, saith he, that thou make all things according to the pattern shewed to thee in the mount". In what we build for God, let us build carefully and obediently, according to the inspired instructions which have been given to us (1 Cor 3:9-15).

However, the main thrust of these verses is that the old tabernacle order of things was but a copy and a shadow. It would be sad to be occupied with shadow, when the substance is available to us, in Christ.

6 Christ has obtained a more excellent ministry. There are three "more excellent" things in this epistle (though the original word is different in ch.11). There is:

1. A more excellent name   (1:4)
2. A more excellent ministry   (8:6)
3. A more excellent sacrifice   (11:4)

A more excellent name has been inherited by the Son. A more excellent sacrifice has been offered by the Saviour. A more excellent ministry is now exercised in the Sanctuary.

The ministry of the Minister of the sanctuary is a surpassing, superior, excelling ministry, and the measure of its abounding excellence is the measure of the greatness of Him who is the Mediator of a better covenant.

Now this was a bold thing to do: to speak to Hebrews about a better covenant. But it is the writer's way of continuing to wean these Jewish believers away from Judaism, and to bring them to a desirable maturity. There had been an old covenant, of which their Moses had been mediator (Gal 3:19). This they knew very well. But there was now a better covenant and a greater mediator. The word "mediator" (*mesitēs*) is an interesting word. W.E.Vine explains, in his *Expository Dictionary*, that it is a combination of *mesos*, meaning "middle", and the verb *eimi*, meaning "to go". The mediator is therefore one who goes between. Did not Job long for "a daysman betwixt us, that he might lay his hand upon us both" (Job 9:33)? "Now there is a requirement implicit", says Vine, "that the mediator should Himself possess the nature and attributes of Him towards whom He acts, and should likewise participate in the nature of those for whom He acts (sin apart); only by being possessed of both deity and humanity could He comprehend the claims of the One and the needs of the other; further, the claims and the needs could be met only by One who, Himself being proved sinless, would offer Himself an expiatory sacrifice on behalf of men". "There is one God, one mediator also between God and men, Himself man, Christ Jesus, who gave himself a ransom for all" (1 Tim 2:5). The mediator is also one who acts as guarantor, a surety between the parties concerning the thing guaranteed in the covenant. Christ is therefore both the surety and the mediator of the better covenant (7:22), and we have already observed in ch.7 in how many respects the new covenant is better than the old. (See also 9:15; 12:24)

It is a better covenant. It is a new covenant. It has been established upon better promises. The word "established" has a legal connotation. The new covenant has been ordained righteously; we might almost say, legally. It has been enacted on a perfectly proper basis, upon better promises. These better promises will be enlarged upon in the verses that follow and since there is now so much to be said about this new covenant perhaps here the word needs to be defined and explained.

"Covenant" (*diathēkē*) in its primary meaning has to do with the disposition of property. This may be by means of a will or testament, or by any other means. It is derived from a verb meaning "to divide", a possible allusion to an old custom of dividing the sacrifice when making a covenant (see Gen 15:10). The word is to be distinguished therefore, from the English word "covenant", which implies a mutual agreement or pact between two parties. The word *diathēkē* does not require this. It is the solemn vow of one who puts himself under a binding obligation to another. Although there are many covenants in the history of God's dealings with men, yet the covenants here referred to are called simply, "the first" and "the second". Men may speak of the Edenic Covenant; the Adamic Covenant; the Noahic Covenant; the Abrahamic Covenant; the Mosaic Covenant; the Palestinian Covenant; and the Davidic Covenant; but strictly speaking there are but two, the first and the second, the old and the new. The following verses expound in more detail upon these two covenants, and upon the better promises of a God who keeps saying, "I will ... I will ... I will".

2. A Better Covenant
8:7-13

v.7 "For if that first *covenant* had been faultless, then should no place have been sought for the second.

v.8 For finding fault with them, he saith, Behold, the days come, saith the Lord, when I will make a new covenant with the house of Israel and with the house of Judah:

v.9 Not according to the covenant that I made with their fathers in the day when I took them by the hand to lead them out of the land of Egypt; because they continued not in my covenant, and I regarded them not, saith the Lord.

v.10 For this *is* the covenant that I will make with the house of Israel after those days, saith the Lord; I will put my laws into their mind, and write them in their hearts: and I will be to them a God, and they shall be to me a people:

v.11 And they shall not teach every man his neighbour, and every man his brother, saying, Know the Lord: for all shall know me, from the least to the greatest.

v.12 For I will be merciful to their unrighteousness, and their sins and their iniquities will I remember no more.

v.13 In that he saith, A new *covenant,* he hath made the first old. Now that which decayeth and waxeth old *is* ready to vanish away."

7   The first covenant was not faultless. If it had been, there would have been no need for a second. But substantially and intrinsically there was nothing wrong with the covenant itself if men had had the moral strength to rise to its demands. The story of its inauguration is told in Exod 24. Moses and Aaron, with Nadab and Abihu and seventy of the elders of Israel, approached Jehovah, worshipping. While the others stayed afar off, Moses drew near, and as the mediator of that first covenant he represented God to the people and the people to God. He rehearsed to the people all the words of the Lord and all the judgments, and with one voice the people answered, at the foot of Mount Sinai, "All the words which the Lord hath said will we do". Moses wrote all the words, the terms of the covenant, and in the early morning he built an altar and raised up twelve pillars representing the twelve tribes. There were offerings; there were burnt offerings and peace offerings; blood was shed. Moses took half of the blood and put it in basons. The rest of the blood he sprinkled on the altar he had built. He then took what he had written, the book of the covenant, and read the terms in the audience of the people. Again they said, "All that the Lord hath said will we do, and be obedient". The mediator then took of the blood and sprinkled it on the people, calling it "the blood of the covenant". The representatives of the covenant people then ascended the mount; seventy-four men there were, nobles of Israel. And they saw the God of Israel. They saw God! They saw the glory like as of sapphire and crystal. The saw Him; they fellowshipped with Him. They did eat and drink. At the call of Jehovah, Moses and his minister Joshua,

rose up, and Moses went up higher into the Mount of God, as Sinai had now become. A cloud covered Mount Sinai, and the glory of the Lord abode upon it; a glory which the people below beheld as a devouring fire.

This was a glorious occasion indeed, but how thoughtlessly and rashly had the people cried, "All that the Lord hath spoken will we do". Centuries later Jesus expounded those words of the law very simply. There were, in essence, two commandments, He taught. The first demanded, "Thou shalt love the Lord thy God with all thy heart, and with all thy soul, and with all thy mind, and with all thy strength" (Mark 12:30). This was a serious demand. Had the people not realised that there were such solemn implications in the law? Yet this was not all. The second commandment had a certain similarity with the first. "Thou shalt love thy neighbour as thyself" (Mark 12:31). In one word, the law was demanding perfection. Here was the weakness; it was demanding what men could not give. Jehovah knew it. He would prove to them their inherent depravity and moral weakness, and their total inability to rise to perfection. The second tables of stone were put under a mercy seat. A priesthood was constituted, and a series of offerings, including sin offerings now. Provision was made for the guilt of a covenant people, who, in spite of all that they had promised at the mount, would often be disobedient.

What was wrong with a covenant which asked for perfection? Was there any fault in requiring such holiness as the law outlined in such detail? What could be wrong with a covenant that placed such high value upon moral integrity and implicit obedience? There was nothing wrong with the covenant itself, but, as Paul has reminded us, "It was weak through the flesh" (Rom 8:3). The human failing material with which it had to work could not give what the law was demanding. This was the fault. The terms were too exacting for fallen men with a sinful nature, and though it made demands which were right and proper and good, the law did not, and could not, give to the covenant people the moral strength to rise to the required perfection.

So the history of the people of the covenant is a sad history. They were disobedient. They rebelled. They murmured. They complained. They forgot God and forsook Him. They turned to idolatry and to the worship of Moloch and Baal and other gods. He chastised them. He pleaded with them. He judged them. They repented. There was often revival and recovery, only to be followed by renewed departure. The covenant had not changed them. It could not empower them to live for Jehovah's pleasure. He had brought them out of Egypt because He wanted a people who would serve Him and fellowship with Him, and worship Him. He brought them out and covenanted with them at Sinai. It was like a marriage. "We will", they said, but their history is a tale of unfaithfulness and infidelity. Indeed it was national adultery (Ezek 23:37; Matt 12:39). The covenant must be replaced with another; with a better; a new covenant was necessary.

8   From a very early stage every godly Jew must have known that the first covenant could not continue. Its ultimate demise was inevitable. It could not produce that which it demanded but only exposed the inherent sinfulness and weakness of man.

Jehovah Himself had found fault with "them". At first glance it may be imagined that the pronoun "them" has reference to the disobedient people. But the word is apparently in the neuter gender, which indicates "things" rather than "persons". Jehovah is here finding fault with the terms of that old covenant, with the details of the Sinaitic legislation, rather than with the people. In some sense, the terms of that covenant were not profound. In another sense they were most complex and difficult. Observe how they are rehearsed in Lev 26, "If ye walk in my statutes, and keep my commandments, and do them; then I will give you rain in due season, and the land shall yield her increase, and the trees of the field shall yield their fruit ... And I will give peace in the land ... and I will rid evil beasts out of the land ... and I will have respect unto you, and make you fruitful, and multiply you ... and I will set my tabernacle among you ... and I will walk among you, and be your God, and ye shall be my people".

How infinitely precious were these promises of blessing. But they were conditional upon obedience: "But if ye will not ... ": there was another side to be considered. Disobedience would bring with it the terrors of disease, sorrow, famine, subjugation, fear, weakness, plagues, desolation, death, pestilence, chastisement, dispersion, perdition (Lev 26:14-26). How literally has poor Israel experienced the truth of Lev 26. In the sorrows of successive pogroms she has learned that disobedience is a difficult pathway, a foolish pathway. It robs of blessing and brings only heartache and tears. The nation knows this, and the worst is yet to come before she enters nationally into the millennial blessings of the new covenant.

Jehovah then has found fault with the terms of the old covenant. Its blessings were dependent upon an obedience that the people could not render. Man's deceitful heart and sinful nature were barriers and prohibitions to the enjoyment of that which would be given in exchange for implicit obedience. "I will", said Jehovah, "if you will". It seemed so simple and straightforward, but the depravity and contrariness of the human heart made it all so complicated, and indeed, impossible. Jehovah decreed to replace the old covenant with a new.

Notice that in keeping with a pattern already observed, the writer will now quote from their OT Scriptures without identifying the source of his quotation. We have thought earlier that there were at least two reasons for this omission. Firstly, he was giving his readers credit, as Jews, for knowing their Scriptures. Did he really need to tell them that he was now quoting fron Jeremiah? Secondly, the human penman is not important. When he quotes the oracle and writes "saith the Lord", then it does not quite matter who the prophet or poet or psalmist is. It is the oracle of God. There may be yet a third reason for not identifying the source of the quotations, and that is to encourage and promote a desire to search. It would be good for those who did not know, or were not sure, to search for themselves and discover from where the citation was drawn.

So he now quotes four verses from Jer 31: "Behold, the days come, saith the Lord, when I will make a new covenant with the house of Israel and with the house of Judah" (Jer 31:31). The nation is viewed as a whole. The first covenant was made with Israel as such, and the second covenant will be also. This is not here developed. The writer is quoting Jeremiah for the purpose of showing that there was indeed to be a new covenant. It will be enacted formally with Israel in the millennium, but the details of that are not here necessary to the argument of the epistle.

The covenant will be established with the nation. It has been described as a principle of relationship with God on earth – conditions established by God under which man is to live with Him. Strictly speaking then, the gospel is not a covenant. It is the glad tidings of a salvation for guilty men. But we who believe the gospel are brought prematurely into the essential privileges of the new covenant, as will become more evident in the succeeding verses. Our salvation is based upon the shedding of that precious blood of Christ which is called in this epistle, "the blood of the covenant" (10:29; 13:20). Paul describes himself and his preaching colleagues as "competent ministers of a new covenant" (2 Cor 3:6). We have covenant blessings and covenant privileges. We have been brought, even now, into the joy of that for which Israel yet waits.

9   Jehovah now recalls again the bringing in of the first covenant. It is remembered in order to see afresh the superiority of the second, the new. There is something of a sad and tender rebuke in the remembrance of the circumstances in which the first covenant had been introduced. The people had been a nation of slaves. Egypt had become to them a house of bondage. By compulsion they had served Pharaoh. In humiliation they had made bricks for Pharaoh and had groaned under the whips of the taskmasters. They were a helpless subjugated people until Jehovah heard their cry and decreed to emancipate them. He gave them a deliverer in Moses. He gave them His faithful word, and by the blood of the lamb and the power of His arm He redeemed them. He destroyed their enemies. He brought them safely over the Red Sea and set them singing on course for Caanan. But how tenderly is all that described in this verse, "I took them by the hand to lead them out of the land of Egypt". The word "lead" is a shepherd word. It is the word of the Good Shepherd Himself in John 10:3 where He calls His own sheep by name and "leads" them out. It is the word used by Paul in speaking of the exodus in Acts 13:17: "The God of this people of Israel chose our fathers, and exalted the people when they dwelt as strangers in the land of Egypt, and with an high arm *brought* he them out of it". It is the word too, used of our Lord in Luke 24:50, "He led them out as far as to Bethany". They were His little flock. He led them. There is a quiet calm dignity and tenderness with the word.

So had Jehovah led Israel out of Egypt, taking them by the hand and bringing them, a redeemed people, to Sinai. What gratitude ought to have filled their hearts. How powerfully they ought to have been motivated by desire to be His people exclusively, to render due worship to Him alone, and to bring Him pleasure who had redeemed them. And, indeed, so it seemed at the mountain: "All that the Lord hath said will we do, and be obedient". Thus they entered into covenant relationship with Him who had shepherded them safely out of bondage. But the pledged obedience was not forthcoming. They were not true to their vows.

"They continued not", was the indictment, "and I regarded them not", was the judgment. The pronouns are emphatic. "They" did not ... and "I" did not. They did not continue. They did not stay in the terms and conditions of the covenant. They did not abide in a fulfilment of their profession of obedience. They had broken their vows made at the mount. The result was sad, "I did not regard them". Literally, "I disregarded them". The same word is translated "neglect" in 2:3. Jehovah did not care for them. They had spurned His care. They had rejected His advances of love and affection towards them, and, so spurned, He says, "I disregarded them". Jehovah had literally said, "I will, if you will". The people had answered, "We will". But they were not true to their promise and the covenant failed. How willing He had been; how unwilling they. The sadness and tragedy of it all was re-echoed centuries later by One who wept over their capital city and cried, "How often would I ... but ye would not" (Luke 13:34).

The thrust and purpose of this verse is to state again that the new covenant will not be like the old. It will not fail as did the first covenant. And again we hear the sure word, "saith the Lord".

10 With this verse the "better promises" of v.6 are introduced. The promises are seven-fold.

1. I will put my laws into their minds
2. And write them in their hearts
3. I will be to them a God
4. They shall be to me a people
5. All shall know me
6. I will be merciful to their unrighteousness
7. Their sins and their iniquities will I remember no more.

The word "covenant" is emphasised twice in this verse. Literally Jehovah says, "This is the covenant that I will covenant with them". Jeremiah had spoken of "days to come". These would be days of anguish and travail. They would be "the time of Jacob's trouble" (Jer 30:7). It would be "after those days" that Jehovah would covenant a covenant with His people. Israel will be saved, remnant-like, out of the tribulation of those days. The Sun of Righteousness will arise with healing in His wings for the troubled land. A new day will dawn for the reborn nation. Israel nationally will enter into that which presently we enjoy individually in Christ. The better promises will be made good to them as they are now to us.

"I will put my laws into their mind" imparts a spiritual intelligence of the desires of God for us. That which was once written legislatively on tablets of stone, is written, under the new covenant, in the mind of the saints. There is an instinctive, intuitive understanding of righteousness without any legislation. So will it be with Israel in those millennial days. So is it now with those who enjoy the blessings of the new covenant.

The promised knowledge of God's law is not just an academic knowledge. It is not just an intellectualism. It is indeed in the mind (*dianoia*), in the thinking, in the thought, but it is also in the heart: "And write them in their hearts". Israel had ever been encouraged to teach and learn and memorise God's laws (Deut 6:6-9). To this very day they bind them ceremonially on their arms and to their foreheads, and write them on the door-posts of their houses. But more than this is needed. To quote F.F.Bruce's helpful comment, "The original wording of Jer 31:33 is: I will put my *torah* within them. The Hebrew *torah* means more than statutory law; it embraces the ideas of guidance, direction, and instruction. The NT fulfilment of the promise is nowhere better expressed than in Paul's words in Rom 8:1 ff. of the work of the indwelling Spirit of God in the believer". In the mind, and in the heart: thus intelligence and devotion are wedded together in the children of the new covenant. Theirs is intelligent devotion and devoted intelligence, a knowledge of what is required and an affectionate desire to do it, and the gracious enabling of the indwelling Spirit to accomplish those spiritual desires.

In such happy circumstances this ancient promise of the old covenant, "I will be to them a God", now renewed, will be brought to fulfilment for Israel, as it is even now for us. Jehovah ever desired to be known as the God of His people, the God of Israel. In a special way He had been the God of certain noble individuals. He was the God of Abraham; the God of Isaac; the God of Jacob; the God of Shem; the God of Daniel; the God of Elijah. To the people of the new covenant He is:

1. the God of glory   (Acts 7:2)
2. the God of love   (2 Cor 13:11)
3. the God of patience   (Rom 15:5)
4. the God of comfort   (2 Cor 1:3)
5. the God of grace   (1 Pet 5:10)
6. the God of hope   (Rom 15:13)
7. the God of peace   (Rom 15:33)

But He is, supremely, the God and Father of our Lord Jesus Christ, and it is He, risen from the dead, who says to us, "My God, and your God" (John 20:17). The ancient promise is fulfilled, "I will be to them a God". So it is now (2 Cor 6:16), and so will it be in an eternal state (Rev 21:3).

Now if God is their God, then it follows that they should be His people. This brings upon us great privileges with great responsibility. His people! God's people! So does Paul use it to exhort the Corinthians to holy living (2 Cor 6:14-18). There were other gods. There were mere idols. These were ever associated with uncleanness, impurity, corruption, darkness. But with such the people of God can have no communion. Those whom He calls "my people" must be separate. "Wherefore", He saith, "come out from among them". Because you are "my people ... my sons ... my daughters", be ye separate saith the Lord. To receive the promises is to accept the obligations.

11   The next promise has a beautiful simplicity with it: "All shall know me". The law which was written in stone at Sinai is often referred to as "the Decalogue", the ten words, the ten commandments. These however were the basic tenets of a legal system which was very complex and intricate. There were multitudinous ceremonies and rituals which must be observed. The precepts were legion. They were so numerous that it could hardly have been expected that the common people could have intimate knowledge of every commandment. Yet the plea of ignorance was not acceptable. Even sins of ignorance, when they came to light, required offerings. To a certain extent conscience may have been a guide in matters of morality, but in things ceremonial even the most tender conscience could be no guide if there was not knowledge of the required ritual. It became necessary therefore that there should be men educated in, and familiar with, the law, who could teach, direct and guide others through the innumerable precepts which affected every sphere of private, domestic, family, and religious life. So arose the scribes and the rabbis, the teachers and interpreters of the law. Men were dependent upon them, and they upon each other, for a knowledge of the law which they were obliged to observe. A man might be morally right and yet ceremonially wrong for lack of knowledge of ritual law.

   Now the recognised leaders were not always helpful. They often complicated the already complex laws. They added to them. They bound heavy burdens on the people, grievous to be borne. As the copiers and preservers of the law they were necessary, if not indispensable. As interpreters of the law they were needful too, when they interpreted aright. Either way, the common people were dependent upon them, and upon fellow-citizens, neighbours and brothers, for a knowledge of the law and of the Lord. To know Jehovah in personal experience was perhaps a rare thing under the old covenant. Jehovah had indeed revealed Himself, and was known nationally, but individual and personal knowledge of the God of the Decalogue was a different matter. He was a thoughtful scribe who once said to Jesus, "Well, Master, ... there is one God; and there is none other but he: and to love him with all the heart, and with all the understanding, and with all the soul, and with all the strength, and to love his neighbour as himself, is more than all whole burnt offerings and sacrifices" (Mark 12:32-33). This was knowing the Lord.

   With the new covenant the complexities are gone. The rituals are a thing of the past. The law has been abrogated. Of the people of the new covenant it may be said, "All shall know me". They have become partakers of the divine nature. It is consistent with that nature to desire the things that He desires, so that the requirements of the law are lived out instinctively and without law, by those who enjoy the better promises of the new covenant. Without legislation they live as Jehovah ever intended and desired His people to live. And this is true of all of them, from the least to the greatest; from the oldest to the youngest; male or female; rich or poor; literate or illiterate; high or humble. Each and all are indwelt by that same Spirit who produces in their lives that for which the Decalogue was legislating. It is the fruit of the Spirit now. There is love, joy, peace, longsuffering, gentleness, goodness, faith, meekness, and temperance. These lovely features were all seen in Christ and are reproduced in those who love Him. Without law, under the new covenant, godliness is formed in their lives. They need not that any man teach them. They have an unction from the Holy One (1 John 2:20, 27).

12   There comes to us now that most delightful and precious of promises: "I will be merciful". W.E.Vine's expository definition of "mercy" (*eleos*) deserves to be quoted in full: "*Eleos* is the outward manifestation of pity; it assumes need on the part of him who receives it, and resources adequate to meet the need on the part of him who shows it. God is rich in mercy (Eph 2:4). Wherever the words mercy and peace are found together they occur in that order, except in Gal 6:16. Mercy is the act of God; peace is the resulting experience in the heart of man. Grace describes God's attitude toward the law-breaker and the rebel; mercy is His attitude toward those who are in distress".

It is interesting to note that the words are to be found in Exod 33:19, in association with the first covenant: "I will be gracious", says Jehovah, "and will shew mercy on whom I will shew mercy". The circumstances are very touching. Moses had come down the mount with the tables of the law. He had come down, with Joshua, to the noise of a people who had corrupted themselves in his absence. They were singing and dancing shamelessly, and worshipping a golden calf. The first and second commandments of the Decalogue were already broken. There was a judgment; there was a slaughter and three thousand men died. There followed a national mourning and a repentance as Moses mediated for the people. How early had they broken those vows that they had made. How soon had they become unfaithful. Yet it is even at this time that Jehovah affirms, "I will shew mercy". Moses ascended the mount again "And the Lord descended in the cloud, and stood with him there, and proclaimed the name of the Lord. And the Lord passed by before him, and proclaimed, The Lord, The Lord God, merciful and gracious" (Exod 34:5-6).

Well it was for Israel that the God of Israel was a God of mercy. How often, in the centuries that followed, did they have cause to lean on that mercy. Yet, though the mercy was real, and Jehovah bore with them, and went along with them, and there was a measure of forgiveness, there was no perfecting of the conscience under the old covenant. Sins accumulated. They were atoned for. They were covered. Days of Atonement came and went annually, but with the forgiveness they brought there was also a remembrance of sins. The new covenant has better promises.

"Their sins and their iniquities will I remember no more". Three word are used to describe the wrong-doings of the people. They are all plural words; unrighteousnesses; sins; iniquities. W.E.Vine distinguishes them and defines them as follows:

a.   Unrighteousnesses (*adikiais*): injustices; deeds violating law and justice.
b.   Sins (*hamartiōn*): literally, a missing of the mark.
c.   Iniquities (*anomiōn*): lawlessness; wickednesses.

Now it was a great weakness of the old covenant that it could not effectually deal with the problem of sin. It could, and did, define sin, and denounce it, but it had no power to restrain it, and no means of removing it. How welcome then is this assurance of the new covenant, "Their sins and their lawlessnesses I will never remember any more" (JND). The blood of Christ, which is now about to be mentioned seven times in the epistle (from 9:12), is the blood of the everlasting covenant. "The new covenant in my blood" the Saviour said on that last evening in the upper room (Luke 22:20 JND). It is the righteous basis upon which God can now remit sins. He can justify the guilty and yet remain just (Rom 3:26). He can pronounce the unrighteous man righteous because the unrighteousnesses have been thoroughly dealt with in the death of Christ. It is the promise of the new covenant that the sins thus dealt with are never remembered any more. "Never" is a strong, double negative: "I will never never remember"; "I will in no wise remember". This is a divine prerogative, to choose not to remember. Men may forget, but men cannot choose not to remember. Indeed a man's efforts to forget a matter may serve only to fix that matter more permanently in his memory. God does not forget. He chooses not to remember. Our sins are gone, and for ever! "I will never never remember any more".

These then, are the better promises of the new covenant. We bow in adoring wonder as we remember the cost of them. "Christ died for the ungodly" (Rom 5:6); He "bare our sins in his own body on the tree" (1 Pet 2:24); "He was wounded for our transgressions" (Isa 53:5); He "gave himself" (Gal 2:20). Well do we sing:

> All our sins were laid upon Him;
>   Jesus bore them on the tree;
> God, who knew them, laid them on Him;
>   And believing we are free.

13 It is a "new" covenant, and in that He says "new" He has made the first "old". The sentence of death and of obsolesence had been pronounced upon the first covenant even in the days of Jeremiah the prophet. Its weakness and inabilities were obvious even then, and already its days were numbered. It was to be superseded. The bringing in of a new covenant would make it antiquated, old, and obsolete. Who wants an obsolete covenant when there is a new one? Still the writer is endeavouring to draw his Hebrew readers away from any lingering attachment to Judaism. The old system is finished because it is old; it belongs to the past. There is a better thing in Christ. It was understandable, and they need our sympathetic appreciation of it, that these Hebrews, steeped in the aesthetic beauties of the old religion, should yet be prone to cling to it and hanker after it. There was a certain appeal in the ornate architecture, the ceremonies, the feasts and rituals, the music, the incense-laden atmosphere of the synagogues, the chanting, the vestments, and, of course, the temple itself. But it was "old" for it had been made so by the introduction of the new. And indeed these very outward attractions of Judaism were about to disappear. The shadows of AD70 were looming large when this epistle was written. The destruction of the city and the temple was now very near.

It must have been but a little while after the writing of the epistle that Jerusalem, in revolt against the Romans, was besieged by Titus and the Roman legions. It was a fearful and frightening time, recorded in awful and horrible detail by Josephus the historian: "It was a miserable case", he writes, "and a sight that would justly bring tears into our eyes". The conditions were almost indescribable. Famine and hunger reduced men and women to an animal state: "Children pulled the very morsels that their fathers were eating, out of their very mouths, and what was still more to be pitied, so did the mothers do as to their infants: and when those that were most dear to them were perishing under their hands, they were not ashamed to take from them the very last drops that might have preserved their lives ... Nor was there any commiseration shown either to the aged or to infants, but they lifted up children from the ground as they hung upon the morsels they had gotten, and shook them down upon the floor ... They also invented terrible methods of torment to discover where any food was ... and a man was forced to bear what it is terrible even to hear, in order to make him confess that he had but one loaf of bread, or a handful of barley meal".

"It is impossible to go distinctly over every instance of these men's iniquities", continues Josephus. Despite the pleas of Josephus, a Jew, and the sympathy of Titus himself, who called upon God to witness that this was not of his making, the siege continued. Every day saw hundreds of Jews fleeing the city and falling into the hands of the Romans. "It was a miserable procedure", says Josephus, "while they caught every day five hundred Jews; nay, some days more ... The soldiers, out of the wrath and hatred they bore the Jews, nailed those they caught, one after another, to the crosses, by way of jest; when their multitude was so great, that room was wanting for the crosses, and crosses wanting for the bodies".

It was a terrible answer to the prayer of those who had cried, "His blood be on us, and on our children" (Matt 27:25). It was an ironical sequel to the cry, "We have no king but Caesar" (John 19:15). "With that cry" says Edersheim, "Judaism committed suicide". Our Lord foresaw it all and wept over the city (Luke 19:41-44). Perhaps the writer to the Hebrews did not have detailed knowledge of the pending events, but he knew this, that the outward vestiges of Judaism were ready to vanish away. They would soon disappear in the destruction.

Josephus himself again pleaded with them in the Hebrew tongue, earnestly praying them to spare their own city, and to prevent that fire which was just ready to seize upon the temple. His words brought a great sadness and silence among the people as he called for repentance, to save the sanctuary and the sacrifices. He records how he spoke with groans, and with tears in his eyes, his voice interrupted with sobs.

The famine and the misery continued, with happenings that made even some of the hardened Roman soldiers pity the distress which the besieged Jews were under.

Eventually the fatal day was come. "It was the 10th day of the month Ab", records the historian, the very day upon which the first temple had been burned by the king of Babylon. "It was the revolution of the ages" says Josephus. "As for that house, God had for certain long ago doomed it to the fire". Titus would have saved the temple if he could, but one of his soldiers, without any orders, set fire to one of its golden windows. The conflagration spread rapidly. There was the utmost confusion and noise. The flame was also carried a long way, and made an echo, together with the groanings of those that were slain. Blood was larger in quantity than the fire. Those that were slain were more in number than those who slew them.

So was the holy house destroyed. It was the last vestige of an antiquated covenant. The inspired writer of the Epistle to the Hebrews had anticipated it as he wrote. The whole thing was waxing old and was ready to vanish away. To every thoughtful Jew this was a matter of great sadness. How tenderly and aptly does A.B.Bruce comment upon their situation. He writes, "Think of this, ye Hebrews, who cling to Levitical ordinances! See; the high priest's head is white with age; his limbs totter from feebleness; the boards of the tabernacle are rotten; the veil of the sanctuary is moth-eaten. Everything portends approaching dissolution. Let it die then, the hoary system, and receive from devout men decent burial. Shut not your eyes to the white hairs and tottering steps, fanatically striving to endow the venerable with immortality, embalming that which is already dead. Accept the inevitable, however painful, and find comfort in the thought that when the old passes away something new and better takes its place. It is sad to lose such a one as Simeon the just and devout; but why mourn for him when a Christ is born?"

So does this section of the epistle draw to a close, but the grand argument of Christ's superiority continues in the next chapter. Christ, who is a high priest of good things to come, has an abiding ministry in a greater and more perfect tabernacle. In the enjoyment of the better covenant and its better promises we may now enter where He has gone, with purged consciences and an acceptable service.

The holiest now we enter
    In perfect peace with God;
Regaining our lost centre
    Through Christ's atoning blood:
Though great may be our dulness
    In thought and word and deed,
We glory in the fulness
    Of Him who meets our need.

IX. A Better Tabernacle (9:1-28)

1. The Old Sanctuary
9:1-5

v.1 "Then verily the first *covenant* had also ordinances of divine service, and a worldly sanctuary.

v.2 For there was a tabernacle made; the first, wherein *was* the candlestick, and the table, and the shewbread; which is called the sanctuary.

v.3   And after the second veil, the tabernacle which is called the Holiest of all;
v.4   Which had the golden censer, and the ark of the covenant overlaid round
      about with gold, wherein *was* the golden pot that had manna, and
      Aaron's rod that budded, and the tables of the covenant;
v.5   And over it the cherubims of glory shadowing the mercy seat; of which
      we cannot now speak particularly."

1   The grand theme of superiority is a consistent one in this epistle. Whether it be the superiority of the Son, or of the Priest, or of the promises, or the covenant, or the sanctuary, or the sacrifice, it is always superiority, and the same theme continues now.

"Then verily the first covenant had ordinances of divine service, and a worldly sanctuary", so reads the AV, but several words in this rendering require comment.

The particle "verily" is not quite the familiar "verily" of the Gospels. It is similar however, and is the same as that translated "surely" in 6:14. The RV rendering will suggest that it is "even" so, and J.N.Darby will translate the word "indeed", and reinforce it with the word "therefore"; Thomas Newberry's *Interlinear New Testament* will render it similarly. Whichever way we may render it, the intended meaning is that there can be no doubt about the truth of what he is going to say; they all knew it; it is not questioned.

The word "covenant" though not in the Greek text, as all agree, has been supplied by translators (AV, RV, but not JND). "The first had ordinances of divine service" is the literal translation. The first what? Most are happy to understand that it is the first covenant that is intended, and so the supply of that word to make intelligent English reading.

Dikaiōmata ("ordinances") is an interesting word, found again in v.10 of this chapter. It is cognate with *righteousness* and *justification*. It signifies regulations which ensure that all is done properly and righteously. Such were the regulations governing the rituals of the old covenant services and ceremonies. There were just requirements which had to be observed. The "service" which was thus regulated was the *latreia*, a word found again in a plural form in v.6, and again in v.14. We have already commented upon this word in 8:5. It is the priestly word which describes the service of the tabernacle.

The word "divine" has no direct equivalent in the original text. The translators who use it (AV, RV), have appended it to the word "service" to indicate to us that this was service connected with holy things and the Holy Place. It was not just ordinary service; it was service of the sanctuary. Hence, "divine service" is most expressive.

Now the first covenant had, with this divine service, a sanctuary, a worldly one. That is to say, the sanctuary was "of this world". We have become accustomed to using the word "worldly" in a bad sense, as we use the word "carnal". This, of course, is not what is intended here. The old sanctuary belonged to this world in that it was material and tangible, and therefore temporal. Belonging to this world stamped a kind of earthly transience upon it. It was not an abiding structure at all. Notice that it is the wilderness tabernacle about which the writer always speaks in this epistle, and not the temple. But the same thing might well have been written of the temples, whether Solomon's temple, or Zerubbabel's, which was later known as Herod's. With all their grandeur of architecture and magnificence and costliness, they were still "of this world" just like the tent in the wilderness. They were not to remain. They may have looked more permanent than the tabernacle. They may have seemed more durable and lasting, but the fact remained that they belonged to this world and were therefore destined to pass away. A.B.Bruce renders the expression "a mundane sanctuary". This may not appear to be a very complimentary way of speaking of the tabernacle in the wilderness but it is most expressive. The word "mundane" means earthly, banal, or ordinary, and that is basically what the old tabernacle was in itself. Its wealth and richness of typical teaching was another thing, but in itself it was quite an ordinary tent belonging to this material world. It was material indeed, and therefore perishable.

2   Now there were, in that old tabernacle structure, three compartments, the first of which, the outer court, is not involved in the current discussion. The tent itself was divided into two chambers or compartments. Entrance to both of these was through a veil. The first veil barred the way for most mortals into the first chamber which was known as the Holy Place. Priests alone entered there. The second veil, to which we usually refer when we speak of the Veil, was the dividing curtain between the Holy Place and the Most Holy, often called, properly, "the Holy of Holies" or "the Holiest of all". Only the high priest entered here. This same general plan was preserved with the building of the temples which succeeded the tabernacle. Although they were much more ornate and elaborate and had several outer courts for priests and Levites and women and Gentiles, yet the house itself consisted of a Holy Place and a Most Holy.

So, says the writer, a tabernacle was set up. He is looking back beyond the temple period to the tabernacle in the wilderness. A tent was prepared for the divine service to which he has alluded.

The writer will soon tell us that he cannot now, at this point, speak particularly or in detail about the holy vessels and furniture which belonged respectively to these holy places. In keeping with this we must therefore ourselves curtail any present comment upon them, interesting as this would be. Some commentary, however, is necessary.

The outer compartment, the Holy Place, measured twenty cubits long by ten cubits wide. Assuming the cubit at twenty-one inches then the Holy Place was a chamber some thirty five feet long by seventeen and a half feet wide approximately. The Holy of Holies was a perfect cube, measuring ten cubits long, ten cubits wide, and ten cubits high. These two holy places were divided, as we have seen, by a beautiful curtain of blue, purple and scarlet upon fine twined linen skilfully adorned with embroidered cherubim. This curtain we call the Veil.

The passage before us in this chapter is initially concerned with the furniture of the Holy Place, the foremost of the two compartments, referred to simply as "the first". In this compartment, the writer reminds us, there was, first of all, the candlestick. A better translation is "lampstand". It is the same word *luchnia* as that used to describe the seven assemblies in Rev 2, 3. No measurements are given of the lampstand. We know only that it was beaten out of a talent of pure gold. Indeed, all the articles of furniture in the Holy Places had gold about them. The golden lampstand must have been beautiful, with three branches springing out of each side of a central stem. Each of these, central stem and branches alike, held a lamp; seven lamps in all. If it were our present study we would see this as a lovely type of Christ as the Light of the sanctuary, not here "light of the world" as the Saviour presented Himself in John's Gospel (8:12; 9:5). He was that as long as He was in the world. Now He has gone. The world is in moral darkness now, though believers shine in it (Matt 5:14-16; Phil 2:15). The Lord Jesus is now the Light of the sanctuary.

The table was golden also. It was not of solid gold as was the lampstand, but was constructed of acacia wood and overlaid with gold. This typically is the Christ in whom God and His people fellowship with satisfaction and delight. The table is ever a symbol of fellowship and upon this table were displayed constantly the twelve cakes known as "the shewbread". Darby calls it "the exposition of the loaves". The table measured two cubits long, one cubit wide, and one and a half cubits high. The twelve loaves were literally "bread of the face", or "bread of the presence", or "bread set in order". The thought intended is that the bread was ever in the presence of God, set in order before the face of God. It was holy bread, to be eaten only by the priests in the holy place. The loaves were replaced every Sabbath day by fresh loaves baked of fine wheaten flour. They were displayed before God in two rows with pure frankincense upon each row. So were they freshly arranged every Sabbath and the old cakes became the food of the priests. Such is Christ to us. He in whom the wood and gold of true manhood and very Godhood are combined, is the One in whom both God and saints find mutual satisfaction. He is, in truth, the "bread of God" (John 6:33).

This chamber or compartment containing the lampstand and the table was called the sanctuary (AV). It is, quite literally, called "Holy". The RV will render it "the Holy Place". There now arises somewhat of a problem, the resolution of which will determine our understanding of yet another problem which presents itself in v.4. The present difficulty is that the writer appears to have concluded his inventory of the furniture of the Holy Place and yet he has not mentioned the golden altar of incense. This was, of course, a most important piece of the furniture of the Holy Place and it is almost inconceivable that the writer should not make reference to it. But as we have intimated, the matter will arise again in the interesting problem of v.4.

3   The curtain or screen which divided between the Holy Place and the Most Holy is here referred to as "the second veil". It is that curtain to which we usually refer when we speak simply of "the veil". There were however two veils. The first veil was of blue and purple and scarlet and fine linen embroidered as damask. It was artistic and beautiful. It hung at the entrance to the first compartment of the tabernacle. The

second veil was similarly of blue and purple and scarlet and fine twined linen, but it had the additional beauty of cherubim embroidered upon it. It hung, suspended upon four pillars of acacia wood which were overlaid with gold. They had hooks of gold and they stood upon four bases of silver. This curtain, or veil, or screen, was distinctly said to be for "a division to you between the holy place and the holiest of all" (Exod 26:31-33 JND). J.N.Darby comments that literally this is, "holiness of holinesses". It was indeed the Most Holy. Only but a few privileged men, in high priestly ministry, were ever permitted to pass beyond the second veil into the inner holiness, and then only once every year.

4   These opening words of v.4, "which had the golden censer", present us with the first real difficulty in this chapter. The writer is now enumerating the articles which belonged to the Holy of Holies, and if "golden censer" is the correct rendering there are a number of problems.

Firstly, we never read of a golden censer in those chapters which deal with the construction of the tabernacle in the wilderness. Nor indeed is there, anywhere in the Pentateuch, any mention of a golden censer. That there may have been such a vessel in later years is a possibility, but there is certainly no such vessel referred to in any of the five Books of Moses.

Secondly, if this means, literally, a golden censer, then why is there here no mention at all of the golden altar of incense? It must surely seem strange that reference should be made in this important passage to every other piece of furniture in the Holy Places but no reference to the golden altar.

Thirdly, if this supposed golden censer was kept in the Holy of Holies, behind the veil, then how, and when, did the high priest retrieve it for his use, since his first entrance into the Holiest on the Day of Atonement was with burning incense (Lev 16:12-13)? He dare not enter otherwise, "that he die not".

These problems may be resolved by a careful look at the word translated "censer", and by making a change in this translation, but it must then be acknowledged that other problems arise. The word for censer (*thumiatērion*) means, literally, a vessel for burning incense. Now it will be at once observed that this does not necessarily imply or demand a "censer", but could be a direct reference to the golden altar, which was, of course, a vessel for burning incense. This is the rendering preferred in the RV margin, and also in the text of the ARV, and RSV, and others. If "golden altar of incense" is the correct rendering, then the problems now are two-fold.

Firstly, it is argued that the word *thumiatērion* is never used by the LXX to indicate the incense altar. This is so, but does not mean that the word cannot so be used. F.F.Bruce and others will point out that both Josephus and Philo use the word in this sense, describing the golden altar. It must be conceded that the word simply indicates a vessel for burning incense, as we have already remarked, and this description adequately suits the golden altar.

Secondly, we have the difficulty that this golden altar of incense did not actually stand in the Holiest, but in the Holy Place, before the veil, whereas the AV text appears to suggest that the vessel under consideration was in fact in the Holiest. We will not of course, stand in the company of those modernists who charge the writer to the Hebrews with having made a mistake in locating the golden altar within, rather than without, the second veil. There can be no such mistake entertained by those who accept the plenary inspiration of Holy Scripture. It is too, a slur upon the accuracy and knowledge and integrity of the unknown author of the epistle. There is no mistake.

Notice carefully the words "which had", at the beginning of this verse. Note that they are not the same as the words which introduce the Holy Place with its furniture in v.2. There we read, "wherein" was the candlestick, and the table. But here it is not "wherein". It is "which had", or, "to which belonged". The writer is not saying that this vessel stayed in the Holy of Holies. He is not saying that it was located there, or that it was kept there. What he says is that it belonged there. This is a different thing. The phrase belongs peculiarly to the golden altar among the other items in the Holy Place. It had a ministry which belonged to the Holiest. The altar itself may indeed have been located outside the veil, but its fragrant ministry belonged inside. There was a special relation between the incense-altar and the Holy of Holies. It is distincly called in 1 Kings 6:22 "the altar that belonged to the inner shrine" (see RV and RSV). Indeed it may be said that the golden altar belonged to the Holy of Holies as much as did the holy ark with which it is now associated.

The ark is here called "the ark of the covenant". Its full title is "the ark of the covenant of the Lord". Sometimes this was abbreviated to "the ark of the Lord". Sometimes it was "the ark of the covenant". See the title in full, with the two different abbreviations, all variously used in Josh 6. But is is fitting here, in such an epistle, to such a people, and at such a point in the epistle, that it should be "the ark of the covenant". We are reminded that the ark was overlaid round about with gold. How have teachers, preachers and expositors revelled in the gold and wood of the tabernacle. The holy ark, made of the incorruptible wood, was encased in the most precious gold. It is not difficult to see, in symbol, the holy humanity and the very deity of Him of whom the ark was but a foreshadowing. Chs. 1, 2 of this very epistle are the gold and the wood respectively, of Christ's Godhood and manhood. But the writer will not indulge in interpretation of the sacred symbols. He proceeds to the contents of the ark.

There were, at the beginning, three items contained within the ark. There were the golden pot of manna, Aaron's rod that had miraculously budded and the two tables of stone on which were written the commandments. No one now knows what ever happened to the ark. It is never heard of after the destruction of the first temple by the Babylonians in 587 BC. There are legends and stories and rumours, but no one knows. Some rabbis in Jerusalem cherish the hope that it might be concealed somewhere in the temple area, under the temple mount, where there are numerous alleys, corridors, and rooms, deep in the debris of the centuries. No one knows. Not only has the ark disappeared from view but even when it was placed in Solomon's temple as early as 1 Kings 8:9 there was nothing in it save the two tables of stone.

There is something interestingly beautiful about the three items which were at the first contained within the holy ark. They were, at one and same time, memorials of Israel's national sins, and yet foreshadowings of the blessed One who was to come to make an end of sins.

The golden pot holding the manna was a constant reminder of Jehovah's gracious provision for His people in the wilderness. It must also have been a reminder of the murmurings of that people. They murmured after the flesh and food of Egypt. How soon did they forget the sorrows, the whips, the taskmasters, the bondage, and they lusted after the Egyptian flesh-pots. God gave them manna. It was white and sweet, like cake with honey (Exod 16:31). It was freely available in plenteous supply, fresh every day for everyone. But soon they murmured again. "Our soul loatheth this light bread" they complained. Jehovah was wroth with them. They complained of that which foreshadowed Christ, so He sent fiery serpents among them in judgment. It was this manna which was laid up in a golden pot in the ark. If the people did not appreciate it, Jehovah did. It spoke of the coming One, the Bread of God. It was, at one and the same time, a memorial of their sin and yet the promise of the Christ.

Aaron's rod that budded had similar connotations. They had murmured again. This time it was complaint against Moses and Aaron. Korah, Dathan, and Abiram led a jealous revolt against the men whom God had appointed to be leaders of the people. The rebellion ended in a fearful judgment. Many died. The whole story is recorded in Num 16. It was a national tragedy. Jehovah then decreed a divine public approval of the men whom He had ordained. Twelve rods or staves were laid up overnight before Him, each bearing the name of the head of a house of Israel. On the morrow, Aaron's staff, the rod for the house of Levi, had miraculously brought forth, not only buds and blossoms, but ripened almonds too. It is a story of vindication by what was the miracle of new life. So was this rod contained also in the holy ark. It was a testimony to their sin. It was the vindication of the Lord's anointed. It was a fitting emblem too of the Christ who was to come. He too would be rejected of the nation but approved by His resurrection from among the dead. A risen Man in glory was foreshadowed in Aaron's rod.

The tables of the covenant were also there in the ark. Here too was a monument to their oft sinning and backsliding. Had they not broken the first two of those laws even before they reached them (Exod. 32). They had preferred other gods. They had made and worshipped a golden calf. Jehovah's anger burned, and Moses' anger burned too (vv.10,19). Moses had cast down the two tables of the law and shattered them beneath the mountain. Later, God provided replacement tables, and these are they which were contained in the ark. One Man alone would live in the perfect fulfilment of this law. The blessed man of Ps 1 is ultimately Christ. He alone of all men, kept the law in its every detail. He alone loved the Lord His God with His whole being, and His neighbour as Himself. The law waited for Him.

Here then, in these three items, were the symbols of divine provision, divine approval, and divine pleasure, all in Christ.

5   Above the ark, and over it, were the cherubim of glory. They were formed out
of one piece of pure gold with the lid of the ark which was called the mercy seat. Here
at the mercy seat Jehovah would meet with men, but the way was ever guarded by
the cherubim. They stood at either end of the golden mercy seat. They looked
towards each other and towards the ark, and with outspread wings they stood
protectively in the Holiest of all.

The cherubim are first mentioned in Scripture in Gen 3:24. There they were
placed at the gate of the garden of Eden eastward, to keep the way of the tree of life.
This first mention gives us help as to what we should look for in later references.
They are guardians of God's righteous character. God had driven the sinning man out
of Eden. It is as if the cherubim would say Amen, God was perfectly righteous in
driving out the man. The cherubim would guard the way back and vindicate God in
His action. This is their ministry ever afterwards. And so it is in the Holy of Holies.
They will keep the way, looking, as it were, for the prescribed blood upon the mercy
seat if man would dare to draw near. But there is now a real Man in the glory, on the
throne. He has gone up and gone in and sat down, and if the living ones of Rev 5
may be equated with the cherubim, then all they have to say is Amen! (Rev 5:14).
They are satisfied, who are the guardians of Jehovah's righteousness. A Man has gone
in and they acquiesce. The Man has rights to go where He has gone. Indeed He is
there by divine invitation.

However, perhaps we transgress by staying here with details. For the writer himself
says that this is not quite the time to speak particularly or in detail about these same
matters. His main thought is to impress upon his readers the fact of a veil which
barred men out. There was a Holy Place, and there was a Holy of Holies, and as long
as the veil hung between, the way into that Holiest was not open for men in general.
We do however learn this from his comments, that at some other time it would
indeed be both proper and profitable to examine the detail. By his stating that this
is not now the time to do so, he is surely implying that at some other time it would
be right. At such a time we ought to find the mind of the Spirit in the particulars
concerning the furniture and vessels of that ancient tabernacle in the wilderness.

2.   *The Old Ritual*
      9:6-10

v.6   "Now when these things were thus ordained, the priests went always
      into the first tabernacle, accomplishing the service *of God.*

v.7   But into the second *went* the high priest alone once every year, not
      without blood, which he offered for himself, and *for* the errors of the
      pecple:

v.8   The Holy Ghost this signifying, that the way into the holiest of all was not
      yet made manifest, while as the first tabernacle was yet standing:

v.9   Which *was* a figure for the time then present, in which were offered both
      gifts and sacrifices, that could not make him that did the service perfect,
      as pertaining to the conscience;

v.10   *Which stood* only in meats and drinks, and divers washings, and carnal
ordinances, imposed *on them* until the time of reformation."

6   Now when everything had been so prepared and ordered, as described in vv.1-
5, the priests in general moved continually, at all times, into the Holy Place, called
here, the first tabernacle. There was a constant ministry to be performed in the Holy
Place, the outer compartment. Indeed the word "service" as in the AV, should be
"services". It is the word *latreia* as in v.1, except that here it is in the plural, for the
priestly ministrations in this Holy Place were many and varied.

These were the principal services of the priests who ministered in the outer
compartment. Every day, morning and evening, the lamps of the lampstand had to
be trimmed and the oil had to be replenished. Every day also, there was a burning of
incense on the golden altar. Regularly the blood of sin offerings had to be sprinkled
before the veil. There were morning and evening oblations and there were also
individual offerings. Every week the loaves of showbread had to be removed from the
golden table and replaced with fresh loaves.

Everything was ordered and orderly, and in view of the fact that there were many
thousands of priests in Israel in later days, it was indeed a priestly privilege to be
allowed to minister in the Holy Place. Edersheim, quoting Josephus, reminds us that
in our Lord's day there must have been some twenty thousand officiating priests. It
was therefore not physically possible for all of these to be engaged at once in the
ministry. The priesthood was divided into twenty-four courses, but neither was it
possible for even one course of priests to be engaged in ministry all at the same time.
Lots were cast, and so, by lot, the ministrations were allocated. It was likely that a
priest might have the holy privilege of burning incense at the golden altar only once
in his lifetime. (Read the story of Zacharias in Luke 1:9.)

This then was a limited privilege. There was no unhindered liberty of access while
the veil hung and the first tabernacle was still standing. The writer, while showing
the beauty of the old system, is nevertheless showing also its great limitations. He is
here preparing the way for yet another exposition of the greater things which his
readers had in Christ.

7   But even the most privileged of the priesthood in general were barred from the
Holy of Holies. All their ministry was accomplished on the outer side of the veil.
Only one man was permitted beyond that veil where the Shechinah glory was. That
one privileged man entered only once every year, his one entry being on one special
day, and in a particular prescribed manner.

That man was, of course, the high priest. There were those thousands of priests
that we have mentioned, among them chief priests, leading figures in the twenty-four
courses of priesthood. But there was, at any one time, but one high priest, and to him
alone was granted the awesome privilege of entering behind and beyond the veil into
the Holiest.

His entrance into that Most Holy Place was on the Day of Atonement, the tenth day of the seventh month of every year. It was perhaps the most solemn day in Israel's calendar. The whole story of the Day of Atonement is told in Lev 16, the day known among Jews as *Yom Kippur*.

There was a three-fold entrance into the Holiest on that great day, every movement and detail of which must conform to the divine regulations for the occasion.

Firstly, dressed, not in his gorgeous robes of glory and beauty, but in garments of white linen, the high priest entered with incense. He would have carried a censer of burning coals and the incense burning upon these coals produced a fragrant cloud which both enveloped the man and filled the place. This cloud would have shrouded the Shechinah. It was a sweet symbol of the fragrance of that lovely life that was to come with the incarnation of the Son of God. In all the loveliness of His moral glory Jesus has entered in. The perfections of His spotless stainless life and character afford Him the moral right to enter in on our behalf.

The mercy seat having been thus covered with the cloud of incense, the high priest now entered the Holiest a second time. This time he went in with blood, the blood of the bullock, a sin offering for himself and for his house. The Jewish high priest was a privileged man, but he was a sinful man nonetheless, and was required to bring an appropriate offering for himself and his family. He sprinkled the blood of the sin offering upon and before the mercy seat. Once upon the mercy seat, and seven times before it, was the blood sprinkled, so making safe his presence in that inner shrine where holiness dwelt in glory (Lev 16:14).

Having now assured for himself, by incense and by blood, a standing in the Holiest, the high priest entered again, a third time, as a representative man. This time he brought the blood of the goat of the sin offering for the people. There would be, of course, a scapegoat also (Lev 16:8), but the writer to the Hebrews is concerned just now only with the ministry of the sanctuary. He is not particularly expounding the ritual and typology of the Day of Atonement, but rather dealing with the purpose and functions of the veil and the Holy of Holies. The blood of the goat was likewise sprinkled upon and before the mercy seat.

Aaron and succeeding high priests therefore offered both for themselves and for the people. But it is the delight of every lover of Christ to remember that the blessed Man who is our representative and great high priest, needed not to offer for Himself. Aaron was preparing himself to be typically what Jesus was intrinsically. He, whose whole life was fragrant to God, needed no sacrifice for Himself. In all the perfection of His moral glory He went in for us, to offer on our behalf. And when He offered, He offered Himself. The blood which is the basis of our forgiveness and our acceptance is His own blood.

Notice the interesting word "alone": "the high priest alone". There is a dual thought. It may mean simply "the high priest only", signifying that he exclusively, alone among the priests, was privileged to enter the Holiest. It was a singular, solitary dignity to be permitted to enter beyond the veil. But there is another significance. He entered "alone". There was indeed a solemn loneliness with this ministry. How often is the word used of the Lord Jesus:

1. He was "alone" in His supplications. He went up into a mountain apart to pray, and He was there "alone" (Matt 14:23).

2. He was "alone" in His service. Patiently, faithfully, He taught the people, and when He was "alone" they asked Him of His teaching (Mark 4:10).

3. He was "alone" in the glory of His sonship. On the holy mount the voice proclaimed "My beloved Son". and when the voice was past, Jesus was found "alone" (Luke 9:36).

4. He was "alone" in His Messiahship. It was when He was "alone" praying that He asked them, "Whom say ye that I am?" Peter answering said, "The Christ of God" (Luke 9:18-20).

5. He was "alone" in His sufferings. Did He not tell them on that last evening, "Ye shall leave me *alone* (John 16:32)?

There was indeed, during His ministry, a certain solitariness, an aloneness. Well do we remember this as we read, "the high priest alone".

8   Now in all of this the Holy Spirit was signifying a most important matter. He was teaching a most salutary lesson: the way into the Holiest was barred. Veils and altars, incense and blood, bullocks and goats, were His divinely-chosen symbols to teach us that access to the divine presence, however desirable, was not freely available for sinful men. The veil hung, prohibitively, between God and men. Beyond the veil was the glory, the Shechinah, the Holiness. This side of the veil men stood in the guilt of their shortcomings and sins. It mattered not if these were sins of ignorance, as the word "errors" of v.7 seems to imply. They were sins nevertheless, and sins committed unwittingly and in ignorance only served to reveal the terrible fallen condition of human nature and the depravity of the human heart. Such sinfulness could not be permitted into the awful presence. The veil with all its beauty was a barrier.

Note the word "signifying" (from the verb *dēloō*). It means, to make plain; to make evident; to declare; to show. Some have questioned the importance and value, and indeed the validity, of typology. If ever we needed assurance of the spiritual value of the typical Scriptures, this chapter gives it. The tabernacle design and structure, the vessels and furniture, the altars and the ark, the lampstand and the table, have all a certain significance. They all serve to teach us some lesson. But particularly here is the writer dealing with the dividing veil. The hanging veil created two compartments. It closed off the Holy of Holies where Jehovah dwelt, at least in the symbol Shechinah, between the cherubim. To be in His presence, and to enjoy it, would be the ultimate experience for every mortal: "In thy presence is fulness of joy" (Ps 16:11). But man's sinfulness made the desirable impossible, and the veil which closed Jehovah in, closed man out. As long as the veil hung there was a "first" and "second" compartment;

access was impeded. "The way of the Holies" would be a literal translation of this middle phrase of v.8. The way of the Holies was not yet made manifest in such circumstances.

Notice that it is the Holy Spirit who is thus signifying this solemn truth. Not only is He the author of these inspired words to the Hebrews, but it was He who inspired the men who constructed that early tabernacle in the wilderness. "I have called Bezaleel" said Jehovah, "and I have filled him with the Spirit of God" (Exod 31:2-3). To Bezaleel was imparted, by the Spirit, wisdom, understanding, knowledge, skill, and a versatility of workmanship in gold and silver, in brass and stone, and in timber. This chosen workman was divinely equipped by the Spirit of God, who, in all the work, was preparing a typical house. He was "signifying" something. He would teach us lessons. In all the beauty and intricacy of that early tabernacle with its furnishings and rituals and services, He would teach us about God and about Christ, and about ourselves. Well does the writer to the Hebrews assure us that it is "the Holy Ghost" who is thus signifying these lessons of the tabernacle.

The particular lesson here then, is that as long as that veil was hanging the outer compartment, the first tabernacle, was still standing, and the way of the Holies had not been made clear. Jehovah dwells, hidden behind the veil. Man dwells, in his sinful condition, outside. Complete communion with God was not yet granted while the veil was hanging and that first tabernacle still had a standing.

9   The argument continues. The writer now uses a most interesting word to describe the purpose of the tabernacle, both the structure and the system. He says that it was "a parable", the word here translated "figure" in our AV. "Parable" (*parabolē*) is a word comprised of two words, a preposition and a verb: the preposition *para*, meaning "alongside"; the verb *ballō*, meaning "to throw". *Parabolē* therefore indicates a throwing of one thing beside another, perhaps with a view to comparison. That early definition of our childhood days is perhaps hard to improve upon: "A parable is an earthly story with a heavenly meaning". Divine truths are placed alongside familiar earthly circumstances, with the purpose of making them intelligible to our limited human understanding. Such was the tabernacle in the wilderness – a parable. It was a parable, not in words but in fabrics. Its wood and gold, its silver and brass, its curtains and coverings, its rites and ceremonies, all combined to provide a grand object lesson. The whole thing was a parable.

We now meet with a textual problem. There is a certain ambiguity which cannot be resolved with any dogmatism. It will suffice to point it out and to give the varied thoughts of scholarly and saintly translators and expositors, and to leave the reader to judge. Both ways of understanding the expression in question are valuable. It is a matter of what is intended in the context.

The problem relates to the phrase "a figure for the time then present" (AV). Now it must be conceded that the AV translators have supplied the word "then"; it is additional to the text. The literal reading would appear to be "a figure for the time present". Is this the time "then" present, as in the AV, or is it the time "now" present, as preferred, for instance, by J.N.Darby who translates it "an image for the present time"? The ambiguity is acknowledged by all. Is it "the time then present" or "the time now present"? The difference is not fundamental.

If the former rendering is preferred, following the AV, "a figure for the time then present", then the writer is saying that the tabernacle with its dividing veil was a parable for the people of that time, indicating to them the inaccessibility of the Holiest. Its primary teaching for them was that there was a barrier between God and men. Free access and the joy of perfect communion with Jehovah was not possible. For them, this was the meaning of the parable, that the way of the Holies was barred.

If, however, the alternative rendering is accepted, then there is a different shade of meaning. If the writer is envisaging a parable for the time "now" present, i.e. the present time, then his thought is this, that the full meaning of the tabernacle can be properly understood only by those who are now in the enjoyment of the work of Christ.

If this "present time" be accepted as the true import, then Wm. Kelly is worth quoting. He encourages us to observe that it is the tabernacle in the wilderness which is before the writer, and not the temple. The tabernacle, he points out, "differed in some essential respects from the temple, for it (the temple) was the figure of the millennial kingdom and rest, as the tabernacle is of the resources of grace in Christ for the wildernesss and its pilgrimage. Hence the ark when set in the temple had neither the golden pot with manna therein, nor Aaron's rod that budded (2 Chron 5:10) which we find carefully named here in v.4." So, if it be the present time which is in view, it is this emphatically, the time "now" present, and not including the age to come.

Perhaps indeed this latter rendering is to be preferred, but it must be repeated and emphasised that great and good men have differed, and, in the end, both views are possible. The tabernacle was a parable for the time then present, teaching that the way into the Holiest was then barred; it is too, a parable for the present time, being to us a foreshadowing of the Person and work of Christ who for us has made access to the Holiest a possibility and reality.

In this tabernacle, as we have already seen, there were offered both gifts and sacrifices. These have been commented upon in 5:1 and 8:3. The point of their mention here is to indicate again the weakness and the limitations of that which was indeed a parable, but only a parable, the figure of better things to come in Christ. These ministries could not make the minister perfect as to his conscience. There might be a measure of approach to God, there might be a priestly approach which could be termed "worship", but confident approach with a perfectly clear conscience was not possible. The annual Day of Atonement, while dealing with sins nationally, in fact produced an annual remembrance of sins. The gifts and sacrifices were in keeping with the parabolic character of the tabernacle. They were provisional and temporary. They were figures of that which was to come, but they themselves could not give the perfect conscience which is a prerequisite to true worship and to real communion with Jehovah.

10 The "gifts and sacrifices" are now further developed and enlarged upon. They consisted of meats and drinks, divers washings, and carnal ordinances.

"Meats and drinks" were meat offerings and drink offerings. Certain offerings were the food of the altar. Some were also the food of the priests. Drink offerings were poured upon the offerings. All was parabolic and figurative. There was no other value in these offerings apart from a typical value. They spoke of Christ, of what He was and of what He would do. Some think that there may also be a reference to the food-laws of Lev 11.

For both priests and people there were endless ceremonials with regard to purification, "divers washings". The priests were familiar with the laver (Exod 30:17-21). It was required of them that they must wash and be clean for their ministrations. The people, though not washing at the laver, were also required to be ceremonially clean. Note the waterpots at the wedding at Cana, "set there after the manner of the purifying of the Jews" (John 2:6).

"Carnal ordinances" are literally ordinances of the flesh. Leviticus abounds with the most detailed instructions regarding ordinances. These were all "fleshly". They were divinely ordered and there were hygienic reasons for them, but they were not spiritual. They had to be observed but they did not help towards the perfecting of the conscience. Such perfection was not possible under the old economy.

These ordinances were imposed for a specific time. The word "imposed" denotes that they were "laid upon" the people. So is the word translated in John 11:38. Concerning the tomb of Lazarus it is said that a stone "lay upon" it. Jehovah had laid upon the people a system of laws and ordinances. It was incumbent upon the people that they observe these, but they were really a burden, bringing no peace to a troubled conscience.

They were imposed until the time of reformation, this is the present era, the time of setting things right with the coming of Christ. The imposition of fleshly ordinances was a temporary measure, awaiting the advent of the Messiah who would make all things anew. It is the time of reconstruction for every believing Jew. Wm Kelly says, "Ordinances of flesh imposed until a time of rectifying". A.B.Bruce, thinking similarly says, "The expression 'time of reformation' is one of several names given to the new christian era from an OT point of view. For those who lived under the moonlight of Jewish ordinances, conscious of its insufficiency, waited eagerly for the dawn of day; that era, the object of their hope, was the age to come, the time of a better hope, the time of refreshing, the day of redemption, or, as here, the time of rectification. This last designation, if not the most poetical, is very appropriate. For when Christ, the high priest of good things to come, arrived, all defects inherent in that ancient system were remedied. The veil was removed; the multitude of ineffectual sacrificial rites was replaced by one all-availing sacrifice; the problem of pacifying the conscience was thoroughly dealt with". It would not any more be "an affair of mechanical routine, but a rational spiritual service".

3. *The Blood of Christ*
   9:11-14

> v.11 "But Christ being come an high priest of good things to come, by a greater and more perfect tabernacle, not made with hands, that is to say, not of this building;
>
> v.12 Neither by the blood of goats and calves, but by his own blood he entered in once into the holy place, having obtained eternal redemption *for us.*
>
> v.13 For if the blood of bulls and of goats, and the ashes of an heifer sprinkling the unclean, sanctifieth to the purifying of the flesh:
>
> v.14 How much more shall the blood of Christ, who through the eternal Spirit offered himself without spot to God, purge your conscience from dead works to serve the living God?"

11 It has been said of this short section that it "bristles with difficulties". It is a passage of comparisons and contrasts, between Aaron and Christ, between the old and the new, between the tabernacle and something greater, between the material and the celestial, between the sacrifices and Calvary, between the oft-shed blood of animal victims and the once-for-all, never-to-be-repeated sacrifice of Him who procured eternal redemption by the shedding of His own blood and entered into the sanctuary for us.

The first difficulty in the passage relates to the "good things to come". What exactly are these "good things", and when do they come?

Some will equate these "good things to come" with the time of reformation of v.10, and understand them to be those good things which have now come to us in Christ. This view will interpret the good things as being "to come" only as far as the people of the old dispensation were concerned, but as having now come to us who belong to the new.

Others will understand the good things as being things yet to come, and not yet realised. To quote J.N.Darby who espouses this view, he says, "They are yet to come. These good things consist of all that the Messiah will enjoy when He reigns".

But why should we be constrained to accept either one of these interpretations to the exclusion of the other? Is it not true that "good things" have come, and that there are good things still to come, and that all that we have now, together with all that we shall yet enjoy, are together embraced in this phrase, "the good things to come"? They were "to come" to the saints of an earlier day. They are yet "to come" in all their fulness, in a day of glory yet future. This appears to be the understanding of Wm. Kelly, who writes, "While the blessing is fully made known to the believer now, in order to place him in immediate access to God according to the rights of Christ's glory and of redemption actually accomplished for the soul, the phraseology is purposely such as to hold out and ensure 'the coming good things' for His people another day, like 'the world to come' in ch.2, 'the rest that remaineth for the people of God' in ch.4, 'the age to come' in ch.6, and the implied exercise of the Melchisedec priesthood in ch.7, to say no more now".

"Good things" therefore, have come to us already, but good things have yet to come in another future day.

There is a greater and more perfect tabernacle than the structure and system that Israel knew in the wilderness. There are many "great" things in this epistle.

1. A great salvation   2:3
2. A great high priest   4:14
3. A great fight of afflictions   10:32
4. A great recompense of reward   10:35
5. A great cloud of witnesses   12:1
6. A great Shepherd of the sheep   13:20

But there are also two "greater" things. Moses esteemed the reproach of Christ "greater riches" than the treasures in Egypt (11:26). Here there is a "greater tabernacle" than that of the wilderness.

The old tabernacle, though divinely ordained, was man-made. The sphere of Aaron's ministry was material and visible and tangible, but the sphere of our Lord's ministry is heavenly; His is a sanctuary not made with human hands; it does not belong to this creation; it possesses therefore a perfection which Aaron's did not. The persistent, repeated argument of the writer continues, that the old thing was shadowy and typical. It has served its day and taught its lessons and has now been displaced and superseded by something greater and more perfect.

12 Now Aaron's entrance into the Holiest was by the blood of goats and calves. The story of his annual entry into that Most Holy Place is told in Lev 16, as we have already observed. It was by divine ordering that he entered with blood. The shedding of blood was the giving of life. It was death, the death of a substitute victim. Thus was the penalty of sin exacted by the death of another, and on this ground alone, that the penalty had been paid, did Aaron enter in.

> Without blood is no remission
>   Thus the Lord proclaims from heaven,
> Blood must flow – on this condition,
>   This alone, is sin forgiven;
> Yes, a victim must be slain,
>   Else all hope of life is vain.

But there was no intrinsic value in the blood of bulls and calves. It was a ceremonial, ritualistic ordinance that allowed Jehovah to go along with the people. With Christ it was different. He who is our Saviour entered by His own blood: He gave Himself. And He entered in "by" His own blood, not "with" His blood, as some would have it. We have earlier observed in ch.2, propitiation was made on the cross, not in heaven. The argument of some, that Christ entered heaven with His blood to make propitiation there, has no foundation or support in this verse. Our Lord accomplished propitiation on the cross. The work was completed on the tree. In virtue of that finished work He entered the heavenly sanctuary to engage in priestly ministry for His people. Indeed this verse shows plainly that the expiatory work was already complete for He entered in "having obtained" eternal redemption for us. Christ was the offering and Christ the offerer. This sacrifice is of more than ceremonial and ritual value. Its value is intrinsic, measured only by the greatness and preciousness of the blessed One who gave Himself a holy sin-bearer and substitute to bear the sin of many (Isa 53:12).

This is the first reference in the epistle to the blood of Christ. There are seven mentions in all, each one expressive and instructive.

1. "His own blood"   9:12
2. "The blood of Christ"   9:14
3. "The blood of Jesus"   10:19
4. "The blood of the covenant"   10:29
5. "The blood of sprinkling"   12:24
6. "His own blood"   13:12
7. "The blood of the everlasting covenant"   13:20

It is important to note that nowhere in any part of NT Scripture, do we read of "the blood" without some qualifying descriptive word or clause. It is "the blood of Christ", or, "the blood of Jesus", or, "His own blood", or some such, as we have seen, but never simply, "the blood". Hymnology might sing of "the blood". Untaught or unthinking preachers may make bold reference to "the blood". It is not reverent. It is not in the spirit of Scripture so to speak.

The other great contrast in this verse is related to Christ's one entry into the Holiest. Aaron's was an annual entrance. It was a repeated, recurrent event, once every year (v.7). Now the word "once" in this v.12 is not quite the same as the word "once" in v.7. The word of v.12 is a strengthened form of the word of v.7 and denotes "once for all". There need never be, and can never be, a repetition of the work completed at Calvary. Accordingly Christ has entered the heavenly sanctuary once for all. The redemption which He has obtained is, like so many other things in this epistle, eternal. The relief afforded by Israel's Day of Atonement was to be re-established annually. The efficacy of the sacrifice of Christ is eternal.

13   The writer refers back once more to the animal sacrifices of the old dispensation. "The blood of goats and bulls" would have a primary reference to the Day of Atonement (Lev 16), but would undoubtedly embrace other offerings as well. Every Jew was familiar with the story of endless sacrifice and offering over the centuries. They were necessary as the divinely-ordained way for the forgiveness of sins, for atonement and approach to God. But there was no personal value in the victims whose blood was shed. Goats, bulls, sheep, lambs and turtledoves had a ceremonial, ritual value only. There was no intrinsic value in the creatures themselves. The principal offerings are outlined in the first seven chapters of the Book of Leviticus.

Then there was the red heifer. The reference here is to Num 19. A red heifer, without blemish or defect, and upon which never came yoke, was to be brought to Eleazar the priest. Eleazar was directed to bring the animal outside the camp where it was slaughtered before him. Its blood was sprinkled seven times before the tent of meeting and its body was burnt, consumed wholly, in sight of the priest. Its skin and its flesh, its blood and its dung, were incinerated completely while Eleazar watched. The priest then took cedar wood, hyssop, and scarlet thread, and cast them into the midst of the fire as it burned. A ceremonially-clean man gathered up the ashes and deposited them in a chosen clean place outside the camp. Thereafter these ashes were mingled with water which was known as the water of separation. It was sprinkled, for purification, upon those of Israel who had become defiled by association with the dead. This granted a certain sanctifying and purification of the defiled person. The defilement anticipated may have been unavoidable but to neglect the prescribed purification was a most serious offence.

F.F.Bruce has preserved for us the interesting information that Israel last killed a red heifer around AD 58-60, the heifer being slain by a priest Ishmael ben Phabi. The Samaritans continued the practice until the year 1348, the ashes of that heifer being preserved until around the year 1600. It is of sad interest that Israel today is searching again for a perfect red heifer. The Temple Institute, situate in the Jewish Quarter of Old Jerusalem, is dedicated to researching the accurate construction of temple vessels and furnishings. Many of these, with certain priestly garments, are ready for use in a third temple. They are serving an educational purpose until a new temple is built. This Institute talks freely of the search for a red heifer, perfectly red and unblemished, so that the ritual of Num 19 might be revived. But to what purpose?

So, says the writer, the blood of goats and bulls was shed, and the ashes of an heifer being sprinkled afforded a purity for those who had been defiled.

14   If all this was true, and it was, how much more precious was the blood of Christ. Well does Peter speak of "the precious blood of Christ" (1 Pet 1:19). Here indeed is contrast rather than comparison. Here is intrinsic value. Here is incomprehensible preciousness and matchless worth.

Those sacrifices of old effected an external, ceremonial purification. The blood of Christ does more. It has a blessed effect; the believer's conscience is purified, and not just his flesh.

Our Lord offered Himself. How precious! He offered Himself spotless to God. It was the climax of His moral glory. Obedient unto death! For thirty-three years he had lived sinlessly. Those years had brought much pleasure to His Father – a Man in a sinful environment living without sin. It was a requirement with all the Levitical offerings that they must be "without blemish". This is stated and restated again and again in those early chapters of Leviticus. When Christ offered Himself it was in absolute accord with that requirement. There is perfection and purity and preciousness immeasurable in Christ, who offered Himself. Aaron could not do that; he offered another. Every Levitical offering was the offering of a substitute life. Only Christ could offer Himself, and He did. It was the offering up of the only life that had ever brought pleasure to God in its every detail. Every deed and every word; every look and every thought; every movement of every moment; all brought delight to God's heart. It was such an One who offered Himself. There is no comparison with the prior offerings. It is a deep, sharp, unmeasured contrast which bows our hearts in worship.

It was by the eternal Spirit that He so offered Himself. Attempts by some good expositors to make this our Lord's own spirit are interesting, but are not satisfactory. Christ offers in the power of that same Spirit by which He was anointed at the commencement of His ministry (Matt 3:16; Luke 4:16-18; Isa 61:1). By the ministration of that Spirit He had been conceived in the womb of the virgin (Luke 1:35). In the power of that Spirit He had moved and ministered (Matt 12:28). He had lived and laboured in unbroken communion with the Spirit, like a meal offering mingled with oil. Now, by that Spirit, He offered Himself spotless to God. The comments of another are very beautiful; "He offered Himself to God – but as moved by the power, and according to the perfection of the eternal Spirit. All the motives that governed this action, and the accomplishment of the fact according to those motives, were purely and perfectly those of the Holy Ghost; that is, absolutely divine in their perfection, but of the Holy Ghost acting in a man (a man without sin who, born and living ever by the power of the Holy Ghost, had never known sin; who, being exempt from it by birth, never allowed it to enter into Him" (JND).

Observe that the Spirit is here called the "eternal Spirit". Everything in this epistle is stamped with eternality. All is in contrast with the temporary, transient nature of Judaism.

The power of such an offering cannot be properly estimated: "How much more", exclaims the writer. If the blood of goats and bulls, and the sprinkled ashes of an incinerated heifer, brought a certain sanctification for the defiled flesh, how much more is brought to us by the blood of Christ. The believer's conscience is purified. The guilt of dead works is purged. These are not only the "dead works" of ceremonial observances associated with Judaism. They are all works which issue in death; sins which have defiled the conscience and stained the soul. Such inner defilement cannot be removed by the blood of bulls and goats. Those offerings granted an external ceremonial purifying of the flesh. The death of Christ has brought us into a wholly-cleansed condition in which with joy we may serve the living God. What privilege and pleasure is this, to stand wholly cleansed in the presence of the living God, in perfect liberty to worship Him against whom we had earlier offended. We come nearer than any priest of Israel ever did, and are happier too, standing unquestioned in the divine presence, with every defilement of our conscience completely blotted out.

4. *The Perfect Mediator*
9:15-22

v.15 "And for this cause he is the mediator of the new testament, that by means of death, for the redemption of the transgressions *that were* under the first testament, they which are called might receive the promise of eternal inheritance.

v.16 For where a testament *is,* there must also of necessity be the death of the testator.

v.17 For a testament *is* of force after men are dead: otherwise it is of no strength at all while the testator liveth.

v.18 Whereupon neither the first *testament* was dedicated without blood.

v.19 For when Moses had spoken every precept to all the people according to the law, he took the blood of calves and of goats, with water, and scarlet wool, and hyssop, and sprinkled both the book, and all the people,

v.20 Saying, This *is* the blood of the testament which God hath enjoined unto you.

v.21 Moreover he sprinkled with blood both the tabernacle, and all the vessels of the ministry.

v.22 And almost all things are by the law purged with blood; and without shedding of blood is no remission."

15   Christ then, has offered Himself spotless to God, and has procured by His death an opened sanctuary, and a purified conscience for the believer. For this cause, for this reason, and on this basis, He is the mediator of a new covenant. This covenant we have already discussed in ch.8. There was an old covenant; there is a new one. And of this new one Christ is mediator. This new covenant has not yet been ratified with Israel and Judah. For them it is still future; but the mediator has established the basis for it. Even before the cross, in anticipation our Lord gave the cup to His disciples, saying, "This cup is the new covenant in my blood" (1 Cor 11:25). Believers today, whether Jewish or Gentile, are already in the enjoyment of the blessings of a covenant which will be made with Israel in a coming day.

The death of Christ has procured redemption. Every believer knows this in a personal manner and delights to exclaim with David and with Job, "my redeemer" (Job 19:25; Ps 19:14). But the redemption here mentioned has wider implications. It covers retrospectively the sins of centuries under the first covenant. The blood of bulls and goats could never take away sins. They provided an atonement, a covering, which allowed Jehovah to go along with the people. Calvary was ever in view. God would eventually provide in Christ a full redemption, and, knowing this, He was able in righteousness, in grace and in forbearance, to pass by the accumulated transgressions of those past ages (Rom 3:25). Calvary vindicated God in doing this. The death of Christ has declared His righteousness, and now, for those who are called, there is not only redemption but the promise of the eternal inheritance. Past, present, and future are all taken care of in the death of Christ. The work is complete.

No blood, no altar now,
   The sacrifice is o'er;
No flame, no smoke ascends on high,
   The lamb is slain no more;
But richer blood has flowed from nobler veins
   To purge the soul from guilt and cleanse the reddest stains.

This is a privilege of those who are called. There is to all men who hear, a general call in the gospel, but not all who hear will respond to that call. Some will however, and those who do are referred to as "the called according to his purpose" (Rom 8:28). Peter speaks of it too. "Your calling", he writes in 2 Pet 1:10. "Be holy", he exhorts, "as he which hath called you" (1 Pet 1:15); "who hath called us unto his eternal glory (1 Pet 5:10). These Hebrew readers had already been reminded that they were "partakers of the heavenly calling" (3:1). It is then, a priceless privilege to be numbered with "the called", and it is one of the privileges of those that are called that they receive the promise of an eternal inheritance.

Once again we have the word "eternal". It has the same consistent purpose, to contrast the abiding new with the transient old. We who believe have now received, not just the promise, but the thing promised. At least in part we are even now in the enjoyment of the eternal inheritance: "We have obtained an inheritance" (Eph 1:11). On the other hand, there is more to come, for the Spirit indwelling us is the earnest, the pledge, of our inheritance (Eph 1:14), and we wait for that day of glory when Christ will possess His acquired possession. Then shall we enter more fully into all that has been procured for us and promised to us.

16   We enter here upon two verses which perhaps should be viewed as a parenthesis, in which a different meaning from the usual is now attached to the word "covenant". This word we have before seen to be the word *diathēkē*, a word which may be properly translated "covenant" or equally-correctly by the variant rendering "testament". F.F.Bruce explains, "We are almost bound to use two different English words to represent two different aspects of the meaning of one Greek word ... The Greek word is *diathēkē*, which has the comprehensive sense of 'settlement'. As used elsewhere in the epistle, the particular kind of settlement which *diathēkē* denotes is a covenant graciously bestowed by God upon His people, by which He brings them into a special relationship with Himself ... But in vv.16, 17 of our present chapter it is used of another kind of settlement, a last will and testament, in which property is bequeathed by the owner to various other persons on the understanding that they have no title to it until he dies". Some scholars will insist that "testament" is the meaning of *diathēkē* to be preferred throughout the entire epistle. Yet others will maintain that "covenant" should be the consistent rendering. J.N.Darby admits to "a very delicate Greek question", but he agrees in substance with F.F.Bruce, as does Wm Kelly, who, with characteristic definiteness says, "Notwithstanding the doubt cast on the rendering of 'testament' in the last two verses by many eminent Christians and able scholars, there need be no hesitation in deciding for this sense, as here the sole tenable one. That 'covenant' is meant everywhere else in the NT as in the OT is clear from the contextual requirement. The same reason of the context here excludes 'covenant' and demands 'testament', but here only". This he writes "without a shade of disrespect for other commentators"!

W.E.Vine, however, takes the opposing view. He writes, "While the terminology in Heb 9:16-17 has the appearance of being appropriate to the circumstances of making a will, there is excellent reason for adhering to the meaning 'covenant-making' ... The idea of making a will destroys the argument of v.18" (Vine apparently did not observe a parenthesis here). In another place he writes, "In Heb 9:16-17, the translation is much disputed. There does not seem to be any sufficient reason for departing in these verses from the word used everywhere else" (i.e. "covenant"). He has also the support of the scholars Westcott, Moulton and Marcus Dods.

The word however, is undoubtedly capable of the dual rendering, to be determined by the context, and here, in vv.16, 17, it is "testament" which, in our judgment, best conveys the sense intended. This rendering, with the interpretation which naturally belongs to it, we shall therefore follow.

Where there is a testament, states the parenthesis, there must be also the death of the testator. Death is a necessity. The testator must die if there is to be an effective disposition of that which is willed. The execution of the testament is dependent upon the death of him who made it. The problem has been raised as to how Christ might be both the testator and the mediator, or executor, if in fact He must die. There is no problem. Our Lord wills to us an eternal inheritance: He is the testator. He dies to make that testament effective. Now, risen from the dead, He is the mediator or executor, making disposition of the inheritance. As another has said, "He is testator and executor, surety and mediator alike".

17 The same argument is now continued, the facts being repeated in both positive and negative terms: "A testament is of force after men are dead". No matter how clear, how concise, how detailed, how simple, or how elaborate the terms of a will may be, the will comes into force only after death. Some wills are expressed briefly, in simple language. Others are lengthy, couched in legal, technical, and complicated vocabulary. It does not alter this unchangeable principle, that the will is of force only after the death of the testator. Or, to state it the other way, "It is of no strength at all while the testator liveth". As long as the testator lives the will is dead, a lifeless document. It lies silent in legal custody, awaiting his death who made it. No one may make a claim upon it while he lives. It has no strength to make any disposition until he dies. This then is the universally-accepted position: death is a necessity.

We bow in wonder and gratitude as we witness the voluntary death of the great testator and mediator. We hear the recurring declaration of Holy Scripture, "Christ died"; "Christ died for the ungodly" (Rom 5:6); "Christ died for us" (Rom 5:8); "Christ died for our sins" (1 Cor 15:3); "he died for all" (2 Cor 5:15); he "gave himself" (Gal 2:20). The necessary death has taken place; the testament is now

effective; the eternal inheritance is now the portion of those who are called. Well do
we sing:

> And did the Holy and the Just,
>   The Sovereign of the skies,
> Stoop down to wretchedness and dust,
>   That guilty worms might rise?

18 The writer now returns to the more general and usual meaning of *diathēkē*, to
the idea of covenant making. If we perceive a parenthesis in vv.16-17 then we
understand that in this v.18 there is now a connection with, and a progression from,
the end of v.15. There he had spoken of the necessity of the death of Christ as the
basis for the redemption of those early transgressions. He had then moved
parenthetically to the idea of the necessary death of the testator before a will could
be ratified. Now he argues that this necessity for death has ever been a consistent
demand. For that matter, he says, the first covenant was not inaugurated without
blood. "Covenant" is here supplied; it is not in the text. The text reads simply "the
first", but the implication is obviously the first covenant. Christ is the mediator of
a new covenant in v.15. As it is with the new covenant so it was with the first, it must
be introduced with blood: "The life of the flesh is in the blood" (Lev 17:11,14). The
shedding of the blood is the forfeiting of the life; the pouring out of the blood is the
laying down of the life. The shedding of the blood is therefore death. Not without
this bloodshed was the first covenant ratified, and the principle does not change.

There is a certain unpopularity in many places today with the preaching of
salvation by the blood of Christ alone. Indeed it has never been popular, but it is
God's way. We need to proclaim it faithfully, fearlessly, plainly, powerfully, and
unequivocally. It is the only way of salvation for all. To rich or poor, high or low,
small or great, learned or unlearned, educated or ignorant, of whatever class, colour,
creed, or language, we must say to all men as Paul did to the Corinthians, "I
determined not to know anything among you save Jesus Christ and him crucified" (1
Cor 2:2). We must proclaim to all as he did to the Galatians, "God forbid that I
should glory, save in the cross of our Lord Jesus Christ" (Gal 6:14); "The preaching
of the cross is to them that perish foolishness" (1 Cor 1:18), but it is the only evangel
committed to us. It is a consistent principle, the writer is arguing, that death is a
necessity. Whether old covenant or new; whether covenant or testament; whether
testator or covenant-victim, there must be death. This is the clear concise argument
of this verse and of this passage.

19 What follows now is an amplification of the statement of v.18 and a summary
of the events of Exod 24. If there are certain features mentioned here which are not
to be found in Exod 24, this must not cause us any concern. We must not be tempted
to speak of discrepancies or of inaccuracies, as some do. We are reading a God-
breathed text, whether in Exod 24 or in Heb 9. They are from the same divine

author. For those who accept this divine inspiration of all of Holy Scripture there can
be no problem. From what source the writer has acquired his additional facts we may
not know. It is interesting, though not essential, to see some of them confirmed and
justified by Josephus the historian.

The story begins in Exod 19 at Sinai. Moses ascended and Jehovah descended. The
whole of Mount Sinai smoked and shook greatly (Exod 19:18). There were thunderings
and lightnings, cloud and fire. The people trembled with the mountain. In ch.24
Moses came and told the people all the words of Jehovah and all the judgments, and
all the people answered with one voice and said, "All the words that Jehovah has said
will we do". A covenant was being made. Young men (first-born?) of the children of
Israel then offered at Moses' direction burnt offerings and peace offerings, and Moses
took of the blood and sprinkled the people. "Behold the blood of the covenant", he
said (Exod 24:8). The words are reminiscent of the words of the Saviour (Matt
26:28).

The blood of Exod 24 was sprinkled not only on the people but also on the altar,
as if, in symbol, bringing God and the people together under the same blood of the
covenant. Indeed, as the writer to the Hebrews has here written, not without blood
was that first covenant inaugurated (v.18).

The additional fact is now given to us that Moses sprinkled the book as well as the
people and the altar: the book, the terms of the covenant; the people who were the
people of the covenant; Jehovah, the God of the covenant; all were solemnly and
ceremonially joined in a covenant relationship by the sacrificial blood. The book lays
down the basis of the covenant. The altar represented Jehovah, the author of the
covenant. The people entered into a covenant bond when they promised, "We will".
And it was all ratified by blood.

Our epistle now makes reference to three particulars which are not recorded in
Exod 24: water, scarlet wool and hyssop.

Water may have been mingled with the blood to facilitate an easier sprinkling. We
are reminded that from the Saviour's pierced side there flowed blood and water.

Scarlet wool was wool dyed-red, symbolic of those sins of which Jehovah says in
another place, "Though your sins be as scarlet they shall be white as snow (Isa 1:18).
Examples of scarlet wool are exhibited in the present Temple Institute in the Jewish
Quarter of Old Jerusalem, where they avow also from Hebrew writings that scarlet
wool was tied to the horns of the scapegoat of Lev 16, symbolising the forgiveness of
the sins which had been confessed and judged.

With hyssop the blood was no doubt sprinkled, just as with hyssop the blood of the
paschal lamb had earlier been sprinkled on the door posts in Egypt. To us it brings
a remembrance of the Lamb of God, who in His sufferings cried, "I thirst". To His
holy lips they reached a sponge, filled with vinegar, and tied to hyssop (John 19:29).

20 "This is the blood of the covenant". These are the words of Moses at Sinai. They
are almost exactly the words of the Saviour in Matt 26:28, spoken with reference to
His own approaching death. We have already observed that the blood of Christ is

also called "the blood of the covenant" in 10:29, and again "the blood of the everlasting covenant" in 13:20.

So was the first covenant inaugurated with blood. The covenant which was enjoined or commanded, was ratified, of necessity, with sacrifice, with blood, with death itself. It should have been to the people a perpetual reminder of the price of disobedience. Jehovah had spoken the ten words. They were written indelibly and inflexibly upon stone. The nation had promised, "We will", and the penalty for failure was death. The covenant was sealed with blood.

21 But this sealing of the covenant with blood was not the only use of blood under the old dispensation. The writer proceeds now to another use, and, in v.22, to yet a third.

At a time later than the events of Exod 24 the tabernacle was constructed in the wilderness. This tabernacle, and its vessels of service, were also sprinkled with blood, as the people had been earlier. It is important to see that v.21 refers, not to the time of the giving of the law as in Exod 24, but to a later date. The tabernacle was not in existence when the people were sprinkled with blood in Exod 24.

For any OT record of this v.21 we must appeal to Exod 29:12, and to the story of the consecration of the priests in Lev 8:15, and to the Day of Atonement in Lev 16. We have, in fact, no concise OT account of the tabernacle and all the vessels being sprinkled with blood, but in these passages cited we have reference to the mercy-seat and to the altar of burnt offering being so sprinkled. We do of course have a full account of the anointing of the tabernacle with oil. (See Exod 40:9-11, where the tabernacle with all that was in it, its furniture and vessels, were all so anointed.) Since the priests at their consecration were anointed both with oil and with blood, it is suggested by some that a similar anointing or sprinkling with blood as well as with oil applied to the tabernacle at that time also. It may only be said safely that we do not know, but of this we are sure, that somewhere, at some time, the tabernacle and all the vessels of service were indeed sprinkled with blood. 9:21 says so, and 9:21 is God-breathed.

22 Here we have the third use of blood in this section. Not only was the covenant sealed with blood, and the tabernacle sprinkled with blood, but indeed, says the writer, almost all things are purified with blood according to the law, and without shedding of blood there is no remission. Forgiveness is by blood alone. "Almost" has presented a problem to some, but there is really no difficulty. "Almost all things" were purged with blood, but not everything; there were exceptions. After the rebellion and subsequent judgment of Korah, Dathan, and Abiram in Num 16, atonement was made for the congregation by incense (Num 16:46-47). We do not stay to see the significance of this, but only to see that "almost" all things are purged with blood. Again, in the same book of Numbers, there is another example: the spoils of battle were required to be purged by fire and water. Gold and silver, copper and iron, tin and lead, passed through the fire and were then purified by the water of separation of Num 19. Things that could not endure the fire were likewise purified by that water.

However, apart from blood shedding, there was no remission. If other neuter things might be cleansed by fire or water, remission of sins was absolutely dependent upon the shedding of blood. The phrase "shedding of blood" as in the AV, is the translation of one Greek word, *haematekchusia* (*haima*, blood; *ekchunō*, to pour out), used only here in the NT. It is a word comprised of two words. The word is, literally, "blood-shedding", so apart from blood-shedding there is no remission.

Another difficulty now arises. In Lev 5:11 we have, anticipated, the case of an Israelite so poor that he cannot bring for a sin offering either a lamb or turtle doves or pigeons. In such poverty it will be accepted from him that he bring a tenth of an ephah of fine flour: an offering without blood! Jehovah, even under law, makes provision in grace for genuine poverty: "If he be not able to bring a lamb" (Lev 5:7); "If he be not able to bring two turtle doves or two young pigeons" (Lev 5:11). This is poverty indeed. Jehovah accepts the offering of flour, given out of penury, but observe that the flour is carried to the altar where it is burned "with Jehovah's offerings" by fire (JND). It goes where the blood is. It is offered on a blood-stained altar. It is consumed in association with the blood of regular sin offerings. There is thus a recognition of the necessity of blood-shedding and death. It is still true that "apart from the shedding of blood there is no remission".

To this truth we gladly bow. Blood-shedding is death. Our holy Substitute has died: "The blood of Jesus Christ ... cleanseth us from all sin" (1 John 1:7).

> Thy blood alone, my Saviour,
>   Can ease this weight of sin;
> Thy blood alone, O Lamb of God,
>   Can give me peace within.

5. *The Three Appearings*
   9:23-28

v.23 "*It was* therefore necessary that the patterns of things in the heavens should be purified with these; but the heavenly things themselves with better sacrifices than these.

v.24 For Christ is not entered into the holy places made with hands, w*hich are* the figures of the true; but into heaven itself, now to appear in the presence of God for us:

v.25 Nor yet that he should offer himself often, as the high priest entereth into the holy place every year with blood of others;

v.26 For then must he often have suffered since the foundation of the world: but now once in the end of the world hath he appeared to put away sin by the sacrifice of himself.

v.27 And as it is appointed unto men once to die, but after this the judgment:

v.28 So Christ was once offered to bear the signs of many; and unto them that look for him shall he appear the second time without sin unto salvation."

23 It was necessary then, that the tabernacle, the tent with its furnishings and vessels, should be purified, and that this purification should be effected by sacrifice and blood. The tent and furniture were figurative representations of the things in the heavens. They were copies of greater things. They were, as another has put it, "glimpses of the things in the heavens" (Rotherham), and it was therefore necessary that they should be clean and pure. God's holiness must be in evidence in every particular. The divine character required purity.

We have already observed in this chapter (v.9), that the tabernacle was a parable. It was an earthly representation of things heavenly. There had been an earthly sanctuary. It was a material, tangible structure, and the whole visible system associated with it was a great figure or copy of something heavenly. With copious shedding of blood and offering of sacrifice Jehovah had declared His holiness and had demanded the same from His people. The sacrifices of old had demonstrated and maintained the divine standard.

Now if such purity was required in the earthly, and if that earthly thing was a parable of the heavenly, then it follows that any service in the heavenlies must likewise be pursued in absolute holiness. Here, however, we meet with the difficulty as to how, or why, or in what sense, the heavens need to be cleansed.

The suggestion is made by some, with good cause, that the heavens themselves have been defiled during the history of sin. Satan has been there, with his lords of darkness and powers of wickedness (see Eph 6:12 JND). It must be true, though not developed here, that he has profaned the very heavens in his diabolical intentions and designs. Can this be overlooked or forever ignored?

Others see the "heavenly things" here, not as heaven or the heavenly sanctuary in any locational sense, but the whole heavenly spiritual sphere of things related to the new order of service and worship.

It does appear though to be consistent with the context that the writer is thinking of heaven itself as a sanctuary, and that that sanctuary with all its holy activity and the persons concerned in any way with it, have been represented by the tabernacle in the wilderness and the earthly priesthood. The argument is, that if that earthly typical system was all maintained and sustained in holiness by blood, then the spiritual (and heavenly) order, which is the true, must likewise be pure, but this will demand something infinitely better and vastly superior to the ritual animal sacrifices of that old system.

A second difficulty arises in this verse with the use of the plural in the term "better sacrifices". There need be no problem. How else would the writer express what was in his mind? He knows full well that the one sacrifice of Christ has availed. He knows that there was a once-for-all sacrifice when Jesus died. He is simply saying that something better than the sacrifices of preceding centuries is needed for the holy establishment of the heavenly order of things. If a ritual ceremonial purity was obtained on earth by the offering of animal sacrifices then better than these is needed for the heavenlies.

24   In the concluding verses of this chapter there are the three appearings of Christ, to which reference is often made by preachers and teachers. The words translated "appear", and "appeared" by the AV in vv.24, 26, and 28, are, in fact, three different words. The thought is true, nevertheless, and very beautiful, that there are indeed three appearings of the blessed One, related to the past, the present, and the future, and related also to His character as Prophet, Priest, and King. It may be helpful to note these words just here.

1.   v.24. *Emphanizomai* (to shine). This Christ does now, appearing in the presence of God for us, radiant in a present glorious priestly ministry for His people.

2.   v.26. *Phaneroomai* (to be manifested; to be revealed as one is). So He was revealed in incarnation, when He came to preach righteousness in a prophetic ministry, and to put away sin.

3.   v.28. *Horaomai* (to become visible). This is an appearing yet future, associated with His rights as King. It will be the day of His manifestation and of His vindication.

Now in His present priestly ministry Christ has not entered into holy places made with hands. That is to say, our Lord's sphere of ministry is not in any earthly sanctuary built by men, as was that tabernacle of old. That tent of fabric and wood and gold and silver, constructed by men, may suffice for Aaron, and serve as a visible representation of the heavenly sanctuary, but those earthly holy places were the "antitypes" (*antitupos*) of something greater. This word "figures" of this verse, W.E.Vine defines as "a copy of an archetype". The material tabernacle corresponded to the true tabernacle (8:2). It was an earthly counterpart of the heavenly reality. Christ is the true Light (John 1:9); the true bread (John 6:32); and the true vine (John 15:1). The sphere of His ministry is the true tabernacle, the reality, of which the earthly tabernacle was a copy.

"Heaven itself" is an important and beautiful expression. Paul speaks of "the third heaven". There is the heaven of the birds all around us and above us. We call it the aerial heaven. Beyond, there is the heaven of the stars, the stellar heaven. But "heaven itself" is beyond these. Our Lord has gone "higher than the heavens" (7:26). From Olivet, He has passed through the heavens and into the heavens, into "heaven itself".

The verse defines just where that is, "in the presence of God". Christ is before the face of God, and He is there "for us". What holy happy assurance for these Hebrew readers, and for us, that there is a Man in glory, shining before the face of God on our behalf. This was incalculably richer than anything they had ever known, or that could have been known, or had ever been possible, by the ministry of the Levitical priests.

Their range was earth, nor higher soared;
The heaven of heavens is Thine:
Thy majesty and priesthood, Lord,
Through endless ages shine.

25 Christ's sphere of ministry is heavenly, and thus different from, and contrasted with, that of Aaron. But in yet another important particular is our Lord's ministry different. When He entered into the heavenly sanctuary it was once for all, on the basis of a sacrifice that never needed to be repeated. Such is the inestimable and infinite value of that one offering of Himself. What an assuring and comforting contrast is this with the oft-repeated Day of Atonement to which the writer now refers. Israel's high priests came annually. Every year there was a repetition of all the ritual details of Lev 16. There was no end to the recurring sacrificing and shedding of blood because there never was an offering of sufficient value to make an end of sins for ever. Sins accumulated. The Day of Atonement came. The prescribed rituals were carefully observed, and the high priest entered into the holy places on the people's behalf. He might pronounce forgiveness and bless the people, but already the sins had begun to accumulate again. There would be another Day of Atonement next year. *Yom Kippur* would come again, and again, and yet again. There was no end. Last year, this year, next year, and the following year, it would go on and on. The repetition proved the insufficiency of the sacrifices, and demonstrated that there was no abiding value in the blood that was shed year by year.

The Jewish high priest entered the holy places with "blood of others". "With another's blood", says Newberry's *Interlinear Translation*. "With blood not His own" says JND. "With alien blood" says Rotherham, in an interesting rendering. The high priests of Israel may enter in personally and solitarily, but those entrances into the holy places were not at all based upon any personal right or fitness, nor upon any value of their own morality. They entered on the grounds of the shedding of the blood of sacrificial substitutionary victims, but the blood which granted them an annual admission to the Holiest was of limited ceremonial value only, and so required to be shed many many times in endless repetition.

It has not been necessary for Christ to offer Himself often. It is the recurring argument of this epistle that the Saviour died once, yea once for all, because His offering was of Himself, of eternal, incomparable value and matchless worth.

26 Now if it had not been so, there would have been unthinkable implications. If the sacrifice of Christ was such as needed to be repeated then indeed He would have been required to have suffered often throughout the course of world history. At what stage would Christ's sufferings for sins have begun? And how frequently during the centuries would He have had to offer Himself? It is all a sad hypothetical consideration which the writer now raises, to show the absurdity of the thought of any insufficiency in the once-for-all sacrifice of the Saviour.

To answer the first question, it would have been necessary for Him to suffer from the foundation of the world. From the very beginning men have sinned. If Christ is required to suffer more than once for sins (an impossible hypothesis), then that suffering must commence early in man's history, with the first generation of sinners. And how frequently must He suffer? His sufferings would require to be as frequent as the sacrifices of those centuries had been. One sinning generation after another had cried for forgiveness. Christ must often have suffered if His one offering up of Himself was not to be all-sufficient and of infinite value. Had one offering not been enough then He was obliged to suffer often. What completely unthinkable complications this would raise. Repeated incarnations and crucifixions of God's Son! The very thought is to be totally rejected. The truth is a delightful blending of simplicity and profundity, "But now once ..."

"Once in the end of the world", as in the AV, does not adequately or clearly convey the sense. "Once in the consummation of the ages", He appeared. His coming to us was a climactic moment of fulfilment. It was the moment toward which all purpose and prophecy had been moving. But it was not so much an end as a consummation. The Saviour's coming to put away sin was the very climax of history. Ages past and ages future meet here at His cross. All the ages past looked forward to Calvary. All the future will look back to it. The ages meet at Golgotha. When the fulness of the time was come God sent forth His Son. The theological accuracy of the term may be questioned but it has often been said that Calvary was the meeting-place of two eternities. Or, as another has written so beautifully, "Christ bisects the course of time into two parts, appearing as the central figure in the world's history, spreading His healing wings over the whole race of Adam, one wing over the ages before He came, the other wing over the ages after" (A.B.Bruce).

He has appeared; He has been manifested, and for this blessed purpose, the putting away of sin. "Putting away" (*athetēsis*), is elsewhere translated "disannulling" (7:18). It denotes an abolition; a cancellation; a setting aside. Such a cancellation of our sins He has accomplished by His one offering. Our past has been abolished; our guilt has been expiated. Only the sacrifice of "himself" could have made it possible. How foolish and futile to be attracted any more to an obsolete Judaism, or indeed to any other religion. There is an all-sufficiency in Christ and complete efficacy in that one sacrifice of infinite worth, Himself. But the writer will continue to emphasise this once-for-all nature of that offering.

27   Christ died once, because by divine appointment men die once; not that He was entitled to die at all, for death had no claim upon Him. For men death is the wages of sin. He was a perfect Man over whom death had no right.

He was, however, a Man. He had voluntarily taken part in flesh and blood so that He might indeed die. He who, of His own volition, came into manhood, may now lay down His life of His own volition. But only once! It is appointed, divinely appointed, unto men once to die. It is an irrational absurdity to think of the Saviour dying more than once.

For men death is judgment, but there is a judgment still to follow physical death.

It is the portion of men once to die, and after this, judgment. There is, for the unconverted, an immediate judgment. So the Saviour Himself taught. A rich man lived, and died. He lived for time. He lived sumptuously. He lived thoughtlessly, carelessly, materialistically, making no provision for eternity. He died. In hell he lifted up his eyes in torment. (Luke 16:19-23). After death, judgment! This however is not the end. There will be a great white throne. The books will be opened (Rev 20:12). There are degrees of torment to be assessed. For some it will be more tolerable than for others (Matt 10:15; 11:22-24; Mark 6:11; Luke 10:12-14). What is recorded in the books will determine it all. There will be a divine, infallible assessment and men will be judged accordingly in the lake of fire (Rev 20:14-15). It is appointed unto men therefore once to die, and it is in keeping with this that our Lord should die once. And so He did. For Him however, it was a death for others, and in that death He bore the judgment due to others. He who had lived sinlessly, died for sinners, the just for the unjust: He "bare our sins in his own body on the tree" (1 Pet 2:24). Christ died, but voluntarily, and for us.

28   So then, as men die once by divine appointment, so has the Saviour died once for all. He was offered to bear the sin of many. How reminiscent is this of Isa 53:12. It is important that we observe accurately what Scripture says, "the sin of many". It is imperative that we distinguish between substitution and propitiation. Substitution is a truth made good to the believer only. The believing heart may stand at the cross and say, He "gave himself for me" (Gal 2:20). The gospel preacher must be careful with his vocabulary. It is his delight and duty to preach salvation for the "whomsoever", but it is his duty also to remember that the salvation which is "unto all" is only "upon all" them that believe. A sinner may not be told, without fuller explanation, "Christ bore your sins". This is a careless, innacurate vocabulary. "He bare the sin of many" (Isa 53:12). "His own self bare our sins" (1 Pet 2:24). For this He was once offered and faith brings us into the benefit and enjoyment of that finished work. Without the faith which links us with Christ a man will bear his own sins; this is the judgment that follows death. For the believer, this judgment has been meted out to, and borne by, the holy Substitute who was once offered. He exhausted the judgment due to us, in His death for us, and now, risen from the dead, both He and His people live together in a deathless realm.

> Death and judgment are behind us,
>   Peace and glory on before;
> All the billows rolled o'er Jesus,
>   There exhausted all their store.

It was a glad moment for Israel on that Day of Atonement when the high priest, having taken the blood into the Holiest, reappeared. This is undoubtedly the thought with which this chapter closes. Christ has entered. Our high priest has gone within. But He will appear again. See the comments on the word "appear" at the beginning of v.24. The word is never associated with the Lord's coming to the air to catch up His saints, as expounded in 1 Cor 15:51-52; 1 Thess 4:15-17; Phil 3:20-21. The epistle to the Hebrews looks beyond this. This epistle will doubtless be of supreme value to believing Jews after that event which we call the rapture of the church. There will be such a believing remnant, suffering for Christ during the great tribulation, waiting for Him and watching, looking for His appearing. To those who so wait for Him He shall appear in due time, apart from sin, for their salvation. The word "appear" means, as we have seen, to become visible. So it was when first He came. Men saw Him, looked upon Him, but did not recognise Him, and eventually cast Him out. But He will appear visibly a second time, not now to deal with sin as He did before by the sacrifice of Himself. Next time it will be apart from sin. He will appear in glory. Every eye shall see Him (Rev 1:7). It will be the day of His manifestation and vindication, and in that day His people shall be manifested too, and rejoice with Him, sharing in His glory.

X.   The Law is Superseded   (10:1-39)

1.   *The Will of God*
10:1-10

> v.1   "For the law having a shadow of good things to come, *and* not the very image of the things, can never with those sacrifices which they offered year by year continually make the comers thereunto perfect.
>
> v.2   For then would they not have ceased to be offered? because that the worshippers once purged should have had no more conscience of sins.
>
> v.3   But in those *sacrifices there is* a remembrance again *made* of sins every year.
>
> v.4   For *it is* not possible that the blood of bulls and of goats should take away sins.
>
> v.5   Wherefore when he cometh into the world, he saith, Sacrifice and offering thou wouldest not, but a body hast thou prepared me:
>
> v.6   In burnt offerings and *sacrifices* for sin thou hast had no pleasure.
>
> v.7   Then said I, Lo, I come (in the volume of the book it is written of me,) to do thy will, O God.
>
> v.8   Above when he said, Sacrifice and offering and burnt offerings and *offering* for sin thou wouldest not, neither hadst pleasure *therein*; which are offered by the law;
>
> v.9   Then said he, Lo, I come to do thy will, O God. He taketh away the first, that he may establish the second.
>
> v.10 By the which will we are sanctified through the offering of the body of Jesus Christ once *for all.*"

1   There are three features in this Epistle to the Hebrews which must soon become apparent to every careful reader. Firstly, there is the oft repetition and restatement of many truths and doctrines. The writer has no hesitation, nor embarrassment,

about repeating again and again those things which he deems so important for his readers. It is the way to teach and it is the way to learn. His first readers (as so many of his later readers!) were dull of hearing (5:11); they were slow to learn. Repetition of these great matters was an aid to learning. Secondly, there is the constant appeal to the OT Scriptures. There are citations from the OT in every chapter in this epistle. This of course was of the greatest importance to converted Jews. It established the greatness and value of the old writings with which they had been familiar earlier, and it established also the truths of the new order of things which they had now embraced, as that which had ever been in the mind of God for them. Thirdly, there is a recurring and persistent principle in this letter that the writer often makes an early allusion to some matter and then develops it later in the epistle. This same principle is so evident also in the Epistle to the Romans that some have appealed to the similarity to prove a Pauline authorship of the Epistle to the Hebrews.

These three features will all be observed in ch. 10 upon which we have now entered. With its opening words we are reminded yet once more that the law was but a shadow (see also 8:5), and was not the actual reality of the good things. These were, at that time, yet to come (9:11). Paul concurs with this in Col 2:17, where he likewise uses the word "shadow" to describe the character and nature of the old order. Its food-laws, its feast days and its festivals, the whole system, was but a grand foreshadowing of that which was to come. The law which was at the very heart of that old Judaistic system was similarly a shadow. But at least there was this value in a shadow that it indicated that there was indeed a substance. This was the typical value of the law and the system with which it was associated. It told the thoughtful that there was a glorious reality to come. Good things, better things, were being foreshadowed.

The law then had the shadow and not the very image of those good things. There is an important distinction here made between "shadow" (*skia*) and "image" (*eikōn*). This is not the word "image" of 1:3 (that word is *charaktēr*), but it is the word of Col 1:15, which passage makes the meaning of it very clear. Christ is the image (*eikōn*) of the invisible God. He has made God visible and tangible. He is the perfect and complete manifestation to us of the God we have never seen (John 1: 18). The law was never that image, but it was a shadow. Now if it be argued that all this has been dealt with already, that is true. This is exactly what we have been observing, that the writer repeats himself again and again. These are matters of the utmost importance, and his Hebrew readers in particular needed to learn them. It would make any thought of a return to Judaism seem a most foolish thought. They would be abandoning the substance for the shadow. They would be giving up the good things in Christ for the now-obsolete religion which had served its purpose and had been superseded.

But the repetition will now continue. The law, being but the shadow that it was, could never bring perfect peace to any conscience with its prescribed sacrifices. Doubtless the ritual of the Day of Atonement is still in the writer's mind, but his argument need not be restricted to that great day alone. There was an apparently endless sacrificing and offering of animal victims. It was a constant, continual exercise. Rotherham expresses it in a most telling way, "the same sacrifices which year by year they offer evermore". Their sacrifices were offered in variety and in perpetuity, but in insufficiency. They could never afford perfection of conscience to those who so approached God. Men came, and came, and kept coming, but never with consciences completely at ease. The sacrifices which could never take away sins (10:11) could never make the conscience perfect. But at least they had this usefulness, that they were shadows of a perfect thing to come.

> Not all the blood of beasts
>   On Jewish altars slain,
> Could give the guilty conscience peace,
>   Or wash away the stain.

With such knowledge of the insufficiency of those sacrifices, how foolish to be attracted in any way to obsolete Judaism, to the shadow. Is it not infinitely better and happier to sing with enlightened saints:

> But Christ, the heavenly Lamb,
>   Takes all our sins away;
> A sacrifice of nobler name
>   And richer blood than they.

2   A question is now raised: if what the writer is saying regarding the insufficiency and inability of those Jewish sacrifices is not true, then, at some time, would they not have ceased to be offered? They could not bring peace and perfection, he had argued, otherwise, if they could, would they not have been discontinued as being no longer necessary? It is better to read this as a question, as in our AV. Some marginal readings will render the expression as a statement rather than a question, "they would have ceased to be offered"; but the question form is better. The writer is teaching by interrogation. If it had been otherwise; if those sacrifices could indeed have brought perfection then would they not have ceased to be offered, as having fulfilled a purpose and being no longer necessary? If we are correct in dating the epistle prior to AD 70 then even at the time of writing the offerings were still being brought to the Jerusalem temple which must have been still standing. This then, the continuing offering up of sacrifices, was a testimony to their insufficiency, and to their inability to bring the peace of mind and conscience which men sought. Men brought their offerings because of a conscience of sin. The very fact of his bringing an offering betokened a consciousness of sin on the part of the offerer. If a man could be perfectly cleansed from all sin then the need for offerings disappeared. But the animal sacrifices of Judaism could not do that. There was no such perfect cleansing, so there was no easy conscience, and so the sacrifices continued.

The writer refers to "worshippers once purged". It is the "once for all" word which we have observed earlier. To be purged "once for all" would indeed have been a blessed experience for any worshipper. It would have brought with it a holy joy in communing with God with a clear conscience. "Blessed is the man to whom the Lord will not impute sin" (Rom 4:8). But alas, such blessedness was not possible under the law. The continuing offering up of sacrifices proved that. There was no once-for-all cleansing. A man sinned; he brought his offering; he received forgiveness; he sinned again; he offered again; he sinned again. There was no complete cleansing or perfecting of the man or his conscience. There was no easy mind, no heart at peace truly. Else, would those sacrifices not have ceased to be offered?

3   But there was yet another sad deficiency with that system of sacrifices, and perhaps particularly with those Days of Atonement. Not only did they not remove sins, but they actually created a remembrance of sins. They prompted, in the mind of the offerer, a recollection of the sins of the past. How many a man must have stood in the solemn assembly at *Yom Kippur*, and thought to himself, "I was here last year, and the year before that, and the year before that!" If he was spared, he would be present the next year, and the next year, and the year following that, and it would go on and on. It was a perpetual reminder of his sinfulness. In every exercised heart there would be a recalling of sins that had been confessed in former years. There was a remembrance of sins year by year, and there would be the sad but correct conclusion that there would be no end to these confessions and offerings. They would continue just as long as he was a sinning man and they would keep reminding him that he was just that.

   For the believer it is now different: not that we have no conscience about sinning, but we are no longer burdened with a conscience of sin. "If any man sin we have an advocate with the Father" (1 John 2:1). We no longer stand accused and guilty, bowed and cowed, fearful in the presence of God. Our sins, all of them, have been judicially and penally dealt with at the cross. Past, present, and future sins have all been accounted for.

   All my sins were laid upon Him;
      Jesus bore them on the tree;
   God who knew them laid them on Him,
      And believing I am free.

If a man sins, communion is interrupted, but we have a *paraklete* who assists us towards the Father in contrition for the wrong that we have done. With His gracious aid confession is made and communion is restored. The question of penalty or judgment is never raised. It is not a guilt problem any more. It is an erring child being restored into communion with his Father. This is the portion and joy of the Christian. It was not possible for the Jew under the old economy.

4   There is a holy abruptness in the manner with which the writer now dismisses the animal sacrifices of the old Levitical order. With a certain brevity, and clarity, and finality, he declares that it is impossible for the blood of bulls and goats to take

away sins. Those sacrifices had indeed been decreed and ordained of God, and they provided an atonement for the sinner, but they could not remove the sad fact of sin and sinning. They covered up the sins (with Calvary in view) but men continued sinning as they continued offering. There was no power or virtue in the blood of bulls and goats to remove sin. How blessed it would have been if both sin and the desire to sin could have been removed from the hearts and lives of men. How blessed for a man to be able to live wholly and always in the will of God, never sinning at all. But there was no such power in the blood of bulls and goats to effect such a happy state as that would be. There were limitations and there were impossibilities. The animal sacrifices were ordered for a purpose, and men were obliged to offer as they sinned, but the blood that they shed could never take away sins nor produce a man who would not sin. Sins and sinning persisted concurrently with the sacrificing of those innumerable victims, until He would come whose holy life and purpose in living, would be unique, and different from all others in the accomplishment of the will of God for the pleasure of God.

5 "Wherefore ..." is the word which continues the argument to its conclusion. Wherefore, because of the insufficiency of the blood of bulls and goats, and because of the inability of these animal sacrifices to remove sins, there comes into the world a Man, a blessed Man, to do the will of God perfectly. There had never before been such a man as this. He "came into the world". This clause gives assurance, if assurance were needed, that here was One with prior existence, now voluntarily coming into the world: "In the beginning was the Word, and the Word was with God, and the Word was God. He was in the beginning with God ... And the Word became flesh, and dwelt among us" (John 1:1,2,14 JND). He who ever dwelt in the Father's bosom, came, and dwelt among us. His coming not only brought Godhood to earth, but also took true manhood to heaven. He brought deity to men and presented pure humanity to God.

As He comes into the world this unique One is heard to say to God, "Sacrifice and offering thou wouldest not". Now what does this mean, since God Himself both commanded and demanded these same sacrifices and offerings? How then can it be said that God did not desire them, that He did not will them, if He comanded them? The answer is simple. God ordained them and ordered them that He might be enabled, in righteousness, to go along with a sinning people. But the will of God was for much more than a sinning people bringing sacrifices. The ultimate desire of the heart of God was for a life so lived that offerings for sin were not necessary. God demanded sacrifice, but He desired more. He desired such a dedication to His will in holiness of life and pursuit of His pleasure that offerings would be unnecessary and superfluous. Such devotion as He desired had been foreshadowed in the whole burnt offering of Lev 1, which was a life given in entirety to God, consumed wholly in the sweet savour of a devotion to His will and a desire for His pleasure. Men had not been able to live like this and in the consciousness of their shortcomings and failures they brought burnt offerings, type of Him who was now come into the world to do the will of God.

These words of Messiah, "A body hast thou prepared me", with the earlier clause in this verse, are a quotation from Ps 40, but as we have already observed, the OT citations in the Epistle to the Hebrews are not from the Hebrew Scriptures but from the Septuagint, the Greek translation (see note on the LXX at the end of ch. 1). This often creates a difference in renderings which to some is confusing, but there need be no confusion or difficulty when we once remember that the Epistle to the Hebrews is equally inspired with the Psalms by the same Spirit, and that it is His divine prerogative to quote His word either from the Hebrew original or from the Greek translation, as it pleases Him. The Hebrew of Ps 40:6 is correctly rendered, "Mine ears hast thou digged". The connection between "A body hast thou prepared me" and "Mine ears hast thou digged" is eloquently and lucidly explained by J.N.Darby, who writes, "The psalm says, in the Hebrew, 'Thou hast digged ears for Me', translated in the Septuagint, 'Thou hast prepared Me a body'; words which, as they give the true meaning, are used by the Holy Ghost. For 'the ear' is always employed as a sign of reception of commandments, and the principle of obligation to obey, or the disposition to do so. 'He hath opened mine ear morning by morning' (Isa 50), that is, has made me to listen to His will, be obedient to His commands ... Now in taking a body, the Lord took the form of a servant (Phil 2). Ears were digged for Him. That is to say, He placed Himself in a position in which He had to obey all His Master's will, whatever it may be". Or, as W.E.Vine comments, "The body prepared by the Father for the Son was the instrument of His self-surrender and His entire and devoted submission to the Father's will. The Son Himself, in partaking of flesh and blood, put Himself into the position for rendering perfect obedience. We are on holy ground. We are listening to the Son's most intimate communion with the Father as to the way in which the Son would become incarnate, in obedience to the Father's will, and all for the fulfilment of the counsels of sovereign grace".

6 "In burnt offerings and offerings for sin thou hast had no pleasure"; yet the pleasure of God must be the desire of every spiritually exercised soul. It should be the compelling motive of our every movement and the object of our every deed. To bring Him pleasure must be the ultimate goal of every truly loyal heart, but it must surely be a knowledge common to all such hearts that animal sacrifices, in themselves, could never bring that desired pleasure to God. We have seen that He required such offerings. He prescribed them and ordered them and accepted them, but their only value was a typical value. The writer will enter shortly into more detail with respect to these offerings. The broader reference to them here in this verse embraces two kinds of offerings, sweet savour and non-sweet savour. But it does not matter which. Neither burnt offerings nor sin offerings brought pleasure to God's heart. Offerings brought implied shortcoming and sin on the part of the offerer and this could not be pleasing to God. Even the burnt offering, the offering of a worshipper, presented by a devoted heart, was given out of a sense of personal failure. The offerer had desired sincerely to live a life wholly yielded to the will of God for God's pleasure. But that had not been possible. So he brings another life, to be consumed wholly upon the altar for God as he had wanted his life to be. Jehovah accepted it, but there was no pleasure. Real pleasure would have come with the life of the offerer himself lived out all for God.

With the sin offering it was all so obvious. Every sin offering offered was an offering brought out of a sense of guilt. The man had sinned; he had a conscience; he brought his offering. Jehovah required such, and accepted it, but again, there was no pleasure. Jehovah's pleasure would rather have been assured if the man could have lived without sinning at all, and therefore without the need to bring the offering. And so, the sad indictment of the whole sacrificial system: "no pleasure!" The offerings were necessary, but Jehovah desired something more, something better. He wanted a life that needed no offerings, which was in itself a body presented as a living sacrifice, holy, acceptable unto God. This would bring Him pleasure, but not the endless animal sacrifices of old Judaism and the law.

7   And so He came: "Lo, I come ... " Voluntarily, willingly, He came. Long promised, long predicted, and long awaited, He came: "Christ Jesus came" (1 Tim 1:15); "I am come" (John 10:10). He came, in humble circumstances, born in a scene of poverty and lowliness. Bethlehem was the beginning of an earthly human story that was to bring infinite pleasure to God. These words, as spoken by the Messiah at His incarnation, describe the whole pattern and purpose of His life, "I come to do thy will, O God". The word of the holy Child in the temple, when but twelve years old, likewise sums up His whole reason for living, "Did ye not know that I ought to be occupied in My Father's business?" (Luke 2:49 JND); literally, "I must be about the things of my Father". At last there was such a life as would bring pleasure to God. This life would require no offering for itself but would be in itself the fulfilment of all that the offerings had foreshadowed and typified. It would be a life wholly yielded to God and to His will, and this would mean that ultimately it would be laid down vicariously .

Our Lord's incarnation and ministry, with His eventual sufferings and death, were all "according to the scriptures" (1 Cor 15:3-4). There is a parenthesis in this v. 7, "In the volume of the book it is written of me". "In the roll of the book" doubtless refers to the inspired scroll of OT writings, the Holy Scriptures. All had predicted His coming. Prophets, poets, and psalmists, had, in their own personal styles, pointed forward to the Christ. They had told of His virgin birth (Isa 7:14); of His birth-place (Micah 5:2); of His tribe (Gen 49:10); and of His family (Isa 11:1). They had predicted His rejection (Isa 53:3); and His death by crucifixion (Ps 22:16). He rode into Jerusalem on a donkey as prophesied by Zechariah (Zech 9:9). Men gambled for His garments in fulfilment of Ps 22:18. They gave Him vinegar to drink according to Ps 69:21. They pierced His side with a spear in keeping with Zech 12:10. His burial would be in perfect accord with Isa 53:9.

Well does He exclaim at His coming into the world, "In the volume of the book it is written of me". The whole life of this lovely Man would be lived in the accomplishing of the will of God. He alone could truly say, "I delight to do thy will, O my God: yea, thy law is within my heart" (Ps 40:8).

8   The writer will now go into more detail regarding the sacrifices of which he has spoken so much. He is still quoting from Ps 40. When he writes, "Above when he said ...", the reference may simply be, as some will have it, to something further back, or higher up, in the text from which he is quoting. The Messiah says, "I come to do thy will O God", but higher up in the text of the Ps 40, or, "above" this expression, we have the other words about to be cited in this verse. This is how certain scholars understand the word "above", as meaning "higher up" in the text of the Psalm.

There may however, be a better view. Why should this not direct us "above", to the heavens, to the holy converse between Father and Son, to the mystery of eternal counsels and divine communications in the Godhead? "Above", in those heavenly courts, and in the holy exchange of thought between divine Persons, it is the Son who voluntarily offers Himself, and, in light of the insufficiency of the sacrifices and offerings, says, "Lo, I come, to do thy will O God". Above, in glory, there is One who offers Himself for the pleasure of God. The sacrificial system could not bring that pleasure. The law, while demanding it, could not produce it. But "above" there is One who says, "Lo, I come". He undertakes to do what all else and all others have failed to do. He will empty Himself, take a bondman's form, and in a scene of failure will do always and only those things that please the Father. Hearts that love Him will sing of Him:

> Faithful amidst unfaithfulness,
>   Midst darkness only light;
> Thou didst thy Father's Name confess
>   And in His will delight.

The characteristic diffferences of the various offerings are now specified. In a concise and compact manner words are chosen to embrace and distinguish the principle kinds of offerings as prescribed in Lev 1-7. Four distinct words are used:

1. *Sacrifice.* This word may be employed in a general sense to describe any of the main offerings, but it is more particularly used to indicate the peace offering. This was a fellowship offering, in which Jehovah, and the priestly family, and the offerer and his house, all had a part. It was offered as a thanksgiving, or at the making of a vow, or just as a voluntary expression of worship (Lev 3; 7:11-35).

2. *Offering.* While again capable of being used in a general sense, "offering" would appear to be directing us here to the meat offering. This is often called the "meal" offering, because, substantially, it was an offering of flour in various forms. It was a "meat" offering, however, because it was a presentation of food for both altar and priest. God and the priests shared in this offering (Lev 2; 6:14-23).

3. *Burnt offering.* The burnt offering may have been from the herd, the flock, or the fowls. But whether it was a bullock, a sheep, a goat, or birds, the great characteristic of this offering was that it was all for God. It was burnt whole on the great altar, a fitting foreshadowing of One whose whole life would be lived, and laid down, in and for the will of God (Lev 1; 6:8-13).

4. *Offerings for sin.* The guilt offerings were of two kinds. There was a sin offering for sins which had been committed in ignorance and which later came to light. There was a tresspass offering for sins committed knowingly and wilfully. With one notable exception (Lev 4:31) there was no sweet savour from these offerings for sin. They expressed Jehovah's displeasure and His judgment of sin, whether committed ignorantly or wilfully (Lev 4:1-6:7; 6:24-7:7).

These were not all the offerings, but they were the principle ones, but neither in any of them nor in all of them did Jehovah find His desired pleasure. They were indeed prescribed by the law and they were accepted when offered, but in themselves they were not the fulfilment of His will. "Thou wouldest not". Jehovah willed more than all that the sacrifices could ever yield. They were, after all, the involuntary sacrificing of irrational animals. His delight would be found rather in lives dedicated and willingly pledged to His will, lived for His glory. Such a life was the life of Christ, of whom the Father proclaimed publicly, "My beloved Son, in whom I have found my delight (Matt 3:17 JND).

9 " Then", said He. When? It was above, in those divine counsels. When He said, "Sacrifice and offering and burnt offering and offering for sin thou wouldest not, neither hadst pleasure therein", it was then that He also said, "Lo, I come to do thy will O God". And in this He takes away the first that He may establish the second. The first is that covenant based on law and on sacrifice. It was not sufficient, as we have seen. It must be superseded.

Now if it is God's mind and purpose that the new, second covenant should be a covenant in which the covenant people have His will (and the desire to do it) written in their hearts and not on stone, then it is befitting and proper that He who inaugurates it should be of such a character also. And so the blessed One of whom it is said, "He takes away the first that he may establish the second", is the same One who says, "To do thy good pleasure, my God, is my delight, and thy law is within my heart" (Ps 40:8 JND). The Son comes to earth, incarnate in a servant's form, to do on earth what He had ever done in heaven. He fills the Father's affections, He fills the Father's heart. He dwells ever in the bosom of the Father. This spirit then, which characterises the Son, will characterise the people of the new covenant also, a heart-desire to do God's will. In holy submission and in glad devotion, both He and they live for God's glory and for God's pleasure. This is the blessedness of the new covenant, and this blessedness is seen first in Christ. Others will take character from Him. And even, as we have seen, if this obedience to the Father's will involves eventual suffering and death and the cross with all its shame and deep sorrow, He will still say, "Lo, I come to do thy will". That obedience which was enjoined and imposed upon the people of the first covenant is a willing obedience on the part of the Son. That which was commanded on graven stone at Sinai is ever in the heart of Christ to do. It is His very nature to live for God's pleasure. This Man and this spirit displace the old covenant. So He lived, and so in the garden He faced death, saying, "Not my will, but thine be done". By such a life and such a death, superseding all, the first covenant is taken away and the second is established.

10 In the will of God, and by the will of God, and for the will of God, believers are sanctified. They are set apart from the world for His pleasure. The world is in revolt. Men yield Jehovah no joy. But there is a people separated unto Him for His glory. This He desired Israel to be, a nation apart and different, but they became quite like the nations around them, and failed Him. The blessed effects of the accomplishing of the will of God by Christ are now seen in the believers of the new dispensation. They are set apart for Him. Their sanctification is threefold.

1.   There is a sanctification by the Spirit (1 Pet 1:2). This is God's work of grace in the heart of a man by the gracious ministry of the Holy Spirit.

2.   There is a sanctification by the Word (John 17:17). This is a practical separating of the man by the daily application of the Scriptures to his life.

3.   There is a sanctification by blood. This is the sanctification referred to in our present verse. Christ's doing of the will of God has resulted in the sacrifice of Himself and the shedding of His blood. This has forever set apart those who belong to Him . His cross makes a difference between them and the world.

In the context, and in keeping with it, Calvary is viewed as "the offering of the body of Jesus Christ". The body in which He lived for God, and pleased God, and accomplished the will of God, is now, in that same will, offered up. It is the appreciation of this that causes us to love Him and this sets us apart, sanctified, for Him.

Again in keeping with the context, it is a once-for-all offering. He gave Himself in a sacrifice which is unrepeatable. In doing the will of God He became obedient unto death, even the death of the cross. That cross stands forever between us and the world. We are sanctified. We are His. From henceforth the people of the new covenant will delight to do the will of God, as He delighted. In some measure they may now say, as He said, "Thy law is within my heart".

2.   *The Work of Christ*
   10:11-14

> v.11   "And every priest standeth daily ministering and offering oftentimes the same sacrifices, which can never take away sins:
> v.12   But this man, after he had offered one sacrifice for sins for ever, sat down on the right hand of God;
> v.13   From henceforth expecting till his enemies be made his footstool.
> v.14   For by one offering he hath perfected for ever them that are sanctified."

11   The writer now returns to the question of the on-going sacrifices of Judaism. He writes in the present tense, for the temple was still standing and the sacrifices were still being offered. "Every priest standeth". This was the first weakness. In a moment we shall be reminded again (for the third time in the epistle) that Christ has sat down. See 1:3; 8:1. The priests of Judaism were standing ministering day by day. It was a continuing repetitive ministry which had, for them, no end in view. Christ's work was different. They offered "oftentimes", and they offered the same sacrifices every day. There was a sadness in it all, for the sacrifices which they offered could never take away sins. The sadness and weakness of it all was therefore fourfold, at least.

1.   The priests stood. They never sat. There was no provision for their sitting down. They must always be standing, ever ready to engage in their never-ending ministry.

2.   They ministered day by day continually. Every succeeding day brought its demand for sacrifice. Every new dawn anticipated another quota of victims and offerings. The great altar was never satisfied.

3.   The sacrifices were therefore multitudinous. It would be accurate to say that they were innumerable.

4.   They could never take away sins. This was the greatest sadness of all. Sin offerings there were, and tresspass offerings, but they could never take away the sins and the tresspasses for which they were brought. In the past they had provided an atonement. They had covered up (with Calvary in view). But they could never take away the sins that occasioned them.

   Now if all of this was true of those many sacrifices prior to Calvary, how indescribably sad and foolish was this continuing offering up of animal victims in a temple which was now but an empty shell, and about to be destroyed. Oh the folly, the futility, and the utter absurdity, that any of these Hebrew readers should ever be attracted back to such. There was weakness and sadness and emptiness in the whole system. Yet still the priests stood, and still they ministered day by day, and still they offered the apparently endless round of sacrifices which were of no avail at all. It is refreshing to leave the frustration of v.11 to enjoy that which follows the important "But" at the commencement of v.12.

12 "This man", our blessed Lord, is portrayed again in contrast to the insufficiency and imperfection of the old order, and although the two words may be in question in the original text, how have preachers and teachers alike delighted to point men and women to "this man".

"This man receiveth sinners"	Luke 15:1
"This man hath done nothing amiss"	Luke 23:41
"I find no fault in this man"	Luke 23:4
"Never man spake like this man"	John 7:46
"This man hath an unchangeable priesthood"	Heb 7:24

Here, in our present verse, "this man" has sat down after the offering up of one sacrifice for sins. Those priests stood; this man sat down. They offered often; He offered once. There is a disagreement among expositors as to the words "for ever". It is but a question of the placing of a comma. Does this mean, as in the AV, that He offered one sacrifice for sins for ever, and sat down. Or does it rather mean that having offered one sacrifice for sins, He for ever sat down? Of course both statements are true. He has offered once-for-all and for ever, and, as far as sins are concerned, He has sat down for ever, nothing remaining to be done. It is a matter of deciding which thought is here contextually and grammatically the more accurate. Opinions are divided, but both context and grammar seem to be weighted in favour of the latter view, i.e. that He has sat down for ever. J.N.Darby's *New Translation* will reveal his mind on it and express what many feel to be the correct meaning of the verse, "But He, having offered one sacrifice for sins, sat down in perpetuity at the right hand of God". There is therefore a double contrast between "this man" and the priests. They offered many sacrifces; He offered one. They stood; He has sat down. And His sitting down is for ever, because of the infinite value of the sacrifice He has offered.

Now if it be objected that Stephen saw Him "standing" on the right hand of God (Acts 7:56), the objection is neither valid nor serious. Christ sits for ever as to the question of our sins. That work is done. He will never rise again to deal with the sin-question which He has settled for ever. If He is seen standing in Acts 7 it is that He has risen to welcome graciously and tenderly His martyr Stephen. He has not risen to engage Himself at all with the matter of sin.

He has sat down then at the right hand of God: "I am sat down", He says in Rev 3:21. The right hand is the place of honour, and with personal, filial, mediatorial, and redemptive rights our Lord has seated Himself in that place of honour at the Father's invitation (Ps 110:1). This then is the confidence of every gospel preacher and the assurance of every believing heart, that Christ's work is finished. He has offered one sacrifice, Himself. That offering is of such inestimable worth that He now sits in glorious perpetuity while His saints sing:

> Done is the work that saves,
>   Once and for ever done;
> Finished the righteousness
>   That clothes the unrighteous one.
> With boldness let us now draw near,
>   His blood has banished every fear.

13 From henceforth, from the day of His ascension to the Father's right hand, Christ waits expectantly for another day. In the spirit of the Ps 110 we are now directed to His patient waiting. His enemies shall be made His footstool. What terrible indictment of men is this, that among them the Christ should have enemies. Alas it is true. He who came in gentleness and grace, and who said, "I am meek and lowly" (Matt 11:29), could also say, "They that hate me without a cause are more than the hairs of mine head: they that would destroy me, being mine enemies wrongfully, are mighty" (Ps 69:4; John 15:25). In awful fulfilment of Ps 2 they arrayed themselves against Him, Jehovah's anointed. Without a cause they hated Him and hunted Him, until, in the cruelty and agony of crucifixion, they cast Him out. His claims were refused. His rights were denied. He who was rightful King wore only a crown of thorns and a purple robe and was nailed to a cross. Some six weeks later He was received up in glory, from Olivet to the Father's right hand, and since then He waits.

His enemies will be made a footstool for His feet when He comes to His throne. In another metaphor He tramples them like as grapes are trampled in a winepress (Isa 63:2-3). It will be a day of vengeance. But today is a day of grace and He sits in longsuffering while the gospel appeals for acknowledgement of His person and of His rights. Many hearts respond and enthrone Him. Many will yield glad allegiance to Him and bow in willing confession of His Lordship. But many will not. The day of grace will end and the day of vengeance will come. Until then He waits. Patiently and expectantly He awaits His vindication and the judgment of those who have elected to be His enemies.

14 The words "for ever" which appeared in v.12 now appear again with a most beautiful connotation. Christ is seated for ever and we are perfected for ever. That one offering of Himself is of infinite worth and has linked us with Him in glory. Our salvation is as assured as is His seat in the heavens. As long as He is seated, His work relative to sin finished, so long are we safe. He has for ever sat down and we are for ever perfected. Conscience of sins will never burden us again. We have been sanctified, set apart, by that once-for-all sacrifice of Him who now sits in glory. As long as He so sits, the sanctified are safe; and He sits for ever. Glorious truth, that He has made us as Himself.

There is another most interesting and assuring relation of words to be observed in this chapter. Christ is seated "in perpetuity" (v.12). Believers are perfected "in perpetuity" (v.14). But notice that those priests of Israel offered "in perpetuity" (v.1). As long as they lived, they offered, but the sacrifices which they offered could not bring the perfection which has now come with Christ's one offering. And observe yet another thing. When the Saviour finished His work on the cross, He cried "*Tetelestai*" (John 19 :30). Finished! Fulfilled! Perfected! This perfect work has perfected the saints. We stand complete in a perfect relationship to God on the ground of that perfect finished work. The perfection of that work, the perpetuity of Christ's sitting down, the perfecting of the saints in that same perpetuity, these are all bound up together in a holy, happy interdependence the one with the other.

3. *The Witness of the Spirit*
   ### 10:15-18

> v.15 "*Whereof* the Holy Ghost also is a witness to us: for after that he had said before,
> v.16 This *is* the covenant that I will make with them after those days, saith the Lord, I will put my laws into their hearts, and in their minds will I write them;
> v.17 And their sins and iniquities will I remember no more.
> v.18 Now where remission of these *is, there is* no more offering for sin."

15 We are now further encouraged by the witness of the Spirit. It must ever be a cause of worship and of wonder to us that divine Persons should be interested in mortal men. We are again and again reminded of this holy interest throughout the NT. The Godhead, the Tri-unity, has, in unity, graciously moved towards us. The foreknowledge of God the Father, the sanctifying ministry of the Holy Spirit, and the blood of Jesus Christ, the Son, as in 1 Pet 1:2, these represent divine interest in men. "The grace of our Lord Jesus Christ, and the love of God, and the communion of the Holy Ghost be with you all" (2 Cor 13:14). In a dispensation past Jehovah had been intent upon teaching His people the unity, the oneness, of the Godhead. This was a vital and necessary lesson for them, surrounded as they were by idolatrous nations with many gods. To the saints of the new dispensation the same Jehovah now reveals the truth of the Trinity. Believers are baptised in the name of the Father, and of the Son, and of the Holy Ghost (Matt 28:19). Notice the singular "name" for the three Persons in Godhood, preserving the holy unity while, at the same time, teaching plurality of Persons.

This then is encouragement indeed, both to the early readers and to us, that having observed the will of God at the beginning of the chapter, and the work of Christ later, we are now assured by the witness of the Spirit.

There is too, an added assurance here with regard to the inspiration of Holy Scripture. It is the Holy Spirit who has spoken in Jeremiah (Jer 31:33), as indeed He had spoken in David (Heb 3:7; 4:7). God has spoken (1:1-2). So also has the Son spoken (2:3); and so also the Holy Spirit. Inspiration is a breathing into the minds of chosen men of the thoughts of God. This has been the gracious ministry of the Spirit, that holy men should be so borne along in inspired thought, then putting into holy script for us what God has breathed into them. It is that Spirit who now brings His divine witness to us yet once more with regard to the new covenant and its blessed effects. He again gives us His holy confirmation of all that the writer has been teaching us respecting this new and better covenant.

16   This verse, with that which follows, is the citation from Jeremiah (31:33) which has already been quoted in this epistle in 8:10,12. But we have before noticed the principle of repetition which is so prominent throughout the epistle. We are reminded yet once again of the promise of the new covenant and of its character. It is indeed a spiritual order, its character being effected in the lives of its people by the ministry of the Spirit. It is no longer laws written on stone. It is not any more a people living by rules and regulations, observing ceremonials and rituals. The desires of Jehovah which once were engraven upon stone tablets are now written on the hearts and minds of the covenant people, so that, instinctively, they live so as to please God and to fulfil His desires in holy living. What were once His demands are now their desires. They are a spiritual people, indwelt by the Holy Spirit, with natures intent upon pleasing God. The righteous requirement of the law is fulfilled in them, who do not walk after the flesh, but after the Spirit (Rom 8:4). If these saints do not steal, it is not because there is a law which says, "Thou shalt not steal". If they do not tell lies, it is not because there is a law which says, "Thou shalt not bear false witness". They are sons of God. They are partakers of the divine nature (2 Pet 1:4). Jehovah's desires are theirs also. They mind the things of the Spirit. The law is written in their hearts and minds. This covenant will be ratified with the house of Israel and with the house of Judah in a day yet future (Jer 31:31-34). That will be a day of millennial bliss, a saved nation being in holy fellowship with Jehovah. But the Spirit, with divine prerogative, does not here say, "with the house of Israel". He says simply, "This is the covenant that I will make with *them* after those days". These Hebrew believers had privilege and advantage. While the "house of Israel" to which they had belonged, still engaged itself with sacrifices and offerings, and laws and ceremonies, and priests and temple, they had entered (if only they would enjoy it) into all the blessings that Jehovah had in mind for the nation in a happier day to come. They, with us, are now, prematurely, in the glad possession of all that will be ratified with Israel in a coming day.

17   After saying this, i.e. the word about the covenant in v.16, the Holy Spirit now has something more to say. To give the sense of the passage from vv. 15b to 17 it is helpful to insert the words "it is said" or "then said he" at the commencement of v.17. See, in this connection, the RV, and other marginal readings, with JND's footnote at this verse. After He has spoken as in v.16, He also says, in v.17, "their sins and iniquities will I remember no more".

This is very blessed. In the light of all the perfection which has come to us by the death of Christ it is difficult to understand those who are still unsure of the eternal security of the believer. Some will doubt it. Some will even deny it. Here is both a promise and a bold statement, "their sins and iniquities will I remember no more". There is a grand finality about it. Sins and lawlessnesses, sins committed either ignorantly or wilfully, are blotted out for ever under the new covenant. The old covenant could not do this. The Day of Atonement, as indeed all the other offerings, brought continual and repeated remembrance of sins. The new covenant, established in the blood of Christ (Matt 26:28), removes not only the sins but every remembrance of them. They will never be charged to us again. Since they are remembered "no more", then there can be no more fear of condemnation or of judgment. The Holy Spirit bears witness to this. It is His word, that our sins will be remembered no more.

To choose not to remember is a divine prerogative. Men may forget, but they cannot choose not to remember. A man may say, "I did not remember", but he did not order or arrange it so. He forgot! Only Jehovah may say, "I will remember no more". This is the will of God now fully realised. It is founded upon the work of Christ. And the Holy Spirit bears witness to us that because of that one offering, perfection is now possible. This is not, of course, a present moral perfection; it is not sinless perfection now. But it is a perfection of conscience, in the knowledge that our sins and our iniquities have been blotted out. It is perfection too in the matter of our relationship with God; this is now complete. Such blessedness could never have been attained under the old covenant. It is ours now, as a present possession, and the Holy Spirit bears witness of it to us.

18 "Now", says the writer, "where remission of these is, there is no more offering for sin". Yet another conclusion is arrived at in the argument, and yet another proof of the obsolescence of the Levitical offerings. The argument is simple, but logical, and final. If there are no sins, then there is no need for offerings. Our sins have been remitted. Why then should there be offerings? One "no more" logically follows another. If there is no more remembrance of sins, then there can be no more offering for sins. No more sins and no more offerings are inseparably linked together.

What impact must this have had on these first Hebrew readers of the epistle, whose national fellows were yet engaged in temple ritual. To what purpose, with what intent, could there still be a bringing of animal victims to the great altar? How the simplest believer ought to have recoiled from the very idea of it. It was all a denial of, or an ignorance of, the perfection of the work of Christ. Everything had been accomplished by that one offering of the Son of God. Redemption was procured; sins were remitted; the conscience was purged; and Jehovah was satisfied. There could be no more sacrifice for sins now. The continuing sacrifices at the Jerusalem temple were to no avail. They were no longer needed nor accepted. The whole system was obsolete and ready to disappear. It would be complete and utter folly to be attracted to it or by it. Perfection was in Christ.

4. *The Way to the Holiest*
   ### 10:19-22

> v.19 "Having therefore, brethren, boldness to enter into the holiest by the blood of Jesus,
> v.20 By a new and living way, which he hath consecrated for us, through the veil, that is to say, his flesh;
> v.21 And *having* an high priest over the house of God;
> v.22 Let us draw near with a true heart in full assurance of faith, having our hearts sprinkled from an evil conscience, and our bodies washed with pure water."

19   Though we shall treat them separately, it is important to notice that vv.19-22 are one unbroken sentence. The heart of the sentence is the exhortation, "Let us draw near" (v.22), and for those who respond there are two encouragements with the exhortation. Having boldness, and having a great Priest, we may, with confidence, approach into the Holiest. The reasons for our boldness will be developed. The truth of our great high Priest has already been fully expounded in the epistle.

Notice again the word "therefore". It is the word so prominent in the Epistle to the Romans, the word used so much in argument, bringing propositions to a conclusion. Each time we read "therefore" we should ask "wherefore?" This will take us back in mind over that which has been developed in the earlier part of the chapter. There divine Persons have wrought for our salvation. The will of God has been fully accomplished by the incarnate Son. His unique sacrifice has made an end of all others, and He has sat down in glory. The Holy Spirit bears witness to us of a new covenant, a remission of our sins, and a perfection of conscience and of relation with God. With such sure blessings it seems but right to say, "therefore".

Having therefore a befitting and proper boldness, we may draw near. "Boldness" must not be confused with irreverence or arrogance, or with an undue familiarity. The word (*parrhēsia*) originally indicated the liberty to speak boldly, freedom of speech. Later it came to denote confidence. (See 3:6; 4:16.) Such confidence, such freedom, such liberty to approach God we now have on the basis of all that has been accomplished for us. This was never the portion of saints of old, not even of the privileged high priests. The masses of the people could never draw near at all. For them the Holiest was inaccessible. They were kept at a distance. The priesthood in general could minister only in the Holy Place, between the two veils. The high priest alone went beyond the inner veil, and that only once every year. With what reticence and awe, and perhaps indeed with trembling, must those men have passed through the veil into the Holiest where the glory dwelt. It is ours to approach with confidence. But our approach is neither physical nor localised. We draw near in spirit, in thought, in affection, in devotion, in love, in trust, and in worship. In the Epistle to the Ephesians we are viewed as being already seated in the heavenlies. In this epistle we are pilgrims in a wilderness, but with full liberty of approach into the presence of God.

It is by the blood of Jesus that we enter the Holiest. For the first reference to the blood of Christ in the epistle see 9:12. There are seven references to His blood. It is the basis of all that we are and all that we have. It is the price of our redemption and it is the blood of the covenant whose blessings we now enjoy.

20   Our entry into the Holiest is now doubly described as being both a "new" and a "living" way. The word "new" (*prosphatos*) originally and literally meant "freshly-slain" or "newly-killed". Some have seen in this an oblique reference to the sacrifice of Christ, to the blood of Jesus. The word however had come very early to mean simply "new", "newly made", "fresh", or "recent". It is a new way because it was unknown in a past dispensation. We have a way to God of which the people of the past knew nothing; an approach which they did not have.

It is a "living" way, as is everything else in the new order. It is the way of One who was the Son of the living God, who said, "I am the way ... the life" (John 14:6); "I am the living bread" (John 6:51), and also, "I am He that liveth ... I am alive for evermore" (Rev 1:18). His people are living stones (1 Pet 2:5). They have a living hope (1 Pet 1:3).

This new way has been opened for us by Christ. He has consecrated, dedicated, or inaugurated the way for us. Whatever other difficulties may arise in the verse, it is reminiscent of 6:20. Our high Priest is forerunner. He has gone in, going before. He is the first Man to enter. He has entered by His own blood, in virtue of His sacrifice, having obtained eternal redemption (9:12). So entering, He has consecrated a way for us; we may follow where He has gone. In the imagery of the old tabernacle He has gone within the veil, into the Holiest.

A problem arises with the clause "that is to say, his flesh". Does this clause qualify "the veil" or "the new and living way"? There is a certain ambiguity which not even the Greek text will clear up. There are two views which must be considered. Some will read, "the veil. that is to say, His flesh", understanding that the veil was, in symbol, His flesh. Others will rather understand that "the new and living way through the veil" is His flesh.

In favour of the first view it is argued that the wording of the verse suits this better, that it reads the more easily to say, "the veil, that is to say, His flesh". It is maintained that there is a kind of awkwardness of reading if we try to connect the clause in question to "the way". This first view will interpret the veil as symbolising our Lord's flesh, i.e. His humanity, and there is of course something beautiful in this. The blue and purple and scarlet and fine twined linen of the veil have been ever understood as foreshadowing the various glories that were seen in Christ, the lovely Man. But the veil, with all its beauty, represented a prohibition. It closed man out from the Holiest. Men may come near to it, and admire it, and even touch it, but it was a barrier. So with the humanity of Christ. Men came near to Him. Little children and even outcasts might touch Him. But the moral beauty that was seen in Christ was the holiness that shut men out from the presence of God. Until, eventually, at Calvary that veil was rent. His holy body was rent in sacrifice, and through that veil, that is to say, His flesh, a way is now opened for our approach to God. This is the first view, and perhaps it is the traditional and majority view. But there is another.

A lesser known translation will offer a rendering which fairly well expresses the second viewpoint. "The new, living way which He has opened for us through the curtain, the way of His flesh". This is to say that the new and living way is the flesh, the incarnation, the humanity, the body of Christ. This view does not necessarily depend upon any rending of the veil (which is not mentioned here anyway). The way into the Holiest in the old economy was "through the veil". It was the only way into that inner sanctuary. Maintaining that tabernacle imagery the writer is showing that there is now a newly-made way through the veil. There is liberty now, a boldness, and we may come freely. That way through the veil has been consecrated for us by the Lord, in His flesh. Like as we have been sanctified through the offering of the body of Jesus Christ (v.10), so, because of that same offering of His body, His flesh, we now have a new and living way through the veil into the Holiest. He who offered Himself, a spotless victim, now has gone up in resurrection, in a body into glory. The flesh, the manhood, of the incarnate One has consecrated for us a way into the presence of God. And so we sing:

> Lamb of God, through Thee we enter
>   Inside the veil;
> Cleansed by Thee we boldly venture
>   Inside the veil:
> Not a stain; a new creation;
> Ours is such a full salvation;
> Low we bow in adoration
>   Inside the veil.

21 The encouragement to draw near, and the basis upon which we may draw near, are continued. We have a dual reason for our bold approach. We have a new and living way, and we have a great Priest. We have, as A.B.Bruce so beautifully expresses it, "an open way and a friend at court".

References to Christ's priestly ministry are now drawing to a close. Is this the last reference to it in the epistle? The truth has been fully and richly expounded, and the value of it has been applied in power to the readers. From its first mention in 2:17 the ministry of that merciful and faithful high priest has been made good to them. His sacrifice, His intercession, His personal greatness, His sorrows and suffering in life, His ascent to the heavens, His superiority over Aaron and the Levitical priests, His perpetuity in a priesthood after the order of Melchisidec, these excellencies all have been urged upon the readers as encouragement and assurance of the greatness of their inheritance in Christ. Now there is this final exhortation, "Let us draw near ... we have a great priest over the house of God".

We have viewed Christ earlier as the forerunner in 6:20. He is already there. Our great high priest has gone in bodily to where we enter in spirit in our worship and intercessions. If He were not there we should have no right to enter. If there be not a Man in the glory already we have no grounds upon which we may draw near. But He is there indeed, a great priest, and we may come to where He is.

His priestly presence in the Holiest is universally beneficial to all believers. He is a great priest over the house of God. This term has been discussed at length at 3:6. It embraces all believers in the Lord Jesus. Sadly, many saints on earth today gather where the character of the house of God is not expressed in a local practical way. The well-ordered scriptural assembly has "house of God" character. God may dwell there. He may indeed rest there. And His authority is recognised there. But not all believers choose to gather in such a manner, with such assemblies. Nevertheless, essentially every believer belongs to that house and is accordingly afforded the ministry of that great high priest who is "over the house of God". To exclude a believer from the house of God is to deny to that believer the ministry of the great high priest. For any company to claim to be "the house of God" to the exclusion of other saints, is a high claim to high ground, with no sanction in Scripture.

22 With the exhortation to draw near there are now associated four important particulars. These are not necessarily conditions, nor impositions. They should be regarded as a four fold gladsome characteristic of those who are entitled to draw near. They are essentially true of every saint: "a true heart ... full assurance of faith ... hearts sprinkled ... bodied washed ...".

Two things are here implied in the expression "a true heart": firstly, the heart, and secondly, the sincerity of that heart. We draw near in heart. It is not a cold, legal, ceremonial entry into a material holy place of boards and curtains. Those hearts that enter so are true hearts. They are genuine and sincere. They are in keeping with the true tabernacle into which our Lord has already entered (8:2). Such is the "true heart", and such hearts draw near with gladness and boldness.

We approach with a holy confidence in "full assurance of faith". We boast nothing of personal worth or natural rights to draw near, but we come with an assurance begotten of simple but absolute trust. In faith we began. By faith we live and walk. In full assurance of faith we come to the Holiest, never doubting our acceptance there, since He is there whom we love.

With "hearts sprinkled from an evil conscience", the writer now resorts to typical language. It is undoubtedly the truth of 9:14. Our consciences, once heavily laden and stained by sin, have now been purged and perfected. We may be conscious of sinning, but we have no conscience of sin. There is a difference. Our hearts are heavy no more with the matter of guilt. All has been removed and we may in a holy and happy spirit enter the Holiest as purged worshippers.

In "bodies washed with pure water", some have seen a reference to baptism, but that interpretation is strained and unnecessary. The reference is obviously to the laver washing with which the Levitical priests were so familiar. The priest must be clean as he entered the Holy Place in priestly service. So have we been cleansed and fitted to draw near. Notice "hearts" and "bodies". Internally and externally we have been fitted to draw near. And so we worship in spirit and in truth.

Having had such privileges conferred upon us, well does the writer exhort, "let us draw near".

5. *The Walk of the Saints*
   ### 10:23-25

> v.23   "Let us hold fast the profession of *our* faith without wavering; (for he *is* faithful that promised;)
>
> v.24   And let us consider one another to provoke unto love and to good works:
>
> v.25   Not forsaking the assembling of ourselves together, as the manner of some *is*; but exhorting *one another*: and so much the more, as ye see the day approaching."

23   We have observed already in the epistle that there is a going in, and a going out. As a holy priesthood we go in to a sanctuary ministry, and as a royal priesthood we go out in testimony. Along with the privilege of drawing near in the Holiest there is the corresponding responsibility of living in the world in keeping with the dignity of our priestly standing. Privilege and practice are joined together, as are doctrine and devotion, dogma and duty. Having instructed us as to the way into the Holiest the writer will now exhort us as to our walk in the world.

For the AV expression "the profession of faith", maybe "confession" a better word, as in 4:14. It is an avowed consent and assent, a frank declaration that we have made, and we must hold it fast. Perhaps too, it may be "hope" here, rather than "faith" (see RV, JND, Newberry, and others). But the two are closely related. What we have grasped by faith gives us the hope that characterises us as Christians. We must hold it fast, unwavering, steady, with an undeclining firmness.

"For" is the connecting and assuring word. We have great reason to cling steadily to the hope for it is the word of Him who cannot lie. He is faithful. He whose promise it is, is a faithful God. We cannot do else but rest in His word and on His promise. Paul links all these matters together in Titus 1:2. "In hope of eternal life, which God, that cannot lie, promised before the world began". That promise has been manifested through preaching. We have responded to that preaching and we have believed the promise and inherited the hope. With such a promise, from such a God, it is incumbent upon us to hold it fast without wavering. To waver and doubt must surely be an irreverent slight on the divine character. To rest on His word with unqualified trust is the way to peace and blessing. Why should one waver in a hope which is based upon His unfailing promises?

24   But in all of this, let us have consideration for one another. This completes a threefold exhortation in this section. "Let us draw near ... Let us hold fast ... Let us consider one another". Mutual consideration of one another is the way to harmonious relationships in the assembly. It is, after all, only but right and proper that fellow members of the same body should feel for one another. Such consideration will promote and preserve a desirable unity among the saints, and such dwelling together in unity is both pleasant and precious to God and to us, and it is prosperous too (Ps 133).

But the consideration to which we are here exhorted has a more particular end in view. It is for the provocation of one another to love and to good works. The word "provoke" (*paroxusmos*) is normally used by us in a bad sense. Indeed Paul uses the word in that way in 1 Cor 13:5, where he says that love is not easily provoked. Here the word is used with a good connotation. We are to provoke, or stimulate, each other to love. Men may be provoked to jealousy, or to anger, or to strife. It is a happy situation when brethren seek to provoke each other to love. If I can so live, and so behave towards my fellow believers as to provoke them to love me, then that is the fulfilment of this present exhortation.

The provocation is not only to love, but to good works. We have earlier read of "dead works" (9:14). These characterised us in our unregenerate past. We should now be a people of good works. Let us "eschew evil, and do good" (1 Pet 3:11). "Who is he that will harm you if ye be followers of that which is good?" (1 Pet 3:13). We ought therefore to provoke each other to good works. We must endeavour to live as He did, who "went about doing good" (Acts 10:38). If we can provoke one another to increased love and good works, this will foster the desired harmony and will prosper our testimony to the world.

25   In the furtherance of this mutual helping of one another it is therefore necessary that we give diligence to attend meetings of the saints. We must not neglect or forsake the gatherings. For those Hebrews who were wavering under persecution and reproach and ridicule because of their faith in Christ it would have been tempting to stay away from the recognised gatherings of the Christians. But it is to the profit and encouragement of all that we all should attend the arranged meetings. The word "assembling" used here by the writer, is an interesting word. It is a form of the word "synagogue", but with the prefix *epi* – *episynagōgē*. Some have seen in this a suggestion that some of these Hebrew believers were yet "synagoguing" with their Jewish compatriots, and were neglecting the "episynagoguing", the additional "synagoguing" with their brethren in Christ. It was already, sadly, the practice and manner of some to be neglecting the gatherings of the saints and this was to the detriment of all concerned. Why should there be any such forsaking of the christian gatherings? Have we not been reminded earlier that there was with some of them an immaturity which may have been indicative of a lack of real spiritual life. If with some there was a profession only, without reality, then there would be an attraction back to the old synagogue and little heart to share in the reproach which attached to the christian assembly. It would be a logical sequence to forsake the gatherings in favour of the Jewish synagogue.

And so, appeals the writer, exhort one another, encourage one another. Some would apostatise. An academic, intellectual profession of Jesus as Messiah would not be sufficient in the day of testing, and some would go back. For the rest it was necessary that there should be a constant encouraging of one another, and so much the more as they saw the day approaching.

The shadows of AD 70 were looming large. To those with spiritual intelligence and discernment it was evident that the day which our Lord had predicted was now not far distant. The siege and fall of Jerusalem was at hand. Jesus had sat with a little remnant on the Mount of Olives and had outlined the impending destruction of the city. That was nearly forty years earlier. Now the day was approaching. It would be a fearful day for the nation. But believers would remember His words, and even now, before the event, but with the day in view, there should be a constant desire to encourage one another and to meet together for that purpose. The old system with which they had been associated earlier as Hebrews, was indeed waxing old. It was ready to vanish away with the burning of the temple and the destruction of the city by the Roman legions. It was foolish to be attracted any longer by such a doomed system. Stay together as believers in the Lord Jesus. Consider one another. Encourage one another. Do not forsake the gatherings. Strengthen and support and stimulate and comfort each other, and do this the more diligently as the fearful day approaches.

6. *The Word of Warning (The Fourth)*
10:26-31

> v.26 "For if we sin wilfully after that we have received the knowledge of the truth, there remaineth no more sacrifice for sins,
>
> v.27 But a certain fearful looking for of judgment and fiery indignation, which shall devour the adversaries.
>
> v.28 He that despised Moses' law died without mercy under two or three witnesses:
>
> v.29 Of how much sorer punishment, suppose ye, shall he be thought worthy, who hath trodden under foot the Son of God, and hath counted the blood of the covenant, wherewith he was sanctified, an unholy thing, and hath done despite unto the Spirit of grace?
>
> v.30 For we know him that hath said, Vengeance *belongeth* unto me, I will recompense, saith the Lord. And again, The Lord shall judge his people.
>
> v.31 *It is* a fearful thing to fall into the hands of the living God."

26 The awful sin here referred to is not moral sin. It is neither the trespass which overtakes a man, as in Gal 6:1, nor the grievous sin which required the ultimate discipline as in 1 Cor 5:9-13. It is the sin of apostasy. It is the crime of rejecting revealed truth in a wilful, coldly-intelligent manner, and this though there may have been an earlier mental assent to it, and a certain sympathy with it, even a profession of adherence to it. Apostasy is an abandonment of truth and principles previously professed and owned. Receiving the knowledge of the truth is not the same as receiving the truth. A man may be granted the knowledge of the truth and yet never in heart embrace the truth to the saving of the soul. Judas Iscariot is the great example. He had received the same knowledge of the same truth as had the others.

Together the twelve had listened to the Master's unfolding of divine things. They had heard His parables and His expositions of truth. He had instructed them as to sin and salvation, as to grace and faith and hope and eternity. Judas had listened with the eleven. He received the knowledge of the truth. But while the others embraced the revealed truth and believed it, Judas rejected it. The love of silver was preferred over love to the Saviour. The material loomed larger than the spiritual. He had received intellectually all the knowledge that was necessary for salvation but he rejected what had been taught him. It was a wilful sin indeed, the sin of apostasy.

The warning of ch.6 therefore is repeated here. To sin wilfully in rejecting the truth and returning to Judaism placed one in an impossible situation. There was, for such, no more sacrifice for sins. Where could a sacrifice for sins be found for the apostate? God had rejected the sacrifices of Judaism. The apostate had rejected the sacrifice of Christ. The wilful sin of the apostate, once enlightened, left that apostate in a vacuum. There was nothing left for him anywhere as far as salvation was concerned. There was nowhere to go and no one to whom he could now look or turn. He was doomed; and damned. He was condemned by his wilful rejection of revealed truth.

27   There was something, however, which did remain for such a one. There was a certain and fearful expectation of judgment. After all the apostate had chosen judgment by refusing salvation. It was certain. To reject the Saviour who bare the sin of many is to expose one's self to one's own judgment. There is no third option. The glad language of the believer is, He died for me. Our judgment has been borne and is past. The rejection of Christ as Saviour is a deliberate decision to bear the consequences in one's own self, even the penalty of one's own sinning. The judgment is certain.

It is also fearful. The pains of hell and the lake of fire are fearfully indescribable. Thirst; torment; loneliness; darkness; remorse; memory; hopelessness; an eternally fixed gulf: these all make the expectation of judgment to come a fearful thing indeed.

> O awful day, who would not be
>   Sheltered O Lamb of God in Thee;
> Safe at Thy side while wild and loud
>   The shrieks of that unnumbered crowd
> Shall rend the heavens and fill the skies
>   Till judgment's doom shall close their cries.

The Christ rejector is rightly regarded as an adversary, and for the adversary there will be revealed a devouring fiery indignation. There will be a heat of fire (JND). For those who are found in apostasy at the appearing of the Messiah there will be the most fearful revelation of One who will be manifested in flaming fire, taking vengeance on them that know not God and that obey not the gospel (2 Thess 1:8). A similar outpouring of devouring fire will be the portion of the adversaries at the close of the millennium (Rev 20:9). At the appropriate time there will be a certain judgment for every adversary. It is a fearful expectation.

28   The writer now appeals to conditions as they were under the law of Moses which his readers knew so well. They would have to agree that disobedience in that realm was deemed to be most serious and was accordingly punished. To disregard Moses' law was indeed akin to despising it and if such disregard was proven then there was no mercy. He had already referred to this law as "the word spoken by angels" (see comments at 2:2) and had emphasised that the gospel was greater in that it first began to be spoken by the Lord personally. Jehovah was righteous and required any disregard of the law to be evidenced by the testimony of two or three witnesses (Deut 17:6). When such witness was available, and the breach of the law was proven, then there was certain judgment. Neither was there any mercy. Sin must be dealt with, and it was. So was evil put away from among the people (Deut 17:7). It could not and would not be tolerated. When once proven it must be punished. The offender died without mercy or compassion. There was no such feeling with the law. This was the principle which, as Hebrews, these readers knew so well and the writer now draws a parallel.

29   Think of it, he literally says, how much more serious is it, and how much sorer punishment is due, if one should despise the Son of God? To disregard Moses was serious enough. To despise the Son of God is infinitely worse. To set aside Moses' law was a solemn offence. To refuse Christ's gospel is unspeakably more offensive. Of how much sorer punishment then shall he be counted worthy who so lightly esteems God's Son?

The apostate is indicted and is guilty of three most serious charges: he has callously trampled upon the Son of God; he has despised the blood of the covenant, the blood of Christ; he has insulted the Spirit of grace. The apostate despises the Son, the Sacrifice, and the Spirit.

To be trampled underfoot (*katapateō*; to trample upon) is cruel rejection indeed. It is a deliberate, definite, calculated refusal to acknowledge the Person of the Son of God. It is not simply a failure to recognise His greatness; it is a wilful rejection of that greatness. The apostate had been enlightened. He had received the knowledge of the truth of Christ's Person. But he has chosen to trample that blessed One underfoot in rejection, and has constituted himself worthy of sore punishment.

The blood of the covenant has been esteemed by the apostate as common. That precious blood which has set those men apart who have professed the Saviour's name, is regarded by the apostate as unclean, as unholy. Such is the meaning of the word *koinos* here rendered "common" in the AV. It is the word used to describe the defiling thing of Rev 21:27. The death of Jesus, the sacrifice of infinite worth, is counted by the apostate as being of no value. Such rejection of the Man of Calvary must inevitably call for wrath upon the rejector.

The Spirit of grace is insulted. It was grace that brought the Son of God to earth, to Bethlehem and to the manger. It was grace that took Him to Golgotha, to the death of the cross. In the exercise of that same grace the Spirit of God pursues a ministry to guilty men. He convicts of sin. He creates a consciousness of God and a fear of eternity; He shows Christ to be the only answer to the revealed need. To reject this gracious ministry is to insult the Spirit of grace. It is to do despite to that divine Person.

On these three counts the apostate is guilty. His punishment will be sore and deserved, and will be administered without mercy. He has rejected God. God will reject him. Apostasy is wilful sin, a coldly-intelligent refusal of revealed truth.

30 Jehovah's character does not change with the dispensations. His ways in His dealings with men may vary dispensationally but His character remains the same. For this reason the writer to the Hebrews is able to quote their OT writings freely. They knew Him who had spoken through the prophets, and they knew that He had said, "Vengeance is mine, I will repay" (Deut 32:35). As Hebrews they would be familiar with the Song of Moses (Deut 31:19, 22, 30). It was a song of great principles, of truth, justice, righteousness, sovereignty and divine rights. Several times in that song Jehovah had asserted His rights to judge: "To me belongeth vengeance" (v.35); "the Lord shall judge his people" (v.36); "I will render vengeance to mine enemies: and will reward them that hate me" (v.41); "he will avenge the blood of his servants" (v.43); "and will render vengeance to his adversaries" (v.43). Paul quotes the Song of Moses in Rom 12:19. Jehovah has sovereign rights. His desire is to heal and to make alive, to be merciful and to bless, but when His proffered grace is spurned He retains the right to whet His glittering sword and take hold on judgment (Deut 32:41). These Hebrews must acknowledge this truth they had known so long. Apostates were adversaries and Jehovah would inevitably rise against His adversaries in righteous vengeance.

31 Well does the writer conclude this section with the sobering observation, "It is a fearful thing to fall into the hands of the living God". "Fearful" (*phoberos*) is the word of v.27 and of 12:21, where we read of a fearful looking for of judgment and of the "terrible" sight which Moses saw at Sinai.

And God is the living God. He is not like the dead and impotent deities of the heathen. He has life and energy and power to judge, and it is a fearful thing to fall into His hands.

7. *The Watchfulness of the Faithful*
   10:32-39

> v.32 "But call to remembrance the former days, in which, after ye were illuminated, ye endured a great fight of afflictions;

> v.33 Partly, whilst ye were made a gazingstock both by reproaches and afflictions; and partly, whilst ye became companions of them that were so used.
>
> v.34 For ye had compassion of me in my bonds, and took joyfully the spoiling of your goods, knowing in yourselves that ye have in heaven a better and an enduring substance.
>
> v.35 Cast not away therefore your confidence, which hath great recompence of reward.
>
> v.36 For ye have need of patience, that, after ye have done the will of God, ye might receive the promise.
>
> v.37 For yet a little while, and he that shall come will come, and will not tarry.
>
> v.38 Now the just shall live by faith: but if *any man* draw back, my soul shall have no pleasure in him.
>
> v.39 But we are not of them who draw back unto perdition; but of them that believe to the saving of the soul."

32   The writer now repeats the pattern of ch.6. Having sounded a solemn warning concerning the danger of going back in apostasy, he would now encourage and comfort those who were truly Christ's. They were enduring continuing hardship and reproach in the cause of Christ and he would not add to their sorrows or discourage them in any way. Rather would he now encourage, and fortify them, and commend the watchfulness of those who genuinely looked for the coming One.

"Call to remembrance" is the exhortation, although it is not always good to dwell upon the past. Sometimes it is better to forget the things which are behind and press on (Phil 3:13-14). But at other times there is good reason to remember, to sit still and recall the past. It is always good to remember the day of conversion. For these Hebrews those had been days of enlightenment, days of illumination, when the light of the gospel had first shed its rays across their pathway and then illumined their dark hearts and minds. Into their darkness the knowledge of the truth had come. It was the light of the glad tidings of the glory of Christ (2 Cor 4:4). That was an experience never to be forgotten. He who at the beginning had brooded over the dark waters and who had commanded "Let there be light" (Gen 1:2-3), in the gospel had shone His light into their hearts in what the writer calls "the former days". This they could not fail to remember.

With them, however, as with many others, those former days had been associated with persecution and reproach. The joy of knowing the Saviour and the decision to live for the rejected One had stirred the inevitable enmity of the world and particularly that of their Jewish brethren, and they had been called upon to endure "a great fight of afflictions". There are six "great" things in the epistle.

1.	A great salvation	2:3
2.	A great High Priest	4:14
3.	A great fight of afflictions	10:32
4.	A great recompense of reward	10:35
5.	A great cloud of witnesses	12:1
6.	A great Shepherd of the sheep	13:20

The word "fight" (*athlēsis*) will be easily noted as the word from which we derive our English word "athletics". It is a contest, a conflict, and they would well remember the conflict of those early days. Since we cannot determine precisely the identity of these first Hebrew readers, neither can we determine exactly to which particular persecution the writer refers. There had been those early persecutions during which Stephen had been brutally martyred. That persecution continued after Stephen's death. There had likewise been persecutions, imprisonments, and martyrdoms under Herod, when James was slain (Acts 12:1-2). Hebrew believers were no strangers to persecution, and whatever the precise identity of these particular readers, they, like so many of their brethren, had endured persecution after conversion.

It must have been to their great encouragement that the writer here uses the word "endure" (*hupomenō*). The word *menō* means to abide. We believers have an "enduring", abiding substance in heaven (v.34). But of *hupomenō* W.E.Vine says that it is a strengthened form of *menō*. It indicates not only an abiding, but an abiding under strain, bearing up courageously under suffering. Taking it patiently, says Peter (1 Pet 2:20). They had bravely and patiently borne the suffering of those early days. They had endured indeed. "Remember!" says the writer. They must not forget the courage of those former days. Afflictions there had been, but they had borne up with courage. Let the remembrance of that early courage now fortify you and strengthen your resolve still to live for Christ, come what may.

33   The sufferings of those former days had been twofold, for not only had they themselves been made a spectacle to the world, but they had been companions too of those who were being similarly reproached. By the reproaches and afflictions which were heaped upon them they had been made a gazing-stock (*theatrizō*). The connection with the English "theatre" is obvious. They had been made a public spectacle. They had been put on show for the world's perverted enjoyment. Their reproaches and afflictions drew the contempt and scorn of unbelievers. Reproach (*oneidismos*) implies defamation. Their reputations had been slandered. Their characters had been defamed. But then, their great forebear Moses, had similarly borne reproach (11:26). He counted it greater riches than Egypt's treasures. Let us therefore go forth unto Christ, without the camp, bearing His reproach (13:13), even though that does imply being made a gazing-stock for the world.

The afflictions which they bore are described by the word *thlipsis*. It indicates pressure; it is that which burdens the spirit. It is variously rendered anguish, distress, persecutions, tribulation, and trouble. All this was their burden of affliction in those early days of following Christ. It had made them a spectacle, but they had endured it. They had courageously borne up under the pressure of it all in those days of first love.

But there was that other part to the reproach of those former days. Not only had they known such suffering themselves, but they had willingly become companions of those who were passing through similar trials. They had been happy to share the reproach of the reproached. They had fellowshipped with sufferers for Christ. They had become partakers in the afflictions of others. This is the nature of true love, to weep with them that weep (Rom 12:15), and it was the spirit of Christ Himself (John 11:35). There was something noble about this and the writer appreciates the memory of it. To suffer affliction in themselves was something thrust upon them by others, but to become companions of others in reproach was a bold courageous gesture. To fellowship voluntarily and willingly with those who were suffering for Christ was an indication of their genuine resolve as Christians. The memory of it all should now encourage them to stand firm again, though some, professors only, were apostatising and returning to Judaism.

34 If the text of the AV is acceptable here, then, in this their companionship with other sufferers, the writer had been personally involved. It was not just hearsay to him that they had become partakers in the afflictions of others. He had known experientially their compassion while he had been in bonds. They had shown him kind attention when he had been in prison, and had been unafraid of the consequences. Some manuscripts will not favour this personal "of me", as in the AV text, but will prefer the more general "ye had compassion on them that were in bonds". Whichever is the true rendering, the tribute which the writer pays to his readers is just the same: they had voluntarily chosen to suffer with others. This is the meaning of the word "compassion" (*sumpatheō*, to suffer with another). It is the origin of the English "sympathy", and, as has already been observed, it is the spirit of Christ. The word is used in 4:15 to describe His high priestly feelings towards us. He is "touched" with the feeling of our infirmities.

Prisoners of those days were very much dependent upon the sympathy of friends. A prisoner of no personal means might easily starve in prison. Those who were imprisoned for Christ's sake relied upon the visitation of christian friends, who, at great risk to their persons and to their reputations, braved the scorn of the world and the synagogue and ministered to alleviate the sufferings of their brethren in bonds. This brings not only the commendation of the inspired writer, but also the high commendation of Christ Himself who says of some, "I was in prison and ye came unto me" (Matt 25:36).

Now these Hebrew believers had not only suffered affliction, and fellowshipped with others who were also in affliction, but they had suffered materially in the loss of goods and properties. Persecution of Jewish communities in those days was often accompanied by wholesale looting of the properties of the persecuted. Indeed JND here uses the very word "plunder": "ye accepted with joy the plunder of your goods".

How literally did these believers respond to our Lord's exhortation of Luke 6:22-23. "Rejoice", He said, "when men shall hate you ... and shall reproach you ... Rejoice ye in that day, and leap for joy: for, behold, your reward is great in heaven". How firm a hold did these Hebrews have on heavenly things in those early days, enabling them to hold loosely to the things of earth. How great their appreciation of things spiritual that they could part so cheerfully with things material, for Christ's sake. Is it to be wondered at that the writer should say, "call to remembrance the former days"? Those were days of great love to Christ and of utter devotion to His cause. The memory of that early fidelity and loyalty must now encourage them to abide faithful still.

35 "Cast not away therefore your confidence". Remember the courage and confidence which you displayed in those former days and do not be tempted to be any different now. Why indeed should they now be tempted to abandon that for which they had suffered so much in times past? The substance which they had in the heavens was as great now as it had been then. The celestial treasure was still there, superior now, as ever it had been, to the possessions of earth. It is as if he would say to them, "You have suffered much, and sacrificed much; you have endured so much, and borne it all cheerfully. What has changed? Has anything changed, that after all that you have sustained, you should abandon the confidence of those early days?" "Oh remember", he is saying, "remember your bold and fearless loyalty to Christ. Remember with what confidence you then professed His name. Do not now jettison that confidence because of present difficulties. Persevere in the spirit of the former days. Continue stedfastly in the way in which you began".

Such confidence will have great recompense of reward. Notice the earlier usage of this same expression in 2:2. The God who justly recompenses evil will likewise recompense the good. He will judge unbelief and He will reward faith. The one is as sure as the other. Great recompense indeed for the unbeliever, but great recompense too for the man of faith. It is an added incentive to maintain the confidence with which we began, and to continue faithfully for Him.

36 This reward, however, was not an immediate or present reward. It belonged yet to the future, perhaps to the bema, the judgment seat of Christ (Rom 14:10; 2 Cor 5:10). This being so, there was an interim, waiting period, during which they had need of patience. *Hupomonē* ("patience") is a word so similar to that translated "endured" in v.32. As we noticed in that verse, it means literally, "an abiding under". It is patient endurance under trial, perseverance in suffering. They had need of patience now. They had suffered much and had been objects of much persecution and derision. They must not give up now, but continue patiently in the path of faith.

After all, it was the way of the will of God for them. It is a blessed thing to be found in the path of His will. It may not be comfortable or easy; it may be positively difficult. But it is the way of blessing, and that promised blessing awaited them. They would receive assuredly the promised blessing in due time, for the Saviour was coming.

37 The promise of blessing is as sure as the promise of His return, and the waiting time is really just "a little while". It is, more accurately, "a very little while". W.E.Vine suggests that a very literal rendering would be, "A little while, how little, how little!"

A little while for patient vigil keeping,
To face the storm and wrestle with the strong;
A little while to sow the seed with weeping,
Then bind the sheaves and sing the harvest song.

A little while to keep the oil from failing;
A little while faith's flickering lamp to trim;
And then the Bridegroom's coming footsteps hailing
We'll haste to meet Him with the bridal hymn.

"He that shall come will come" is a quotation from Hab 2:3-4. There it has to do with the coming, or fulfilment, of a vision, "It will surely come". The LXX however, from which the writer to the Hebrews always quotes, makes it the coming of a person, "Wait for him, he will surely come". It is undoubtedly Messianic, anticipating the appearing of the promised Messiah. Since this quotation is from the OT, it cannot be primarily, if at all, a reference to the rapture of the NT church as expounded in 1 Cor 15 and 1 Thess 4. Believers of this present day however will make the promise good to themselves and by application they will enjoy here the thought of the coming of Christ after a little while. How precious however will these words be to that Jewish remnant, after the rapture, who in the midst of suffering will persevere and wait for their Messiah. What comfort to them to read Hab 2:3-4, and to read the divine interpretation of it in Heb 10:37, "Yet a little while, and he that shall come will come".

"He that shall come" is literally "He that cometh", or, "He that comes", or, "the coming One". So did John Baptist and his disciples refer to the coming Messiah, "Art thou the coming One?" (Matt 11:3 JND).

The coming One will surely come, whether as Bridegroom for His church or as Messiah for a remnant of Israel. He will come and will not tarry. He will not delay. He will not be late. This was their encouragement then to continue in the will of God. There was a promised blessing, a reward. It would come with the coming One, and He would not delay. Let us, with them, wait with expectancy, and serve with loyalty, looking eagerly for that moment when He will come.

38 Still referring to Habakkuk the writer now quotes, "The just shall live by faith". This phrase is quoted three times in the NT epistles, here, Rom 1:17 and Gal 3:11. It is often pointed out that the emphasis, and the reason for the quotation, is different each time. In the Epistle to the Romans the predominant theme of the early chapters is righteousness and justification. The emphasis in Rom 1:17 is on the word "just". The *just* shall live by faith. In Galatians the emphasis is on "faith", to refute the errors of the Judaisers who taught that salvation was by law-keeping. The just shall live by *faith*. Here in Hebrews the emphasis is on "live". Those who lived and walked and waited for Christ would do so in faith. The just shall *live* by faith. Of course righteousness and faith and life are necessarily involved in all of these passages. It is the particular emphasis in the quotation that differs.

Some there were, sadly, who had once been numbered among those who professed faith, but who had now gone back. Such apostasy could bring no pleasure to the heart of God. This in no way contradicts the great truth of the eternal security of the true believer. Those who are truly Christ's are members of His body (Eph 5:30). They are children in His family (Heb 2:13). They are sons in His house (Gal 4:7). They are lambs in His flock (John 10:14, 16, 27). They are stones in the building (1 Pet 2:5). It is impossible that such should ever be lost. True, they may be side-tracked, and they may backslide. But they can never be lost. The way to assure others that we are truly the Lord's is to live by faith. "The Lord knoweth them that are his" and, "Let everyone that nameth the name of Christ depart from iniquity" (2 Tim 2:19).

39 How tenderly and thoughtfully does the writer ever find a balance between his warnings and his encouragements. No sooner does he issue a solemn warning to them than, anxious not to discourage, he appends a word of comfort: "We are not of those who draw back". It is reminiscent of ch 6, where, after the warning of the early verses there, he will say, "But we are persuaded better things of you". We do not belong, he is saying, to those who apostatise, who draw back. Is it not again like Ruth and Orpah? Some will go on, as Ruth did, to life and to blessing. Others will go back, as Orpah did, to darkness and to death. Perdition! What a fearful thought, that some had professed what they professed, and had seemed to enjoy what they enjoyed, but were shrinking back to perdition. "We are not of them", he says. The "we" is emphatic. And to add weight to the encouragement which he offers, he readily includes himself with them, and they with him, in the pronoun "we". "We" belong to each other, we do not belong to them who draw back.

Note the parallelism in the "of them", twice repeated in this verse. There are they "that shrink back". We are not "of them". He identifies "them that believe to the saving of the soul". We are "of them". Their's is salvation in its fulness, salvation in its completeness. We are of course "saved" now. It is a present possession. We are also being saved, as we make our way in pilgrimage through a wilderness world. One day we shall enjoy salvation in its fulness. In faith and by faith we continue, going on to that complete salvation which will be realised fully when we see Him whom now we love without seeing.

In the chapter that follows the writer will enlarge upon this great principle of faith, telling us what it is and what it does, and he will review for our encouragement, the lives of a great number of the faithful of earlier generations. With these faithful ones of the past we walk the same path of faith, and their example is indeed an assurance and an encouragement to us all. Dispensations come and go. God's dealings with men may vary as He moves towards His purpose. But the principle of faith is an abiding principle in every dispensation and generation. It is an inestimable privilege to be associated with those who trust Him and it must surely give Him pleasure to be trusted. How well did that good man capture the spirit of it all who wrote:

What powerful, mighty Voice, so near,
  Calls me from earth apart –
Reaches, with tones so still, so clear,
  From th'unseen world, my heart?

Lord let me wait for Thee alone;
  My life be only this –
To serve Thee here on earth, unknown;
  Then share Thy heavenly bliss.

XI The Triumphs of Faith (11:1-40)

1. *The Character of Faith*
11:1-3

> v.1 "Now faith is the substance of things hoped for, the evidence of things not seen.
> v.2 For by it the elders obtained a good report.
> v.3 Through faith we understand that the worlds were framed by the word of God, so that things which are seen were not made of things which do appear."

This great chapter, the longest in the epistle, has often been likened to an illustrious roll of honour, or to a grand portrait gallery hung with the portraits of the great. Sixteen names of the faithful of ages past are listed, with brief accounts of their deeds of faith and with appropriate comments. There are fourteen men and two women explicitly named. Exactly half of these, seven men and one woman, are from the book of Genesis, thus showing us that faith is as old as the earliest records of the word of God. As well as those who are particularly named there are memories of those who did similarly great exploits but who remain in anonymity. No doubt this is for the encouragement of so many of us whose names may never be known or numbered publicly among the great ones, but who nevertheless are privileged to live and serve and witness faithfully for God in our own spheres.

1   It is often said that the chapter here begins with a definition of faith. This is not strictly correct. These opening words do not constitute a definition of what faith is but rather a statement of what faith does. It is the character and the nature of faith which is here being explained and expounded.

Faith is the substance of things hoped for. "Substance" (*hupostasis*), a word found only five times in our entire NT, and twice more in this epistle, is used in 1:3 of the Son, the exact expression of God's "substance" (rendered "person" in the AV). In 3:14 the word is rendered "confidence", and also in 2 Cor 9:4; 11:17. It is the character of faith to give substance to our hope. We trust for things which as yet are unseen but faith gives assurance and confidence to such hope. It is, in the rendering of JND, "the substantiating of things hoped for". Some have likened it to a title-deed. We have already, by faith, the title-deed to our inheritance, the assurance of the unseen things for which we hope as believers.

It is, likewise, the evidence (*elenchos*) of things not seen. This word is elsewhere found in the NT only in 2 Tim 3:16. Although rendered "reproof" in the AV of 2 Tim 3:16, it has the underlying sense of "conviction" (see JND). This reinforces the thought of the preceding phrase. There is so much which we, as believers, cannot see with the natural eye. There are unseen things for which we hope. Faith is the proving of these things. Faith gives substance to our hope and conviction relative to the things which we cannot see. By faith we have assurance and confidence, and so has it been with the faithful of all ages, as the writer will show.

2   In the power of this faith the elders received the divine commendation, heaven's testimony. They obtained heavenly approval, but they obtained it by faith. Doubtless "the elders" are those whom he calls "the fathers" in 1:1. Faith is, and ever has been, what he has just declared it to be. The writer, in his recounting of the triumphs of faith, will go back almost to the beginning, to Abel, and from there continue through the history of the patriarchs and judges, prophets and kings, to demonstrate that the faith of his Hebrew readers is no new thing. There may be fresh revelation, and a new dispensation, but the character of faith is just the same. This faith of yours, he is saying, is the principle by which the elders, the fathers, obtained the approval of heaven. It has been so from the beginning; it was so for these Hebrews of the first century AD; it is true for us of these latter times. It is an unchanging principle, as he will later say, that without faith it is impossible to please God.

3   By this faith we understand what the intelligentsia of the world cannot understand. Every believer, even the simplest of believers, may apprehend the mystery of creation. The faithful do not rationalise; they do not reason; they simply believe. The man of faith takes God at His word and everything is simplified. We understand that the worlds were framed by the word of God. Three words here need comment: "worlds", "framed", and "word".

"Worlds" is that word *aiōnes* which we have met formerly in 1:2. Literally it means "ages", but includes all that the ages have brought forth as they have rolled their course. It has been described as the universe of time and space. The word primarily signifies a period of time, an age, but embraces all that the successive ages contain. It is to be distinguished from *kosmos* which is world order.

"Framed" (*katartizō*), means, in the words of W.E.Vine, "to make fit, to equip, to prepare". These cycles of time, with all that they have brought forth, have been fitted together and suitably prepared by God's word.

"Word" is not the usual *logos* but *rhēma*, indicating the declaration by which the creation, the divine will, was brought into being. W.E.Vine equates it with the expression "The Lord said" of Gen 1.

Such is the wonder of it all, and the true meaning of what the writer is now saying, that the things which are seen, the visible creation, were not formed out of any pre-existing material. The word of God, this divine *rhēma*, called them into being out of nothing. As another has put it, "the visible came forth from the invisible". This is, of course, too great for the reasoning mind of the rationalist, but again we say that the simplest believer in the Lord Jesus apprehends what the world does not. How? By faith.

2. The Antediluvians
11:4-7

v.4   "By faith Abel offered unto God a more excellent sacrifice than Cain, by which he obtained witness that he was righteous, God testifying of his gifts: and by it he being dead yet speaketh.

v.5   By faith Enoch was translated that he should not see death; and was not found, because God had translated him: for before his translation he had this testimony, that he pleased God.

v.6   But without faith *it is* impossible to please *him:* for that cometh to God must believe that he is, and *that* he is a rewarder of them that diligently seek him.

v.7   By faith Noah, being warned of God of things not see as yet, moved with fear, prepared an ark to the saving of his house; by the which he condemned the world, and became heir of the righteousness which is by faith."

4   Having expounded briefly the nature and character of faith the writer will now bring forth the first of the great examples. For these first three he will go back beyond the flood of Gen 7. So we say "antediluvian", before the flood. From those iniquitous days, when the sins of men rose obnoxiously before God, the writer will bring the names of three men who lived by faith in a sinful scene, and who became examples for the men of faith who would follow.

It must be worthy of note that the first example of faith is that of a man whose name is ever associated with sacrifice. All that we are and have, who are the faithful of these later times, is firmly based upon that great sacrifice of which Abel's was but an early foreshadowing. There had undoubtedly been a divine revelation and instruction concerning sacrifice. Indeed the parents of Cain and Abel had been clothed with skin after the Fall (Gen 3:21). The death of a victim is implicit. Abel's offering was therefore an act of faith in that he acknowledged and obeyed the word of God which he must have learned from his parents. His shedding of the blood of a sacrificial victim was an acknowledgement that his sinful condition meant a forfeiture of life. The divinely-appointed substitute was slain and offered in his stead. Another life was given for his, and so by faith approach to God was possible. There was divine testimony to his righteousness in that God accepted his gifts. Abel's offering is accepted and Abel is accepted in the acceptability of his offering and declared righteous. Note that "gifts" is in the plural. Is there a suggestion here that this was Abel's practice, his custom, to approach God by faith with sacrifice? It was not so with Cain's offering. He was rejected, for he was not of faith.

Abel has died long since, but as an example of faith he lives on. Being dead he yet speaks. His manner of life cost him his life. Our Lord speaks of "the blood of righteous Abel" (Matt 23:35). The first murder in Scripture and in human records, is not that of a rebel, or of a thief, or of an agitator, or of an enemy of his fellow-men, but of a man of faith who believed God and was accounted righteous. In the annals of example Abel lives on and speaks to us who follow.

5   For three hundred and sixty-five years Enoch lived in an exceedingly sinful environment, and he pleased God. In the Hebrew of Gen 5:24 it is said of Enoch that he "walked with God". The LXX, translating the Hebrew into Greek, renders it, "Enoch pleased God". How indissoluble are these two principles. To walk with God is to please God. To please God we must walk with God. So did God grant to this man of faith that which is our hope also who are the faithful of this dispensation, God translated him that he should not see death. In the will of God he may do for us what he did for Enoch and take us to glory without dying. As another has beautifully said, "The power and the rights of death are entirely destroyed – Christ has undergone them. Thus, if it please God, we go to heaven without even passing through death … God did this for Enoch, for Elijah, as a testimony" (JND).

But what does this mean, "He was not found"? Does it mean no more than that he was gone? Or is there an implication that men searched for him, a man who walked with God and who mysteriously and miraculously went to be with God? Will it not indeed be so after the translation of the Church, that men will enquire and search and fail to find those men and women who in their thousands will be suddenly caught away to be with Him whom they loved in faith (1 Cor 15:51-54; 1 Thess 4:16-17; Phil 3:20-21)? Men knew this man of faith, who had prophesied while he lived (Jude 14). It was before his translation that he had this testimony, that he pleased God. There had been divine witness borne to him during his lifetime. His life and his preaching were pleasing to God and it is said of him with a beautiful simplicity that "God took him" (Gen 5:24).

6   There is now a brief interlude, occasioned by the memory of this life which was lived for God's pleasure. It was by faith that Enoch pleased God and was translated, for apart from faith it is not possible to please God. "They that are in the flesh cannot please God" (Rom 8:8). The mind of the flesh is enmity against God, therefore it follows that there can be no pleasing of God except by faith.

"He that cometh to God" implies the approach of a worshipper as in 10:22. There can be no such approach apart from faith, for in drawing near of necessity we must believe that God is, and this is faith. There are three indispensable things in this Epistle to the Hebrews:

1. "Without shedding of blood is no remission"   9:22
2. "Without faith it is impossible to please God"   11:6
3. "Without holiness no man shall see the Lord"   12:14

So then did Abel approach, in the same faith as Enoch. Faith also believes that God becomes the rewarder of them that seek after Him. The word rendered "seek" is a strengthened form of the simple verb "to seek" (W.E.Vine). For this reason the AV translators have supplied the adverb "diligently". To those who in faith seek Him out, who seek Him diligently, God ever says, as He did to another man of faith, "I am thy shield, thy exceeding great reward" (Gen 15:1).

7   Five things are here said of Noah, a man who in his day was a righteous man like Abel, and a man who walked with God as did Enoch (see Gen 6:9):

1. He was warned of God.
2. He was moved with fear.
3. He prepared an ark.
4. He condemned the world.
5. He inherited righteousness.

For the second time in the chapter we have the expression "things not seen". God's warning to Noah concerned unseen things. Men had never seen such a deluge as that which was to come. Faith alone would respond to such a warning. Faith alone would see the approaching danger, and suitably respond, while the faithless would continue careless and unheeding until the judgment flood would overtake them (Matt 24:38-39).

Well might such an enlightened conscience move a man to fear. Noah's fear, however, was hardly the fear that he might personally perish in the predicted judgment. He knew God better than that. He had found grace in the eyes of the Lord (Gen 6:8). Here, in vv.8-9 of Gen 6, are the earliest references in our Bible to the great gospel truths of grace and righteousness. Noah's fear would have been a holy, reverential, befitting awe which recognised the majesty and purity of God and His right to act in judgment against sinful men. Such recognition of God would recognise too that both he, Noah, and his family were part of that fallen race of sinners, and in holy fear prompted by faith Noah determined to do whatever had to be done by divine direction.

He prepared an ark. Faith is ever and always associated with obedience. "Make thee an ark", Jehovah had said, and Noah, obediently and unquestioningly "prepared an ark". The obedience of faith assured his deliverance and that of his household, his family. And so it is recorded that when every living substance was destroyed which was upon the face of the ground, Noah only remained alive, and they that were with him in the ark (Gen 7:23). They were spared, in God's plan and purpose, for a new world.

By his faith Noah condemned the world of men around him. As he builded, he preached. He was a preacher of righteousness (2 Pet 2:5). It can hardly be doubted that the good man soon became an object of scorn and ridicule. But he persisted in his preaching, and he prepared as he preached, and walked his path of faith while the world of the ungodly persisted too in a path of iniquity and sin and unbelief. The faith of the man of faith was a condemnation of that unbelief.

By faith Noah became heir of that righteousness which is according to faith. Like another after him, he believed God and it was accounted to him for righteousness (Rom 4:3; Gal 3:6). He was justified by believing, and so is introduced an early example of a principle which prevails still in our gospel preaching. There is a righteousness, a justification, which is by faith alone; Noah believed, and inherited that righteousness.

3.   *The Patriarchs*
11:8-22

v.8   "By faith Abraham, when he was called to go out into a place which he should after receive for an inheritance, obeyed; and he went out, not knowing whither he went.

v.9   By faith he sojourned in the land of promise, as *in* a strange country, dwelling in tabernacles with Isaac and Jacob, the heirs with him of the same promise:

v.10   For he looked for a city which hath foundations, whose builder and maker *is* God.

v.11   Through faith also Sarah herself received strength to conceive seed, and was delivered of a child when she was past age, because she judged him faithful who had promised.

v.12   Therefore sprang there even of one, and him as good as dead, *so many* as the stars of the sky in multitude, and as the sand which is by the sea shore innumerable.

v.13   These all died in faith, not having received the promises, but having seen them afar off, and were persuaded of *them,* and embraced *them,* and confessed that they were strangers and pilgrims on the earth.

v.14   For they that say such things declare plainly that they seek a country.

v.15   And truly, if they had been mindful of that *country* from whence they came out, they might have had opportunity to have returned.

v.16   But now they desire a better *country,* that is, an heavenly: wherefore God is not ashamed to be called their God: for he hath prepared for them a city.

v.17   By faith Abraham, when he was tried, offered up Isaac: and he that had received the promises offered up his only begotten *son,*

v.18   Of whom it was said, That in Isaac shall thy seed be called:

v.19   Accounting that God *was* able to raise *him* up, even from the dead; from whence also he received him in a figure.

v.20   By faith Isaac blessed Jacob and Esau concerning things to come.

v.21   By faith Jacob, when he was a dying, blessed both the sons of Joseph; and worshipped, *leaning* upon the top of his staff.

v.22   By faith Joseph, when he died, made mention of the departing of the
children of Israel; and gave commandment concerning his bones."

8   It is doubtless to be expected that the name of the father of the faithful should
rank high in this listing of the worthies of faith. Abraham's faith made him a friend
of God. His faith has been lauded and lifted as an example, not only by the writer
to the Hebrews, but by Paul and James (Heb 6:15; Rom 4:3ff.; Gal 3:6ff.; James 2:23).
He was called of God. The God of glory appeared to him (Acts 7:2). The facts are
recorded for us in the narrative of Gen 12.

It has been said that the call of God to Abraham consisted of two parts: there was
a command and a promise. The command was "Get thee out ... unto a land that I
will show thee" (Gen 12:1). The promise was "Unto thy seed will I give this land"
(Gen 12:7). The operative word, the great principle with Abraham, as with Noah
and the others before him, was that he obeyed. "Get thee out," said Jehovah; "And
he went out", says the writer to the Hebrews. Abraham's faith took him out not
knowing whither he was going. It was indeed a step of faith that separated him from
his country and kindred and propelled him towards a land that he did not know and
had never seen. Dr John Brown of Edinburgh draws a most interesting analogy. He
writes, "Let us suppose a person, previous to the discovery of America, leaving the
shores of Europe, and committing himself and his family to the mercy of the waves,
in consequence of a command of God, and a promise that they should be conducted
to a country where he should become the founder of a great nation, and the source
of blessings to many nations; and we have something like what actually took place
in the case of Abraham". Jehovah called; Jehovah promised. Abraham believed;
Abraham obeyed. So is he held up to these Hebrew readers (and to us) as an example.
For them particularly was this a great encouragement, that they should abandon old
Judaism with all its religious and natural ties, and in the power of faith trust God for
the blessings He had promised in Christ.

9   Abraham's faith made him both a pilgrim and a worshipper. He pitched his tent
and he built an altar (Gen 12:8). He built his altar between Bethel (the house of
God) and Hai (the heap of ruins). He became a sojourner in response to God's call,
and even in the land of promise he was still a sojourner, a pilgrim by faith. Having
received the promise of the land, and being now even in the land which had been
promised to him, yet he sojourned as a nomad amid the people of that land. This was
faith.

Abraham lived in tents with Isaac and Jacob. What does this mean "with Isaac and
Jacob"? Are we to understand it to mean that quite literally Abraham, Isaac, and
Jacob, dwelt together in tents contemporaneously? Or is the writer simply saying that
Abraham lived nomadically, as did Isaac and Jacob after him? Perhaps both things
are true. Abraham lived for seventy-five years after the birth of Isaac, and during that
time Jacob too was born. Abraham was contemporary with Isaac for over seventy
years, and contemporary with both Isaac and Jacob for perhaps fifteen years. (Cf. Gen

21:5; 25:7; 25:26.) It is indeed highly probable that they dwelt together, family-like, moving their tents together by mutual agreement.

It is certainly true that neither Isaac or Jacob, heirs of the same promise with Abraham, lived to see the actual fulfilment of the promise which their faith had received. Like their father and grandfather they sojourned as aliens in the promised land. But they must have lived in the enjoyment of the promise, as did Abraham, owning nothing of it but a burying place at Hebron (Gen 23:3-20), but knowing that, although deferred, the promise was not denied, but would be redeemed in God's own good time.

10 It has been said that faith brings the future into the present and brings the invisible into view. In such faith Abraham sojourned as an alien in the land of promise. The promised land was as a foreign country. All the time of his sojourn, he was looking for a city. "Looking" does not tell the whole story. The word is *ekdechomai*, signifying that he was not only looking, but awaiting with eager expectation. Notice too, the definite article. It was not just "a" city, but "the" city. And it was "the city which hath foundations". How does faith rise above circumstances! Dwelling in tents awaiting the city! Tents so transient and so temporary, so moving and so moveable, would one day give place to the city with foundations.

Of this city God was both designer and builder. He is the artificer and constructor (JND). Men built the first city (Gen 4:17), and cities have ever been centres of corruption and violence. How different from the Edenic paradise which man had lost. But the last city of Holy Scripture is the heavenly, holy, happy city for which the patriarch waited with eager anticipation. It is the stable, eternal, immutable, abode of the redeemed. Some day, Abraham's faith told him, his wanderings would be over, his pilgrimage past. He would be finished with tents and with travels and would rest happy in the city prepared of God. Faith made all this a pleasant reality to the patriarchs. Happily, they dwelt in tents, awaiting the city.

11 It is an instance of the great kindness of God that here the lapses and failings of the men and women of faith are overlooked completely. Mention is made only of the obedience and patience which generally characterised them as the faithful. They may, at times, have been beset by fear, and at times there was friction, and yet again there were doubtings and misgivings. But these shortcomings are here ignored. This is evident with most of them, if not all, but it may be especially noted in the case of Sarai (who at this time became "Sarah"). See Gen 18:1-15; 17:15-17.

In the tent Sarah overheard the word of the heavenly messengers. It was a repetition of the promise already given to Abraham that Sarah was to bear him a son. Sarah laughed incredulously. The messenger charged her with laughing and this she denied. She was guilty both of unbelief and of falsehood. "I did not laugh", she protested. "Nay, but thou didst laugh", replied the messenger. The question is asked of her, "Is anything too hard for Jehovah?" All this is graciously forgotten in the record of Heb 11. Sarah was brought to faith in the faithfulness of Jehovah: "She counted him faithful who had promised". By faith she received strength to bear the promised son at the appointed time. She trusted Him who possessed the right and the power to give them seed, though both she and her husband were advanced beyond the seasonable age for childbearing. It is an encouragement to us to believe God when natural circumstances seem to militate against us.

12 When a man's faith links him with the promises of God the consequences are incalculable. Abraham, already naturally dead as far as offspring are concerned, becomes the father of a nation. On the principle of faith, Abraham, a hundred years old, and his wife Sarah, ninety years old (Gen 17:17), together become the progenitors of a multitude innumerable. Against hope he believed with hope, this man as good as dead (i.e in reference to these things), and the power of God operating in them imparted strength and gave him the promised seed. Together Abraham and Sarah, by faith, were privileged to lay the foundation of a family and of a nation.

In accord with the early promises (Gen 15:5; 22:17), Abraham's seed have become as the stars of the sky and as the sand of the sea shore for multitude. Many have seen in the two similes here employed an allusion to both a heavenly and an earthly posterity. An earthly nation of Israel, with an earthly history and destiny, was indeed born at that time, for multitude like the dust of the earth and like the sand of the sea shore. Abraham however, is the father of the faithful, and not all the faithful are of that Israel. By faith an innumerable company of believing Gentiles have come to a knowledge of Abraham's God through the promises of the New Testament gospel. A Church has been born, a heavenly body with a heavenly destiny, with members as the stars of the sky for multitude. The effects of Abraham's faith in the faithfulness of God have therefore been far-reaching, and will yet reach far into a millennial glory and into the very day of God itself.

13 "These all" does not refer to all those who have just been named in the chapter, for of course Enoch did not die at all. The verses 15 and 16 make it clear that the writer is referring to those named in v.9. Abraham and Sarah, Isaac and Jacob all died according to faith.

They "died" in faith. There is a double lesson for us in this word "died". Firstly, they died in faith, having only the verbal promise but not the actual fulfilment of it. They lived in patient waiting but died not having received the fulfilment of the promise in which they trusted. They trusted, but they died. Secondly, they died in faith, indicating that they persevered to the end, not wavering, not doubting, but trusting until the end of life. They died as they had lived – in faith. So is it true of us of a later day. We live according to faith, and, if the Lord be not come, may we too die with faith as strong as ever in a faithful God, singing as we do:

Trusting Him while life shall last;
Trusting Him till earth is past;

Till within the jasper wall;
Trusting Jesus, that is all.

But though they did not receive the actual fulfilment of the promises, they did see them afar off. We have already observed that faith brings the future into the present. So near did the promises seem to these men of faith that they virtually embraced them. Many manuscripts omit the phrase "and were persuaded of them", but they did, albeit from afar, both see and greet the sure fulfilment of them. The promises were the objects of their desire and their affection and they embraced them.

This made them different from the men of the world and they readily confessed that they were strangers and pilgrims on the earth. Abraham so confessed to the sons of Heth (Gen 23:4). And this was too, the language of king David himself, centuries later, "I am a stranger in the earth" (Ps 119:19). So do the faithful of this present day confess, as being in the world but not of it:

This world is a wilderness wide;
I have nothing to seek or to choose;
I've no thought in the waste to abide;
I have nought to regret or to lose.

Tis the treasure I've found in His love
That has made me a pilgrim below;
And tis there when I reach Him above
As I'm known all His fulness I'll know.

14 There now follows a very beautiful tribute to these pilgrims. They that say such things, they that talk like this, they that confess that they are but sojourners, make it clear to all others that they seek a country which is their own country. The word which is here translated "country" (*patris*) signifies a fatherland. The heart and affections of a pilgrim can never be satisfied in the land in which he is a sojourner. He is passing through to his home country, his fatherland. His language makes this clear. He speaks with longing of his own country. He has yearnings for it. His accent here is that of a foreigner; he is not at home. And so do we, like them, make manifest by our confession and by our speech and behaviour that we do not belong here. We are travelling through and travelling on to a better land which is our fatherland, singing as we travel:

Heaven is my fatherland,
Heaven is my home.

15 Now it is important to observe that these men were not pilgrims and sojourners in Canaan by compulsion. If their mind had been set on the country from which they had come, there was ample opportunity to return. Abraham had left Chaldea voluntarily. That sight of the God of glory had called him out. But at any time they could have returned, had they been so minded. Another comments thus, "From the call of Abraham to the death of Jacob was a space of 200 years. During this period they might easily have returned to Chaldea. The distance was no obstacle. There does not seem to have been any external obstruction. But they gave clear evidence that they were not disposed to return. Abraham takes an oath of his servant that he will not endeavour to induce Isaac to return to that land ... they were indeed seeking a country, but it was a better country, even a heavenly one. They looked for true happiness in a future state" (Dr John Brown). They were indeed seeking a country, but it was not the country from whence they had come. They were sojourners in the land of promise seeking a better country, their home country, a heavenly fatherland.

16   Jehovah recognises the holy ambitions of the faithful and, knowing the desires of their hearts, has prepared for them a city, for "they desire a better country". The word "desire" indicates an eager desire that reaches after the thing desired. So did they dwell in tents in Canaan, with heart longings reaching out after a better country. This in no wise invalidates the promise of the land for the nation. There can be no doubt that Israel nationally will yet inherit the land which was promised to Abraham's seed. But for Abraham personally, as for Isaac and Jacob, there is the promise of an inheritance in the heavenly city for which they looked (v.10).

God is therefore not ashamed to be called the God of Abraham, the God of Isaac, and the God of Jacob. For a dual reason He is not ashamed to be called their God. Firstly, He has prepared for them all that for which they had hoped and trusted and aspired. He has prepared for them, in the heavenly city, more than their finite minds could ever have conceived. Wherefore, He is not ashamed to be called their God. He has done for them all that a faithful, covenant-keeping God could do. Secondly, they have brought pleasure to Him by trusting Him and believing Him. They have rested on His word and thus honoured Him. They live as strangers and pilgrims, in patience looking for the fulfilment of His promise to them. He recognises their faith and their faithfulness and is not ashamed to be called their God. They acknowledge the faithfulness of God, God acknowledges their faithfulness to Him.

17   It is a principle that God does not tempt men. However He does sometimes test and try the faith of His believing people with the purpose of proving the quality and calibre of their faith. For Abraham, the greatest trial of his faith came on the day that Jehovah asked for Isaac: "Take now thy son, thine only son Isaac whom thou lovest, and offer him for a burnt offering" (Gen 22:1ff.). The patriarch had more than one son, but he had only the one Isaac. "Take now thine only Isaac", Isaac, the child of promise; Isaac the beloved; Isaac who was the repository of the promises concerning the nation that was to be. Isaac upon whom everything depended, was to be given back to Jehovah.

But Abraham had already believed God with reference to the miraculous conception and birth of Isaac. He had not staggered when the promise of a son was first given to him, but, without wavering, had believed God, and received the fulfilment of that early promise with the eventual coming of Isaac. The faith that believed God then, trusted him now. Jehovah would not make a promise and then deny it. Had he not declared that in Isaac Abraham's seed would be assured and that from Isaac and through Isaac the promised nation would spring. And so we read that Abraham, who had gladly received the promises was offering up his only begotten son (RV).

18 Of this same Isaac Jehovah had promised "In Isaac shall thy seed be called". Now what a test of faith was this, that Abraham should now be asked to offer back to Jehovah, as a burnt offering, that Isaac, that son, upon whom rested the fulfilment of the promise of a seed innumerable. It is the nature and character of faith to believe when it cannot understand. We are not asked to rationalise or to question. We are not asked to always comprehend. We are asked to trust when at times we cannot see.

Through the mind of Abraham many thoughts must have passed. Why would Jehovah demand the death of that son who was the divinely-given repository of the promises? How would those promises be redeemed if Isaac died? What was Jehovah's purpose in giving and then demanding back again?

What a lonely walk that must have been for the patriarch, three days into the hills of Moriah. While the young men tarried at a distance, Abraham must have gazed wonderingly on Isaac. What reminiscences must now course through his aged mind as he recalled the dealings of God with him. The God of glory had called him out, and he had obeyed. The same Jehovah had appeared to him by the oaks of Mamre, and he had believed. Promises had been made to him and promises had been fulfilled. But the promise of a great nation was to have been fulfilled in Isaac and his seed. Why should Jehovah now bring him this way, to the place of sacrifice and death? What held the future now? Without faith the prospect would doubtless have been dark. To unbelief it was all bewildering. But of Abraham it is said again and again that "he believed God".

And so, with resolution, he made his lonely way to Moriah, not knowing, as we do now, that centuries later another Father and Son would walk together, as it were, to the same Moriah, for if we identify it correctly, Golgotha is indeed the northern crest of that Mount Moriah where stood the temples and the altars, and where burnt offerings without number were offered by the nation through the long centuries of Israel's history.

19 Abraham's conclusion, by faith, was this, that God was able to raise Isaac even from among the dead, if that were necessary. Had not Jehovah, in effect, already given Isaac miraculously to them, as to those who were as good as dead as far as conceiving and bearing children was concerned? And by the same power, could He not raise Isaac up again from among the dead if indeed he were now to die as a burnt offering? So was faith able to say, "I and the lad will go yonder and worship and come again to you".

In the obedience of faith Abraham took the wood, the fire, and the knife, and walked resolutely with Isaac to the place of sacrifice. Jehovah-Jireh would order things aright. Abraham built an altar, laid the wood upon it, bound Isaac and laid him upon the wood, and took the knife to slay his son. He that had received the promises was indeed offering up his only-begotten upon whom the fulfilment of the promises depended. This was faith in action.

At the crisis moment of the severe trial Jehovah intervenes. The patriarch has demonstrated his faith and has proved his love for Jehovah. God will ask no more: "Now I know that thou fearest God". The ram is provided, taking Isaac's place upon the altar. It will be as Abraham's faith had said, "I and the lad ... will come again to you". In a figure, Isaac had indeed been received back from the dead.

The trial of Abraham's faith had been most severe. It is difficult to think of another quite so severe as this. Did he bear it alone in his heart? Did Sarah know? Or did the patriarch conceal from the aged mother the awful thing that Jehovah had demanded of them? What effect would the knowledge of it have had upon Sarah? But faith obeyed and responded and Abraham's God proved himself to be Jehovah-Jireh indeed, providing at the right and appropriate moment for the man of faith. So is He Jehovah-Jireh still to His people, at times testing their faith to the limit, and proving their obedience and love, and in the trial showing Himself to them as a faithful covenant-keeping God who will always fulfil His promises to those who believe. What encouragement must this have been to those earliest readers of this epistle. Were their trials more severe than this of their father Abraham? Were their difficulties greater than his? No child of faith need expect to find exemption from trial or immunity to suffering, but there is One who sustains in the trial, and suitably rewards after the trial, and ever orders everything for our good and for His glory. May we all find grace and courage to trust Him as Abraham did.

20   Isaac's name means "laughter". In connection with his birth and boyhood there was at least a fourfold laughter. Abraham laughed (Gen 17:17); it was the laughter of holy joy, of faith. Sarah laughed (Gen 18:12); it was the laughter of unbelief, of incredulity. But Sarah laughed again (Gen 21:6); she was now sharing in the believing joy of her husband. Ishmael laughed (Gen 21:9) the laughter of mockery, so translated by the AV.

Faith is not hereditary; it is not naturally transmitted to offspring; but God does often graciously permit parents to see the development of faith in their children and grandchildren. This is a great blessing, and it is a great sorrow when it is otherwise. So was Timothy a son and grandson of two women of faith (2 Tim 1:5), and so did Isaac now reflect the faith that he had seen in his father Abraham.

By faith Isaac blessed Jacob and Esau, his twin sons. It is an interesting observation that while we read of Isaac blessing his sons, and of Jacob blessing his, we never read of Abraham blessing Isaac. Perhaps this would not have been typically suitable. Isaac, the beloved son, the only-begotten, miraculously conceived, heir of all things, laid upon the altar as a burnt offering, and received back, as it were, from the dead, is such a foreshadowing of Another that it may not be fitting that he should be blessed by Abraham.

Note the order in which the names of the sons are here recorded, Jacob and Esau. This is not the order of seniority, but it is the order in which Isaac blessed them (Gen 27:27ff.). Nothing is said here of the deception which was practised at that time, which brought to Jacob the blessing of the firstborn. And indeed, when the deception is revealed Isaac makes no attempt to reverse or revoke what he has done. By faith Isaac blessed both his sons, but in the sovereignty of God the firstborn blessing was given to Jacob and not to Esau. It is a recurring principle that the second man often gets a firstborn place, so illustrating and confirming the purpose of God as expounded by Paul in (1 Cor 15:45-47).

Isaac blessed them "concerning things to come". Isaac, nearing death himself, still looked for that bright future promised to the posterity of Abraham his father. In Isaac, and through Jacob now, the promise would find its fulfilment. Faith believed that there were good things "to come", and in that hope Isaac blessed his sons. (See the whole interesting story in Gen 27:1-40.)

21   The facts of v.21 are similar to those of v.20. Jacob is a dying. He has sojourned for a long hundred and forty-seven years (Gen 47:28). Now he is sick and the day of his death is approaching. Joseph visits his sick father, taking with him his two sons, Manasseh and Ephraim. The aged Jacob (or Israel), strengthened himself and sat upon the bed. He reminisces. He recalls the past. The Almighty God had appeared to him at Luz (Bethel), and had blessed him with a restatement of the promises made to Abraham and to Isaac. He recalls the death of Rachel and remembers how he had buried her at Bethlehem. At one time he had thought never to see Joseph again, but now he was seeing also Joseph's children. "Bring them", he says, "that I may bless them". Joseph brought them near, Ephraim in his right hand towards Jacob's left hand, and Manasseh in his left hand towards Jacob's right hand. But the old man, guiding his hands intelligently, crossed his right hand to the head of Ephraim. Joseph tried to correct what he thought was a mistake, attempting to remove that right hand from the head of Ephraim to the head of Manasseh. But his father refused to be corrected, and said, "I know, my son, I know; he also will be great; but truly his younger brother will be greater than he". By faith Jacob blessed them, knowing exactly what he was doing, and thus again, the first man is displaced, the second man being brought into blessing.

That which follows in this verse, that Jacob "worshipped, leaning upon the top of his staff", is a translation from the Septuagint version of Gen 47:31. The Hebrew text renders it, he "bowed himself upon the bed's head". This belongs, chronologically, a little earlier than the occasion of the blessing of Joseph's sons, but is associated with that event as being a similar instance of the faith of the aged Isaac. The difference in the two renderings is apparently occasioned by the simple matter of a vowel point. Is the Hebrew word *mittah* (bed), or is it *mattah* (staff)? The difference is negligible since both ideas may well be envisaged in the picture of an old man sitting on his bed leaning on the top of his staff.

22   The facts of this v.22 are gathered from the closing verses of Genesis. Joseph has lived for a most interesting hundred and ten years. He had risen to great heights in the land of Egypt and his privileged position, in the sovereignty of God, had been most beneficial to his father and to his brethren. But Joseph's heart was not in Egypt. Joseph in Egypt predicted the future exodus of the nation from that land. As yet he would know nothing of the pending bondage. Nor would he have details of the exodus as are now recorded in Exod 12. But by faith he knew that there were promises to be fulfilled with regard to the land which had been sworn to Abraham, to Isaac, and to Jacob, and accordingly he knew that God would sometime, somehow, bring them up out of Egypt to Canaan.

Joseph died. They embalmed him, and he was put in a coffin in Egypt, but not before he had given commandment concerning his bones. "God will certainly visit you", he had predicted, "and ye shall carry my bones hence". This was the language of faith. Who, at that time, could have envisaged the departure of a nation, the children of Israel, from out of Egypt? Faith saw it, and Joseph, desiring even in death to have a part in it, gave the appropriate commandment and took an oath of his brethren concerning his bones.

The nation honoured the oath. They carried Joseph's bones with them out of Egypt (Exod 13:19). They carried them with them through all their wilderness wanderings, and eventually buried them decades later in Shechem in the promised land (Jos 24:32).

4.   *Moses, the Passover, and the Exodus*
     11:23-29

> v.23   "By faith Moses, when he was born, was hid three months of his parents, because they saw *he was* a proper child; and they were not afraid of the king's commandment.
> v.24   By faith Moses, when he was come to years, refused to be called the son of Pharaoh's daughter;
> v.25   Choosing rather to suffer affliction with the people of God, than to enjoy the pleasures of sin for a season;
> v.26   Esteeming the reproach of Christ greater riches than the treasures in Egypt: for he had respect unto the recompence of the reward.
> v.27   By faith he forsook Egypt, not fearing the wrath of the king: for he endured, as seeing him who is invisible.
> v.28   Through faith he kept the passover, and the sprinkling of blood, lest he that destroyed the firstborn should touch them.
> v.29   By faith they passed through the Red sea as by dry *land:* which the Egyptians assaying to do were drowned."

23   Thus far in the chapter, reference has been made to eight persons, seven men and one woman. These are, Abel, Enoch, Noah, Abraham, Isaac, Jacob, and Sarah. They represent exactly half of the persons named in the chapter, and their stories are all drawn from Genesis. Another seven men and one woman are yet to be introduced, and now, with Moses and those associated with him, there begins a new phase in the history of the faithful.

Much has transpired between Joseph and Moses. The children of Israel had multiplied and had become a strong nation in the land of Egypt. There arose a new king of Egypt who had not known Joseph. He felt threatened, and in his fear of the children of Israel he inaugurated a period of severe oppression of them, making them virtually a nation of slaves in his land. In their bondage they bore grievous burdens, labouring in the brick fields of Egypt, building store-cities for Pharaoh, serving with harshness, and daily becoming the more embittered under the whips of the task-masters.

But the more they were afflicted, the more they multiplied and spread. The Hebrew midwives were then instructed, that when they attended at the birth of a baby, they must kill the male children while allowing the female babies to live. The brave midwives, however, frustrated the plans of the king and saved the male children alive. This brought a strengthening of the decree and there was now a plain command to the Egyptian people that all Hebrew male infants were to be cast forthwith into the river at birth.

But there was at least one Levite who with his wife was prepared to defy the cruel edict. The woman bore a son. They saw that he was a goodly child, a fair child, a beautiful child. If it is the nature of faith to bring the future into the present, then it must be believed that these parents saw beyond the physical, and recognised a moral worth in their child, and indeed a prophetic destiny, and they were determined to save him from death in the river. Stephen says in Acts 7:20 that the child was exceeding fair. JND points out that this is literally, "fair to God", and with this comment the RV margin agrees.

For three months the parents hid the baby in the house. It is often said incorrectly that he was hidden in the bulrushes by the river's side. He was hidden in the house until they could hide him no longer and it was then that the mother made a tiny ark of reeds. She "plastered it with resin and with pitch, and put the child in it, and laid it in the sedge on the bank of the river. And his sister stood afar off to see what would happen to him" (Exod 2:3-4 JND). It was an act of great faith.

There is a tender phrase in Exod 2:6: "The babe wept". It has been beautifully said, "A baby's tears decided the destiny of a nation. and changed the course of the world's history". Those tears touched the heart of the daughter of Pharaoh. She had compassion on the babe and in the plan of God he became her adoptive son but was nursed by his own mother who was, in turn, paid wages for nursing her own child (Exod 2:7-10). How wondrous are the ways of God. In the sovereignty of God, Egypt provided for the welfare and future education of him who was later to be instrumental in the destruction of the Pharaoh. They called him Moses. And all this because of the faith of a husband and wife who were not afraid of the injunction of an Egyptian king.

24 Moses grew up in the court, in the palace of Pharaoh, the adoptive son of Pharaoh's daughter. He was instructed in all the wisdom of the Egyptians and rose to great heights, mighty in words and deeds (Acts 7:22). But perhaps more important than his Egyptian schooling was the godly instruction which he must have received from his mother in those early impressionable years. How faithfully she must have rehearsed to her son the stories of Jehovah's dealings with the nation, and with Abraham and Isaac and Jacob. And how she would have impressed upon him his essential relationship with the Hebrew people. The faithful instruction was not lost on Moses. "When he was come to years" is in contrast with "when he was born" (v.23). It means simply, "when he reached maturity". He came to full manhood and to greatness, and at the age of forty he manifested, though violently and prematurely, his true position with regard to the oppressed Hebrews (Exod 2:11-12; Acts 7:23-25). His brethren did not understand and a little later Moses had to flee Egypt, leaving behind him, groaning and sighing under the weight of the bondage, the people whose deliverer he was to be.

But the break was made. It may not have been by faith. It may not have been the right time or the right way, but it was the beginning of that renunciation of Egypt and the palace. It was to bring him eventually in God's time into direct conflict with all the might of the Egyptian throne. But he would then act and move by faith. By faith he would indeed refuse to be called the son of Pharaoh's daughter.

25 There was a choice to be made. It was a costly decision. Perhaps we should ever keep in mind that the constant design of the writer was to help and encourage his Hebrew readers. How would the great examples of Abraham, Isaac, Jacob, Joseph, and now Moses, stimulate them to greater faith and obedience, seeing how God in His own good time, rewarded the courage of those who were prepared to trust Him.

Moses chose: on the one hand there were the pleasures of sin; on the other hand there were afflictions with the people of God. Egypt had its corrupt pleasures, and a son of the Pharaoh with impunity could have enjoyed them all. In the luxury of the court Moses might have indulged in that strange blending of refinement and vulgarity, of sophistry and immorality, which so often characterised the courts of the heathen. There were not many saints on earth at that time, but any that there were might have been found among the despised Hebrews. They were "the people of God".

A man of the world, making choice with natural reasoning and human ambitions only, would have had no hesitation or doubt, but faith sees things differently. Faith has wider horizons. The pleasures of Egypt would not last. But then, neither would the afflictions of the people of God! The pleasures of sin, in their transience, would result eventually in eternal loss and woe. Suffering with God's people was a short avenue to glory and to bliss. To faith the alternatives were simple. It was pleasures now for a season and eternal suffering afterwards, or suffering now for a little while, with pleasures for evermore.

26 It was faith that recognised that suffering with the people of God was really bearing the reproach of the Christ. Messiah would come. He would come of the tribe of Judah. How much did Moses then know (taught by his mother?) of that which he was afterwards to record (Gen 49:10)? This influenced his choice. Messiah would come indeed. Moses would not hesitate to suffer with the people of God who waited for that Messiah. Suffering with them was suffering for Him and faith accepted it.

Adversity with Christ was greater than prosperity in Egypt. Egypt's mighty empire would fall. Egypt's treasures would not last. The reproach of Christ was greater riches than were in all the coffers of Egypt. It was the inestimable privilege of sharing in the reproach and mockery that one day would be meted out to the Messiah Himself. And there was great reward. Moses looked off, away into the future. He saw far beyond the horizons of Egypt and the temporary pleasures which would have been afforded him as an Egyptian prince. They were too transient. He made his choice.

27 By faith Moses forsook Egypt. It is difficult to relate this comment to any particular moment or specific event in the career of Moses. It does not appear to describe the circumstances of his flight into Midian after the murder of Exod 2. At that time no doubt there would have been a fear of the wrath of the king. He fled from the face of Pharaoh (Exod 2:14ff.). Neither does it seem to be related to the exodus, the national departure from Egypt. Perhaps it ought to be seen as a state of mind, a conscious decision to which Moses came when, with some understanding of what Jehovah was about to do, and of the part that he was to have in it all, he determined in his heart to abandon Egypt and the court and his adoptive mother, and be associated wholly with the people who were God's people. Moses knew, and supposed his Hebrew brethren should know, at the time when he smote the Egyptian in Exod 2, that God would by him deliver the people (see Acts 7:25). He must have known that his decision to be identified with the children of Israel would indeed incur the wrath of the king. But he did not fear that. His choice was made.

His courage was not of himself. It was by faith that both he, and so many others, were enabled to endure. Faith makes the invisible visible. That which is not comprehensible to human thought and reasoning becomes crystal clear to the eye of faith. Is there here an appeal to his Hebrew readers that they should not be attracted by that which was visible and tangible in Judaism? The real things, the eternal things, were the invisible things. Their own Moses had endured as seeing Him who was invisible. So should they, refusing to be influenced by any material temple or priesthood or system, however attractive that may all be. The material was temporal and transient. He had pointed this out to them before. Like Moses himself, let them endure the present reproach with faith's eye upon the invisible.

28 The writer now passes over the years spent in the land of Midian. He omits the experience of the burning bush and the return of Moses to his brethren in bondage in Egypt. Faith, that had preserved Moses in his infancy, and that had enabled him in maturity to make the choice that he did, now makes him in the purpose of God deliverer of the oppressed people. By faith he kept the passover, and the sprinkling of blood. It would have been, to the reasoning mind, a most strange and unusual way of redeeming the nation. A slain lamb and blood-sprinkled door posts would be appreciated only by faith. But it was Jehovah's way and we have seen that faith is manifested by obedience. He "kept" the passover.

The perfect tense of the verb "kept" apparently indicates the continuance of the passover as a perpetual memorial to the exodus. That historical night of the original passover must never be forgotten. Jehovah had decreed the destruction of all the firstborn in the land of Egypt. But He had also decreed the redemption of those firstborn ones who were sheltering behind that sprinkled blood. Faith accepted the warning that judgment was coming and faith also accepted the ordained means of salvation from it. "When I see the blood I will pass over you" (Exod 12:13). The message of the blood upon the door posts was that death had already entered that particular home and family. A substitute for the firstborn had died in that homestead. Faith obeyed. Faith rested on the trustworthiness of the word of God and the destroyer of the firstborn did not touch them.

It is not the writer's purpose here to expound the interesting details or typical meaning of the passover. This would be profitable at other times but the Day of Atonement is the background to this epistle rather than the passover. The present purpose is to encourage faith as the faith of Moses who believed and obeyed God and who, by such unusual means as the death of the lamb and the sprinkling of blood was enabled to lead a nation of bondmen out of Egypt.

29 It can hardly be supposed that every individual that came out of Egypt that night came out by faith, but the faith of Moses and Aaron and the leaders of the nation appears to be credited to the great company as a whole. It was indeed a great multitude that went up out of Egypt on that memorable night, six hundred thousand men with their women and children, estimated by some to be in the region of three million souls (see Exod 12:37). Four hundred and thirty years of Egyptian history was now drawing to a close for the children of Israel. They moved out and journeyed from Rameses to Succoth, and from Succoth to Etham. eventually encamping near Migdol by the Red Sea. It was perhaps here, so soon, that the sad story of their oft murmurings began. Pharaoh pursued them with horsemen and chariots and in their fear they upbraided Moses. Had he brought them out here to die in the wilderness because there were no graves in Egypt? Why had he done this to them? Were they not indeed right when some of them had said, in their bondage, "Let us alone" (Exod 14:11-12)?

The reply of the man of faith is now preserved immortally, the grand text of many a gospel preacher, "Fear not: stand still, and see the salvation of the Lord". It was a word of faith truly. The hosts of Pharaoh were behind them; the waters of the Red Sea were before them. To the rational mind they were trapped. It is in just such impossible situations that faith provides the necessary courage and comfort. Jehovah hid them from the Egyptians with an intervening pillar of cloud. He divided the sea with a strong east wind until the waters stood up on either side, a wall of water on the right side and on the left, and the sea bed became as dry land for them. How wide this break in the waters was we cannot tell: one mile? two miles? or several miles? We do not know. It was wide enough to allow the thousands of Israel to pass to safety while Jehovah was confusing and confounding the pursuing Egyptians (Exod 14:23-25). It was as if the promise of a later date was even now being made good to them, "When thou passest through the waters, I will be with thee; and they shall not overflow thee". Such a promise would still be made good to the early Hebrew readers of this epistle in their times of reproach and persecution.

And so by faith they passed safely through. The Egyptians, assaying to do the same thing, were swallowed up by the returning waters and perished. It is to all a solemn and fearful lesson that man cannot, in the energy of the flesh, walk the path of faith.

5 Rahab and Jericho
11:30-31

> v.30 "By faith the walls of Jericho fell down, after they were compassed about seven days.
> v.31 By faith the harlot Rahab perished not with them that believed not, when she had received the spies with peace."

30 The writer now moves at once from the Red Sea to the conquest of Jericho on the other side of Jordan. There is not a word concerning the events of the wilderness. Those forty years were not characterised by faith. This verse brings us then beyond the death of Moses and into Canaan. The descending waters of the Jordan had been cut off and had stood up in a heap until the hosts of Israel were safely passed over. Now they were indeed in the land, and on the plains of Jericho they held the passover and ate the old corn of the land and the manna ceased (Jos 5:10-12).

The story of what Jehovah had done for the children of Israel was soon well known to the inhabitants of the land so that fear took hold of them, their hearts melted, and Jericho was shut up and barred. But in a way which must have been thought ludicrous to the worldly strategist Jehovah was about to give Jericho into the hand of Joshua. The well-known story is told in Jos 6.

For six days Israel's men of war encompassed the city once every day, accompanied by the ark of the covenant and seven priests carrying ram's horns, or trumpets. They marched in silence except for the continual blowing of the trumpets. On the seventh day they rose at dawn and compassed Jericho seven times. As they went round the city for the seventh time the trumpeting priests made a long blast with the ram's horns. This was the signal. "Shout", said Joshua, "for Jehovah has given you the city". And so did they shout, with a great shout, and the walls of Jericho fell flat, and they took the city.

By whose faith was the conquest of Jericho accomplished? Certainly there was the faith of Joshua personally. But if faith is evidenced by obedience then there was faith indeed on the part of the people who obeyed, apparently without question, the commands of Jehovah given through Joshua.

It is sad to hear the pathetic endeavours of infidelity to explain away rationally the conquest of Jericho and the rolling back of the seas, as well as the other divine interventions of those days. How pitiable indeed that, rather than accept in faith these thrilling accounts of what has been wrought by faith, men of intellect and learning should search in vain for explanations of these phenomena. How much better to bow simply to the authenticity and infallible accuracy of God's word.

31   Now Jehovah has His servants everywhere and even in Jericho there was one who was destined to be forever after cited as an example of simple faith. That one was Rahab, a Canaanitess and a harlot. If there is any lesson to be learned from the examples of faith which are given in this great chapter it is that faith knows no boundaries. There are no barriers, neither racial, national, social, cultural, nor dispensational. Men and women, antediluvians and postdiluvians, Israelites and Canaanites, kings and judges, princes and prophets, rich and poor, young and old, alike find a mention in faith's grand roll of honour.

It is not to be supposed that the Biblical records condone all that Rahab did or said. But she acted in the simplicity of a basic elementary faith and Jehovah acknowledged that. The two spies had visited her when Israel was yet on the other side of Jordan (Jos 2:1ff.). She had bravely concealed them from the king's men and actually told lies to ensure their safety. Why did she do it, risking her own life for them? It was indeed the obedience of faith. Listen to her testimony. "I know that the Lord hath given you the land ... we have heard how the Lord dried up the water of the Red Sea for you ... the Lord your God, he is God in heaven above and in earth beneath ... shew kindness ... give me a true token ... save alive my father, and my mother, and my brethren, and my sisters ... deliver our lives from death". This was the language of faith, and it was the obedience of faith that bound the scarlet line in her window and so effected her deliverance (Jos 6:17, 22, 23, 25).

6   *More Victories and Victors*
   11:32-40

> v.32   "And what shall I more say? for the time would fail me to tell of Gedeon, and *of* Barak, and *of* Samson, and *of* Jephthae; *of* David also, and Samuel, and *of* the prophets:
> v.33   Who through faith subdued kingdoms, wrought righteousness, obtained promises, stopped the mouths of lions,
> v.34   Quenched the violence of fire, escaped the edge of the sword, out of weakness were made strong, waxed valiant in fight, turned to flight the armies of the aliens.
> v.35   Women received their dead raised to life again: and others were tortured, not accepting deliverance; that they might obtain a better resurrection:

v.36   And others had trial of *cruel* mockings and scourgings, yea, moreover of
        bonds and imprisonment:
v.37   They were stoned, they were sawn asunder, were tempted, were slain
        with the sword: they wandered about in sheepskins and goatskins; being
        destitute, afflicted, tormented;
v.38   (Of whom the world was not worthy:) they wandered in deserts, and *in*
        mountains, and *in* dens and caves of the earth.
v.39   And these all, having obtained a good report through faith, received not
        the promise:
v.40   God having provided some better thing for us, that they without us
        should not be made perfect."

32   The writer acknowledges that his present account of the exploits of the faithful
is by no means exhaustive. Nor can it ever be. Neither time nor space would suffice
to tell all. "What more do I say? The time would fail me telling of Gideon, and Barak,
and Samson, and Jephthah, and David and Samuel, and of the prophets" (JND):
Gideon of Judges 6, who threshed wheat by the winepress in defiance of Midian;
Barak of Judges 4, who believed the prophecy of Deborah and delivered the nation
from twenty years of oppression under Jabin and Sisera; Samson of Judges 13-16, who
rent a lion apart as if it had been a kid; who slew a thousand men with but the
jawbone of an ass; who broke the strongest cords with which the Philistines could
bind him; who carried away the gates of Gaza; who, though blinded by his enemies,
pulled down the pillars of the temple of Dagon and thereby slew more at his death
than in his life; Jephtha of Judges 11, a man of low birth and of disadvantage, the son
of a harlot, who, when circumstances seemed to be against him personally, delivered
Israel from the oppression of the Ammonites; David of 1 Sam 16:12, the shepherd
boy of Bethlehem who slew the giant Goliath and who became psalmist and sweet
singer and king of Israel and Judah (1 Sam 18:16); Samuel of 1 Sam 1, the temple
child who became a prophet and who anointed the nation's first kings; the prophets
too, a long line of faithful men who, often in times of oppression and danger, boldly
conveyed the mind of God to the people, whether a ministry of rebuke or of comfort,
of commendation or of condemnation.

The closing list of names is not in a chronological order, as will be noticed, but
neither is it an order of importance or of excellence. Men and women from every
walk of life have been used of God by reason of their faith. What an added
encouragement should this have been to these early Hebrew readers of the epistle.
Jehovah was still the same. And there was nothing mystical about faith. It was
always, in every age, a simple matter (though costly) of taking God at His word, of
believing and responding in obedience as these did who had now been mentioned.

33   No more names will now be added to the list. But there is of course the great
anonymous multitude of faithful ones who have done exploits for God similar to
these mentioned, often incurring much personal suffering and pain. What has God
wrought by the faith of men and women like these. The trials and triumphs now
being recounted have been duplicated again and again in the lives of the faithful

through the ages, though the events and circumstances as narrated in these verses may be directly associated with the judges and kings and prophets just mentioned.

By faith kingdoms had been subdued since the days of Joshua. Through the period of the judges and into the days of monarchy Jehovah had given victory after victory to his people. How often did their triumph seem, logically, but a vain hope, yea even a military impossibility. But with Jehovah on their side enemy kings and kingdoms were subdued indeed, until, in the reigns of David and Solomon, Israel's territory extended from the Euphrates to the Negev.

By faith they wrought righteousness. Not only did the men of faith live out a personal righteousness but the bold prophets fearlessly demanded it of the nation. Such established righteousness was the prayer for Solomon in Ps 72:1-4. It was a most desirable, if not essential, characteristic of the king, for did not the nation usually take character from the throne? The righteous character of a good monarch was so often reflected in the behaviour of the people, and, conversely, the unrighteousness of an evil ruler was often reflected too.

By faith promises were obtained. We may think of Abraham, Elijah, Elisha, Daniel, Nehemiah, and so many of the faithful to whose intercessions Jehovah lent His ear and granted them promises because of their faith.

Faith stopped the mouths of lions. We immediately and instinctively think of Daniel (Dan 6:16, 22); but he was not the only one so to do. Remember Samson (Judges 14:5-6); and David (1 Sam 17:34-37); and Benaiah, one of David's mighty men, a man great in exploits (2 Sam 23:20).

34   For some, the violence of fire was quenched by faith. Particularly do we think of Daniel's faithful companions in Babylon, Shadrach, Meshach and Abednego (Dan 3). These young men defied the edict of king Nebuchadnezzar, knowing that a fiery furnace awaited them for such rebellion, and not knowing whether it would please God to deliver them or not. How much were they like the leper of a later day who cried in earnestness to the Saviour, "If thou wilt, thou canst" (Mark 1:40). Like the young men in Babylon the leper had no doubts about the divine ability, but was there divine will and willingness? Shadrach, Meshach and Abednego said simply, "Our God is able" (Dan 3:17). This was faith. Whether Jehovah in His sovereignty would choose to deliver them or not, they did not know, but in any case they would not bow. Their faith and courage was rewarded. The violence of the fire was quenched.

Some escaped the edge of the sword. We remember particularly David's deliverances from the sword of Saul; Elijah's deliverance from the wicked Jezebel (1 Kings 19); Elisha was delivered too, from the sword of Jehoram, son of Ahab and Jezebel (2 Kings 6); and Jeremiah was delivered from Jehoiakim (Jer 36).

It seems to be a principle and a delight with God that "from weakness he makes strong". If men will but trust Him He has ever been pleased to use small things. "God hath chosen the weak things of the world to confound the things that are mighty" (1 Cor 1:27). His strength is made perfect in weakness. How many of these who did exploits for Him by faith were naturally weak when He found them. But He has been pleased to take up these unlikely vessels, and use them mightily, that the excellency of the power which is demonstrated may be plainly seen to be of Him and not of us (2 Cor 4:7).

So then, by faith they waxed valiant in fight. They became mighty in war, and, as JND so beautifully renders it, they "made the armies of strangers give way". This may be illustrated again and again in the history of the nation, in stories of heroism from Joshua onwards.

35 Women received their dead again by resurrection. There are two notable instances (see 1 Kings 17 and 2 Kings 4). One woman was poor; the other was rich. One was an Israelite; the other was not. One was from Zarephath; the other from Shunem. One was a widow; the other had a husband. One was given back her child by the ministry of Elijah; the other through the ministry of Elisha. We have seen that faith knows no boundaries and this fact is illustrated again in the cases of these two women. A poor widow of Sarepta and a rich woman of Shunem will alike share in the blessings that faith can bring. Alike they received back their dead sons, raised to life again.

Others, that is, others who have not yet been specifically referred to, were tortured. The word rendered "tortured" is from the verb *tumpanizō*. It indicates not just general torture but a particular kind of torture. The word signifies a stretching upon a wheel or rack for a beating, probably to death. As the skin of a drum may be stretched upon the frame and beaten, so does this word indicate that some of the faithful suffered so. It was therefore a double torture, being stretched cruelly and then beaten. Since such instances are not recorded in the Biblical accounts it may well be that the writer is thinking of the Maccabees who were tortured and martyred for their faith under Antiochus Epiphanes. Josephus the historian says of them, "They every day underwent great miseries and bitter torments; for they were whipped with rods, and their bodies were torn to pieces, and were crucified while they were still alive and breathed".

They would not accept deliverance since that was usually dependent upon their renunciation of the faith for which they were suffering. The account of the sufferings of that famous Maccabaean mother and her seven sons is most moving. When that mother was urged by the evil king to counsel her son, her youngest, she replied, "I will counsel my son", and turning from the king to her boy she said, "Fear not this tormentor, but, being worthy of thy brethren, take thy death". Such was the faith that would not accept deliverance.

They did it that they might obtain a better resurrection. What does this mean, a better resurrection? Perhaps its primary and true interpretation may be seen more easily if we notice the RV and JND rendering of the first clause in this verse. "Women received their dead again by resurrection". Great blessing as that was, it was a resurrection back to normal life on earth, with this prospect, that sometime they must die again. The "better resurrection" is that resurrection which will introduce us to that sphere of bliss where we shall never die again. It may also mean, as some contend, that resurrection for those who have been faithful unto death will bring greater reward than could have been expected if they had relented under pressure and accepted deliverance on their tormentors' terms.

36 Then there were yet others. There were others who endured mockings and scourgings and bonds and imprisonment. The story of such is so vast and the persons are so numerous that it is scarcely feasible to begin to mention names. But as we think of them it can hardly escape our notice that all of these cruelties here mentioned were borne by our Lord Himself. He is, after all, the great exemplar of every God-pleasing trait. As we sing:

> Thou, O Son of God wert bearing
> Cruel mockings, hatred, scorn;
> Thou, the King of Glory, wearing,
> For our sake, the crown of thorn.

Would the remembrance of what they suffered, and of what He suffered, be of some comfort and encouragement to these Hebrews, and an incentive to endure? May it be so too, to us and to all.

37 Many were stoned. This cruelty was continued into NT days, and well would these Hebrew readers recall the stoning of Stephen.

They were sawn asunder. There is no Biblical record of this but tradition has it that Isaiah the prophet was put to death in this most cruel manner by Manasseh. F.F.Bruce has the following interesting comments, "The apocryphon called the *Ascension of Isaiah*, which records the prophet's death, is a composite work, Christian in its completed form; but the record of Isaiah's martyrdom which it incorporates is of Jewish origin and exhibits affinities with the Qumran literature. It tells how Isaiah, to avoid the wickedness rampant in Jerusalem under Manasseh, left the capital for Bethlehem and then withdrew to the hill country. There he was seized and sawn in two with a wooden saw".

In that some "were tempted" we are probably to understand the attempts which were made by their tormentors to make them recant and renounce their faith.

We have observed that, by faith, some escaped the edge of the sword (v.34), but it is most important to note that it was also by faith that some were slain by the sword. God does not always deliver. In His sovereignty, He may choose to deliver some and not to deliver others. It is ours to obey in a simple trust, and not to question the ways of God. This may at times be difficult, but it is the path of faith. His ways are past tracing. Happy are those saints who can trust Him and rest, knowing that sovereignty makes no mistakes and always arranges what is best for our good and for God's glory.

So many of the faithful lost homes and friends and creature comforts. They went about in sheepskins and in goatskins, being destitute, lacking the basic necessities of life. They were afflicted (*thlibō*), suffering under the extreme pressure of their circumstances. They were tormented (*kakoucheō*), suffering injustices and being evilly treated by their persecutors.

38 The bracketed parenthesis at the beginning of this verse is very beautiful. The world which oppressed these believers would not have worded it quite like this. Their oppressors would have said that these saints were not worthy of the world, but the testimony of heaven is that the world was not worthy of them! The enemies of faith and truth cast them out as not being worthy to be in the world. The truth of the matter was that heaven received them because the world was not worthy to have them.

And so while they were here they wandered in deserts and mountains and in dens and caves of the earth. The world had its palaces, its stately homes, its society and its luxuries, but the world was not worthy to have the company of these, the aristocracy of heaven. They were cast out from the world as being not worthy of it, but heaven's verdict is best, the world was not worthy of them.

39 We have read earlier of those patriarchal saints that "these all" died in faith (v.13). But "these all" of this v.39 is much wider. All these saints of OT times, from righteous Abel through until the last believer of that earlier dispensation, had witness borne to them by God. Jehovah saw and appreciated, and has witnessed to their witness for Him. He has testified to their testimony. But having obtained assurance that God had appreciated and recorded what they had done for Him, yet they lived and died without receiving the promise. This does not contradict either that which is said of Abraham in v.17, or that which is said of the faithful in v.33. Those promises received by the patriarch and by others who followed were promises of a more temporal and personal nature. That which is spoken of here is *the promise*. It was the promise of a coming Messiah who would bring life and immortality to light through His gospel. It was the promise, not just of future earthly blessing, but of a life that would never die, a glory that would never fade, a bliss that would never end, a resurrection splendour. These faithful saints lived in earnest expectation, believing God, but they did not receive the fulfilment of that promise.

40 But delay is not denial. Jehovah had foreseen a better thing for us, who are believers of a new dispensation. The writer does not enter into detail with regard to the church. The church and the hope of the church is not the purpose or subject of this epistle. But these Hebrew Christians must know that even now, while here on earth in pilgrimage, we already have better things than did those earlier saints. We may indeed be linked with a rejected Messiah, who Himself waits for a day of manifestation, but while we wait with Him and for Him, we are in the present enjoyment of heavenly blessings. We have an opened sanctuary; we have a Man in the glory as our great high priest; we have consciences purged and perfected as far as sins are concerned; we are actually seated in the heavenlies and have within us the earnest of an indwelling Spirit. Neither Abraham or Moses, or Isaiah or Daniel, or David or Samuel or any of the OT worthies, were in the enjoyment of any of these blessings. God had foreseen a better thing for us. Other epistles, of course, will develop our standing in Christ more fully than this epistle.

The OT saints therefore, could not, in the purpose of God, be made perfect without us. Indeed they have not been perfected yet in the fullest sense of that word. It is true that they may be viewed as "the spirits of just men made perfect" (12:23), but that is perfection as to their present state which of course is not a resurrected state. For that they wait, with all those who have died in Christ. One day all these that have died in faith shall be raised out from among the dead. One day, in bodies of glory, with us they will be perfected. And although there may well be eternal distinctions in the families of the saved (Eph 3:15), with the church, the mystical body of Christ enjoying a unique and peculiar intimacy, nevertheless for His glory there shall be a great united company of the redeemed, altogether like Him and for His glory. Well do we sing with JND:

And is it so! we shall be like Thy Son,
Is this the grace which He for us has won?
Father of glory! (thought beyond all thought)
In glory to His own blest likeness brought.

Not we alone, Thy loved ones all, complete,
In glory round Thee there with joy shall meet,
All like Thee, for Thy glory like Thee, Lord,
Object supreme of all, by all adored.

XII. Encouragements to Faith   (12:1-29)

1. *The Supreme Example*
12:1-3

v.1   "Wherefore seeing we also are compassed about with so great a cloud of witnesses, let us lay aside every weight, and the sin which doth so easily beset *us,* and let us run with patience the race that is set before us,

v.2   Looking unto Jesus the author and finisher of *our* faith; who for the joy that was set before him endured the cross, despising the shame, and is set down at the right hand of the throne of God.

v.3   For consider him that endured such contradiction of sinners against himself, lest ye be wearied and faint in your minds."

1   The connecting "Wherefore", or "Therefore", with which this chapter now continues the treatise, causes us to pause and consider the content of the chapter just concluded. That lengthy chapter had extolled the virtues of simple unswerving faith in Jehovah, and had seen that faith in action in the lives and ministry of patriarchs, judges, kings, and prophets, as well as in the innumerable host of the anonymous who had served God well by faith and had so often suffered for it. But it must not be

supposed that such faith belonged only to the record of the past. It was a present continuing thing, spanning the ages and knowing no boundaries, and the writer is now intent on encouraging his Hebrew readers to emulate the faith of the elders and live for God as they had done.

So, he says, we are surrounded by so great a cloud of witnesses. The witnesses are doubtless the faithful of the past, of whom he has just been writing, but the word "witnesses" has presented some difficulty and has occasioned a certain disagreement as to the writer's meaning. The word (*martus*) is capable of two meanings, both of which may be correct in context. It may indicate a person who sees, or is a spectator to, or witnesses something; or it may indicate a person who bears testimony to something. But which meaning is to be understood here? Commentators are not agreed. JND says, "Witness, in English, has two senses: 'seeing, so as to bear witness', and 'giving testimony to'. The last only I apprehend is in the Greek here". William Kelly, with characteristic frankness, echoes JND and writes, "The witnesses .. are not spectators of us as some have unintelligently imagined, but men that obtained testimony from God in virtue of faith". F.F.Bruce, rather more graciously, writes, "But in what sense are they 'witnesses'? Not, probably, in the sense of spectators, watching their successors as they in turn watch the race for which they have entered; but rather in the sense that by their loyalty and endurance they have borne witness to the possibilities of the life of faith". W.E.Vine, however, sees it differently, writing, "As to the persons mentioned in ch.11, their lives of faith are so recorded in the OT narratives that they seem to be living spectators urging us on to run as they did". F.F.Bruce concedes that the word is capable of this sense, which it probably bears in other places, and he cites as an example 1 Tim 6:12.

Perhaps Dr John Brown of Edinburgh deserves to be quoted at length. He writes, "The allusion is here ... to those public agonistic or gymnastic games, which among Greeks had less the character of a frivolous amusement than that of a grave civil institution ... The most imposing form of this singular custom was perhaps that presented at Olympia, a town of Elis, where games were celebrated in honour of Jupiter once every five years. An almost incredible multitude, from all the states of Greece and from the surrounding countries, attended these games as spectators. The noblest of the Grecian youths appeared as competitors ... The victors in the morning contests did not receive their prizes till the evening, but, after their exertions, joined the band of spectators, and looked on while others prosecuted the same arduous labours which they had brought to an honourable termination ... The ancient worthies whose actions are recorded in Scripture are represented as spectators; their deeds, and sufferings, and triumphs, as recorded in Scripture, being calculated to have the same influence on the minds of the believing Hebrews, as the interested countenances and encouraging plaudits of the surrounding crowd had on the minds of the Grecian combatants ... A countless host of venerable countenances beam encouragement, and ten thousand times ten thousand friendly voices seem to proclaim, 'So run that ye may obtain: we once struggled as you now struggle, and you shall conquer as we have conquered. Onward! Onward!' "

Note that the writer numbers himself with those in the race: "we are compassed about"; "let us lay aside every weight". And note too the word "also". Those worthies of faith of earlier days were surrounded by witnesses in their day, and we also are surrounded as they were, with the encouraging hosts. He sees these hosts as a cloud, a well-known figure describing the vastness of the company. See Isa 60:8; Ezek 38:9 for the same figure. In 1 Thess 4, when the Saviour comes, we shall be caught up together in clouds to meet Him in the air. "Behold, He cometh with clouds" (Rev 1:7) may well have reference to those clouds of saints which have been earlier caught up to Him in 1 Thess 4.

In light of all these considerations, let us lay aside every encumbrance. The serious contestant will not handicap himself by carrying superfluous weight. The race is on and we must divest ourselves of every hindrance, even though that thing may appear quite legitimate to others. How many saints are often hindered by weights of which they will ask, "Is there anything wrong with it?" Of course there would likely be no law against an athlete wearing clumsy footwear, or heavy winter clothing, while he runs in the games, but such is unthinkable! How many believers are encumbered by business, by hobbies, by sport, by taking on unnecessary additional secular studies, by other pursuits which may make demands on time and interest and energy that should be given to the race. We must be disciplined, and lay aside every impediment, and earnestly devote our time and energies to the race before us.

But above all we must beware of sin. The AV suggests some particular sin of which a man may say, "It is my besetting sin". This is not the thought. It is sin of every shape and form which may so easily, at any time, entangle us. The word "beset" (*euperistatos*) is found only here in the NT. It has the thought of encircling or surrounding, even to the point of clinging to. The propensity to sin is ever with us. We must lay it aside. It will deftly and subtly entangle us and hinder us in the race as a runner may be impeded if he were to wear a long loose robe clinging to him as he ran.

With so much to hinder then, it is not surprising that we are constantly in need of patient endurance. And so the writer's exhortation, "Let us run with patience". Let us run the race before us with persistence and with perseverance, ever determined that nothing, whether legitimate or sinful, will entrammel us in our endeavour.

2   Believers are therefore encompassed, not only by the great cloud of witnesses but also by the ever-present possibility of being entangled by that which would hinder and impede. The greatest safeguard and incentive is to look away from all of these and be in constant occupation with the supreme example, Jesus Himself. "Looking" (*aphoraō*) signifies "looking off" or "looking away". We must fix our eyes exclusively on Him, who has trodden the path of faith before us and who is now in glory.

"Jesus"! Note the lovely human name of Him who began life in such lowly circumstances, and who, from Bethlehem to Golgotha, walked humbly as a dependent Man, accomplishing the will of God in every detail of His life and in every step of the path He trod. We shall never live as perfectly as He did, but He is our example (1 Pet 2:21) and our encouragement. He is now, as we love to call Him, the Man in the glory, and the writer's exhortation is that we should look away off unto Him. With our eyes on Him it will be easier to cast aside the weights that would hinder. "In fact", writes J.N. Darby, "when we look at Jesus, nothing is easier; when we are not looking at Him, nothing more impossible".

Jesus is the author and finisher of faith. The pronoun "our" as in the AV should be omitted. It has been supplied by the translators, but it narrows the meaning of the text. It is faith in its entirety that is in view. The word here rendered "author" is *archēgos* which we have noted before in 2:10. It denotes a leader. To quote J.N. Darby's helpful note on the occurrence of the word in Acts 3:15, he writes, "This word is difficult to render in English. It is a 'leader', but it is more. It is used for one who begins and sets a matter on. The Greek word occurs four times in the NT, (Acts 3:15; 5:31; Heb 2:10; 12:2). In Heb 12:2 it means, 'He began and finished the whole course'; 'the origin' or 'originator' ... The word is only used of our Lord". He is the great exemplar of faith. His enemies said of Him, "He trusted in God" (Matt 27:43).

"Finisher" (*teleiōtēs*) denotes completer or perfecter. It is akin to His word from the cross, "It is finished" (John 19:30). He has triumphantly walked the whole pathway of faith from the manger to the cross, from cattle-shed to Calvary. Greater therefore than all the worthies of faith, the witnesses of ch.11, He is the supreme example and we ought ever to be looking off unto Him.

For the fourth time in the epistle we are reminded that our Lord has sat down at the right hand of God. It is the repeated quotation of Ps 110:1. We have observed it in 1:3; 8:1; 10:12. He has arrived in glory by way of a path of suffering which involved the shame of the cross. But He endured the cross and despised the attached shame. There is no article before either cross or shame. It is the awful character of His sufferings that is before us, so that we may read it, "He endured crucifixion, despising shame". We remember Phil 2: He became obedient unto death, even the death of the cross. Crucifixion was a most shameful form of execution. It was reserved by the Romans for slaves and aliens, their own Roman citizens being exempt from it. He endured it. There is an implicit encouragement for those Hebrew believers who were suffering reproach, that they should disregard the shame even as their Lord did. There would be glory at the end.

Now Jesus endured both cross and shame for the joy that was set before Him. The preposition "for" has occasioned some diversity of opinion among expositors. It is the preposition *anti*. Does it mean, "in view of the joy lying before Him", or does it mean, "instead of the joy that was before Him"? Perhaps a majority will see the former meaning as the true one. This indeed is JND's translation, to bring the sense, as he saw it, into the text, and eliminate any ambiguity. W.E.Vine states categorically, "The preposition *anti*, rendered 'for', does not here mean 'instead of'! The joy set before the Lord was the anticipation of His glory with the Father and all that was to be the outcome of His finished work on the cross, both in the present age and in the ages to come. Because of the value He set upon all this He endured the cross". Vine points out that the same preposition is used again in v.16 concerning Esau, who *for* one morsel of meat sold his birthright.

The view of others however, is perhaps ably expressed by M.R.Vincent, who says that this is *anti* in its usual sense, "in exchange for": "The joy was the full, divine beatitude of His preincarnate life in the bosom of the Father; the glory which He had with God before the world was. In exchange for this He accepted the cross and the shame". He continues to say that it is, "renouncing a joy already in possession in exchange for shame and death".

Doubtless both of these considerations are doctrinally true but most readers will understand the former view as being, contextually, the more correct meaning here.

3   There follows now a befitting and timely exhortation, an antidote to weariness and fainting, "consider him". We have been encouraged once before to consider Him (3:1) though the word "consider" is different there. Here it is *analogizomai*, found only here in the NT. It means to consider well, to contemplate and compare and contrast carefully, to meditate upon. As we take into account all that is recorded of Him for us we remember the great contradiction of sinners that He endured. What comfort this would afford to these first Hebrew readers of the epistle. They too were enduring contradiction or gainsaying from the enemies of the gospel and it would be so easy to become disheartened and dispirited, to weary and to faint. "Consider him" was the safeguard against weariness and fainting. The word rendered "contradiction" essentially denotes gainsaying, scornful language, haughty words of insolence; but it is probably here used in its wider sense of opposition. How they opposed Him, both by words and actions, accusing Him falsely and treating Him most cruelly.

All this contradiction was against Himself. If the RV text is preferred then this was the contradiction of sinners against themselves. Men were really against themselves when they opposed Him. But the most ancient manuscripts are apparently divided between the plural "themselves", and the singular "himself". It may be better to understand the contradiction as being from sinners against Himself.

2. *The Chastisement of Sons*
   12:4-11

v.4   "Ye have not yet resisted unto blood, striving against sin.

v.5   And ye have forgotten the exhortation which speaketh unto you as unto children, My son, despise not thou the chastening of the Lord, nor faint when thou art rebuked of him:

v.6   For whom the Lord loveth he chasteneth, and scourgeth every son whom he receiveth.

v.7   If ye endure chastening, God dealeth with you as with sons; for what son is he whom the father chasteneth not?

v.8   But if ye be without chastisement, whereof all are partakers, then are ye bastards, and not sons.

v.9   Furthermore we have had fathers of our flesh which corrected *us*, and we gave *them* reverence: shall we not much rather be in subjection unto the Father of spirits, and live?

v.10   For they verily for a few days chastened *us* after their own pleasure; but he for *our* profit, that *we* might be partakers of his holiness.
v.11   Now no chastening for the present seemeth to be joyous, but grievous: nevertheless afterward it yieldeth the peaceable fruit of righteousness unto them which are exercised thereby."

4 That these first Hebrew recipients of the epistle had suffered much could not be denied. The writer has already recalled the persecutions of those earlier days when they had endured so much (10:32-34). He would not minimise what they had suffered but it must all be kept in context. They had not yet been asked to shed their blood. They had not yet suffered martyrdom as had so many of the worthies of faith referred to in the previous chapter. They had not suffered as much as He had suffered for whom they were now privileged to maintain testimony. The Saviour had given His life for them. He had endured even the death of the cross.

It was true that in faithfulness they were in a continuing battle with evil. There was an ongoing wrestling with opposing forces. Sin, in a variety of forms, was against them. They had to agonise like the combatants in the games, resisting the evil in whatever form. They had resisted; of this there is an implicit acknowledgement in the text, but they had not yet resisted to the shedding of their blood, to death itself.

Observe the word "yet": "ye have not *yet* resisted unto blood". Is there a concealed warning that the fiercest storm was yet to come. They must use the present trials as a preparation for greater struggles. Like as a tree in the storm may put down its roots for greater stability and security, so must they use the present persecutions to strengthen them for what may lie ahead.

5 And had they quite forgotten the exhortation of Prov 3:11-12? This Scripture was "speaking" to them, (*dialegomai*) reasoning with them, dialoguing with them, discussing with them, persuading them. Had they forgotten it? That Scripture was addressing them as sons (*huioi*). "Children", as in the AV, does not adequately convey the sense and the force of the writer's thought. The Proverbs text was reasoning with them as with those who could intelligently understand the dealings of the Father with them. It was the Father's prerogative to use circumstances for the training of His sons. Here was a mature way of looking at their persecution and suffering. A true father will discipline his sons for the moulding and building of character. "My son", reasons the Scripture, "despise not the chastening of the Lord". In His sovereignty, in His wisdom, and in His love, the Father will chasten and admonish us, and will turn adverse and hostile circumstances to our good in this respect. So then, rather than faint under the adversity and the difficulties of the way, we ought to view them as the Father's means of teaching us something. This would make them easier to bear, if we could apprehend just what particular lesson we are to learn in the sorrows that inevitably come our way. We must not despise this discipline. We must not make light of it, nor treat it carelessly. The Father is instructing us and it is, ultimately, all for our good and for His glory.

6 In fact, the writer will now argue that, when once we reckon our sufferings to be the chastening of the Lord, we have, for our consolation and encouragement, an inherent evidence of His love for us, for whom the Lord loves he chastens. As W.E.Vine so helpfully remarks, "The verb *agapaō* signifies to love, not merely by way of affection, but in a practical way by approbation, and this is indicated here in the chastening and its motive and object". It may make the burden lighter to recognise that it is His chastening, which is an indication that we are indeed sons, and that we are loved of the Father.

And He scourges every son whom He receives. Scourging is not pleasant. Our Lord predicted it for His faithful disciples (Matt 10:17; 23:34). The Jewish method of scourging with which these Hebrew readers would have been familiar was a beating with a rod. We are reminded of 1 Cor 4:21 and of 2 Cor 11:25. Every son requires such discipline at some time. It will be administered in love by every wise father, and when the Father uses prevailing circumstances to so scourge us it is good to remember that this is, in fact, His recognition of our sonship and a proof of His parental love for us.

7 The writer continues in the same strain. The encouragement now is that they should indeed recognise their afflictions as chastisement or discipline and not as wrath. They must not necessarily see their sufferings as being an expression of divine displeasure with them. This it might be at times (1 Cor 11:30), but it is not always or necessarily so. It is well with us when we can see the tender love of the Father in our afflictions. He is but building character in us. It is well-known that the sweetest and choicest saints are those who have suffered. Out of the refining furnace of affliction there comes a purer life, a more fragrant character, a greater dependence, and a deeper devotion to the Father. Recognise then that when you suffer, God is conducting Himself towards you as towards sons, in whom He is desirous of developing likeness to Himself and to that Son who is His only-begotten, the Son of His love and of His eternal bosom.

Who is the son who is not chastened by his father? Where there is real fatherly care and genuine parental ambition for the moral welfare of the son, every true father will exercise discipline. It is not kindness on the part of a father to give unrestrained liberty to his son. Such liberty will end in ruin. Who has not watched a boy flying a kite? Have we not seen the kite pulling at the cord, straining, struggling, to be free? What will be the outcome if the boy grants the liberty for which the kite is straining? What will really happen if the restraining cord is cut or broken? The kite will flutter and tremble and fall. It may seem paradoxical but it is fact, that that which appears to be holding the kite down is really keeping it up. It would not be in its best interest to give to the kite the liberty for which it strains. It would not survive without the restraint of the cord. So the restraining influence of a kind father, though often resented at the time, is best for the son. It will produce real virtues and will bring moral prosperity which will eventually be appreciated by all.

8   But what if a man lives without chastisement from God. This is most serious, for if we are without chastening, if we know nothing of the disciplining hand of God in our lives, then the solemn conclusion must be that we are not His sons. How would such an observation be received by these Hebrew readers? Were there not those among them who were spurious children? Have we not already had warnings that there must be some among them who had given but mental, intellectual assent to the truths of the gospel but who had no heart experience of the Saviour? We are reminded of the opening warning section of ch.6. What would such know of a Father's care and correction in their lives? What would they appreciate of a loving Father's kind restraint, with the purpose of developing godly character in them? Such were not true sons. They were, professedly and outwardly, in the family, but of true sonship they knew nothing. The writer's conclusion is both sad and solemn, "Then are ye bastards and not sons". All true sons are partakers of chastisement. If we do not partake of chastisement then we are not true sons, but illegitimate, though in the family by profession.

9   Furthermore, what the writer has been saying in a sense should be already well known. It is all in perfect accord with normal family life. We have had natural fathers who have corrected us when necessary. The word "corrected" (AV), or "chastened" (RV) is not a verb, but a noun. Literally, "We have had the fathers of our flesh as chasteners" (JND). They were our chasteners when chastisement was needed. They corrected us when correction was necessary. We may have resented the correction at the time, but in ideal family relationships the son will reverence the father and submit to the chastisement. The dutiful son will know that a caring father does not correct his child needlessly. All correction from our natural fathers was training for a desirable quality of social and familial behaviour in us. Our fathers sought to mould us, and their pleasure was to see the development of sons of whom they would not be ashamed.

   Now if we have reverenced our fathers after the flesh, our natural fathers, shall we not much rather be in subjection to God our Father? "The Father of spirits" is a title of God found only here in our Bible. It is doubtless in contrast to the "fathers of our flesh" that God is now seen as "the Father of our spirits". True living, life in its fulness and dignity, may be attained by subjecting ourselves to Him whose chastening of us is for our spiritual welfare. He, the Father of our spirits, will never make a mistake when chastening us. Those fathers of our flesh, whom we reverenced, at times may have erred. Was their chastisement not at times too severe? And were there not other occasions when, due to moods and circumstances, we received less chastisement than we expected or deserved? It is not so with the Father of our spirits. His assessment of what is necessary is always correct and befitting. We ought then to subject ourselves willingly to Him and enter into that life which He desires for us.

10   Now those earthly, natural fathers who chastened us, were not only fallible, and liable to err sometimes, but the time of their chastening of us was brief, just that short period of childhood and youth. It was, relatively speaking, but for a few days that we were under their jurisdiction. The time of our subjection to them was fleeting and transient; it quickly passed. And the training they gave us was for behaviour in this life. They did what seemed good to them during the short period of their responsibility for us, though, as we have already seen, sometimes, during that short period, they did make mistakes. So then, their chastening and discipline of us was characterised by fallibility and brevity.

But our Father in heaven has eternal interests in us and His judgments and corrections are infallible. All that He does, all that He causes us to bear, is for the development in us of that holiness which is His own nature. Did not His own beloved Son address Him as "Holy Father? (John 17:11). Without holiness there can be no enjoyment of Him or fellowship with Him. So would He see in His sons that holiness which is characteristic of Himself, and if at times He chastens us it is in order to the partaking of His holiness. It is always for our profit that He chastens.

11   The theme continues, and concludes. No chastening at the time is a matter of joy. No one likes correction or chastisement. Human nature resents it. It is a burden to the flesh. While it lasts it is grievous to the individual concerned. But there is an "afterwards". It will yield something to the exercised soul. The word "yieldeth" means "to give back". There is some return from the pain of the discipline for those who are prepared to be exercised by it.

But note that there is an implicit warning here that not everyone will be suitably exercised by discipline. It would be possible, as we have observed in v.5, to despise the correction. That is, we may treat it lightly and carelessly. There are no returns from it for those who so despise it. Then again, it would be possible to faint under it, as again in v.5. These are opposite reactions to the chastening of the Lord and both are unprofitable. There will be no returns for such attitudes.

For the exercised soul discipline will yield fruit. As a farmer may speak of the "yield" of the land, meaning that which the land gives back to him in return for the seed sown and the labour expended, so will there be a yield of fruit for the chastening administered to an exercised believer. The fruit which is yielded is righteousness. This, after all, was the whole purpose of the chastening, as we have already observed, that it might produce in us likeness to the Father. Note that He who called His Father "Holy Father", did on the same occasion, and in the same prayer, say, "Righteous Father" (John 17:25). It is the Father's purpose in all disciplining of us that we might become righteous, live in dignity, and be partakers of His holiness. This is the desired fruit.

It is called by the writer, "the peaceable fruit". How blessed is such peacefulness after the trauma of chastisement. The God who chastens us is called in this very epistle "the God of peace" (13:20). Our Saviour is "the Prince of peace" (Isa 9:6) and "the Lord of peace" (2 Thess 3:16). Our gospel is "the gospel of peace" (Eph 6:15). Peace is of the fruit of the Spirit (Gal 5:22). It is not to be wondered at that the Father would have us know righteousness in peace. The word rendered "peace" is the corresponding Greek word to the lovely Hebrew *shalom*. This denotes rather more than our English word "peace", which at times may simply mean a cessation of hostilities. The peace to which we are here enjoined embraces the thoughts of quietness and tranquillity, with wholeness and prosperity. All this the Father desires for us and it will indeed be the assured portion of those who are exercised by His chastening.

3. *Working, Walking, and Watching.*
   ### 12:12-17

> v.12 "Wherefore lift up the hands which hang down, and the feeble knees;
> v.13 And make straight paths for your feet, lest that which is lame be turned out of the way; but let it rather be healed.
> v.14 Follow peace with all men, and holiness, without which no man shall see the Lord:
> v.15 Looking diligently lest any man fail of the grace of God; lest any root of bitterness springing up trouble *you,* and thereby many be defiled;
> v.16 Lest there *be* any fornicator, or profane person, as Esau, who for one morsel of meat sold his birthright.
> v.17 For ye know how that afterward, when he would have inherited the blessing, he was rejected: for he found no place of repentance, though he sought it carefully with tears."

12   The writer now returns more definitely to the athletic metaphor and speaks of the hands, the knees, and the feet of those who are in the race by faith; not that he has ever completely left that metaphor for it is well known that discipline is an important factor in the progress of every athlete. So although for a little while he has dealt with chastisement in relation to sonship, yet that correction, and willing submission to it, are very much linked with our training as we run in the race of v.1 and engage in the wrestling of v.4. Now keeping in mind that we may falter under discipline, that we may grow weary and faint, there follows his exhortation that we strengthen the hands that hang down and that we make firm the failing knees.

There is a little difficulty here as to whether the writer is exhorting those who are actually flagging, or is appealing to others to help such as are in need of encouragement. To whom are his words addressed? There is an obvious allusion here to Isa 35:3, and if we stay in the context of that chapter then it would seem that the appeal is to the strong, that they come to the aid of those who are feeling discouraged and dispirited.

On the other hand, the exhortation may be a direct challenge to those who are drooping under the unpleasantness of chastening: hands hang down; knees are feeble and failing. Some there may be who have lost sight of the Father's purpose in the discipline and have lost too the sense of His love. Such must renew their confidence and trust in Him. Brace yourselves anew. Revive your determination. "Lift up the hands that hang down, and the feeble knees". Encourage yourselves in the Lord as

David did, who knew so much about depression and weariness of soul.

But if the appeal is to others to help the discouraged then here is a ministry in which all can surely engage. The Lord has given gifts to His people. He has given certain gifts to individuals for particular ministries, and He has given these gifted individuals to the saints for their profit. How often, when thinking and speaking of "gift" do we have in mind only the spectacular and vocal gifts which bring men into public view. There is however, a most necessary gift in the assembly which is neither spectacular nor public. It is called "helps" (1 Cor 12:28). W.E.Vine, in his *Expository Dictionary*, says that it signifies "rendering assistance, perhaps especially of help ministered to the weak". To such as would be helps among the saints, the writer exhorts, "Lift up the hands that hang down, and the failing knees" (JND). Encourage your discouraged brethren. "Support the weak" (1 Thess 5:14).

13   We are to make straight paths for our feet. It is symbolically interesting that the newly-converted Saul of Tarsus was early found by Ananias in the street called Straight (Acts 9:11). It was to characterise the whole course of his after life. It is imperative for our testimony to the world, and also for our good influence and example to the saints, that we walk in straight paths. There must be nothing dubious or suspicious or shady or crooked about our walk. All the faithful of past ages knew the importance of a right walk before God and men. "Ponder the path of thy feet", wrote the wise man in Prov 4:26. "He leadeth me in the paths of righteousness" David had sung in Ps 23. "Thy word is a lamp unto my feet, and a light unto my path" (Ps 119:105). The path of godliness is charted out for us in His word. How we need to pray, in the spirit of David, "Teach me thy way, O Lord, and lead me in a plain path" (Ps 27:11).

> Teach me Thy way, O Lord,
>   Teach me Thy way;
> Thy gracious aid afford,
>   Teach me Thy way:
> Help me to walk aright,
> More by faith, less by sight;
> Lead me with heavenly light,
>   Teach me Thy way.

Faith will obey and grace will assist us to walk that path for His glory.

Our walk and example is of the utmost importance for those who are already lame. Those who are walking feebly may be further injured if we are not walking right. How many weak and dispirited souls have been finally stumbled in the path of testimony by the unrighteous walk of others of whom they expected better? We are responsible to walk such a beaten path that others following are not caused to stumble. For the straight path is not necessarily a path that has no windings; it is the well-trodden, beaten, proven path of faith. There are no impediments or causes of stumbling on this path. If we walk right then others may follow safely, and not be turned out of the way.

If we set such a good example to those fellow-believers who may be walking lamely or feebly, then, following our footsteps in the path of faith, they may be helped and healed. Many are weak, and easily turned aside into bypaths. Let us not be the cause of their straying by the path that we walk, but by good and wholesome example, let us rather be that godly influence which will help and guide them, and be the means of their being strengthened and healed. The character of our walk will affect, for good or bad, those who look to us for example and guidance.

14   We are now exhorted to follow peace with all men. This AV rendering does not convey the whole sense of the writer's exhortation. It is not just a matter of following peace, but rather of pursuing it. We are to make it our business, our duty and endeavour, to earnestly follow after peace, pursuing it as a most desirable thing. And it is not just peace among ourselves as Christians that we seek after, it is, where and when possible, peace with all.

We have observed earlier, in reference to that peaceable fruit of v.11, that peace is in the very nature of God who is the God of peace. It is characteristic of God, of Christ, and of our gospel, and it is just a consequence and corollary of our salvation that we should be at peace. We are at peace with God and we ought to be at peace with our brethren, with one another. But there is even more to be sought after, as Rom 12:18 makes clear: "If it be possible, as much as lieth in you, live peaceably with all men". Now at times men may make this difficult, and even impossible, but as JND renders Rom 12:18: "as far as depends on you" live peaceably with them. We are not altogether naive; we are not ignorant of the nature of the world and of men about us. We were once part of that system and we know that there are those in it who will refuse to co-exist peaceably with believers. The pure and honest lives of believers condemn the sinful behaviour of many of those around them and this engenders hostility to the saints. Did not the Lord Jesus predict, "In the world ye shall have tribulation" (John 16:33)?

It is for this reason that the exhortation continues with this most important qualification, "and holiness". We are to pursue peace, but likewise we are to pursue holiness. Note that peace and holiness are together the desired consequences of chastening (vv. 11, 12). Now at times it may be that, much as we desire to be at peace with the men of the world, it may not be possible without compromising our holiness. In such cases sadly we must forfeit peace; we cannot have it at the expense of holiness. Let us by all means seek to cultivate peace with all. Let us endeavour to be helpful and kind to our worldly neighbours and pursue peace with them, but when this is not compatible with practical holiness we must compromise.

"Holiness" is better "sanctification"; it is a setting apart for God. It is separation unto Him. Such is the essential importance of this sanctification that without it no man shall see the Lord. This is just what our Lord Himself taught in that early Sermon on the Mount (Matt 5:8): "Blessed are the pure in heart for they shall see God". It is the highest, greatest privilege and blessing imaginable, to have visions of

God. But revelations of Himself are given only to the pure in heart. Those who despise holiness and live for self and sin cannot have part in such enjoyments as this. Jehovah has reserved glimpses of His glory for those who set themselves apart in holiness for Him.

This then is the whole exhortation of this verse, that we should diligently seek to cultivate peace, not only with each other, but also with the men of the world, and endeavour by our harmless and helpful relations with them as neighbours to maintain peace when it depends upon us. But such peace, however desirable, must never be incompatible with practical holiness, for without this we lose the sense of God's presence and are robbed of continuing revelations of Himself.

15   The path of faith is constantly beset with dangers and the believer needs to be ever watchful. Now each man must watch himself, of course, but the appeal here may be wider than that. It may be that each of us should watch with a care for others. The word rendered "looking diligently" (from the verb *episkopeō*), is the same word as is used by Peter in relation to overseers in 1 Pet 5:2, "taking the oversight". Perhaps then, there is indicated here a responsibility which devolves upon all of us that we should all have a care for one another, watching over each other lest there be in any a lack of that grace which is so necessary. In our own strength we must certainly fail. We are ever dependent upon the grace of God for the maintaining of that holiness which we desire. So, while pursuing peace and holiness we must always be looking carefully, watching diligently, lest any should fail of that grace. It was grace, the undeserved kindness of God, His loving disposition towards us, that first started us on this pathway of faith and it is only by that grace that we shall attain the peace and holiness that we pursue. And so we sing with Philip Doddridge:

> Grace taught my wandering feet
>   To tread the heavenly road;
> And new supplies each hour I meet,
>   While pressing on to God.

How then may a man fail, or fall short of, the grace of God? There are two considerations, which we have before observed in the epistle. Firstly, a man may be genuinely the Lord's and may be enticed and ensnared by sin and fall from that state which grace intends for him. On the other hand, we have seen that there must be some whose profession of Christ is intellectual only, and such will fall short of that which grace desires for them by returning to the old life and the old religion. Each man who reads the writer's warning ought to know how to interpret it in relation to himself. Either way, it is a sad and serious situation for which we are all responsible to look carefully, so that both the individual life, and the life of the testimony, may be preserved in purity.

The warning now becomes reminiscent of the warning of Moses in Deut 29:18. Indeed such is the similarity that the writer might almost be quoting from that passage. Moses was warning Israel against the idolatries of the Canaanites among whom they lived: "Lest there should be among you man, or woman, or family, or tribe, whose heart turneth away this day from the Lord our God, to go and serve the gods of these nations; lest there should be among you a root that beareth gall and wormwood". Sin is indeed a root of bitterness; a root bearing bitter leaves and poisonous fruit. Such will be a certain trouble to the believer and such in the company will be a trouble to the assembly. Whether it be the sin of eventual apostasy or that sin which spoils the testimony of the true saint, the root of bitterness is a contaminating, corrupting element to be prevented at all cost, or to be dealt with when it appears. Is not this but an echo of the writer's warning back in 3:12, "Take heed, brethren, lest there be in any of you an evil heart of unbelief, in departing from the living God"?

The writer would not have them "troubled " with the bitterness of sin among them. The word "trouble" (*enochleō*) means "to crowd upon"; it is rendered "vexed" in the AV of Luke 6:18 and "beset" by JND. Sin in an individual would not end there. It would crowd upon the whole assembly, upon the testimony, and vex them all indeed. It is the principle that "a little leaven leaveneth the whole lump" (1 Cor 5:6). The sin of one was likely to defile many and they must therefore watch over one another with care and diligence.

16 The solemn warning continues, speaking now of fornication. There is some difference of opinion as to whether the writer is referring to fornication in the literal sense of the word, or to a spiritual fornication which would be idolatry or apostasy. Whether it be filthiness of the flesh or spirit (2 Cor 7:1) is of no account. Both things are, of course, obnoxious, and to be avoided, but it is likely that the writer has actual fornication in mind. Israel had once been plagued by idolatry but had long since been cured of that plague by long captivity in Babylon. Sexual impurity however was an ever-present danger, and against this the constant warning was necessary. The same watchfulness applied therefore, lest there should be any fornicator among them. Such had been in the assembly in Corinth and they had not had the moral strength to judge it, and the apostle deals with the subject in the utmost severity throughout the whole of 1 Cor 5.

It is neither implied or proven here that Esau was a fornicator. He is indeed so designated in extra-Biblical literature and this charge against him is likely derived from the fact that he married two Canaanitish women, to the sorrow of his parents. They were a grief of mind unto Isaac and Rebekah (Gen 26:34-35). Esau is here called a profane person. W.E.Vine says of the word "profane" that it denotes that which lacks all relationship or affinity to God. It means "unhallowed", the opposite to sacred. That such should be, or could be, among the saints, was almost unthinkable, but was yet a sad possibility, and indeed in some instances a reality.

Esau's profanity, his great failure, was his despising of the birthright. In a moment of sensual desire he sold his birthright for a morsel of meat. The story is told in Gen 25. For one meal, referred to as a "mess of pottage", to satisfy his fleshly appetite, he sold his rights in the patriarchal family. To satisfy the hunger of a moment he gave up the rights of the firstborn, the title to land, and the ancestorship of the Messiah. These great privileges and blessings he undervalued profanely and is now held up as a warning. Is it possible for believers now to act similarly? For these Hebrews, being constantly attracted by the aesthetic beauty of Judaism, it was verily possible. For all believers, of every age, it is always a real possibility that to indulge the flesh in a moment of sensual pleasure the testimony of a lifetime may be bartered away. Is it to be wondered at that the writer should exhort us to watch carefully and diligently?

17   Like many another since, Esau lived to regret what he had done. For a moment of carnal satisfaction he had given away too much and he regretted it. In the calmer light of a later hour he could now assess the cost of that moment's fleshly pleasure. He had lost the firstborn's blessing with all that it entailed. It had been a bad bargain. He had been influenced foolishly by the desires of the moment. It had been a sad and deplorable choice that he had made and now he was sorry.

Esau's sorrow, however, was not the sorrow of repentance. It was the sorrow of a self-pity that he had so foolishly lost so much. What Esau sought with tears was not a place of any repentance on his part for what he had done, as our AV might imply. He sought for the blessing which he had lost to Jacob (Gen 27:1-40). In his *New Translation* J.N. Darby will make this clear, as will the RV, by putting brackets around the words "for he found no place for repentance". Such parenthesising of these words will make the main sentence then read, "For ye know how that afterward, when he would have inherited the blessing, he was rejected ... though he sought it carefully with tears". Esau's tears were exceeding great and bitter (Gen 27:34): "Bless me – me also, my father!" he had cried to Isaac. But Isaac had to simply say, of Jacob, "I have blessed him; also blessed he shall be".

There is an acceptable thought however that Esau did in fact seek repentance, a change of mind, this though, not on his part, but on the part of Isaac his father. For yet again he cried, " ... one blessing, my father? bless me – me also my father! And Esau lifted up his voice and wept" (Gen 27:38). But while it is true that Esau did so plead with his father, it is more likely that what he sought for with tears was the blessing. In any case, there could be no change of mind on Isaac's part. There was no room for second thoughts now. The blessing had been lost, and given to another, and it was regrettably final. Esau had despised his birthright and he must suffer the consequences.

Alas, the bitter, bitter "afterward" that followed that moment of profanity. How many dear saints of God have reaped sadness in the same fashion as Esau; how many have forfeited the testimony of a lifetime for a moment of sensual satisfaction, a testimony never to be regained, though there be genuine sorrow and many tears.

The inherent warning to these Hebrews would be concerning apostasy. Some who were professors only, would sell their privilege and potential like Esau. How foolish; how exceedingly, indescribably foolish, to barter an eternity of bliss and glory for the attractions of an old obsolete Judaism which was about to vanish away.

4. *The Two Mountains*
12:18-24

v.18 "For ye are not come unto the mount that might be touched, and that burned with fire, nor unto blackness, and darkness, and tempest,

v.19 And the sound of a trumpet, and the voice of words; which *voice* they that heard entreated that the word should not be spoken to them any more:

v.20 (For they could not endure that which was commanded, And if so much as a beast touch the mountain, it shall be stoned, or thrust through with a dart:

v.21 And so terrible was the sight, *that* Moses, said, I exceedingly fear and quake:)

v.22 But ye are come unto mount Sion, and unto the city of the living God, the heavenly Jerusalem, and to an innumerable company of angels,

v.23 To the general assembly and church of the firstborn, which are written in heaven, and to God the Judge of all, and to the spirits of just men made perfect,

v.24 And to Jesus the mediator of the new covenant, and to the blood of sprinkling, that speaketh better things than t*hat of* Abel."

18 The words that now follow are again intended as a warning to the potential apostate, and at the same time as an encouragement to the true and genuine believer. They are related to the preceding verses by the connecting "for". They contain reasons for godly living and also a renewed warning against both moral laxity on the part of the believer and a going back on the part of those not wholly committed to Christ and the gospel. They revive and continue the comparison and contrast of earlier chapters concerning law and grace, Judaism and Jesus. The two principles will be seen as symbolised or personified by the two mounts, Sinai and Sion (or Zion).

The writer begins the section with a fearful reminder of all that was introduced and intimated at Sinai. The story of Exod 19-20 they would all know very well; it had been recounted by Moses in Deut 4:10ff. Mount Sinai was a literal, material, tangible mountain, "the mount that might be touched". This is not at all at variance with Exod 19:12, where the people were forbidden to touch the mount. "Not a hand shall touch it" (Exod 19:13). The fact that they were forbidden to touch it then, only indicates that it could be touched at other times. Those few "interpreters" who argue that a negative particle has been lost here, and that the phrase should read, "the mount that might not be touched", have missed the meaning entirely. It is the materialism of Sinai, and of the system which it represented, that is here intended. It was indeed "the mount that might be touched". We have not come to that. We, believers of a new dispensation of grace, have nothing to do with Sinai.

Sinai, on that awful inaugural day, was wrapped in smoke. Jehovah descended on it in fire. The fire descended and the smoke ascended, and the whole scene was shrouded in obscurity, blackness, and darkness and tempest. It was all a most befitting foreshadowing of what the law would bring. Moses and the people trembled like the mount. There was no beauty or grace in that scene, but the glory of Him who is a consuming fire (Heb 12:29). It was a frightening occasion, and it was in such fearful circumstances that the law was given, and Judaism as a system was born. How grateful we are that we have not come to Sinai! Who, having known the blessings that grace has brought, would now want to be caught up in the tempestuous and smoky atmosphere of Judaism?

19 Trumpet sounds rent the air at Sinai. In the years that followed the trumpet call would be a familiar sound to the nation. There would be trumpet calls to service, to warfare, to worship, to the great convocations, and to the onward march through the wilderness. Would the blowing of the trumpet ever be a reminder to the thoughtful among them, of that day when the trumpet of Jehovah sounded through the smouldering atmosphere of Sinai? We, who wait for the last trump, the trump of God, have no fear of the warning trumpet of that awful mount (1 Cor 15:52; 1 Thess 4:16). The last trump will summon us to Himself.

The voice of words, announcing and enunciating the tenets of the law amid the accompanying thunderings and flames, was so intimidatory that the people intreated that they should not be so addressed directly by God. They shrank back, pleading with Moses, "Speak thou with us, and we will hear; but let not God speak with us, lest we die" (Exod 19:18-19).

Who, having known the sweetness of His presence and the joy of listening to His voice through His word to the heart, would not be grateful beyond words for all that has come to us in Christ? How we give thanks in glad acquiescence as we hear this writer say, "Ye are not come to the mount that might be touched"! They intreated that the word should not be spoken to them any more. What contrast with those who now sing sincerely:

Speak, Lord, in the stillness,
    While I wait on Thee;
Hushed my heart to listen
    In expectancy.

Speak, O blessed Master,
    In this quiet hour;
Let me see Thy face, Lord,
    Feel Thy touch of power.

20 In the form of a parenthesis the writer now enlarges upon the scene at Mount Sinai. Such was the emphatic holiness of the mount that the whole congregation stood in fear. They could not bear, or endure, the demands of it all. It was not, at that moment, the actual demands of the law that terrified them, but the demanding, frightening manner and atmosphere of awful holiness in which the law was being delivered to Moses for them. If either man or beast touched the holy mount then immediate death must ensue (Exod 19:13). It was easily possible that one of their beasts, bullock or sheep or goat, could accidently touch the mountain, and in such cases it had to be stoned or shot through with a dart. "Or thrust through with a dart", as in the AV text, is omitted in many manuscripts and by the RV and JND. Some manuscripts however do have the phrase, and it is of course part of the narrative in Exod 19. The thought seems to be that, such was the majesty of the occasion, if so much as a brute beast strayed to the mountain, it must be killed from a distance, shot through. There must be no attempt to touch or recover the trespassing beast. The awful holiness must be recognised and guarded.

21 The parenthesis continues. So terrible was the sight that not only the people, but Moses himself, stood in fear. Moses, already acquainted in some measure with Jehovah, is afraid. He had trembled before, at the burning bush in the same Sinai area (Acts 7:30-33). There had been fire then too, and a voice, and the ground was holy. Since then there had been repeated converse with Jehovah throughout the days of the plagues in Egypt and the negotiations with Pharaoh. Moses was indeed privileged above other men in the matter of acquaintance with God. He had already witnessed demonstrations of Jehovah's power. One might be tempted to think that he would now be accustomed to such scenes of awful majesty and holiness. But even Moses said, "I am exceedingly afraid and full of trembling" (JND). These actual words of Moses are not recorded in the Exodus account of those days, but the inspired writer to the Hebrews has now preserved them for us.

Now was not the terror of that mount characteristic of the law that was being handed over? Was it not typical of the dispensation that was being introduced? Sinai has become a synonym for the dispensation of law. The awful circumstances of the giving of the law were characteristic of the law that was being given. What a scene that was: a howling wilderness! a rugged mountain! thick clouds! tempest wind! the trumpet sound! the lightning flash! the flaming fire! the divine voice! It was all emblematic of the law that was being delivered to them, indicating the solemn and severe demands that holiness was to make upon them! "And mount Sinai was altogether on a smoke … The mount quaked … All the people that was in the camp trembled" (Exod 19:16-18).

We must rejoice with the writer that we are not come unto that material, symbolical, awful Mount Sinai.

22 This verse, and this new section of the chapter, begin with a welcome "But". The writer, having dealt with the negatives, will now turn our attention to the positives. He has recounted those awful happenings at Sinai, and with these we have nothing to do. He will now remind his readers of the glory of the gospel and of the new economy. He doubtless describes conditions which are intimately related to a future millennium, but to these happy conditions we who now believe have already come in spirit, by faith. We are, even now, in the enjoyment of blessings which for Israel and the saved of the nations are yet future.

For a clear understanding of the verses now before us it is necessary that we see the punctuation correctly, particularly noting the correct placing of the important conjunction "and". Some of this accuracy has been lost in the AV rendering, but it is recovered for us in the RV marginal reading, and preserved with more clarity in the text of J.N. Darby's translation. It will be of profit to include that rendering here:

"But ye have come to mount Zion; and to the city of the living God, heavenly Jerusalem; and to myriads of angels, the universal gathering; and to the assembly of the firstborn who are registered in heaven; and to God, judge of all; and to the spirits of just men made perfect; and to Jesus, mediator of a new covenant; and to the blood of sprinkling, speaking better than Abel".

It will be observed now that there eight considerations. These may be suitably arranged in four pairs, in which pattern we have:

1.   The Mount and the City.
2.   The Angels and the Church.
3.   The Judge and the Just men.
4.   The Mediator and the Sprinkled Blood.

Mount Zion was, of course, a literal and beautiful hill with Jerusalem on its northern side: "Beautiful for situation, the joy of the whole earth, is mount Zion, on the sides of the north the city of the great King" (Ps 48:1-2). It became a synonym for Jerusalem and symbolically it represents, in the words of another, "the intervention of sovereign grace (in the king) after the ruin, and in the midst of the ruin, of Israel, re-establishing the people according to the counsels of God in glory, and their relationships with God Himself. It is the rest of God on the earth, the seat of Messiah's royal power". Priests and people and judges had all failed. King Saul and prince Jonathan had been slain in battle. The holy ark was in Philistine hands. All was Ichabod, a departed glory. The days were dark. But it was then that Jehovah intervened. David, anointed king in Hebron, went to Jerusalem against the defiant Jebusites. He took the stronghold of Zion, which is the city of David (2 Sam 5:1-7). Jehovah had intervened indeed. "And David became continually greater; and Jehovah the God of hosts was with him" (2 Sam 5:10). So has David become a foreshadowing of the greater Son of David, and Zion has become a symbol of royalty and rest, established by God in grace.

Now for Israel this is all a prophetic foregleam of what Jehovah has in purpose for the nation. There can be no greater contrast to Mount Sinai than Mount Zion. But we have not come to any material or physical mount, neither to Sinai or to Zion. We have come to Zion spiritually and morally. We have come to that which Zion represents. We have come, even now, into the enjoyment of that same grace which one day will bring Messiah to the throne, Israel into rest, and the millennial earth into blessing. This is ours now, by faith.

The hill of Zion yields
A thousand sacred sweets,
Before we reach the heavenly fields
Or walk the golden streets.

We have come also to the city of the living God, the heavenly Jerusalem. Earthly Jerusalem is the centre of the land masses of earth. It was Israel's national centre and meeting place. It will one day be the centre of government for a millennial earth. But all that Jerusalem represents, like all that Zion represents, is our heritage now who have already arrived by faith. The heavenly Jerusalem is, literally, "a living God's city". It is the city of which God Himself is the architect and builder. It is the heavenly capital, a city with foundations, holy centre of worship and service, and the seat of glory for men who are pilgrims and strangers on earth. Abraham looked for it (Heb 11:10). It is described in greater detail in Rev 21, 22.

23   The writer now sees, in the glory to which we belong, an innumerable company of angels. An innumerable company indeed; another NT writer records that the number of them was ten thousand times ten thousand, and thousands of thousands (Rev 5:11). Keeping in mind the correct punctuation, which we have earlier observed, these hosts of angels are in fact, the same general assembly of which the writer now speaks, "myriads of angels, the universal gathering". The word rendered "assembly" by the AV, is not the word *ekklēsia*, which is the usual word for assembly in the NT. This word *panēguris* found only here in our NT, denotes a festive gathering. It is doubtless to be understood here in contrast to the angelic ministry at Sinai. The law was handed over in their presence, adding to the solemnity of that awesome occasion (Gal 3:19). Jehovah came to Sinai with ten thousands of His holy ones (Deut 33:2). But the angels are now in the holy festal joy of a new dispensation, and are ministering spirits to those who inherit salvation.

The church of the firstborn is now mentioned. Two words need comment. Firstly, "church" (AV) is, more correctly, "assembly", and this is now the familiar *ekklēsia*, denoting a "called out" company. Secondly, for the first and only time in the NT we now have the word "firstborn" in the plural. The word in the singular is, of course, used many times of Christ, and we have commented on this in ch.1 of this epistle. It is also used of Israel whom Jehovah calls, "my firstborn" (Exod 4:22). But here it is, literally, "firstborns", or "firstborn ones". We can hardly be in any doubt that this assembly of firstborn ones is the church of the NT, of which our Lord spoke when He predicted that He would build such an assembly that the gates of hades would not prevail against it (Matt 16:18). It is the church which is His body, the mystery more fully expounded in the Epistle to the Ephesians.

These firstborn ones are enrolled in heaven. They did not belong there by right or by nature, as did the angels, but by grace, and in the sovereign purpose of God, they have been enregistered in the glory. We are now, even now, citizens of that glorious sphere where angels live. We may yet sojourn on earth but our citizenship is in heaven (Phil 3:20). What encouraging words for these early Hebrew readers in their persecutions and suffering: rejected on earth but enrolled in heaven! "Rejoice! because your names are written in heaven" (Luke 10:20).

We have come also to God who is the Judge of all. The Judge of all is our God. We are not afraid. It is He who has inscribed our names in heaven and this assures us of our security and of our justification before Him. Others will one day stand to be condemned before Him in His judicial character, before whose face the earth and the heaven will flee away. For us there is no such dread of judgment. The Judge is our God. We have come to Him.

The spirits of just men are a different company from the assembly of firstborn ones. They are undoubtedly the faithful of past ages. They are OT saints who looked for the fulfilment of the promise but did not receive it. They are the great company represented by the men and women of faith of ch.11, who have now arrived in glory. They are not yet made perfect in the absolute sense for they must wait for resurrection before receiving their bodies of glory. But in the spirit state in which they now dwell they have been perfected. Compare 11:40.

24 Jesus is the mediator of the new covenant. In one short phrase does the writer here bring together three of the great themes of his epistle.

1. "Jesus". The loved and lovely human name of Him who is greater than all the patriarchs, priests, princes, prophets, psalmists, and poets of Israel. The precious name given to Him at His birth has already been used several times in this epistle in a supreme solitariness. It is so again, and will yet be used one more time in 13:12. It is the name of the rejected One, but we have come, by faith, to Him, Jesus.

2. "Mediator". What gracious and holy ministry He has undertaken for those at a distance from God and estranged. The covenant has not yet been established with Israel. But the Mediator is in glory and everything is in readiness when the nation is ready. Meantime, all the blessings that Israel will have in that coming covenant relation with Jehovah are ours now.

3. The new covenant has been explained and expounded in ch.8. Its zenith is reached in that Jehovah has said, "Their sins and their iniquities will I remember no more". He will be their God and they shall be His people in millennial joy. But we have already come to this joy, for we have come to Jesus, mediator of the new covenant.

The blood of sprinkling is the blood of Christ. It is the ground of all our blessings. For the first reference to the blood of Christ in the epistle, see 9:12, and note comments there on the several ways in which reference is made to His precious blood. It is "his own blood"; it is "the blood of Jesus" (10:19); it is "the blood of

Christ" (9:14). Again in the epistle it will be called "the blood of the everlasting covenant" (13:20), and here the "blood of sprinkling" is reminiscent of the blood of the covenant as in ch.9.

The blood of Christ here speaks better things than that of Abel. Cain shed his brother's blood. Abel's blood cried for vengeance, for the punishment of the murderer (Gen 4:10). Cain became a fugitive on the earth for what he had done. He is a most remarkable type of the Jew, guilty of the death of Christ, and ever since dispersed and hunted on the earth. "His blood be on us, and on our children", they had cried (Matt 27:25). The blood of Christ however does not cry for vengeance, but in grace calls for pardon for the guilty. One day, on the basis of that precious shed blood of Christ, the dispersed nation will be regathered, and re-established in the land. But we already have come to an appreciation of that blood of the Saviour and are in the enjoyment of covenant blessings.

5.   A Closing Appeal
12:25-29

v.25   "See that ye refuse not him that speaketh. For if they escaped not who refused him that spake on earth, much more *shall not* we *escape,* if we turn away from him that *speaketh* from heaven:

v.26   Whose voice then shook the earth: but now he hath promised, saying, Yet once more I shake not the earth only, but also heaven.

v.27   And this *word,* Yet once more, signifieth the removing of those things that are shaken, as of things that are made, that those things which cannot be shaken may remain.

v.28   Wherefore we receiving a kingdom which cannot be moved, let us have grace, whereby we may serve God acceptably with reverence and godly fear:

v.29   For our God is a consuming fire."

25   The great message of the Hebrews from the very beginning has been that God has spoken. Again and again the readers have been warned against any neglect of that spoken word: "Today, if ye will hear his voice ...". To despise, or disregard, when God is speaking, is a most serious offence. So does the writer now raise the warning note once more, "See that ye refuse not him that speaketh". The word "refuse", is the same verb as that used in v.19, where the people at Sinai "declined the word being addressed to them" (JND). There, however, it was the overpowering sense of the awful presence of God which instilled fear into the congregation and caused them to feel their inability to bear any more of the divine voice. They were prepared to listen if Jehovah would speak to Moses and he relay the words to them. The scene is though, a sad foreshadowing of the fact that for other reasons the nation in the months and years to come would refuse to hear that voice. Throughout their sojournings in the wilderness, through all the centuries in the land, and, finally, through three and a half years of gracious ministry of the Son Himself, they had been repeatedly guilty of refusing the divine communications. These Hebrews now being addressed were the descendants of disobedient forebears. The rebellious tendency is in all men, but these Hebrew readers in particular must have felt the import of the exhortatory warning, "See that ye refuse not him that speaketh". Again the thought is in the background, that perhaps among them there were those who were not genuine and real, and who might neglect the word and face an awful apostate end.

For those who refused to hear there was no escape. The word spoken on earth, that is, the commandments, the law of Sinai, was unbending, unyielding, inflexible: "The word spoken by angels was stedfast, and every transgression and disobedience received a just recompense of reward" (2:2). Now if they could not escape who refused the oracles uttered on an earthly mount, how shall they escape who neglect the great salvation which at first began to be spoken by the Lord and was confirmed unto us by them that heard Him (2:3)? This is now, in the gospel of the glory, a word from heaven itself, from mount Zion as it were. The people at Sinai sought to "excuse themselves" (v.19 JND), as they declined to hear the word. And men yet seek excuses for not hearing. But there is no acceptable reason for refusing the word from heaven. For those who will not hear there is no escape. To refuse to hear, for any proffered reason, is to turn away. This "turning away" is apostasy.

26 The voice that now speaks to men from heaven in gospel grace is the voice that once shook the earth. "The earth shook ... even Sinai itself was moved" (Ps 68:8). "He hath promised ..." seems a strange word to use in such a context as this. To those who are unprepared it comes rather as a threatening, warning, intention of divine judgment. But to those who by grace are able to enter into the thoughts of God and appreciate the divine purpose, it is a promise. Those who have obeyed His voice and who have responded to His words of warning and invitation, and have come to know Him, can appreciate that this word also, though announcing terrible judgment, is His promise nevertheless, and will most surely come to pass.

What then is this promise? It is that once more He will shake, not the earth only, but heaven also. The prophecy which is here quoted is from Hag 2:6 where the prediction is that Jehovah will shake the heavens and the earth and the sea and the dry land and all nations, and that He will fill His house with glory. This, paralleled with the passage in 2 Peter 3:10-13, will find its ultimate fulfilment in the day of God, when God will shake and change all things, and introduce a new creation. Earth has been corrupted by sin. Satan, who introduced the corruption, originated in heaven, thus defiling the heavens also. All nations have been perverted and rebellious, Israel included. Jehovah will shake everything in that day.

Now although this all points forward to what Peter calls "the day of God", nevertheless, as with many other prophecies of Scripture, there is a near and a distant fulfilment. It would appear that the promise begins to be fulfilled at the manifestation of Christ and in the establishment of that earthly kingdom of righteousness under the government of the Son of man. In that day God's house will be filled with glory, and the desire of all nations will come, but the glory of the millennium will be preceded by judgments, by earthquakes and flaming fire and fearful signs in the heavens (Matt 24:7, 29; 2 Thess 1:8). When the earthly, millennial phase of the kingdom is complete then will Jehovah again shake all that is of the first creation and there will be a new heaven and a new earth in which righteousness will dwell.

27 Now this "Yet once more" has reference to the shaking of all those things which can be shaken. This then means the shaking of all things related to the present creation. The "things that have been made" are created things, and are temporary in their nature. That word of 2 Cor 4:18 is relevant here, "The things which are seen are temporal". All that is visible here, all that we can observe and lean upon, is transient and passing and shakeable. The old creation is doomed to be shaken and to be set aside. It would be foolish to cling to that which is to pass away.

There is however another purpose in the removal of the things that can be shaken. It is that the things which cannot be shaken may remain and be made manifest. There is a new creation. There are things which will abide, unchanging and unchangeable. It is to this sphere that the true believer belongs, so that the promise of the shaking and the removing of the old creation holds no dread for him. Rather does he enter into the thoughts of God concerning it all and looks forward with confidence to that day when all that remains will be headed up in Him of whom it was said in the first chapter of the epistle, "Thou remainest". Things that will abide after the dissolution of the present creation will be for Him and for His glory. All will be permanent and immovable in the new order.

28 The familiar "wherefore" now appears again. Some conclusion is about to be reached; some decisive point in the argument is about to be stated. It is, in essence, that we Christians are privileged to be part of a kingdom which cannot be moved, and that we ought to offer service which is in keeping with this great privilege.

Our service is offered in gratitude. It is the believer's response to the high favour which has been conferred upon him, that he should be in the enjoyment of things that can never be shaken. This is not the service of deacons. Nor is it the service of bondslaves. It is the willing service of worshippers (*latreuō*).

We must serve with reverence and godly fear. Our service should be characterised by the piety which was characteristic of the Son Himself (5:7). "Reverence" (*eulabeia*) indicates a sense of the holiness of God. Such service is marked by dignity, and by a demeanour suited to the presence of the holiness which we serve. There can be nothing light or loud or frivolous or over-familiar, in service which is acceptable to Him. This is in no sense incompatible with the fact that we are His children and that He is our Father, and that we enjoy intimacy and liberty in His presence. We must approach with reverence and godly fear, remembering the awful holiness to which we come to offer service.

Only service so characterised will be acceptable, that is, well-pleasing, to God. In the modern lightsome days in which we live it is well to cultivate a real sense of His majesty and of His hatred for sin, and approach Him with manners and language befitting. Service which has not these two characteristics, of reverence and awe, is not acceptable. Every grateful believer would truly desire to render service which would be well-pleasing. Is this why we sing:

> Consecrate me now to Thy service Lord,
>   By the power of grace divine;
> Let my soul look up, with a stedfast hope,
>   And my will be lost in Thine.

29   There is yet one concluding and conclusive argument for dignity and veneration in our approach to God. It is that our God is a consuming fire. Once, when we were in our sins and exposed to His righteous wrath, such thought made us tremble. This "consuming fire" is His essential holiness.

Now this holy character of God is unchanging and unchangeable. The fact that He is now our Father does not alter the fact of His holiness of nature. Of course we do not now stand in His presence with the dread of judgment that once we had. We are no longer in terror as we remember the demands of that holiness. We rest in the remembrance of this, that another has taken our place in judgment. The Just One has died for the unjust. The righteous, judicial demands of that holiness have been fully satisfied by another, and here we rest. Like the throned elders of Rev 4 we may sit in the presence of thunders and lightnings and voices and lamps of fire, and be unafraid. Indeed, like the saints of Rev 15, we may stand upon the sea of glass mingled with fire, and sing! This is the song and the confidence of those who, though fully aware of the holiness of God, have entered into the joy of redemption and have no fear.

But though we no longer dread the consuming fire as sinners exposed to judgment, yet we must ever remember that our God is unalterably holy and that we must always approach and serve Him accordingly. It is, as we have said, the final argument for a proper and suitable service from those who love Him. He is our Father indeed, but let us ever be mindful of His eternal holiness, His absolute purity, His inflexible righteousness, and His uncompromising hatred of sin. Our God is a consuming fire. Remembering this we shall serve Him acceptably.

Here ends a weighty and powerful portion of the epistle. Matters both practical and doctrinal have been considered. The chapter that follows has to do with what used to be called "divers admonitions". It is a series of encouragements and appeals to those who have learned the great truths of the preceding chapters, that these truths might not be doctrine only, but that they may be wrought out morally and practically in the home and in the assembly and in the world.

XIII Concluding Exhortations and Greetings (13:1-25)

1. *Concerning Hospitality and Holiness*
13:1-4

> v.1 "Let brotherly love continue.
> v.2 Be not forgetful to entertain strangers: for thereby some have entertained angels unawares.
> v.3 Remember them that are in bonds, as bound with them; *and* them which suffer adversity, as being yourselves also in the body.
> v.4 Marriage *is* honourable in all, and the bed undefiled: but whoremongers and adulterers God will judge."

It will have been noticed by many that the last three chapters of Hebrews are an exposition of the three great principles of faith, hope, and love; and in that order. Ch.11 is that great account of faith in action, its power being demonstrated in the lives and exploits of the faithful of past ages. Ch.12 deals very largely with the believer's hope, pointing us upward to the seated Saviour, and onward to the unshakeable kingdom. Ch.13 combines a series of moral and spiritual exhortations, which, if obeyed, will prove to be a very practical outworking of the abiding principle of love.

1 "Let brotherly love continue" is a certain recognition here that such love did indeed already prevail among these saints. The one word translated "brotherly love" is the familiar *philadelphia*. It is found, apart from the name of the city in Rev 3:7, only five times more in the NT:

1. Rom 12:10   "Be kindly affectioned one to another with *philadelphia*".

2. 1 Thess 4:9   "As touching *philadelphia*, ye have no need that I write unto you".

3. 1 Pet 1:22   "Ye have purified your souls unto ... unfeigned *philadelphia*".

4. 2 Pet 1:7   "Add ... to godliness, *philadelphia*".

5. 2 Pet 1:7   "And to *philadelphia* charity".

An overview of these Scriptures will suffice to show the great importance of brotherly love among the saints. It is associated, in these various references, with kindness, purity, truth, godliness and sincerity. How it must have rejoiced the heart of Paul that the Thessalonians had learned the value of it instinctively, being taught of God. They needed no exhortation or instruction from him concerning it, but were living and serving in the enjoyment of it (1 Thess 4:9).

Love of the brethren is not a NT feature only. Did not the Psalmist have the same thing in mind as the writer of our epistle when he exclaimed, "Behold how good and how pleasant it is for brethren to dwell together in unity" (Ps 133:1)? Perhaps the Psalmist envisaged those earlier people of God travelling up to Jerusalem and to the house of God for seasons of worship. It must have been a most delightful scene to see the caravans of pilgrims making their way to the divine centre in harmony with each other, singing as they travelled, and in a spirit of brotherly love rising to the high privileges of praise and worship as in Ps 134.

Brotherly love is not only requested of us, it is incumbent upon us and expected of us. The world will look for it too, and will recognise by it our association with the Lord Jesus: "By this shall all men know that ye are my disciples, if ye have love one to another" (John 13:35). It has often been called "the badge of discipleship".

Now it is well known that love of the brethren will thrive and abound in seasons of adversity. Whenever saints have been persecuted by the world they have been drawn closer to each other in a holy dependence in a bond of mutual love. When however conditions are easier, or when circumstances are less taxing due to either affluence or apathy, then *philadelphia* needs to be cultivated and fostered. It is easy, in the luxury of physical and material ease and security, to turn to criticism and to bickering and strife. These Hebrew readers knew what persecution was, and they knew therefore what comfort and encouragement there was in brotherly love. Now, exhorts the writer, whatever the future holds, in prosperity or adversity let brotherly love abide. Let it remain and continue.

2   Where there is love of the brethren there will be a ready willingness to offer hospitality. This is ever appreciated, not only by ministering brethren away from home, but also by those who must travel on secular business. The world's inns are not always the most congenial places for saints to lodge in, and believers away from home are very grateful for the hospitality of christian homes. In the pagan world in which many of the earlier saints lived, travellers were often exposed to temptations and corruptions, and a kind offer of accommodation with a believing family must have been most welcome. The corrupting influence of the pagan world is now also with us in what is called the "permissive society" of the civilised world, and the extending of hospitality to visiting and travelling saints is a most commendable ministry.

The ministry of hospitality will not be limited to those whom we know, but will be extended also to strangers. It may be well for us to remember that it is the habit of many races who are not christian to extend gratuitous hospitality to strangers. It is an unwritten law among Bedouin tribes people that strangers should be entertained. For one, two, or three days and nights, the visiting stranger will be afforded without question food and a place to rest and sleep. Only after three days will the stranger be asked of his intentions, and enquiry be made as to his identity and purpose. If such kindly disposition prevails among the Bedouin, surely it ought to prevail among saints who profess greater revelation and privilege.

There is, of course, great reward for those who show themselves hospitable. We are at once reminded of Abraham and Sarah in Gen 18, and of Lot in the chapter that follows. Abraham freely entertained three strangers, two of whom were angels, and the other the Lord of the angels Himself. What unsought reward was there for his kind ministry of hospitality. Lot also entertained strangers who proved to be angels. But what of that couple who lived at Emmaus long ago? They constrained the Stranger to come into their home, humble though it probably was. "Abide with us", they had said, and they prepared supper. They had the priceless privilege of having the risen Christ at their table. Who can tell what great reward, unsought and unexpected, may be the portion of those whose love expresses itself in practical hospitality? Hospitality is required of overseers in the assembly (1 Tim 3:2; Titus 1:8). But it is desirable and commendable in all believers.

3   The saints are now exhorted to remember prisoners. The word "remember" is not the same as that in v.7. It is not just a matter of remembering in the sense of mentally recollecting or calling to mind. The word indicates, in the language of J. N. Darby, "an active recollection because the object is cared for". It is the same word as in 2:6 where it is asked of Jehovah, "What is man that thou art *mindful* of him?" With what love and care did God remember His creature. How mindful He was of man's needs, and He accordingly remembered him and ministered to him. So were these readers to be mindful of those who were in bonds. Indeed, says the writer, "Remember them as bound with them". Enter into their sorrows. Put yourselves in their place. Suffer with them. Let their afflictions and pains be yours also. Love weeps with them that weep.

Does it need to be pointed out that these prisoners were not criminals? They were not in bonds for their crimes, but for their faith and testimony. It was not for common law-breaking that they were in chains, but for their fidelity to Christ. Remember them. Think of them with affection. Pray for them. Visit them. Take to them such comforts as food and clothing as is permissible. Be mindful of them in an active practical manner. Perhaps Onesiphorus is the great example, in his ministry to the imprisoned apostle. Of Onesiphorus Paul says, "He oft refreshed me, and was not ashamed of my chain: but when he was in Rome he sought me out very diligently, and found me ... and in how many things he ministered unto me at Ephesus, thou knowest very well" (2 Tim 1:16-18).

How many of the saints, though not in prison, were nevertheless suffering adversity. These too were to be similarly remembered and cared for. Some had lost homes and properties, employment and wealth, goods and friends. The winds of adversity were blowing cold for many. They were being evil treated. We are exhorted to remember such, with this in mind, that we ourselves are also in the body. "In the body" is variously interpreted. Some think that this is that spiritual body of which Paul says "The members should have the same care one for another. And whether one member suffer, all the members suffer with it" (1 Cor 12:25-26). Now while this is true in other contexts, it is neither probable or necessary here. Neither is that body the subject of this epistle as it is in the epistles to the Ephesians or Colossians. Rather should we see the writer's meaning as, "Remember your brethren who are being evil treated, keeping this in mind, that you yourselves are still in the body, that is, still alive. You may yet, yourselves, be called upon to suffer as they now suffer, and you may yet be grateful for someone to care for you and comfort you". Remember them accordingly.

4   From hospitality the writer now turns to holiness. There is, of course, a connecting thought, in that if we are to be hospitable, extending the fellowship of our homes to other saints, then it is imperative that our homes should be marked by holiness. There ought to be no restraint in the opening of our homes to others. There ought to be no fear of a discovery in our homes of that which is inconsistent with our confession as Christians.

The reference to marriage and to marital purity is probably not so much a statement as a directive. The writer is not simply saying that marriage is honourable, as the AV would imply. He is rather exhorting that marriage, and the marriage bed, should, in every way, be held in honour. Believers of our day, equally with the saints of that day, should be encouraged to hold both the institution of marriage and the purity of the married state in the highest regard. "Let marriage be held in honour" (see JND and cf. also RV). The union of one man with one woman for life was the divine purpose from the beginning, from the dawn of human life and society. It was the divinely-ordained way of maintaining order and purity in the race. Polygamy was not envisaged. Neither was divorce, but for Jews this was eventually made easy by the liberal teachings of certain Rabbinical schools, and for Gentiles the licentious practices of a permissive society have made it similarly easy.

The institution of marriage is older than either Christianity or Judaism. It is as old as mankind. It is most important to remember this. In a world that despises marriage and treats it lightly, believers must hold it in honour. If the learned judiciaries of the world now grant divorces and annulments on the easiest of easy terms then the believer must disregard this. (The same courts sanction the marriage of homosexual partners!) Marriage is for life: "Until death us do part" (cf. Rom 7:2-3). The re-marriage of one already married and divorced is adultery. The only exception recognised by our Lord was that possible case, in Jewish culture, where fornication by the betrothed wife was revealed at the consummation of the marriage. Such an unclean wife could be put away, and this in accord with Deut 24:1-2. (See Matt 5:32; 19:9.) The unchastity of a betrothed wife was a sad possibility. Consider the fear of Joseph in Matt 1:18-19. Note that fornication and adultery are not synonymous terms. Adultery demanded death, not divorce (Deut 22:22).

In such a world of confusion then, the believer will desire to be pure. Neither imposed sacerdotal celibacy on the one hand, nor moral licentiousness on the other hand, are in accord with the divine purpose. Let marriage be held in honour. Hold in the highest esteem both the marriage bond and the marriage bed. Let chastity and holiness reign in our homes.

The two words which we have already noted, fornication and adultery, are now included together in the verse, confirming that which we have observed, that they are not synonymous interchangeable terms. "Fornicators and adulterers God will judge". Believers do not belong to such an impure world. To quote J.N. Darby again, "The world goes its way and I am not part of it".

2. *Concerning Covetousness and Contentment*
   13:5-6

> v.5 *"Let your* conversation *be* without covetousness; *and* be content with such things as ye have: for he hath said, I will never leave thee, nor forsake thee.
> v.6 So that we may boldly say, The Lord *is* my helper, and I will not fear what man shall do unto me."

5   Our conversation is to be without covetousness. "Conversation" in old English meant much more than it means today. It meant our manner of life, our character, our conduct, our converse socially and morally with our fellow-men. The whole life and behaviour of the Christian ought to be without covetousness.

"Thou shalt not covet" was, of course, among the Sinai commandments (Exod 20:17). What heartbreak and trouble might have been avoided had this tenth commandment ever been observed among men. But alas, covetousness has been the source of every kind of evil. "Covetous" is *philarguros* (literally "money-loving"). Is there a play upon words here? We should have *philadelphia* and *philoxenia*, but not *philarguros* ! *Philadelphia* is "love of the brethren". *Philoxenia* is "love of the stranger". *Philarguria* is "love of money". As in the matter of hospitality, there is an important and peculiar application to the overseer (1 Tim 5:3), but the advice is good for all of us, for every kind of evil finds its root in the love of money (1 Tim 6:10).

"Be content" for covetousness and contentment cannot dwell together in the one heart. It must be covetousness or contentment. Contentment is satisfaction. We cannot have satisfaction and avarice at the same time. Well is it for that believer who knows not greed or envy, but is satisfied with his circumstances and with his lot. Godliness with contentment is great gain (1 Tim 6:6). "I have learned", says Paul, "to be content" (Phil 4:11).

What powerful, divine encouragement to contentment now follows: "He hath said, I will never leave thee nor forsake thee". It is the application to us of the word spoken to Joshua (Jos 1:5). And how especially precious this must have been to these early readers of the epistle. They were Hebrews. They had abandoned Judaism, and, in that sense, they had lost Moses. But here was a promise for them, given initially to a young man who had also lost Moses: "I will never leave thee nor forsake thee". As Jehovah was with Moses, so would He be with Joshua, and so would He be with them. With such assurance there was no reason to be envious of others. There was no need to be covetous. The word "never" is very strong: "In no wise will I leave thee nor in any wise forsake thee".

6   The response of the believing heart is as an echo of the promise. We may say, and say boldly, "The Lord is my helper". Speaking boldly means, "taking courage". This is not a brash boldness begotten of self or self-confidence. It is a courage instilled into us as we remember God's promise to us. It is always good to rest in His word. If He has said, "I will never leave thee", then we may say, "The Lord is my helper", and if He is my helper then I can say, "I will not fear". For that heart then, that can believe His word and rest on His promise, there need be neither covetousness, greed, nor fear. Indeed the verse concludes with a triumphant challenge, "What can man do unto me?" This is a citation from Ps 118:6. Note the preciousness of the word of God. He gives His word to us that He will not leave nor forsake us. We trust His promise and respond to it in the language of His word again. 13:5-6 is a beautiful bringing together of the divine promise of Jos 1:5 and the human response of Ps 118:6.

3.   *Concerning Grace and Truth*
    13:7-9

> v.7   "Remember them which have the rule over you, who have spoken unto you the word of God: whose faith follow, considering the end of *their* conversation.
> v.8   Jesus Christ the same yesterday, and to day, and for ever.
> v.9   Be not carried about with divers and strange doctrines. For *it is* a good thing that the heart be established with grace; not with meats, which have not profited them that have been occupied therein."

7   We have before noted the difference between the words translated "remember" as in vv.3, 7. The former is an active practical remembrance of those that are in certain need, being in bonds or under trial. This latter is a calling to mind of those who had been the guides of earlier years. There are three references to guides, or leaders, in this chapter. In v.17 there is an exhortation to obey them. In v.24 the writer requests that they be saluted. It is his greeting to them. But here in v.7 they are to be remembered. The guides here spoken of are leaders of past days: "them that had the rule over you". They had run their course, and had served their generation, and were now departed this life. They were to be remembered. It is possible that some of them had been martyred, but that it is not here stated or relevant. Their lives and ministry and good example were to be remembered.

It is a large part of a leader's ministry to speak the word of God to the saints. In both 1 Tim 3 and Titus 1, as in 1 Pet 5, it is envisaged that the guides will be "apt to teach", and able to "feed the flock of God". Such men may not be public ministers of the Word, nor may they be known as teachers in the sense of Eph 4:11. But they will be personally familiar with the truth of God and be able to counsel the assembly in all things relating to faith and doctrine. They will be equipped to teach and exhort, to encourage and comfort, and to generally direct the saints by the ministry of the Word. These departed guides had done this and they were to be remembered.

We are not only to remember, but, in remembering, we are to consider well "the end of their conversation". "Conversation", as we have observed in v.5, is manner of life. What was the end, the issue, the result, of the manner of life of these former guides? Consider what was the outcome of their lives and their ministry. Have they not powerfully influenced the saints? Did they not faithfully serve among you and leave you a good example? Is not the memory of these good men an incentive to us and an encouragement to godly living? This was the issue of their conduct among the saints. Remember and consider.

Now in reflecting upon the lives of these former guides there should be begotten within us a desire to follow them and to be imitators of them. "Whose faith follow". By their manner of life, by their ministry of the Word to us, and by their good example, these leaders of earlier days have left the saints a legacy and a challenge. We remember what they taught us. We consider what they were. We reflect upon their faith. We recall their shepherd love and care for the flock. And we desire to be like them, to imitate them, to follow them. In this way your holy living and good conduct will be but a part of the issue of theirs.

8 "Jesus Christ, the same yesterday, and today, and for ever". These beautiful words, well known and much loved by all the people of God everywhere, take on a new beauty when considered in their context. How often do we spoil the lustre of precious gems of Holy Scripture by lifting them out of their setting. Those guides, whom we knew, have departed. Those good men who served us well for so many years are gone. We loved them and we mourn their passing. They have loved us and left us, and we miss them. But it is not so with Jesus. He is the same yesterday, and today, and for ever. We may say of Him, as in ch.1, "Thou remainest" and, "Thou art the same". He abides. He was with us yesterday, a dependent Man, living amongst us, teaching us, loving us, and suffering for us, even unto death. Today He is in glory, interceding for us, our Paraclete, our Helper, if we sin (1 John 2:1). Tomorrow, yea, and for ever, throughout the ages to come, He will be ours unchangeably, and we shall be with Him and like Him. Our earthly friends may come, and go. We appreciate them; we bid them farewell and we remember them. Jesus remains the same. It is as if He would say to us, with the keys of death and of Hades hanging at His girdle, "Fear not ... I am he that liveth, and was dead; and, behold, I am alive for evermore" (Rev 1:18).

9 So then, we need not, we must not, be carried away, or carried about, with every wind of doctrine. Strange and varied teachings will ever beset the people of God in every age. Our guides help us while they are with us. But the greatest safeguard against shipwreck is occupation with Christ. Winds of doctrine will assail us. Some saints, alas, will be blown off course to disaster. Others will be tossed about, unsettled and unsure. Our haven of rest is Christ. Let us resort to Him in times of adversity and storm. Let us test every doctrine in relation to Him and to His glory. Let us anchor ourselves in Him and we shall be safe.

It is good that the heart be established, or confirmed, with grace, and not with meats. By "meats" the readers would understand those ordinances of Judaism relating to food and drink. Judaism had endless food laws, regulations and prohibitions and rules about eating that every orthodox Jew must observe.

But the instructed believer will be finished with such rules and regulations. He has learned that the kingdom of God is not meat and drink, but righteousness, and peace, and joy in the Holy Ghost (Rom 14:17). External ordinances will never establish the heart. The testimony of those who have walked in them will confirm this. Men have never been profited spiritually by the observance of the demands of Jewish law. How foolish to hanker after such legalities, when there is grace abounding in Christ to establish our hearts. How earnestly did Paul plead with the Galatians, "How turn ye again to the weak and beggarly elements, whereunto ye desire again to be in bondage? Ye observe days, and months, and times, and years. I am afraid of you ... O foolish Galatians" (Gal 4:9-11; 3:1). In the words of Wm Kelly, "O the folly, if we have Him, of hankering after a Caiaphas, or a Sadducean like Ananias".

Many there are in Christendom for whom Judaism will have no appeal, but who are attracted by the ornate buildings, the gorgeous vestments, the music and the litanies, and the sensual religion of a Judaised Christianity, Those aesthetic niceties are but a residue of an obsolete Judaism. They may appeal to the senses; they may stir the emotions; but they will never mature any believer. Grace alone will do that, and this is to be found in Christ. The law was given by Moses, but the dispensation of law is past. Grace and truth have come to us through Jesus Christ (John 1:17).

4. *Concerning Separation to Christ*
13:10-14

v.10   "We have an altar, whereof they have no right to eat which serve the tabernacle.
v.11   For the bodies of those beasts, whose blood is brought into the sanctuary by the high priest for sin, are burned without the camp.
v.12   Wherefore Jesus also, that he might sanctify the people with his own blood, suffered without the gate.
v.13   Let us go forth therefore unto him without the camp, bearing his reproach.
v.14   For here have we no continuing city, but we seek one to come."

10   The writer now speaks of those who "serve the tabernacle". He always speaks of the tabernacle rather than the temple, for even though that magnificent temple was still standing, it was, if the truth be known, as temporary as was the tent in the wilderness. With all its grandeur, it was passing away, but there were priests who still served in it daily (10:12). The argument now is very conclusive and decisive. The writer will prove, by the very laws of Judaism, that a clear choice must be made between Judaism and Jesus. No one could have both.

In "we have an altar", it is not "we Jews", as some see it. It is "we Christians". But what altar do we have, who are a spiritual people, finished with material curtains and altars and lavers and such like? The comments of F.F.Bruce are most helpful. He writes, "The word 'altar' is used by metonymy for 'sacrifice' – as when e.g., we say that a man keeps a good 'table', meaning thereby good 'food'. Our author, who insists throughout that Christians have something better than an earthly sanctuary and animal sacrifice, certainly does not suggest that they have a material altar ... The christian altar was the sacrifice of Christ, the benefits of which were eternally accessible to them. Material food, even if it was called sacred, perished with the using; in this new and spiritual order into which they had been introduced by faith, Christ was perpetually available".

Now, argues the writer, I will show you, even by the very laws of Judaism, that those who serve the tabernacle have no right to eat of our altar.

11 The Levitical priests did eat of their own altar. Of peace offerings and meat offerings and of certain sin offerings they were entitled to partake. But when the blood of a sin offering was carried into the sanctuary for sin, as in the case of the sin offerings of Lev 4:1-21, then the body of that sin offering was carried outside the camp to be burnt. Of such offerings the priests could not eat. Likewise, as is the context here, in the case of the sin offerings of the day of atonement (Lev 16), the blood was taken into the holiest of all by the high priest and the bodies were incinerated outside the camp. The priests were again forbidden to eat of those offerings. The rule was simple. If the blood of the offering was carried in, then the carcase of the offering was carried out, and if the body of an offering was carried outside the camp then of that offering the priests were not permitted to eat.

12 "Wherefore", the argument is about to be proven and the conclusion drawn, "Jesus ... suffered without the gate". The cross stood outside Jerusalem, outside the city, outside the camp. Of the crucified (and now risen) Christ, the adherents of Judaism cannot partake. Their own law forbids it. Jesus suffered outside the gate. We have an offering which is forbidden to those who serve the tabernacle. Their own Levitical law debars them from partaking of the sacrifice of the outside place. So then, it is Judaism or Jesus. This has been the constant argument of the epistle throughout. How powerfully is that argument pressed here, and how equally powerful the appeal to the hearts of those early Hebrew readers of the epistle. A choice must be made. We must be decisive and clear. We cannot have both the old Jewish system with its rules, and, at the same time, enjoy the benefits of the cross of Christ.

The death of Christ outside the city calls us out from all that the city represents. It separates us. We are sanctified by His blood. The place where He was crucified was nigh to the city (John 19:20), but it was outside. To go out to Him meant abandoning the city. The exhortation that follows calls upon us to do just that.

13 "Let us go forth therefore unto him", when it was fully understood, was a powerful call to the believing Hebrew. The implications were solemn and serious and the consequences of obedience would be great. It meant the total abandonment of

286 WHAT THE BIBLE TEACHES / HEB 13

the camp. It meant a complete separation from the Jewish system. The system was now obsolete, but many of their friends were still there. They themselves had been born in it, brought up in it, nurtured in it, and instructed from infancy as to its supremacy over pagan religions. Now, to be called out of it into association with One who had been crucified by it, was a most demanding exhortation indeed.

In the camp there was no place for Jesus. It had so much that it did not need or want Him. So He suffered and died outside. Without the camp was the habitat of the leper and the defiled (Num 5:2). It was the place of condemnation and of execution (Num 15:35-36). To be called outside the camp would have been too hard a thing for any Jew, except for this, that He was there whom he loved. It was the "unto him" that made the difference.

And so does the writer add, "bearing his reproach". It is the inestimable privilege of every believer, to share Christ's reproach. This is not just bearing reproach for Him; it is sharing reproach with Him. His reproach was the reproach of being expelled from the city. It was the city of the great king. The temple was there; "my Father's house", He had called it (John 2:16). It was the very religious and national centre of Judaism. It was the throbbing heart of Israel. And He had been cast out of it. What indescribable reproach was His. "Go out to Him", urges the writer. "Bear the reproach that He bore; share His reproach; be prepared and willing to suffer the shame that was His".

> Outside the camp unto Thy dear Name,
>   Draw me, O Lamb of God,
> Far from the world with its sin and its shame,
>   Hallowed is every sod.
> Outside the camp, 'tis a lonely place,
>   Outside the city wall,
> Here on Thy breast let my soul ever rest,
>   Outside the camp with Thee.

14 In any case, here, in this passing world, the believer has no continuing or abiding city. For the Jew it was Jerusalem, but as another has remarked, "This should be ever true to a Christian's faith, if he dwelt in Rome or in London, as then in Jerusalem" (Wm Kelly). Jerusalem was soon to be besieged and destroyed. All of the world's great cities are similarly doomed. There is no city so established here that it will abide for ever. It is not for us then to be settling here with roots digging deeply. The Saviour said of us, "They are not of the world, even as I am not of the world" (John 17:16). Two things should make it easier for us to go outside the city unto Him. Firstly, He is not in the city. It cast Him out. Secondly, the city is doomed; it will not abide. And so we go out to Him, looking for a city which has foundations. We seek a city to come, and with our hearts already there we may abandon the old associations here and be happy to share the reproach of a rejected Christ for a little while.

5. *Concerning Sacrifice and Submission*
   13:15-17

v.15   "By him therefore let us offer the sacrifice of praise to God continually,
        that is, the fruit of our lips giving thanks to his name.

v.16   But to do good and to communicate forget not: for with such sacrifices
        God is well pleased.

v.17   Obey them that have the rule over you, and submit yourselves: for they
        watch for your souls, as they that must give account, that they may do
        it with joy, and not with grief: for that *is* unprofitable for you."

15   Although we have no material altar, and although we do not offer animal
sacrifices any more, the believer does, nevertheless, have somewhat to offer. By
Christ we have access into the heavenly sanctuary; we have seen this again and again
throughout the epistle and it has been particularly expounded to us by the writer in
10:19-22. We bring the sacrifice of praise; we bring it to God; and we bring it
continually. In another epistle Paul will appeal to us that we present our bodies as
living sacrifices (Rom 12:1). Our lives should be wholly yielded to God in gratitude
for His mercies to us.

But what is this "sacrifice of praise", this "fruit of our lips"? It is the continual,
perpetual spirit of thanksgiving to God for His Son, and for that once-for-all offering
outside the camp. The spiritual mind will constantly find opportunity and occasion
for praise. We must praise of course for daily blessings, for God's provision and
protection, and for the innumerable kindnesses lavished so bountifully upon us. But
in the context this is a priestly exercise of coming to God in a sanctuary ministry,
bearing the sacrifice of praise for Christ. We approach by Christ and through Christ,
and we bring to God our appreciation of Christ, and we give thanks.

In that we do this continually does not mean that we are engaged uninterruptedly
in offering praise to God. But it should be our constant habit and mien, a happy
people ever finding opportunity for praise. "Whoso offereth praise glorifieth me" (Ps
50:23); "Great is the Lord, and greatly to be praised" (Ps 48:1). Through Christ the
spirit of heaviness may be exchanged for the garment of praise (Isa 61:3).

This is the fruit of our lips. The fruit of our lives may be seen in Gal 5:22, 23. The
fruit of our labours is in Phil 4:17. It is for the Father's glory that we bring forth much
fruit (John 15:8). It is for His delight and joy that we bring the fruit of our lips.

"Giving thanks to his name" is rendered by some, "confessing His name". The two
renderings are not at all contradictory, but rather complementary. As we come with
praise on our lips, giving thanks, this is, of necessity, confession of His name. It is our
willing acknowledgement of the Saviour in our thanksgiving to God for Him.

16   There is a holy priesthood and there is a royal priesthood (1 Pet 2:5, 9.) The
holy priesthood goes into the sanctuary in worship. The royal priesthood goes out to
men in testimony. Having been exhorted to a sanctuary ministry of praise and

thanksgiving, we are now encouraged to a very practical ministry. To do good, and to communicate with others in things material, we must not forget. Of two individuals in the NT it is said, "He was a good man" (Luke 23:50; Acts 11:24). This ought to be truly and freely said of every believer. When we were in our sins we were under that awful condemnation, "There is none that doeth good, no, not one" (Rom 3:12). But He came, of whom it was said that He "went about doing good" (Acts 10:38), and since we have come to know Him we have desired to be like Him. "To do good, be not forgetful". It is our christian duty to do good unto all men, especially unto them who are of the household of faith (Gal 6:10). We may do this by sharing with others those material benefits with which we have been blessed of God. With such sacrifices God is well pleased, and James solemnly reminds us that to him that knoweth to do good, and doeth it not, to him it is sin (James 4:17).

So then, we go in to God with the sacrifice of praise, and we go out to men with the sacrifice of the sharing of our substance.

17   Reference is now made again to the leaders. The former reference (v. 7) was to leaders of an earlier day. The exhortation was to remember them. Now it is to contemporary guides that the writer refers. Obey them; be submissive. Such injunctions to obedience and submissiveness are often contrary to the human spirit. There is a rebellious thing in fallen nature which does not take kindly to submitting. "Obey" and "submit" are not congenial words for fallen man.

For the believer, however, submissiveness is the way to blessing. For the younger believer, obedience is the royal road to growth and maturity. It is assumed that these guides are men of such moral stature that they do command obedience. The Pharisees, the guides of Judaism, were not easily obeyed. They demanded one thing but practised another. "Do what they say", said our Lord, "but not what they do" (Matt 23:2). Leaders among the saints would be different. They have been commissioned personally by One who asked, "Lovest thou me?", and when there is indeed love for the chief Shepherd there will be true love for the flock, and He can say, "Feed my lambs ... Tend my sheep" (John 21:15-17). One who was commissioned on that morning by the lake-shore said, "Feed the flock of God which is among you, taking the oversight thereof, not by constraint, but willingly ... neither as being lords over God's heritage, but being ensamples to the flock" (1 Pet 5:2-3).

Submission to the guides will be much easier then, when the guides are men with warm shepherd hearts, loving Christ, and loving the saints, and seeking to order things for God's glory and for the saints' good. At times the true guide will have a word of admonition or rebuke. At other times it may be encouragement, or comfort, or helpful instruction. Whatever the word, obey them, submit yourselves to their godly counsel.

The true guide will ever watch for the souls of the saints with a wakeful, diligent care. "Watch" (*agrupneō*) denotes wakefulness, or, literally, sleeplessness. W.E.Vine says, "The word expresses not mere wakefulness, but the watchfulness of those who are intent upon a thing". As F.F.Bruce comments, "The leaders carried a weighty responsibility ... no wonder that they lost sleep over their responsibility – for the 'watching' could well involve this as well as general vigilance".

But while there is great responsibility here, there is no thought of a clerical authority or of a sacerdotal supremacy. The leaders watch as those that must give account, not of the assembly for which they care, but of the way in which they have carried their responsibility and discharged their duty as leaders. The cleric will often speak of "my flock", and this "giving account" is often interpreted as the pastor rendering account to God concerning the condition of his flock. This is not the thought, neither here nor anywhere else in the NT pattern. The guide does not render account for other men's souls, but for his own ministry among the saints.

Neither is this "giving account" to be projected to the bema, the judgment seat of Christ. It is a present, on-going, rendering of account to God regarding the guide's own labour and toil in the assembly. Well is it when the faithful leader can give account with joy, telling of guidance given and received, and of the assembly profited by his ministry. How sad for that guide who must give account with groaning, with regret that he has not been as vigilant or as diligent as he might have been, or as true guides should be. That would be unprofitable both for him and for the saints. In any case, either with joy or with grief, the guides will give account as to how they have discharged the ministry which was committed to them.

6. *Concerning Intercession*
13:18-19

> v.18 "Pray for us: for we trust we have a good conscience, in all things willing to live honestly.
> v.19 But I beseech *you* the rather to do this, that I may be restored to you the sooner."

18 Pray for us! How often have these words been re-echoed by troubled souls. How often have saints been so implored by others, for a great variety of reasons, in an endless variety of circumstances. The young, the old, the sick, the infirm, the bereaved, the lonely, the discouraged, the evangelist, the busy minister of the Word, the leaders of whom we have been speaking, have all cried, "Pray for us". How precious are the intercessions of the saints for one another. The writer to the Hebrews knew it, and likewise beseeches, "Pray for us".

But why does he say "us"? Is this a literary "us" which really means, "Pray for me"? Or is it indeed intended as a plurality, associating himself with the leaders just mentioned? Perhaps he is indeed saying, "Pray for them"; "pray for me"; "pray for us". He continues with the plural "we" which raises the same question. He has some joy in this, that he writes to them with a good conscience. He has no regrets about his ministry or about the manner in which he has ministered. He has discharged his labour well. He is persuaded that a good conscience about it is in order. He had conducted himself wisely and well; he had lived honourably and had a will to walk rightly among the saints. But he is not unmindful of the dangers of a busy life, even though that life is busy in spiritual things. The busy preacher and teacher is in constant danger of ministering to others and neglecting himself. Many a busy minister has had to lament, in the language of another, "They made me the keeper of the vineyards; but mine own vineyard have I not kept" (Song 1:6). "Pray for us!" He is desirous to continue with a good conscience about himself and his ministry and he covets the prayers of the saints to this end.

19   But there was yet another reason for his request for their prayers. He longed to see them, to be restored to them, to renew the fellowship of former days. We cannot tell with certainty what lies behind this urgent request for special re-union with them, this being "restored" to them. Perhaps there had been an imprisonment which had deprived him of visits to them. Or could there have been some estrangement which had hindered his free fellowship with them? We cannot tell. But his conscience was clear and he longed to be restored to them as soon as possible. He had an obvious confidence in them and he beseeches them the more abundantly to pray for him. It is a plea from his heart to theirs. He greatly values their intercessions and appeals to their affections that they will remember him in these two particular matters, the maintenance of his good conscience as he ministers, and his desire to see them quickly.

7.   *The Doxology*
13:20-21

v.20   "Now the God of peace, that brought again from the dead our Lord Jesus, that great shepherd of the sheep, through the blood of the everlasting covenant,

v.21   Make you perfect in every good work to do his will, working in you that which is well-pleasing in his sight, through Jesus Christ; to whom be glory for ever and ever. Amen."

20   Jehovah has many majestic and glorious titles, but the title "God of peace" was especially and beautifully suited to these Hebrew readers, though this is neither the first nor the only time, that the lovely title is used. Other titles may be found as follows:

1. The God of peace   Rom 15:33; 16:20
2. The God of glory   Acts 7:2
3. The God of love   2 Cor 13:11
4. The God of patience   Rom 15:5
5. The God of comfort   2 Cor 1:3
6. The God of grace   1 Pet 5:10
7. The God of hope   Rom 15:13

It was not only to the Hebrews and to the Romans that the title "God of peace" was given. It was used also in the letters to the Philippians and to the Thessalonians (Phil 4:9; 1 Thess 5:23). It was a title most appropriate for saints in trouble, whether that trouble was difficulty in testimony, or discord in the assembly. These Hebrew readers perhaps knew both. They had experienced the hardship of persecution in the world and there was the internal problem of those who were immature because they were probably not genuine and were potential apostates (chs. 5, 6). Whether their problems were without or within, the writer commends them to the God of peace.

It was the God of peace who had brought the Lord Jesus out from among the dead. Is this the only reference to our Lord's resurrection in the epistle? There are, of course, numerous references to His exaltation to God's right hand, and this demands and implies resurrection, but perhaps this is now the only direct reference to His actual resurrection.

Our Lord has been raised again as the great Shepherd of the sheep. He called Himself "the good Shepherd" (John 10:11). Peter called Him, "the chief Shepherd" (1 Pet 5:4). The good Shepherd laid down His life for the sheep. The God of peace brought Him out again from among the dead. Leaders among the saints are His under-shepherds, but He is the great Shepherd of the sheep now in glory. As the chief Shepherd He will be manifested in a day to come. Intelligent Hebrews would rejoice in these Shepherd titles, remembering that Jehovah was the "Shepherd of Israel" to the nation of earlier days (Ps 80:1). They were the sheep of His pasture in the preceding verse in the Psalter (Ps 79:13).

The risen One is "our Lord Jesus". It is delightfully appropriate to recall that this lovely title is found for the first time at the empty tomb (Luke 24:3). It is, after this, used most frequently in the Acts of the Apostles and in the Epistles. But for thirty-three years the Saviour had lived unrecognised, and unknown except as "Jesus". "Jesus, the carpenter of Nazareth of Galilee" was, in most cases, the limited recognition afforded Him by men. As "Jesus" He was rejected, with that name written above His head on the cross (Matt 27:37). But after three days His tomb was empty. "the Lord is risen indeed", they said. He is "The Lord Jesus" now. And so we sing:

> He is Lord;
> He is Lord.
> He is risen from the dead
> And He is Lord.
> Every knee shall bow,
> Every tongue confess,
> That Jesus Christ is Lord.

Now the righteous basis of His resurrection is this, that in the sacrifice of Himself He has fully satisfied God. His blood is precious blood. The covenant thereby ratified is an eternal covenant. In virtue of this God has raised Him from the dead. What a gospel, and what a benediction is this! Precious blood is shed. The God of peace is satisfied. An everlasting covenant is ratified. The great Shepherd who gave His life has been raised up, out from among the dead, and He is Lord. The appeal of the gospel is therefore, "That if thou shalt confess with thy mouth Jesus as Lord, and shalt believe in thine heart that God hath raised Him from among the dead, thou shalt be saved" (Rom 10:9 JND).

21   The gospel having been believed, the believer now requires to be perfected. This does not mean moral perfection, which will never be ours while living here on earth in these bodies of our humiliation. It is a prayer for these Hebrews that they might be equipped spiritually for the work of the Lord. There was a service to be performed and the will of God to be done, and for the accomplishing of such "good works" they had to be suitably equipped by Him. Natural abilities would not be sufficient for the understanding and undertaking of the will of God. God Himself would need to perfect them for such holy exercise.

If God then would work in them and if they in turn would then work for Him, all would be well-pleasing in His sight and the Saviour would be glorified. Such is the desire of the writer for them, expressed so admirably in this final prayer for them, this benediction and doxology. The God of peace working in them, making them suited to work for Him, and this doing of His will bringing pleasure to Him, and eternal glory to His Son, this is the writer's prayer for his readers, and for us. With him we say sincerely, "Amen", "So be it".

8.   *A Personal Word*
13:22-23

> v.22   "And I beseech you, brethren, suffer the word of exhortation: for I have written a letter unto you in few words.
> v.23   Know ye that *our* brother Timothy is set at liberty; with whom, if he come shortly, I will see you."

22   For the second time in a short section of his epistle the writer "beseeches" them or "exhorts" them (see v.19). He has besought them to pray for him. Now he beseeches them to bear the general exhortations of the letter. We have seen that the epistle abounds in exhortation, as well as edification and consolation. "Bear the word of exhortation", he beseeches. How he has appealed, and expounded, and argued and reasoned. From the Psalms and from the Prophets, like his Lord, he has shown them Christ in all the Scriptures (Luke 24:27).

We of a much later day have divided his letter into thirteen chapters and some three hundred or more verses, but it is only, he says, "in few words" that he has written. Few words! It is a long epistle, but not the most lengthy of the NT letters. It may be read comfortably in one hour. In relation to what could have been written, or what might have been written (5:11; 9:5), it is indeed but a few words. "Bear with me", he asks. It is as if he is saying, "Hear me through". How easily will the flesh weary with prolonged exposition and exhortation. We need to discipline ourselves, determined to suffer the word of exhortation. It is for our profit.

23   The reference to "our brother Timothy" is touching. Many will see the reference as confirmation of a Pauline authorship. Wm Kelly says, "The reference to Timothy suits the apostle Paul fully". But he goes on to add, "No doubt the absence of the writer's name is quite sufficient to show that God is here pointing to the importance of the teaching rather than the teacher".

Timothy had been set at liberty. The phrase almost certainly implies an imprisonment of which we have no account anywhere in the NT. News of his release had reached the writer. He desires his readers to know also. This "know ye" is not a question. It is not "Do you know?", as may be implied in the AV, (though the question mark is omitted in the text). "Know ye" is in the imperative form. He is saying, "Know this; I am telling you this; I would have you to know, so know this". Wherever the writer was at the time, he is hoping that soon Timothy will join him, and that together they may come to visit these Hebrew saints.

9.   *Salutation and Benediction*
        ## 13:24-25

> v.24   "Salute all them that have the rule over you, and all the saints. They of
>   Italy salute you.
> v.25   Grace *be* with you all. Amen."

24   There is now a third and final reference to leaders (see vv.7, 17). "Salute them", he exhorts. "My greetings to them", he is saying. And not only to the leaders does he send his greetings, but to all the saints.

As well as his personal greetings the writer also has greetings for them from believers described simply as "they of Italy". We have earlier observed, in the introduction, that this can mean one of two things. It may well mean that the epistle was written in Italy, and sent from Italy to saints outside that country. In that case this was now just a conveying of greetings from the believers in Italy to those believers to whom he was writing. On the other hand, it may be taken to mean that the writer was writing from somewhere outside of Italy, but that there were Italian believers with him. If this were so then he is but sending on to his readers the greetings of those Italian saints who were with him. This would, of course, be of special interest and importance if the letter was destined for Rome, or for some other part of Italy. The comment of Dr John Brown of Edinburgh is very beautiful.

" 'They of Italy salute you'; that is, 'The Christians in Italy send you the assurance of their cordial regard'. How does Christianity melt down prejudices! Romans and Jews, Italians and Hebrews, were accustomed to regard each other with contempt and hatred. But in Christ Jesus there is neither Roman nor Jew, neither Italian nor

294

Hebrew: all are one. Christians of different countries should take all proper opportunities of testifying their mutual regard to each other. It is calculated to strengthen and console, and to knit them closer in love. Proper expressions of love increase love on both sides".

25 "Grace be with you all" is the final benediction in a letter designed to show the superiority of the gospel of grace over the cold dispensation of law. It is fitting that grace should have a mention in the closing verse and sentence of the letter. And the writer embraces "all" in his benediction. He desires for them, and upon them, the continuing sovereign kindness of God, the blessing of the God of all grace.

Throughout his epistle he has shown them the very heart of that gracious God. God, who had spoken to the fathers, had come out of the mist of early fragmentary prophecies into the blaze of a sunrise of full revelation in His Son. God's love and holiness, His righteousness and truth, yea, His heart, had all been expressed in One who had lived perfectly, who had died vicariously, who was risen triumphantly, who lived eternally, and who would one day appear gloriously. Such a One transcended all that they had ever known in Judaism. The God of grace had been revealed indeed and the writer desires that they might continue and abound in an ever-increasing, loving experience of that God. Of the Son who has revealed Him we delight to sing, and how would these first Hebrew readers of the epistle have sung with us:

Jesus, Thou joy of loving hearts,
Thou fount of life, Thou light of men,
From the best bliss that earth imparts
We turn unfilled to Thee again.

We taste Thee, O Thou living bread!
And long to feast upon Thee still;
We drink of Thee, the fountain-head,
And thirst our souls from Thee to fill.

Our restless spirits yearn for Thee.
Where'er our changeful lot is cast:
Glad when Thy gracious smile we see;
Blest when our faith can hold Thee fast.

Appendix A

The Levitical Offerings

We have read, in Heb 10:8, of "Sacrifice and offering and burnt offerings and offering for sin", and this expression is a summary of the principal Levitical offerings. Detailed instructions with regard to these offerings are given in the first seven chapters of Leviticus. These were not the only offerings associated with the service of the tabernacle, but they were the principal ones, and of these there were five. In the order in which they first appear, they are:

1. The Burnt Offering
2. The Meat Offering
3. The Peace Offering
4. The Sin Offering
5. The Trespass Offering

Each offering is rich in typical teaching. Each offering is a parable (as is the tabernacle as a whole) bringing to us in beautiful symbolism some particular glory of Christ, as touching either His Person or His work. Every offering has its own distinctive features. There is something about each offering which makes that offering unique, so that they do require to be studied both individually and in relation to one another. Associated with every offering there is a priest, an offering, and an offerer. In any fulness of exposition these three aspects would all need to be considered, because Christ is the priest, Christ is the offering, and Christ is the offerer in every case. This brief summary, however, does not pretend to be an exhaustive commentary on the subject, but just a helpful introduction to it, showing in particular how every offering is, in its own way, a presentation of Christ.

The burnt offering represents the very high ground of an appreciation of what Christ means to God. The burnt offering was a "holocaust", called "a whole burnt offering" because the whole carcase of the offering, with its fat and its blood, was laid upon the altar for God. It was all for God. There ascended from it as it burned, a sweet savour. This was a precious foreshadowing of One who was to come, whose entire life, in all its lovely detail, would be fragrant to God, and would be laid down, in a holy climax of obedience, in a death that likewise would be as an odour of a sweet smelling savour to God.

The meat offering, often called the meal offering, was a bloodless offering. While there are symbols of suffering in it, there is neither shedding of blood or death. It is therefore a type of a holy life of perpetual purity and sweet holiness that brought much pleasure, yea satisfaction, to God. There is no thought of atonement in this offering. There is no suffering for sin. It was an offering of fine flour, sometimes baken, sometimes unbaken, which typified that "bread of God" who was to come.

The meat offering was an oblation of food upon the altar, and it was different from the burnt offering in that while it firstly was for God, yet the priests had their portion in it too. It demonstrates the great principle that the food of the altar became the food of the priestly family. Christ for the heart of God is for our satisfaction also.

The peace offering was, like the burnt offering and the meat offering, a sweet savour offering. It was a voluntary offering given from a devoted and grateful heart. It is a high privilege to give to God voluntarily that which is not demanded. And in the peace offering there was the utmost sharing, or fellowshipping. Jehovah had His portion, burnt on the altar. The priests had their portion. The offerer too, and his family and friends, would have their portion. There was a wide enjoyment of the peace offering. It has well been called "the fellowship offering". Here is the communion of saints indeed, not only with one another in a holy union, but with God and with His Son, because of Calvary.

The sin offering was for sins of ignorance. Many are the sins committed in ignorance, and for the Jew, beset as he was with rules and regulations, with prohibitions and with the demands of a complex law, it was altogether too easy to trespass without knowing. When the sin, committed ignorantly, came to light, it required an offering. Because of what we are, in ourselves, we are prone to sin. Such is the state of our hearts, with an old fallen nature, that we may often sin without being aware that we have sinned. Calvary has taken care of this. Christ is the sin offering, propitiating God not only for what I have done, but also for what I am. What I am is probably worse that what I have done, in that what I have done, I would not have done, had it not been for what I am.

The trespass offering was for sins committed willingly, deliberately, and knowingly. We all have within us that rebellious trait, which, even when we know a thing to be wrong, will cause us to sin. In a myriad ways we sin against God, against our fellow-men, and against ourselves. But there is a trespass offering: "The blood of Jesus Christ, his Son, cleanseth us from all sin" (1 John 1:7). He has washed us from our sins in His own blood (Rev 1:5).

These are the main features of these five principal offerings, but it will be noticed that the order in which they first appear is not the order of experience. In the order of experience it is usual for us to begin with the trespass offering. In a consciousness of my sin I appreciate the meaning of the cross, and I appropriate what has been accomplished for me in the sacrifice of Christ. My sins are forgiven. I go on to learn the horror of what I am in myself, with an incurably sinful nature, but I rest in the knowledge that this too has been taken care of in the death of the Saviour. Still progressing I now appreciate the happy and holy fellowship into which I have been brought, and I delight, in my daily life and in my service, to hold sweet converse with God, with Christ, and with my fellow-believers. It will be greater progress still if I can go on to see just how much the lovely life of Jesus meant to God. If I can rise to appreciate that moral glory which ascended like a cloud of fragrant human incense to God, then I am indeed rising to share God's thoughts of His Son. Such appreciation will inevitably bring me to that high ground where I will worship, apprehending a

Christ wholly for God. It will be my delight and my privilege to offer to God, out of a full heart, my appreciation of that Christ. And, in the wonder of it all I will probably sing:

Loved with love that knows no measure
    Save the Father's love to Thee,
Blessed Lord, our hearts would treasure
    All the Father's thoughts of Thee.

All His joy, His rest, His pleasure,
    All His deep delight in Thee;
Lord, Thy heart alone can measure
    What Thy Father found in Thee.

But we must look at the offerings in more detail.

1. The Burnt Offering

The Book of Leviticus begins with the call of God to Moses. This is not the first time that Moses has been so called by Jehovah. In Exod 3 there was a call out of the bush. In Exod 19 the call came out of the mountain. But in Lev 1 the call comes out of the tabernacle, out of the tent. It is the same Jehovah that calls, but for a different purpose each time. In Exod 3 it is a call to service. In Exod 19 it is a call to holiness. In Lev 1 it is a call to worship.

Out of the glory-filled tabernacle Jehovah was calling. It was as if man was being invited to come near, and to bring some offering to God. What a wonder is this, that Jehovah, eternally self-sufficient, should ask something of man. Man, mortal and frail, is being asked to give to Jehovah, eternal and inscrutable! What can he bring?

The offering which God requests may be in any one of five forms, according to a man's resources and his ability to give. He may bring a bullock, or a sheep or a goat, or a turtledove or a pigeon. These are sometimes interpreted as differing "grades" of offering, and since they were indeed offered according to a man's resources, they may, in a sense, be viewed as depicting degrees of appreciation. We must, however, be careful not to introduce market values into such a precious offering. We must ever remember that whether the offering be bullock, or sheep, or goat, or bird, it typifies Christ in some way. A young believer, or indeed an older saint with limited capacity, may appear to bring but a turtledove or pigeon, but if such is given from a full heart, out of a sincere devotion to God and appreciation of Christ, then this is a whole burnt offering just as is the bullock which is offered by one who has vast learning and large capacity and many years of knowledge and experience.

We remember our Lord's appraisal of the two mites cast into the treasury by a poor widow. Man's estimate of her offering would not have been very great, but the Saviour, who knew the resources out of which those two mites had been given, could assess accurately and say, "She hath cast in more than they all" (Luke 21:3)

There is though, in the different forms of burnt offering, a variegated presentation of the many ways in which Christ was precious to God.

a. The *bullock*, or *ox*, was a strong patient servant. In what seemed to be an untiring, unwearying service, the bullock would plod silently a path of obedience. Whether it was ploughing or sowing or reaping or gathering in the harvest or threshing, the bullock was a ready servant. This was a precious foreshadowing of One who was Jehovah's perfect Servant. Did He not daily minister to those around Him, breaking the bread of life to them, bringing tender care and comfort to weary bodies and souls? Do we not hear Jehovah say, with great cause, "Behold my servant" (Isa 42:1)? What a joy is ours, and delight, to bring to God our appreciation of Him who, in a ministry of teaching, preaching, healing, and praying, devoted Himself wholly to the will of God.

b. The *sheep* is ever symbolic of a meek yieldedness, a submissiveness in suffering, that was so characteristic of our Lord Jesus. Was it not as the Lamb of God that He was introduced to the nation by John Baptist? John looked upon Jesus "as he walked" (John 1:36), and said, "Behold the Lamb of God". It is our high privilege too, to gaze upon Him as He walked, to hear Him say, "I am meek and lowly" (Matt 11:29), and to see Him at the end yield Himself to cruel men, to be shorn of all His rights, to be mutilated with thorns and scourge, and to be slain outside the city. This was a holy submission, not to men only, but to His Father and God. "Even Christ pleased not himself" (Rom 15:3). He prayed, "Not my will, but thine, be done" (Luke 22:42).

c. The *goat* is the emblem of resolution and stedfastness. It has "a stately step", and is "comely in going" (Prov 30:29-31 JND). That Scripture ranks the goat with the lion and with the war-horse. What beautiful balance was there in Christ, in that He could be meek and lowly, passive and yielding, and yet be firm and determined, resolute in His walk. This we see when at times men sought to deter Him from the path of obedience and suffering. He could not be deflected: "He stedfastly set his face to go" (Luke 9:51). And though His most devoted followers would say to Him, "Far be it from thee Lord; this shall not be unto thee", His face was set; His mind was stedfast; His step was firm. "He must go ... and suffer ... and be killed" (Matt 16:21-23).

> No unforeseen event
> E'er took Him by surprise;
> Towards the cross with fixed intent
> He moved with open eyes.

d. The *turtledove* is the epitome of an enduring and unwavering devotion. There is an undivided love and loyalty to its partner. The object of its affection will be regarded with a single eye. There is a pure and jealous attachment which commands admiration. So it was with Jesus. In holy constancy of devotion to His Father He lived and died. On the last evening of that lovely life on earth He could say, "That the world may know that I love the Father ... Arise, let us go hence" (John 14:31). Whatever the cost, whatever the consequences, He would continue in love to the Father. Love for His Father motivated all that Jesus did. This was an eternal love, with no beginning, but men were privileged to witness it during the days of His sojourn on earth.

e. The *pigeon* typifies an uncomplaining poverty that was very true of Him who "became poor" (2 Cor 8:9). He began life in a cattle shed or stable, wrapped in swaddling clothes and laid in a manger. He grew up in the poverty of Nazareth. He owned nothing of any value. He had no estate or property. He could borrow a penny, a boat, a donkey, or an upper room. "Ye know the grace of our Lord Jesus Christ". He voluntarily left riches that were incalculable for the penury of earth. He was truly a Man of sorrows. What privilege is ours, that we should be able to recall His poverty, and muse upon it, and bring our appreciation of it as a burnt offering to God.

Now two things were consistently characteristic of every burnt offering, of whatever grade or form. It must be a male, and it must be without blemish. The male is expressive of initiative, of responsibility, of activity and of energy. Later, in connection with another offering, we shall read of female sacrifices, and they will represent submission, subjection, and passiveness. But every burnt offering must be male.

Our Lord's life was an active life. He did not live a monastic existence, cloistered away from the bustle and evil of the world. He lived right in the midst of it. Whether it was society, or family, or synagogue, or business, He was there, busy in it as a Nazareth carpenter, and exposed to it. But He was "without blemish". He was impeccably pure. He was without sin, or the suggestion of it, or the possibility of it. The Lamb of God remained, as Peter declared, "without blemish and without spot" (1 Pet 1:19).

The offerer, a worshipper, brought His offering for his acceptance. It was accepted, and he was accepted in his offering. In all the acceptability of Christ we are accepted too. We are accepted in the Beloved (Eph 1:6). Forgiveness of sins is not at all the primary thought in the burnt offering. It is our acceptance as worshippers because of our association with One who so gave Himself. He is accepted, and we are accepted in Him.

Having presented his offering, it was now the serious duty of the offerer to kill his offering. He became personally responsible for the death of the offering in which he found his acceptance. So do we, as we worship, remember that we were responsible for His death who died for us. Would the very hands of the worshipping offerer be stained with the blood of the offering in which he was accepted? So with us.

But the offerer had done a most important and interesting thing as he had presented his offering. He had leaned his hand upon its head. Two things were happening at that moment. Firstly, the offerer was in effect saying, "This is mine! My offering!" He was identifying himself with it. Secondly, all the acceptability of his offering was now being transferred to him. It shall be accepted for him (Lev 1:4). Note that there are no degrees of acceptance. There may be degrees or grades of appreciation, but not of acceptance. Believers are all, equally and eternally, accepted in the acceptability of Christ.

The death of the offering was now followed by a solemn priestly exercise. The flayed bullock or sheep must be parted into prescribed pieces. The inwards and the legs had to be washed. This was to render them typically what Christ was intrinsically. There must be no defilement with the offering. There must be purity, internally and externally. The portions of the offering were then placed in order upon the great altar. O for priestly ability to bring an orderly, intelligent appreciation of Christ to God, and to assist others to do so also.

The head, the fat, the inwards, and the legs, were all laid on the altar. Notice how these parts of the offering correspond with that well known word of the Lord Jesus when He said, "Thou shalt love the Lord thy God with all thy heart, and with all thy soul, and with all thy strength, and with all thy mind" (Luke 10:27). The inwards of the offering correspond to the heart. The fat, the rich energies, correspond to the soul of man. The legs are the strength, and the head is the mind. This may perhaps be seen more simply and clearly if viewed in a tabulated form.

Luke 10		*Lev 1*
The Heart	...	The Inwards
The Soul	...	The Fat
The Strength	...	The Legs
The Mind	...	The Head

It is all a beautiful picture of Him whose whole life was devoted to the will of His Father. All that He did, all that He was, His words, His ways, His thoughts, His motives, all were dedicated to that which would bring pleasure and glory to His Father and God. With a love that was immeasurable He loved His Father and did always, and only, those things that pleased Him.

All the parts of the offering were then burnt on the altar. There are two Hebrew words for "burn" in these early chapters of Leviticus. One means "to burn up utterly; to consume away; to burn out of sight as one might incinerate refuse". The other means "to smoke; to burn as incense; to turn into fragrance by fire". We shall notice the former word in a later chapter. Here the latter word is used. The whole burnt offering was turned to a sweet savour by the fire of the altar. It was "an offering made by fire, of a sweet savour unto the Lord". Notice in Lev 1, that the vv. 9, 13, 17, all conclude with these identical words. Whether the offering was of the herd, of the flocks, or of the fowls, there was a sweet savour unto Jehovah.

The brasen altar was not a pleasant sight. There was blood, and death, and fire, and ashes. But from it there arose that constant sweet savour. Golgotha was not a pleasant sight either. There was blood and sweat and awful thirst; there were thorns and nails and spear and dense darkness and death. It was not pleasant. But there ascended from it a sweet savour. Calvary was precious to God. It was the climax of His moral glory who had lived in utter devotion to God, and whose life was now laid down, willingly and voluntarily, because that was God's will.

The beauty of the remaining details we must leave.

2. *The Meat Offering*

The meat offering is often referred to as the "meal" offering. It is called the meal offering because the substance of the offering was meal or flour. Neither "meal" or "grain" is, however, a true translation of the word of Lev 2:1. It is *minchah*, meaning "gift; present, donation; tribute". The root of the word probably meant "to give". J.N. Darby will consistently render the word "oblation", which denotes the offering of a worshipper. Another has written, " 'Present' or 'gift' is appropriately used of that offering whose predominant, and indeed almost exclusive, characteristic is, the provision of something grateful to the altar of Jehovah" (B.W. Newton). The meat offering was a gift of food for Jehovah and for the priestly family. It is a delightful principle, which we have noted before, that the priestly house feeds on that which has fed the altar. Christ for the joy of the heart of God is my sustenance also. I feed my soul on Him who has satisfied God.

It has been a problem for some that we have here an offering without blood. How can we reconcile this, for instance, with Jehovah's rejection of the bloodless offering offered by Cain. The answer is that the meat offering was not an offering for sin, and that it was not offered alone. It was a companion offering, or an appendage, to the animal sacrifices, and especially to the burnt offering, so that we may often read, "The burnt offering with his meat offering" (e.g. see Num 29:6 ff). The meat offering was offered in company with the blood of a burnt offering, as if to indicate that purity in life and acceptability in death were inseparable.

There were four ingredient parts in the meat offering. There was flour, oil, frankincense, and salt. Two substances were strictly forbidden. There must be no leaven, and no honey.

a. *Flour*. This was fine flour, the finest part of wheat flour. It was flour fully ground and finely sifted, free from all roughness. It was sometimes offered in its unbaken state, and sometimes as baked cakes or wafers. Sometimes indeed, the green ears of grain were offered, having been dried by the fire. Christ is the Bread of God (John 6:33). His lovely life was a perfect blending of every pleasing feature. There was no inbalance. There was no roughness. All was fine and evenly balanced in His character. There was love, joy, and peace. There was longsuffering, gentleness, and goodness, and there was faith, meekness, and temperance. All these virtues were displayed in equality in the life of Jesus. There was nothing in excess over another, neither was there anything lacking.

> In smooth and silken whiteness
> Without a roughening grain,
> In clear unbroken brightness,
> Without a speck or stain,
> The fine flour in its beauty
> The perfect Man portrays
> In all His path of duty,
> In all His heavenly ways.

b. *Oil*. In three ways was the oil associated with the flour of the meat offering. Sometimes the flour was mingled with oil; sometimes it was anointed with oil; sometimes the oil was poured, the flour being thus saturated. To many, oil will be the familiar emblem of the Holy Spirit. In our Lord's miraculous conception, observe the holy "mingling" of flour and oil. Gabriel said to Mary, "The Holy Ghost shall come upon theee, and the power of the Highest shall overshadow thee: therefore also that holy thing that shall be born of thee shall be called the Son of God" (Luke 1:35).

But see also the "anointing" in John 1:32 and in Acts 10:38: "The Spirit descending from heaven ... abode upon him"; "God anointed Jesus of Nazareth with the Holy Ghost and with power: who went about doing good". So also was the flour saturated with the oil in the ministry of the Lord Jesus: "Jesus returned in the power of the Spirit into Galilee" (Luke 4:14). He declared, "The Spirit of the Lord is upon me, because he hath anointed me to preach the gospel to the poor; he hath sent me to heal the brokenhearted, to preach deliverance to the captives, and recovering of sight to the blind, to set at liberty them that are bruised, to preach the acceptable year of the Lord" (Luke 4:18-19). As the oil was "poured" upon the flour, the same word is used in Ps 45:2, where grace is "poured" into the lips of Christ. He was a Man approved of God by miracles and wonders and signs which God did by Him (Acts 2:22). The gracious and powerful ministry of the Lord Jesus was convincing evidence of His intimacy with the Holy Spirit and of the Spirit's intimacy with Him. It was indeed as if the flour was saturated with the oil. Rejection of Him and His works was a rejection of the Spirit of God (Matt 12:24-32).

c. *Frankincense*. This most precious perfume was rich and rare and fragrant. It was called frankincense because of its whiteness and was a fitting emblem of the sweet pure life of the Lord Jesus. The fragrance of frankincense was enhanced by the action of the fire. The fire did not destroy, but rather developed, the sweetness. Adversity and hostility only but seemed to display the sweetness of the Saviour. The heat of trying circumstances, which would have angered or embittered other men, served only to show how enduringly fragrant His life and character were.

It may be fitting to remember just here that there must be no honey in the meat offering. Sweetness there might be in honey, but it is a corruptible sweetness, a sweetness that may be fermented and soured. Such would not at all be a suitable emblem of that precious fragrance of the life of Christ, which nothing could spoil. "Ye shall burn no honey" (Lev 2:11).

d. *Salt.* This is the fourth ingredient mentioned. Every meat offering had to be seasoned with salt. Here we also recall that leaven was forbidden. Now salt is the great preservative. Leaven is a corrupting element. Here was a dual type, positive and negative, emphasising the essential holiness of the Lord Jesus. Salt is the emblem of purity and perpetuity. Leaven is the emblem of corruption, and was always so understood by Jews, who annually swept their houses clean of leaven at Passover time. Our Lord spoke of the leaven of the Pharisees, the leaven of the Sadducees, and the leaven of the Herodians. This was a warning against the evils of ritualism, rationalism, and sensualism. Paul warned the Corinthians of moral leaven, and the Galatians of doctrinal leaven (1 Cor 5:6-8; Gal 5:9).

Our Lord was incomparable, impeccable, and incorruptible. This double use of the two emblems powerfully guards that moral glory that was His. He was perfectly sinless. He was sinlessly perfect. Salt, yes; leaven, no.

The priest now grasped all that his hand could hold of the flour and oil. It was a memorial handful to be burned on the altar. That which remained of the flour and the oil was the food of the priests. But all the frankincense had to be put on the altar for God. It was as if to say that only the fire of the altar was capable of an adequate appreciation of that fragrance. The frankincense was devoted wholly and exclusively to the altar. We may enjoy, as a priestly family, an appreciation of Christ, and we do. But when all our appreciations are gathered and rendered to God in worship, we know that the Father can say, "There is a fragrance in my Son that only I can fully appreciate. All the frankincense is mine". We respond and sing:

> But the high mysteries of His Name
> An angel's grasp transcend;
> The Father only (glorious claim!)
> The Son can comprehend.

Now while there was no blood-shedding in the meat offering, yet there were emblems of suffering. The offering was often baken, either in an oven, on a flate plate, or in a cauldron. There were sufferings in our Lord's life that were His personal, private, lonely, oven experience. There were sufferings into which we cannot enter because we have no knowledge. Indeed, thirty years of His earlier life have been hidden from us, in the wisdom of God. There were also, sufferings as on a flat plate, when He was exposed to the unpitying eyes of men, and His holy feelings laid bare. But there were sufferings too, as in a cauldron, partly visible, partly concealed. Those who were nearest appreciated most, what He suffered during that last night. Gethsemane! Gabbatha! Golgotha! May we ever draw near in spirit and be helped to view with holy reverence the suffering One of that last sad evening and morning. May we be permitted, with priestly dignity and with becoming awe, to share in an appreciation of such a Christ as is typified in the meat offering.

3. *The Peace Offering*

Peace offerings were offered for three reasons. Sometimes they were a form of thanksgiving for some blessing or favour received. Sometimes they were offered to confirm the making of a vow, as if a man were making a tryst with God. Sometimes they were just voluntary expressions of worship from appreciative hearts.

But why, it may be asked, should a peace offering be the appropriate offering in such circumstances? The reason is that in all of these cases there is a desire on the part of the offerer that others should share his joy, and the peace offering makes provision for such sharing. The offerer is in the joy of fellowship with God as he brings his gratitude, or makes his vow, or renders his worship, but he wants others to enjoy it with him. The peace offering is in this respect different from the burnt offering, in that there was something for the altar, something for the priestly house, and something also for the offerer and his family and friends.

As for God, His portion was taken to the great brasen altar. The fat and the blood and the hidden inner parts were for God. It is relatively easy to see that here we have a picture of God's appreciation of the rich pure motives that energised the ministry of His Son. We have too His appreciation of the tender, inner, sensibilities of that lovely Man whose life was eventually laid down in blood-shedding and death at Calvary.

While the altar fed on these parts of the peace offering, the priests had their portion. The priests fed on the breast and on the right shoulder. The breast is ever the emblem of love and affection. The shoulder is the symbol of strength and power. It is priestly privilege to feed upon the love of Christ and to rest securely in His strength. The breast of the offering is called, "the wave breast", and the shoulder is called. "the heave shoulder". These, though the food of the priests, were first of all displayed to the eye of God in a solemn presentation. If, in priestly exercise, we enjoy thoughts of Christ's love and power, we do well to remember that these were, firstly and primarily, for the pleasure and glory of God. It is that principle again, that the priests feed on that which has already satisfied God.

But if there was a portion for God and a portion for the priests, there was a portion also for the offerer himself. With his family and friends he was enabled to share his joy as they also partook in the eating of the offering, so that now both Jehovah and His priests and the offerer and his friends were all fellowshipping in the one offering. We can say like John, "that ye also may have fellowship with us; and truly our fellowship is with the Father, and with his Son Jesus Christ. And these things write we unto you, that your joy may be full" (1 John 1:3-4).

It will be noticed that in the peace offering there may be offered either male or female (Lev 3:1). The typical meaning of the male we have already observed in the burnt offering. The female portrays that beautiful subjection, that holy submissiveness and devotion and patience, which also characterised our Lord Jesus. It is a delight to trace His pathway through the Gospels and see the moral characteristics of both male and female displayed in Him.

It is interesting to observe that when we come to the laws of the offerings (see Lev 6, 7) the order of the presentation is changed and the peace offering is now considered last of all. We now have to read our way through the accounts of the other four offerings before we arrive at the peace offering. There may be two typical lessons in this. Firstly, is it not so, that to be in the true enjoyment of the fellowship here envisaged, we must be in the good of all the other offerings? When we truly appreciate Christ as our offering for sin, and when we see Him also in His life and death bringing satisfaction and glory to God, perhaps it is only then that we in truth arrive at the peace offering. Secondly, when now we have arrived at the peace offering, this is the ultimate; there is nothing to follow. We have indeed, arrived. It was Jehovah's earliest purpose for man in Eden, that there should be holy communion between Creator and creature. Sin disturbed that Edenic bliss, but now, in Christ, it has been restored. It is a chief pleasure for men to fellowship again with God. Is there anything more for us than this?

4. The Sin Offering

As there were differing grades or forms of the burnt offering, so were there differing forms of the sin offering. As the form of burnt offering was determined by a man's resources, so the form of sin offering was likewise influenced by those resources, but also by the privileges enjoyed and the responsibilities carried, by the person who had sinned. The sin offering and the trespass offering are often viewed together as "the guilt offerings", and together they tell a three-fold story about sin. They relate, typically, the facts as to how by sin God has been robbed and man has been ruined, and they tell how righteousness may be restored.

In Lev 4 we have the four degrees or forms of sin offering. These are presented in order, in relation to the light or privilege possessed by the sinning party. The enormity of the sin is accordingly determined by the measure of privilege enjoyed. It is envisaged that a priest may sin. The whole congregation may sin. A ruler or prince may sin. One of the common people may sin. These are sins of ignorance, sins committed unwittingly, unknowingly, and not deliberately. The person sinning is not aware, at the time, that he has sinned. But this is a sad commentary on the state of the human heart, that a man may sin and not know it. How hard and insensible must our hearts be, that we can sin and not be aware of the wrong until later. But when the sin does come to light, then an offering is demanded – a sin offering.

The sinning priest must bring a bullock. The sinning congregation must likewise bring a bullock. The sinning ruler must bring a male kid of the goats, and one of the common people who had sinned must bring a female kid of the goats or a female lamb. There is a descending scale. The offering is commensurate with the stature and privilege of the sinning party. The priests are more accountable than the common people and must offer accordingly.

Although there were differences in these offerings and in the manner of their presentation, there were, nevertheless, certain principles or features which were common to all. Observe that Jehovah makes provision for all, whether for priest or prince or for congregation or commoner. Sin is grievous in any and in all. The sinning priest robs God of worship. The sinning congregation robs God of testimony. The sinning ruler robs God of government. The sin of the commoner robs God of fellowship with that individual. These are sad and serious deprivations and Jehovah prescribes means whereby atonement can be made and forgiveness extended to the sinner.

It should be noted that in Hebrew there is but one word for "sin" and for "sin-offering". The sin offering was regarded as the very personification of sin. It was treated as sin; it was judged as sin; it was condemned as sin; and it was often carried outside the camp as sin, to be consumed in judgment fire. We are reminded of the Holy One of whom it is written, "He hath made him to be sin for us, who knew no sin" (2 Cor 5:21).

In the case of the sinning priest it should be noticed that, although these are sins of ignorance, it does not say, as with the others in this chapter, "when it is known", or "when it come to his knowledge". It is regrettably expected that such an one as a priest should have known. How sad that one who is anointed, who is in priestly relations with God, and who is possessed of holy knowledge, should sin like one of the common people whose spiritual and moral example he ought to be. Alas it is often so with us.

Observe the recurring phrase, "without blemish". A bullock without blemish is offered by the sinning priest. As in the case of the burnt offering, he leans his hand upon the bullock's head and is then responsible for its death. There is, again, the identification of the offerer with his offering, as if he is saying, "This is mine", but in a different way from that which we saw in the burnt offering. There is a transferring, not now from the offering to the offerer, but from the offerer to the offering. He lays his hand upon its head and there is a transferring of his guilt to his substitute. Another life is to be given for his: another is to pay the penalty for his sin, another is to die. With the guilt of the offerer upon its head the substitutionary offering is slain. Its life is forfeited for his. The bullock dies in the place of the sinner. The typical meaning is crystal clear. We sing, "In my place condemned He stood". John

Newton had the sense of it when he wrote:

> My conscience felt and owned my guilt
> And plunged me in despair;
> I saw my sins His blood had spilt,
> And helped to nail Him there.

"The Son of God loved me, and gave himself for me" (Gal 2:20); He "bare our sins in his own body on the tree" (1 Pet 2:24).

The shed blood of the bullock was now carried into the tabernacle by an officiating priest. It was sprinkled seven times before the veil, and it was applied also to the horns of the golden altar. The residue of the blood was poured out at the bottom of the brasen altar in the court of the tabernacle. The principle is that the blood must go where the sin has gone. Jehovah had been insulted by the sin of the priest. The very sphere of priestly ministry had been defiled. All must be cleansed before priestly exercises can be restored or resumed.

The blood having been carried into the holy place, the fat which was upon the inwards of the bullock, the suet, was then laid upon the brasen altar to be burnt. The carcase of the bullock was then carried outside the camp to be wholly burnt. The entire bullock was burnt, its skin, its flesh, its head, legs, inwards, and dung. All was wholly burnt on wood with fire in a clean place outside the camp. "Jesus also ... suffered without the gate" (Heb 13:13).

At the same time as the carcase of the bullock was being burnt outside the camp, the internal fat of the offering was burning upon the altar. Here it is important to notice again those two different words for "burn", earlier noticed in connection with the burnt offering. See now Lev 4:10, 12. The fat was burnt, being accepted by the altar for Jehovah's satisfaction. The carcase was burnt, being consumed in judgment fire outside the camp. Though our Lord became a sin offering, judged in the stead of others, yet was there ever in Him an intrinsic excellence which rendered Him always precious to His Father, even in the mysterious hours of suffering. The fat burned on the altar while the bullock burned outside the camp.

The procedure for the offering for the sinning congregation was similar to that for the sinning priest, but in the case of the two remaining offerings for sin, one or two interesting variations must be noted. With these offerings, for ruler and commoner, the blood was not carried into the holy place; neither were the carcases burnt outside the camp. These offerings might be eaten by the priests on holy ground in the outer court of the tabernacle. It is like responsible holy brethren grieving in seclusion over the sins of others. Sin is not to be gossiped over in the camp, but to be the subject of meditative sorrow amongst those who lead the saints in service and worship.

One thing more should be observed. There is only one reference to sweet savour in connection with the sin offering (see Lev 4:31). In the matter of a sin offering for one of the common people, the fat was taken off it, as it was taken off from the peace offerings, and it was burnt on the altar for a sweet savour. Does this indicate to us the exceeding preciousness to God of fellowship with even the least of His people? The restoration of this fellowship, after the judgment of the sin that had disturbed it, is now like a sweet savour rising before Him.

Christ, the sin offering, brings righteousness to guilty men, and restores to God all that of which sin had robbed Him. Worship and testimony, government and fellowship, are all now possible in every assembly of the redeemed. The death of the Saviour has propitiated God and has removed the offending transgressions.

5. The Trespass Offering

While many sins were committed in ignorance, and required a sin offering, regrettably there were other sins whose commission was deliberate. These also necessitated an offering if there was to be divine forgiveness. In this category there was a great variety of ways in which a person might sin. There might be wilful violation of the commandments concerning stealing or lying. A man might deceive or defraud his neighbour who trusted him. There may be extortion, or there may be sin in holy things, as perhaps a neglect of tithing, or a failure to observe the ceremonial laws. In whatever way a man was guilty of deliberate sin, he must bring a trespass offering. There were also sins of omission. A man may fail to do what he knew ought to be done. Or he might refuse to tell what he knew should be told. Such sins of omission were just as serious as the sins of commission, and likewise required an offering for their forgiveness.

In every case of wilful sin three things were demanded by Jehovah. There must be:

1. A Full Confession
2. An Offering
3. A Restitution

The confession had to be full and frank. A general admission of failure or shortcoming was not sufficient or acceptable. "He shall confess that he hath sinned in that thing" (Lev 5:5). There must be an explicit acknowledgement of guilt in that particular matter. Such confession is humbling. It is contrary to the flesh. But it is the only way to forgiveness and to blessing.

The offering was accepted, again, in proportion to the resources of the sinner. One man might bring a lamb. Another may find this beyond his ability to give, and he could offer two turtledoves or two pigeons. One of these birds would be treated as a burnt offering, for Jehovah must have his portion. But sometimes a man's resources may have been so meagre that even two turtledoves were not possible. God was very gracious. In such cases He would accept from a man the tenth of an ephah of fine flour. This had no oil or frankincense with it as did the meat offering. It was an offering for sin. A memorial handful of it however, was burnt on the altar, like as with the meat offering, and the remnant of it belonged to the priests.

What singular demonstration of grace was this. Fine flour! No blood! A trespass offering? It was divine recognition of the poverty of the man, and an acknowledgement of his inability to bring more. Does not God still allow for poverty of appreciation and understanding? How many there are who could not explain nor define the difference between atonement and propitiation, or redemption and reconciliation, or substitution and justification, but who, in a simple trust, rest in Him who is typified by the fine flour. Does God reject a simple soul for poverty of knowledge? Will He now demand what a man cannot give, having been so gracious under law? For many in their sincere simplicity it is sufficient to know that Jesus died and Jesus saves. Men with greater priestly capacities may feast upon these things to a greater degree, but for salvation and forgiveness, Jehovah has graciously made provision for all. In any case, the fine flour went to the altar, to the place of sacrifice, where it was doubtless mingled with the shed blood of other offerings.

There must be restitution to the person who had been defrauded by the sin. Stolen property therefore must be returned. But more! A fifth part of the value of the stolen thing must be added to the principal. Our blessed Lord, who has restored that which He took not away, has brought glory to God in abundance. If it might be said with great reverence, God has more glory now than He had before Adam sinned. Adam, as a representative man, robbed Jehovah of a whole creation. Jesus, by His obedience and death, has restored everything, with the added glory of a new creation, a vast assembly of sons after His own likeness, for the Father's pleasure.

It must be observed that sin against my neighbour is sin against the Lord (Lev 6:2). David had learned this when he cried, "Against thee, thee only, have I sinned, and done this evil in thy sight" (Ps 51:4). He had indeed sinned against Uriah, and against Bathsheba, and against himself, but he recognises the awful end of his sin as being sin against the Lord. All sin, in every shape and form and circumstance, is grievous to God. An offence against my fellow-man is an offence against God and must be regarded with the utmost gravity. Only the death of Christ can remove the stain of any sin and give the sinner a standing, justified, before God.

Conclusion

These then, are the principal Levitical offerings. It is important to remember that although there are five offerings, with distinctive features in each offering, and although there are different grades or forms within each offering, yet there is but one object in view – Christ. The Christ who, in His death at Golgotha, meets my need for what I am and for what I have done, is the same Christ who has satisfied all the yearnings of God's heart and all the demands of God's throne. Christ, forsaken of God as my sin offering, is Christ wholly yielded to the will of God as a burnt offering. In the same Christ, God and I, with all my fellow-believers, rejoice together as in the fellowship of a peace offering.

The value of the sacrifice of Christ is infinite. Well does Peter speak of "the precious blood of Christ" (1 Pet 1:19). It is an incalculable, immeasurable, unfathomable, unsearchable preciousness. May these ancient typical foreshadowings help us in some measure towards a deeper appreciation, and may our affection be greatly increased for Him who loved us and gave Himself for us.

Bearing shame and scoffing rude
In my place condemned He stood;
Sealed my pardon with His blood;
   Hallelujah ! what a Saviour.

"And I beheld, and I heard the voice of many angels round about the throne ... and the number of them was ten thousand times ten thousand, and thousands of thousands: saying with a loud voice, Worthy is the Lamb that was slain" (Rev 5:11-12).

Appendix B

The Day of Atonement

The Day of Atonement is called by Jews, *Yom Kippur*, the Day of Covering. It was one of seven "Feasts of Jehovah", instructions concerning which are given in Lev 23. The Sabbath is sometimes also counted with these, making an eighth, but since this was a weekly observance and the others were annual, it is usual to consider it separately. There were as follows.

1. The Passover
2. The Feast of Unleavened Bread
3. The Feast of Firstfruits
4. The Day of Pentecost
5. The Feast of Trumpets
6. The Day of Atonement
7. The Feast of Tabernacles.

"Feasts" is the AV rendering. They were actually "appointed seasons", or "set times", for drawing near to God, and they constituted a kind of religious calendar for Israel as a nation. Five of these were one-day festivals, holy convocations observed on one particular day in the year. The other two, the Feast of Unleavened Bread and the Feast of Tabernacles, lasted for a week, and indeed into an eighth day. The first three feasts were springtime celebrations in the first month of Israel's sacred year. Pentecost was held in the third month, and then, after an interval of some three months or more, the remaining three were autumn festivals of the seventh month.

These divine appointments, spread over the year, are a typical unfolding of the dealings of God with men on the ground of redemption. Since Christ our Passover is, in the purpose of God, the Lamb foreordained before the foundation of the world, and since, in the same divine purpose, everything is moving towards an eternal Sabbath, the rest of God, these feasts have been called, "God's calendar from eternity to eternity". They are a typical foreshadowing of Calvary and the resurrection of Christ, and the descent of the Holy Spirit. They look forward to the regathering of Israel, to the salvation of a remnant nation, and to a millennial kingdom of prosperity and joy.

The Day of Atonement, which is in the background of much of the epistle to the Hebrews, was the holiest day of Israel's year. It may be considered historically, typically, and prophetically, to see, respectively, what it meant to Israel in the past, what it means to believers now, and what it will mean to Israel in the future.

1. *Historically*

The full details for the annual observance are given in Lev 16. Two of Aaron's sons had died, judged for daring to draw near to Jehovah with strange fire (Lev 10). The instructions now given in ch.16 are for the regulating of Aaron's approach into the holiest within the veil. He may not come at all times. He must come only on one particular day in the year to the mercy seat, and he must come in the full and strict observance of the details that follow.

The high priest must be suitably attired. Having been washed in water Aaron must don the linen garments. There was a holy linen vest, linen trousers, a linen girdle, and a linen mitre. Thus bathed and dressed he became a shadow of what Christ is personally and essentially. All was white and clean, a picture of righteousness and purity (cf. Rev 19:8).

Already several offerings had been selected and presented to the Lord, though not yet slain. There was a bullock and a ram, a sin offering and a burnt offering for Aaron and his house. There were two goats and a second ram, a sin offering and a burnt offering for the people. Note that the two goats were, together, one sin offering. Upon these two goats Aaron cast lots. One goat was for Jehovah; the other was to be a scapegoat to bear away the confessed sins of the congregation.

The bullock of Aaron's sin offering was the first to be slain, and Aaron was now ready for the solemn and lonely entry into the holiest of all, beyond the veil. He went into the holiest alone. Before carrying in the blood however, he must first come with a censer of burning coals and with his hands full of sweet incense beaten small. When the incense was put upon the fire a fragrant cloud arose. It filled the sanctuary and it shrouded the mercy seat, and then, in the sweet incense cloud Aaron stood with the blood of his sin offering. He sprinkled the blood with his finger, once for the eye of God upon the gold of the mercy seat and seven times upon the ground where he stood, before the mercy seat. The goat of the sin offering for the people was then killed, and Aaron did with the blood of the goat as he had done with the blood of the bullock. God was propitiated and man was assured and the sanctuary and the tent and the altar were all cleansed from the uncleanness of the nation.

Having completed the reconciliation of the holy things, Aaron now had to attend to the matter of the live goat, the scapegoat. Iniquities, transgressions, and sins, were now confessed as the high priest stood with his hands on the head of the living scapegoat. The guilt of the nation was being transferred to a substitute victim. A chosen man, standing ready, then led the scapegoat away. He took it into the wilderness, and abandoned it in what has been variously called, "a land apart", "a land of separation", "a land not inhabited". It was all a foreshadowing of His sufferings, who out of the darkness cried, "My God, my God, why hast thou forsaken me?"

The ceremonials were now almost complete. Aaron went back into the tent, put off the linen garments, and left them in the holy place. He bathed his flesh in water, attired himself in his other garments, and came forth to offer the two rams, the two burnt offerings. While the burnt offerings and the fat of the sin offering burned upon the brasen altar, the bodies of the bullock and the slain goat were carried outside the camp to be burned with fire.

The Day of Atonement was associated with affliction of soul, with abstinence from work, and with confession of sin. This tenth day of the seventh month was a strict Sabbath. *Yom Kippur* came only once a year (Lev 16:34) and it was perhaps the most solemn event in the year.

2. Typically

The rich typical meaning of the Day of Atonement is expounded in Heb 9 and in other parts of that epistle. The tabernacle, the writer reminds us, was in two parts. In the first part, between the two veils, many priests served in a regular daily ministry. They lit the lamps in the evening. They trimmed them in the morning. They attended to the shewbread on the table every Sabbath, and they burned incense daily on the golden altar. But into the second compartment, the holiest of all, the holy of holies, these priests were not permitted to come. The high priest, alone, once every year, entered that sanctuary with blood. This was that Day of Atonement of Lev.16.

There was a spiritual significance in this, says the writer to the Hebrews. The hanging veil barred man out. There was no manifest way for sinful men into that holy place and holy presence. And the sacrifices offered year by year could never make the people perfect or give them complete rest of conscience. Indeed, every year there was a remembrance made of sins. The blood of those bullocks and goats could never effect an absolute removal of sins.

But those days and those ceremonials only foreshadowed the coming of Christ. Not by the blood of goats and calves, but by His own blood the Saviour has entered into a greater sanctuary. By one sacrifice, the sacrifice of Himself, once-for-all, never to be repeated, He has put away sins for ever and is now in the presence of God for us. Our sins are gone; our consciences are purged; there is an opened sanctuary and a way into the holiest for us by the blood of Jesus. The memory of our sin and guilt will never be revived again. The work is complete. By one offering we have been perfected for ever. We hear Jehovah say, "Their sins and their iniquities will I remember no more", and we sing in joyful response:

> Done is the work that saves,
> Once and for ever done;
> Finished the righteousness
> That clothes the unrighteous one.
> The love that blesses us below
> Is flowing freely to us now.
>
> The gate is open wide;
> The new and living way

Is clear, and free, and bright
With love, and peace, and day.
Into the holiest now we come,
Our present and our endless home.

3. *Prophetically*

Viewed prophetically, the first four feasts of Lev 23 have been literally and actually and punctually fulfilled. At Passover time Jesus died as the true paschal Lamb. There is now a Feast of Unleavened Bread, His people desiring a holiness like unto His own. He has been raised from the dead as the firstfruits of them that sleep. Fifty days after His resurrection, when the day of Pentecost had fully come, the Spirit descended and brought in "a new meat offering" (Lev 23:16) of Jews and Gentiles in one church which is His body (Eph 1:22f).

After Pentecost there was a gap in the sacred calendar of events; there was a prolonged silence. We are living in this gap today. Pentecost is past. Heaven is silent. We wait now for the Feast of Trumpets which broke the silence on the first day of the seventh month. The last trump of 1 Cor 15:52 will call the church home. It will signal also the renewal of God's dealings with Israel and there will be a regathering of the nation to the land.

A remnant of that nation will acknowledge Jesus as Messiah. They will value the blood of the Lamb (Rev 7:13-14). They will preach Him and wait for Him, and when, in power and glory He will be manifested for their salvation they will sing their passion song, "He was wounded for our transgressions, He was bruised for our iniquities". They shall look on Him whom they pierced. A nation will be born in a day. There will be such a national emotion as Jesus is acclaimed as Messiah the Prince, with "the family of the house of David apart ... the family of the house of Nathan apart ... the family of the house of Levi apart ... the family of the house of Shimei apart" (Zech 12:12-13). It is as if the representatives of Israel's prophets, priests, and kings, are gathering in acknowledgement of the anointed One. "And in that day there shall be a fountain opened for sin and for uncleanness" (Zech 13:1).

That will be, for Israel, the grand fulfilment of the Day of Atonement. Calvary will be made good to them. There will then remain only the Feast of Tabernacles to be fulfilled, a time of gladness and rejoicing, of kingdom prosperity and bliss, with the Son of David upon the throne and Israel and the nations basking in the sunshine of His glorious reign.

How grateful are we, who even now, in the day of His rejection, have been drawn by sovereign grace to bow to His claims and to understand the meaning of the cross. We look backward to Calvary and we look forward to glory, and our hearts are at rest. With purged consciences and gladdened spirits we wait for Him and work for Him; we witness to Him and we worship as we sing:

No blood, no altar now,
  The sacrifice is o'er;
 No flame, no smoke ascends on high,
  The lamb is slain no more;
But richer blood has flowed from nobler veins
To purge the soul from guilt, and cleanse the reddest stains.

NOTES

NOTES

NOTES

NOTES

NOTES

NOTES

NOTES